Migrant Citizenship

POLITICS AND CULTURE IN MODERN AMERICA

Series Editors:
Keisha N. Blain, Margot Canaday,
Matthew Lassiter, Stephen Pitti, Thomas J. Sugrue

Volumes in the series narrate and analyze political and social change
in the broadest dimensions from 1865 to the present, including ideas
about the ways people have sought and wielded power in the public
sphere and the language and institutions of politics at all levels—local,
national, and transnational. The series is motivated by a desire to
reverse the fragmentation of modern U.S. history and to encourage
synthetic perspectives on social movements and the state, on gender,
race, and labor, and on intellectual history and popular culture.

MIGRANT CITIZENSHIP

Race, Rights, and Reform
in the U.S. Farm Labor Camp Program

Verónica Martínez-Matsuda

PENN

UNIVERSITY OF PENNSYLVANIA PRESS

PHILADELPHIA

Published by
University of Pennsylvania Press
Philadelphia, Pennsylvania 19104-4112
www.upenn.edu/pennpress

Printed in the United States of America
on acid-free paper

10 9 8 7 6 5 4 3 2 1

Library of Congress Cataloging-in-Publication Data
ISBN 978-0-8122-5229-3

Para mis padres, Esperanza y Liberato Martínez,
que con sus sacrificios me enseñaron a luchar por un mundo más justo,
and for the center of my world, mis amores,
Michael, Joaquín, Lucia, and Oscar Matsuda

CONTENTS

FSA Migratory Labor Camp Locations, July 1942

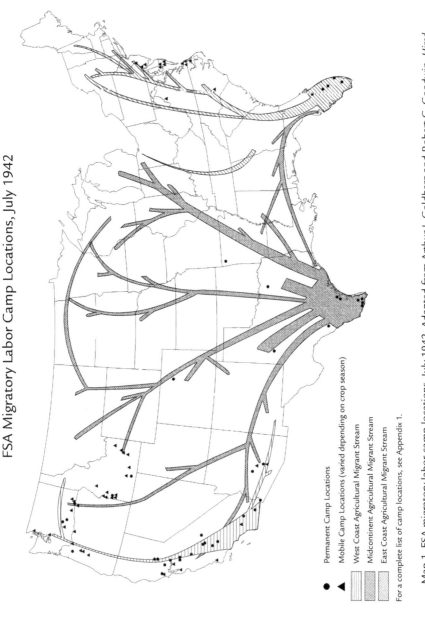

● Permanent Camp Locations

◀ Mobile Camp Locations (varied depending on crop season)

West Coast Agricultural Migrant Stream

Midcontinent Agricultural Migrant Stream

East Coast Agricultural Migrant Stream

For a complete list of camp locations, see Appendix 1.

Map 1. FSA migratory labor camp locations, July 1942. Adapted from Arthur J. Goldberg and Robert C. Goodwin, *Hired Farm Workers in the United States* (Washington, D.C.: Department of Labor, June 1961), 31. Coordinates for some camp locations were slightly adjusted so as to not overlap. Map prepared by Grace Yixian Zhou.

Introduction

On July 2, 1941, 157 farmworkers residing at the Farm Security Administration (FSA) camp in Weslaco, Texas, signed a petition addressed to President Franklin D. Roosevelt demanding that the U.S. government take responsibility for their well-being by defending their right to decent housing, better wages, and "a self Maintainence." The petitioners were contesting the FSA's recent notice of eviction for families who had exceeded the "one-year occupancy rule" aimed at discouraging permanent residency in the federal migrant camps. The individuals who signed the petition were mainly Mexican American farmworkers from South Texas and white Dust Bowl refugees from the U.S. South and Great Plains. They signed the petition as families, clearly indicated by the "Mr. and Mrs." prefix and the grouping of similar surnames on the list. Their appeal declared:

> We as United States Citizens of this Free America, and a Bunch of
> Farmers (Dirt Farmers, not Pencil Pushers) are Now Talking, and
> are Shooting Streight from the Shoulder, Cold, Undeniable Facts;
> FIRST—We are a Bunch of Destitutes; with nowhere to go, Nothing
> to go on; Second—we are not Pleading the Cases of the Factory
> Industry, the Large Farming Industry, nor the Irrigation Industry
> Inc. but we Judge from the *Wages* they offer us for our Labor, they
> must be Somewhat Destitute to. . . . We are yet in Battle and Now
> Asking for a Chance to as Dirt Farmers, Qualified Citizens, and
> Eager to work, earn our living, we are Offering our Labor. . . . As to
> the Up Keep of our little Camp, within our Jurisdiction, we are all
> trying to keep it Looking Nice, With Flowers, and Eats, in front of
> our Respective Shelters; we are not a Bunch of "Dead-Heads"
> "Hobos" or Non-Working People, or "Trash of the Earth" as Proba-
> bly some might Make-believe us to be. Is the Administration listen-
> ing? We are Waiting.[1]

The petitioners' claims dramatically affirmed their status as hardworking, contributing residents and farm laborers entitled to the protections afforded by the camp program and the privileges of American citizenship. Despite their diverse status as "Qualified Citizens"—with some identifying as former farmers, others as longtime migrant workers—they came together, as they explained, "in a Democratic way" to contest the injustice they faced as marginalized, impoverished people. They demanded federal intervention not in the form of charity but as laborers "eager to work" and to "earn" their living. Their claims shrewdly demonstrate the interrelated nature of migrant farmworkers' struggles for expanded civil rights during the 1930s and 1940s in domestic, labor, and democratic terms.

FSA officials in Washington, D.C., responded to the Weslaco families by upholding the one-year rule yet recommending that the FSA camp manager and local regional director determine "the merits of each case" before giving families a notice to move. They conceded largely on the grounds of "unusually adverse weather conditions seriously affecting the crop seasons in Texas," which meant the evicted families would likely struggle to find work and shelter.[2] The agency's position on the issue, though not readily apparent, also revealed the FSA's own battle for survival. By 1941 the FSA was facing intense conservative pressure from commercial growers and their congressional allies seeking to curtail the agency's social reform mission to eliminate any migrant assistance threatening their labor practices. The FSA's one-year occupancy rule represented the agency's efforts to negotiate the shifting federal politics that, with the onset of World War II and the supposed end of the Great Depression, prioritized farmworkers' productive potential over their stability and self-realization. Notwithstanding the FSA's increased role as a labor supplier, the agency remained firmly committed to migrant farmworkers' socioeconomic welfare and political equality. As participants in the FSA's camp program, the petitioners knew the agency was on their side. In demanding federal protection and assistance from Roosevelt's administration, therefore, they were also defending the FSA's political authority.

This book deepens our understanding of the welfare state as it unfolded under the New Deal by focusing on how migrant farmworkers' participation in the FSA's labor camp program challenged the structural forces in agribusiness and rural society that exploited farmworkers as racialized and disenfranchised workers. It also explains how FSA officials fought to extend the promises of New Deal liberalism—in more reformist, rights-based, and democratic terms—into the 1940s. I explore familiar discourses about poor people's relationship to government aid, including concerns over how migrants' dependency on the FSA potentially undermined their self-determination. But I also offer a new perspective on how federal, state, and local governments wrestled over the boundaries of citizenship to define who was entitled to public support. FSA officials argued that the "migrant problem" of the 1930s went far beyond the material consequences of tenant farmers' and sharecroppers' rapid displacement initiated by a crash in farm prices, increased mechanization, and environmental crisis. A more fundamental problem, they claimed, involved the way that this displacement signaled a narrowing of opportunity and equality in U.S. society.

According to Will W. Alexander, the FSA's chief administrator in 1940, the "restlessness" and "instability" produced by migrants' "desperate but vain search for better conditions" made a "mockery of Democracy." As he explained, "under such conditions participation in the affairs of the community and even the enjoyment of the ordinary rights of citizens are virtually impossible. How many of these people attend churches, send their children to school regularly, or even vote?"[3] Carey McWilliams, head of the California Division of Immigration and Housing in 1940, further clarified the problem in an essay titled "Americans Without a Country." Migrant agricultural workers "are 'outlaws' and 'aliens' so far as our welfare programs are concerned," he contended. They are "alien Americans" and part of the "federal homeless," McWilliams asserted, because stringent state and local residency laws, combined with deep-seated racial and class prejudice, made migrant workers American citizens without a place to enact their rights.[4] The Great Depression worsened this problem, but it had always existed. Accordingly, the camp program offers an extraordinary lens into how federal agents and migrant farmworkers aimed to resolve the paradox of migrant citizenship and realize a fuller, more inclusive, and vigorous sense of social democracy in the United States.

At its core, *Migrant Citizenship* blurs the boundaries across labor, cultural, and political history to examine how the FSA's camp program challenged the notion of juridical citizenship as a guarantor of democratic rights for marginalized farmworkers. I see this book contributing to an important discussion among immigration and citizenship scholars interested in the in-between, intervening, ever-changing spaces migrants create for themselves as a way to navigate national belonging.[5] This study builds on race and ethnic studies scholars' examination of the historical limitations of national citizenship, particularly as it rested on the expulsion and suppression of others. It does so by demonstrating how those excluded have nonetheless acted from within the boundaries of state-based notions of citizenship, and alongside state agents, to envision, articulate, and realize their labor and civil rights. In this history, we see how migrants contested the FSA's ideas about their democratic potential, especially in defining them as too ignorant and docile to know and demand their rights, while simultaneously embracing the FSA's mission to include them in the national fold as equal members. To be sure, the relationship between migrants and the state that materialized through the camp program was imperfect. For as extraordinary as the FSA was in its efforts to empower migrant farmworkers, it also suffered from its own set of problems and prejudices that often reinforced the racial, gendered, class, and moral barriers keeping migrants from attaining full citizenship. Ultimately, however, migrant families welcomed the FSA's progressive intervention knowing that the agency's commitment to fulfilling the New Deal's social-democratic possibilities was critical to securing a better life.

Between 1935 and 1946, in more than one hundred permanent and mobile labor camps across the country, the federal government provided thousands of migrant families the essential amenities they needed to regain their dignity, health, and hope for a brighter future. All of the FSA camps offered migrants safe and sanitary housing, full on-site medical service (including dental care), a nursery school program, primary education, home-demonstration instruction, food for a healthy diet, recreational programing, and lessons in participatory democracy through the camps' self-governing councils. The immediate and practical value of these provisions must not be underestimated. Migrant families arriving in the camps in the late 1930s were in absolute dire straits without much recourse for survival. As one California migrant tragically testified in 1940 about trying to save his oldest boy dying of pneumonia, "The state is much more interested in how you die than in how you live."[6] The FSA's concern for migrants' human rights was absolutely unprecedented.

Beyond caring for migrant families within these camps, FSA officials afforded farmworkers the political backing and critical economic security they needed to organize collectively to contest their labor exploitation, chronic poverty, and civic exclusion. And they went a step further by encouraging migrants to do so through the formation of workers' councils, in educational workshops, and by example when advocating on their behalf. Consequently, the camps were never simply labor stations aimed at improving agricultural efficiency. Instead, they represented, as FSA officials frequently expressed, a profound "experiment in democracy."[7] They were spaces to realize a more substantive, participatory, and inclusive sense of U.S. democracy than what existed.

For this reason, the FSA's camp program should be considered central to the civil rights movement that emerged in the 1930s. The program exemplifies the intense struggle for farmworkers' expanded political and socioeconomic power involving diverse migrant families and their communities, state officials at the local and national levels, progressive allies, and radical farm labor organizations. It was a rural movement contesting the exploitive forces of corporate agribusiness at the height of its expansion, and a movement for justice that extended far beyond the South and the nation's black-white racial divide, even as this context was central to the political struggle the FSA traversed. Part of this book's purpose, therefore, entails illuminating how seemingly unrelated groups of migrants—such as Dust Bowl refugees, Mexican and African American farmworkers, and Japanese American internees—were connected in a political fight for civil rights and full citizenship.[8]

When the FSA was created under the U.S. Department of Agriculture (USDA) in 1937, it inherited much of its staff and most of its programing from its predecessor agency, the Resettlement Administration (RA). President Roosevelt established the RA by executive order in May 1935, largely in response to mounting protests by dispossessed black and white share-croppers and tenant farmers across the South. These activists, many of them part of the newly formed Southern Tenant Farmers' Union, blamed the first New Deal for exacerbating their plight by introducing economic recovery measures, such as the Agricultural Adjustment Act of 1933, that favored the region's agricultural establishment. The RA focused primarily on small farmers' rehabilitation in the form of supervised credit, tenure improvements, and debt adjustment. Initially, planters did not wholly object to the RA's intervention so long as it centered on providing tempo-rary relief and did not disrupt the region's social, political, and economic order of white supremacy.[9]

When Rexford G. Tugwell, the RA's first administrator, agreed to fund a migrant camp program in California in 1935, he did so strictly within the rehabilitation framework and felt significantly constrained by agrarian racism at the national and state levels. The first federal camps were intended to provide emergency relief for the Dust Bowl refugees and other white migrants hailing from the U.S. South and Great Plains. Although many of these families did not actually have farming backgrounds, the program began as part of the RA's effort to aid "landless farmers" and restore the "displaced Jeffersonian yeoman," in the words of John Steinbeck, to his rightful status.[10] Consequently, the RA's migrant camps initially excluded the Mexican and Filipino farmworkers who had long labored in California's industrial fields and who demanded government support as they waged several mass strikes in the early 1930s for better labor and living conditions.[11]

The exclusion nonwhite, traditional migrant workers experienced in the program's early phase mirrored farmworkers' deliberate omission from key New Deal labor and social welfare legislation. The National Industrial Recovery Act of 1933, the National Labor Relations Act and Social Security Act of 1935, and the Fair Labor Standards Act of 1938 all failed to guarantee farmworkers the same benefits it did urban industrial workers. Southern Democrats, who dominated Congress and determined the parameters of New Deal policy, purposely denied all farmworkers political rights in their aim to protect Jim Crow.[12] The antiblackness that influenced these New Deal exclusions buttressed the racial hierarchies in California that had historically kept industrial agriculture profitable through the exploitation of noncitizen (irrespective of formal status), mostly Mexican and Asian labor. Simultaneously, the white supremacist discourse that denied black, Mexican, and Asian farmworkers inclusion in the initial camp project helped bolster progressive arguments for why the Dust Bowl refugees deserved federal intervention beyond their class standing as former farmers. As whites and Americans, many progressives contended, these migrants would not tolerate the conditions typically afforded to "foreign peons."[13]

Beginning in 1937, however, the FSA's New Dealers capitalized on President Roosevelt's and Secretary of Agriculture Henry Wallace's increased attention to the crisis of rural poverty to challenge the agrarian status quo by doing more for "the chronic underdogs of agriculture."[14] The FSA's version of rural rehabilitation came to encompass a more expansive and reformist vision that went beyond merely restoring dispossessed farmers' economic security. In a broader sense, FSA rehabilitation involved granting rural poor people the resources and opportunities necessary to better shape their world. Not unlike the RA, the FSA used its financial and administrative authority primarily to aid small farmers and repurpose marginal lands. Yet the FSA's reform goals more readily embraced migratory farmworkers and nonwhites, framing their well-being and civic participation as central to achieving agrarian democracy. Consequently, FSA officials managing the camps supported farmworkers' struggles for improved rights and frequently cooperated with radical unions, leftist organizations, and the progressive media to advance their cause. Commercial growers claimed that the FSA promoted subversive ideas intent on fostering farmworker solidarity. Partly correct in their observations, they understood that the FSA's camp program defied the racist and classist logic behind farmworkers' exclusion from the New Deal and behind migrants' invisibility outside of their economic value. FSA officials affirmed that all farmworkers were entitled to political representation, fair wages, good housing, public education, medical care, and the human dignity they were so often denied.

Despite New Deal scholars' attention to the FSA's reform actions, much of the political history that evaluates the agency's rural development efforts centers on the RA/FSA's planners and the rehabilitation of small farmers during the 1930s. Accordingly, this work has focused on the FSA's programs in the South and Great Plains where the agency was most active.[15] Most studies concerned with the ideological implications of the agrarian New Deal have, therefore, kept migrant farmworkers, particularly those who labored on industrial farms before 1935, marginal to their analysis. In doing so, they have neglected to consider how the FSA's commitment to agrarian reform advanced farmworkers' democratization—especially in racial, labor, and civil rights terms—through the early 1940s. As Jess Gilbert contends, "Historians and social scientists studying New Deal agriculture seemed to have missed the underlying vision of deliberative-participatory planning, intended to foment the democratization of rural America."[16] My book builds on Gilbert's assessment in order to argue that the FSA's social democratic project reached far deeper and wider than scholars have previously acknowledged. In extraordinary fashion, the FSA's experiment also included destitute farmworker families, disenfranchised racial minorities, and the ostracized "alien American" migrants McWilliams described.

This book's chronological focus on the early 1940s also aims to expand on what some scholars have labeled a "Third New Deal." Historians continue to debate the New Deal's political trajectory, particularly "the evolution of liberal priorities and policies."[17] However, the prevailing thought has long been that "by the end of 1937 the active phase of the New Deal had largely come to an end," as Alan Brinkley contends. Although Roosevelt planned to develop a "new New Deal" that included heavy spending on social welfare, reform liberals encountered formidable obstacles to implementing such measures because of the 1937–38 recession, the rise of a conservative coalition in Congress after the 1938 election, and the outbreak of war in Europe in 1939. This context also "muted liberal hostility to capitalism and the corporate world," according to Brinkley.[18]

The FSA's camp program, however, represents an important exception to our understanding of the New Deal's political intent and struggle for survival. It reveals the profound effort by some New Deal liberals to develop meaningful reform action through the 1940s: an action that emerged, contrary to Brinkley's estimation, within a rights-based framework that acknowledged and addressed matters of racial and class injustice as central to the FSA's expanded democratic vision.[19] This reform effort necessarily claimed to serve corporate agriculture by helping better direct the nation's farm labor supply while at the same time significantly challenging agribusiness. Because New Deal scholars typically describe the FSA's farm labor programs as part of the agency's final intervention, they frame the camp program within a narrative of declension. In doing so, they fail to see how the camp program, which materialized most concretely after 1940, embodied one of the New Deal's most remarkable reformist and democratic achievements. FSA officials used the program to defend migrants' right to full political and social participation as citizens. In doing so, they contested the economic forces operating to exploit and marginalize farmworkers.

The FSA built the majority of its camps between 1937 and 1942. In 1936 there were fewer than thirty permanent and mobile labor camps in operation or under construction across the country, with California accounting for close to half of those. At that time, the camps had a combined shelter for approximately seven thousand families. By 1942, however, there were close to 110 camps in operation or under construction, serving an estimated 20,675 families or 89,000 individuals across sixteen states. In 1942 the FSA also had plans to construct 90 additional camps (most of them mobile yet fully equipped) serving up to 140 new locations nationwide. Even more noteworthy, in 1940 there were only fifty-three total camps, meaning that camp construction doubled between 1940 and 1942.[20] This fact underscores how wartime mobilization provided the agency a much-needed reason to expand the camp program rather than curtail it, as was the case for most social federal projects. Indeed, although migrant farmworkers comprised the smallest portion of the FSA's clients, they were the primary reason the agency survived until 1946.

The FSA succeeded in maintaining much of its organizational structure and political power during World War II because it strategically positioned itself as the agency most suited to efficiently recruit and mobilize the farm labor force necessary to meet escalating agriculture demands. Its activities in this regard have led labor scholars to emphasize the FSA's influence mainly as a labor supplier. Don Mitchell, for instance, acknowledges that the FSA cared for migrant farmworkers when the camps first opened, but he stresses how they quickly became mechanisms to dampen labor radicalism. Cindy Hahamovitch similarly explains how the FSA's "apparatus of aid and reform" was "all but abandoned" when the war began. Both scholars focus on the FSA's role in managing the Emergency Farm Labor Supply Program beginning in 1942, under which it negotiated various binational agreements to recruit, contract, transport, and oftentimes house foreign workers, primarily from Mexico and the Caribbean. Most labor scholars conclude, rightly so, that the FSA undermined domestic farmworkers' power to bargain for improved labor rights by importing male guest workers to compete in a quintessential race to the bottom. A key concern in labor studies thus involves the FSA's actions in advancing, not contesting, capitalist agriculture's labor exploitation.[21]

There is no question that the FSA ultimately failed to maintain the labor camp program as a site of farmworkers' democratic inclusion and socioeconomic welfare. However, the FSA's political struggle, especially in the early 1940s, deserves closer attention in order to better understand the material and ideological contradictions it produced within the New Deal, and to more fully appreciate the consequences it had on all farmworkers' labor and civil rights. Because previous studies have too readily assumed that the FSA discarded its social democratic experiment at the onset of the war, they have overlooked how camp officials capitalized on growers' labor demands and on the nation's image of itself as "the great arsenal of democracy" to defend the camps' progressive and reformist interventions. At the same time that Congress pressured the FSA to focus on agribusiness (not migrant) interests, the camps became important symbols of America's commitment to social justice and wartime democracy. What did this ironic development mean for migrant families?

A central part of my analysis thus involves disrupting the gender-class split in labor history to consider how the camps operated as a dual-purpose space of home and work where the dialectical relationship between public and private was always at play and constantly negotiated. As the opening anecdote suggests, farmworkers' struggle for economic and political justice remained intrinsically tied to their domestic environment in a way that varied from the union activism emerging among urban working-class families during the 1930s and 1940s. While New Deal recovery measures concentrated on protecting the vitality of the male head of household and the family wage, migrant farmworkers depended on a family economy where, in most cases, all members (including children) worked alongside one another in the fields. Accordingly, migrants understood their status as laborers and citizens as intimately connected with their identity and responsibilities as fathers, mothers, and members of extended families, which sometimes included their work crews.[22]

A reading of the camps' built environment, monthly population reports, and migrants' oral histories underscores how much the federal camps functioned as vibrant home and community spaces. According to a national survey of the camp population in 1940, for example, of the 68,700 people living in all fifty-three camps, an estimated 30,700 were nineteen years of age and under, 15,400 were between the ages of five and fourteen, and 9,200 were younger than five years old. A study of the Raymondville, Texas, camp for 1941 also shows that of the 4,385 people residing in the camp, 1,574 were men, 1,014 were women, 897 were boys, and 900 were girls (under fifteen years of age).[23] Evaluating the camps in traditional labor terms therefore obscures how the FSA's labor reform actions involved transforming migrants' personal attitudes, domestic behaviors, and cultural practices to mold them into better, more deserving citizens.

Migrant Citizenship is the first study to evaluate the federal camp program from a comprehensive, multiracial, and cross-regional perspective. Some scholars have applied a political economy and cultural studies analysis to their evaluation of the program's impact, yet their work focuses exclusively on California and the experiences of white Dust Bowl families during the 1930s.[24] Beginning in the late 1930s, however, as the program expanded beyond California and Arizona into states such as Washington, Oregon, Idaho, Texas, Florida, and New Jersey, the camps housed an increasingly diverse population. By 1940 the camps accommodated significant numbers of remaining Dust Bowl families (since not all had left the fields for defense work as is often assumed) as well as Mexican, Asian, and African American farmworker families who had long followed the crops. Beginning in 1942, camp inhabitants also included emergency war workers such as Japanese American families recruited from World War II U.S. internment camps as part of the Seasonal Leave Program, and foreign guest workers from Mexico, the Bahamas, and Jamaica. Not all camps housed emergency workers, however, and some that did also continued to house domestic farmworkers. Consequently, many camps remained important family and community spaces where farmworkers benefited from the federal government's effort to improve their health, education, and economic security.

In considering the camps' full demographic diversity, this book contributes to a rich historiography in race and ethnic studies exploring how farmworkers fought for racial equality and full citizenship, and against the disposability of their labor. I utilize my expertise in Chicano/a history to pay particular attention to the camp program as it existed in Texas and as it affected Mexican families. Most farmworker community histories have centered on California and focused on grower-owned or privately funded farmworker housing. They also have paid closer attention to the role of the Mexican government, not the U.S. government, in negotiating farmworkers' rights.[25] In considering the unique dynamic created by U.S. federal intervention, I address the struggle for farmworkers' expanded civil rights at the nexus of juridical citizenship and cultural citizenship. In this way, I hope to revise the standard historical narrative concerning Mexican Americans' experiences under the New Deal—which typically centers on the large-scale, mostly urban efforts to repatriate and deport ethnic Mexicans—to demonstrate how migrants and FSA officials worked to incorporate Mexican Americans in the U.S. national polity.

Texas is central to this study because its agricultural system was at the forefront of national farm labor politics throughout the 1930s and 1940s. The migrant stream of mostly Mexican workers traveling from South Texas to other parts of the nation was far greater than any other interstate flow at the time. Texas constituted, as McWilliams explained, "a great reservoir of cheap labor from which workers were siphoned off in all directions." An estimated 66,100 Mexican migrant workers left Texas annually for seasonal work in the early 1940s. Beyond its scale, the state's agricultural system served as a model for maximizing and regulating industrial farm labor. This model of labor control depended on an oversupply of transitory workers who were denied any basic rights and threatened with deportation if they challenged their condition.[26] When the camp program began in Texas in 1939, FSA officials claimed that it best demonstrated their efforts to adapt their agenda from depression to wartime. Beyond regulating a more established migrant stream, however, FSA officials used the program to challenge growers' practices of farm labor exclusion and abuse. Because the Mexican government refused to send braceros to Texas until 1947—due to rampant racial discrimination against Mexicans in the state—the FSA camps in Texas remained most emblematic of the program's social reform goals.

The camps in South Texas, where I focused my oral histories, also offer a unique opportunity to ground this study through the perspective of migrant families who resided in the area for periods long before and after the camps were built. The fact that most Mexican migrants were from the communities surrounding the camps significantly complicated how FSA officials understood their sense of civic belonging. Highlighting migrants' voices became a central methodological concern in this study to underscore how even the most marginal of actors shape political institutions and operations in significant ways. Migrants' accounts both support and challenge the camps' official records. Even in the camps' federal documents, however, migrants' essential voices appear just beneath the surface. The work involved in bringing their perspectives to the foreground revises the conclusion some scholars have reached about the camps functioning as a "sandbox democracy" where migrants were passive recipients of politicization.[27]

Although Mexican migrants' experiences alone offer an important lens for assessing the program's influence, without a race-relational analysis an evaluation of the FSA's democratic experiment would be incomplete. The extent and limits of the FSA's reformist aspirations become most clear when we consider the way camp officials mediated migrants' specific circumstances of noncitizenship, racial violence, and economic exploitation simultaneously and in relation to one another. A race-relational framework also allows us to see to what extent FSA officials looked beyond class to explain and contest farmworkers' inequity and subjugation. In addition to highlighting migrants' cross-racial coalitions, this book explores how farmworkers' distinct identities and regionally rooted experiences forced FSA officials to reevaluate and adapt their democratic script promising all farmworkers equal opportunity. As they had always done, migrants fought to define, assert, and validate their own identities and political claims.[28] Accordingly, this study illuminates how varied farmworkers, most of whom never met, were linked in a national fight for extended rights.

Though the FSA's social democratic vision was remarkably inclusive, the FSA also contributed to biased discourses and practices that justified migrants' exclusion, racialization, and disenfranchisement. Since the publication of Sidney Baldwin's comprehensive study on the FSA in 1968, scholarly debate continues regarding the FSA's appellation as a "heroic bureaucracy," one "designed to secure social justice and political power for a neglected class of Americans."[29] In the early stages of my research, I was often pressed to conclude whether the camp program reflected a benevolent or repressive hand of the state, and to determine if farmworker families found the program liberating or autocratic. Nevertheless, I resist narrowing my analysis of the program's impact and the interactions it facilitated in this way. Instead, the history that follows reveals the deep complexity in migrants' relationship to the state, and the reality that migrants' experiences typically fell somewhere in between recognizing the camps as promising and limiting. Rather than seeming indifferent to the debate, I want to stress the contradiction as it existed.[30]

As Ira Katznelson contends, we cannot understand the New Deal outside of the fundamental contradiction through which it operated. In particular, he argues, southerners' control of Congress produced "complicated and sometimes unprincipled relationships between . . . democracy and racism." Much of the New Deal's "most notable, and noble, achievements," Katznelson reminds us, rested on "the South's racial hegemony."[31] Women's historians such as Linda Gordon and Alice Kessler-Harris have also demonstrated how New Deal policies relegated women to the margins, solidifying their status as dependent and further nullifying their rights as citizens. The gendered construction of social welfare in the 1930s, they argue, disenfranchised all recipients of public assistance. Recognizing New Deal liberalism's significant incongruities concerning social equality helps contextualize the challenge FSA officials faced in fulfilling their democratic promise. FSA officials were genuinely committed to improving farmworkers' labor and civil rights. Yet in carrying out their program, they also promoted discriminatory policies that further disempowered migrant men and women. The constant political pressure FSA officials were forced to navigate partly explains the agency's contradictory actions. But not all of the FSA's limitations resulted from external opposition to their reform goals. Consequently, one should not overidealize the program's intentions and the extent of FSA officials' progressivism. Doing so would obscure the challenge behind cultivating a more inclusive U.S. democratic society, as well as place too much emphasis on state action as the pathway to economic justice.

Although Congress did not officially terminate the camp program until 1946, most of the FSA's original New Dealers who were invested in the agency's social democratic mission had left or were fired by the end of 1943. In April of that year, President Roosevelt signed Public Law 45, transferring administrative control of the FSA's farm labor programs to the newly established Office of Labor and the War Food Administration (WFA). Essentially grower-led, the WFA favored growers' political and economic interests. Accordingly, the bureaucratic shift, which applied new stipulations on the FSA's ability to regulate farm wages and working conditions, placed significant challenges on the FSA's social welfare goals. Some important services, such as the FSA's comprehensive medical care program for farmworkers, continued until 1946. But, more generally, FSA officials' personal memoirs reveal the profound disillusionment they felt as they witnessed the camps become sites for farmworkers' exploitation, not democratization.

That the camp program failed to guarantee farmworkers the political rights they needed must not eclipse the compelling evidence showing how it successfully challenged actions to deprive migrants of basic entitlements as workers and citizens. Against constant hostility, FSA officials forced corporate growers, discriminatory state agents, and intolerant rural communities to recognize migrant farmworkers' rights to a basic standard of living, equal opportunity, and a political voice. And, when they refused to do so, FSA agents reminded U.S. society of the "mockery of democracy" in the fields. Such a stance was most meaningful to migrant families who needed the government's support to advance their struggle for socioeconomic justice. The program allowed migrant families such as those in Weslaco, Texas, to test federal officials' willingness to listen to their claims, provide for their needs, and view them as deserving citizens.

To best explore the different arenas in which the camps' experiment in democracy took place, and to highlight the diverse historical actors involved in the process, the chapters that follow maintain a chronological structure but are primarily organized around a series of interrelated topics. In Chapter 1 I explain why the camp program emerged by addressing key factors related to the historical context of this era—including farmworkers' strikes in the 1930s, the Great Depression and westward migration of Dust Bowl refugees, and the more progressive political climate reflected in the New Deal. I include brief biographical sketches of some of the FSA's key administrators in discussing the ideologies shaping the program's development. I also consider the central nature of the South's socioeconomic and racial politics that largely determined the RA/FSA's actions in aiding farmworkers nationwide. Additionally, the chapter illuminates why commercial growers opposed the FSA's intervention, including their view that the FSA promoted farmworkers' unions and encouraged migrants to demand undue public welfare. Finally, I end by discussing some of the contradictions in the FSA's democratic promise, especially in race and gendered terms.

Chapter 2 considers the explicit ways the camp space operated to choreograph migrant families' everyday practices. I use camp blueprints, aerial and on-site photographs, and engineering documents to uncover how the FSA's planners and architects constructed the camps to function like "miniature societies" where migrants would develop a democratic, collective outlook. Through a study of the architects' backgrounds, I show how they were invested in the social debates out of which the project emerged and designed each building, road, and landscape feature with their larger political visions in mind. Despite their intended function as community-building spaces, I argue that the camps' design (which was largely standardized across the country) reinforced different racial, gendered, and class-based divisions in U.S. agriculture and society. Lastly, this chapter illuminates how the architects' successful effort in building one of the nation's first public housing projects (the migrant camps) resulted in their assignment to design Japanese internment camps during World War II, which fundamentally questioned their democratic aspirations.

In Chapter 3 I shift our perspective of the camps' built environment as a site of analysis to reveal how migrant families perceived, encountered, and experienced the camp space they occupied. I use migrants' self-produced camp newspapers, letters, songs, and "mental maps" to demonstrate how they constituted their reality of camp life. Migrants ascribed meaning to the camps' built environment through their personal and collective efforts that both challenged and reaffirmed how federal officials understood the process of community formation taking place. Their conceptions of belonging also defied racialized assumptions concerning their willingness to work collectively. Ultimately, I claim that migrant farmworkers exercised significant power as geographical actors in shaping the political and social landscape defining the camp program.

Utilizing the camp clinics' medical records, public health reports, nurses' memoirs, and the FSA's correspondence with physicians, Chapter 4 focuses on the camp program's intervention in migrants' medical care, as well as family and home management. I begin by explaining how FSA officials defended their involvement in migrant health—including their decision to build clinics and hospitals. The FSA stated that the medical program was central to their rehabilitation effort, protected communities from the spread of disease, and improved migrants' efficiency as workers. Ultimately, the FSA's health education program and extensive medical services saved countless lives as it affirmed migrants' entitlement to good health. The medical program was undoubtedly one of the agency's most remarkable human rights achievements. In the process of carrying out their medical project, however, FSA officials often pathologized migrants' domestic and cultural practices as unhealthy, harmful, and degenerative. This promoted racialized views of culture and poverty as a means to reinforce normative American standards of health and hygiene and label certain migrants unfit for citizenship.

In Chapter 5 I examine how migrant families negotiated the different conceptions of American identity, citizenship, and democracy that FSA officials promoted. I pay particular attention to the role of the camp council, the self-governing committee in all of the camps composed of elected migrant residents. Through council minutes and migrants' speeches and writings, I reveal how migrants used the camp bureaucracy to advance their social justice goals and challenge popular assumptions positioning them as "alien citizens" unfamiliar with the principles of American democracy.[32] I pay specific attention to the political struggle that developed between migrants, the FSA, and local communities over migrants' access to public schooling and equal education. This struggle demonstrates the challenge migrants and FSA officials faced in resolving the paradox of migrant citizenship in which even if migrants understood their rights as U.S. citizens, they struggled to exercise them. Finally, I end the chapter by considering the FSA's role in managing the Seasonal Leave Program beginning in 1942. The program allowed Japanese American families (recruited from U.S. internment camps) to live in FSA camps while they engaged in farmwork. Viewed relationally, I argue that the Japanese experience sheds light on the conflicting, unequal, and illusive nature of the FSA's democratic promise.

In the book's final chapter, Chapter 6, I discuss the larger politics surrounding the end of the camp program in 1946. I pay particular attention to the role the nation's farm bloc played in the agency's demise, and I consider the general shift toward political conservativism by the mid-1940s. Additionally, the chapter addresses the irony in the FSA's appointment as the leading agency responsible for recruiting foreign guest workers during World War II, showing how this undercut many of the gains the FSA had

accomplished on behalf of domestic farmworkers. The guest worker programs generated a firmer commitment nationally to industrial farming that
produced adverse effects for domestic workers, including advancing a gendered construction of farm labor that increasingly did away with family
housing. Finally, I examine the camps' political and historical legacy in
terms of farmworkers' civil rights and debates surrounding the welfare
state, particularly during the 1960s. I also illuminate the role FSA officials
went on to play in advancing social reform programs domestically and
abroad.

In closing, the epilogue resituates the book's intervention in debates
about migrant citizenship by revisiting the interplay between domesticity,
labor, and democracy. In more specific terms, I consider how the FSA's
commitment to migrants' security gave way to conditions of risk that have
only intensified in recent decades as migrant farmworkers remain barred
from full labor, civil, and human rights. I also place this discourse within a
broader framework to question migrant workers' status as displaced people
caught in a liminal space of statelessness and noncitizenship, or "illegality,"
devoid of rights. How have migrants contested this condition? What does
their widespread disenfranchisement mean to nations that claim to embody
the virtues of democracy? This book reveals how one experiment to make
meaningful progress in the realization of social democracy unfolded.

CHAPTER 1

Securing (Re)productive Labor

State Intervention in Migrant Housing and Farmworkers' Rights

In 1939 John Steinbeck's publication of *The Grapes of Wrath* brought national attention to, in his words, "the great wave of dust bowl migration [that] was displacing many, though by no means all, of the immigrant, non-white laborers in the California fields." Two other prominent publications appearing that year—Dorothea Lange and Paul S. Taylor's *An American Exodus* and Carey McWilliams's *Factories in the Field*—helped expose the severity of the "migrant problem" at hand. As McWilliams, who was head of the California Division of Immigration and Housing between 1938 and 1942, explained, "With the arrival of the dust-bowl refugees a day of reckoning approaches for the California farm industrialists. The jig, in other words, is about up." All of the authors emphasized this point. According to Steinbeck, these migrants were "white and American labor" who would "refuse to accept the role of field peon, with its attendant terrorism, squalor and starvation." "These despised 'Okies' were not another minority alien racial group," McWilliams similarly contended, "but American citizens familiar with the usages of democracy."[1]

As Steinbeck's novel gained popularity, federal officials working on behalf of President Franklin D. Roosevelt's agrarian New Deal reminded the nation that the grapes of wrath were also stored in the South's sharecropper country.[2] The National Emergency Council's 1938 *Report on Economic Conditions of the South* revealed that in 1934 the average yearly net income on cotton farms in eleven areas surveyed was $417 for tenants, $312 for croppers, and $180 for wage laborers (for an average of $309 per family), while the average net income of the plantation operator was $2,572.[3] The vast inequities in southern farming were aggravated by long-established practices of political disenfranchisement and violent racial subjugation, especially against African Americans. The Great Depression worsened the chronic poverty many experienced and introduced a number of changes, as Lange and Taylor explained, "dealing the old system a series of heavy blows."[4] These developments included a significant drop in cotton prices, a rise in large-scale corporate farming, disparity in crop reduction benefits, and increased mechanization. By the mid-1930s it was evident that these issues contributed to sharecroppers' and tenant farmers' rapid displacement. Indeed, most of the white migrants who traveled to California hailed from the South's western region—primarily Oklahoma, Texas, Arkansas, and Missouri—and not the central Dust Bowl area consisting of the Texas and Oklahoma panhandle and bordering parts of New Mexico, Colorado, and Kansas.

For this reason, federal agents working under the Resettlement Administration (RA), and later the Farm Security Administration (FSA), warned those concerned with California's migrant problem that although a dramatic development—with more than three hundred thousand migrants arriving between 1935 and 1938 in search of work—it was hardly an anomaly.[5] What they were seeing in California, wrote Laurence I. Hewes, assistant administrator for the RA, were "the *effects* of the migrant problem, rather than its causes, although the mechanization and industrialization of agriculture, which is definitely *one* cause, is to be seen here more obviously than in other regions." Various elements in a national process especially evident in the South—including, as Hewes explained, "drought, soil exhaustion, lack of free land, poor methods of farming, and indebtedness"—were fueling the migrant problem. Agriculture was changing, he argued; no longer could the majority of rural Americans draw from it any "semblance of a way of life; or in an increasing number of cases, even a livelihood."[6] As sharecroppers and tenants fell down the proverbial agricultural ladder and became destitute migrant laborers, the RA stepped in to help solve a national crisis.[7] Yet the mythology surrounding the agricultural ladder reinforced federal officials' mistaken notion that the migrant stream was a new phenomenon produced by the economic crisis of the Great Depression.

To best understand the origins of the migratory labor camp program, and why federal efforts to house farmworkers became so contested, one must consider how the depression shaped rural society beyond creating greater economic instability. Beginning in 1933, the New Deal advanced a liberal political agenda allowing progressive reformers, farm labor advocates, and organized workers to demand state intervention to correct the socioeconomic injustices in agriculture. This chapter begins by tracing some of the nation's most volatile agricultural strikes during the early 1930s, to situate the role that noncitizen and nonwhite migrant farmworkers played in demanding federal protection against their repressive employers.[8] Although the 1933 National Industrial Recovery Act and Federal Emergency Relief Administration denied farmworkers the right of collective bargaining and federal aid, such setbacks did not stop migrants from mobilizing. Through farmworkers' activism, housing emerged as a central site of struggle over migrants' labor and civil rights. In 1935 the RA developed the first government-built camps in California to provide emergency relief that would temper existing labor strife and alleviate migrants' suffering, especially their poor health and hunger.

The RA's approach to the migrant camp program seemed initially rather conservative and largely influenced by relief efforts in the South and Midwest where it focused on stabilizing dislocated farmers. Rexford G. Tugwell, who headed the RA until shortly before it became the FSA in 1937, appeared sympathetic to migrant workers' labor unrest. In establishing the camp program, however, the RA remained focused on rehabilitating the nation's "landless farmers." This view, combined with progressive appeals that the federal government intervene in California because the majority of migrants were white American citizens, initially limited the program's radical intervention by maintaining the existing racial biases in agriculture.

As the camp program continued under the FSA through the late 1930s and early 1940s, it increasingly served the nonwhite farmworker families who traditionally followed the crops. The program expanded largely against growers' wishes. While the agency believed that growers would come to realize the program's benefits, most growers felt deeply threatened. The central reason stemmed from the FSA's commitment to social reform, which threatened the status quo. The FSA's camps offered farmworkers critical amenities while encouraging migrants' empowerment through the formation of community councils and cooperative enterprises. Consequently, federal intervention threatened growers' control over farm labor by freeing families from the dependency they had on their employer for subsistence. The camps also undermined the deference migrants were

expected to show growers as expendable, racialized workers. For this reason, growers claimed that the camp program disrupted well-established
employer-employee relations, facilitated labor militancy, and fostered
socialist principles by encouraging idleness and dependency on government
largesse.

Migrant housing came to symbolize more than just a concern over the
nature of workers' shelter. For migrant families, the camps represented an
extension of their identity as citizens worthy of federal protection and equal
representation in society. Yet despite the camp program's promising potential to advance migrants' civil rights, FSA officials drew on strictly gendered
and racialized understandings of democratic inclusion. For as advanced as
they were in their agrarian vision to provide farmworkers with various protections they were denied under the New Deal, FSA reformers maintained
gender-bound conceptions of work that only recognized male breadwinners and affirmed women's status as dependents rather than as central contributors to the nation's (and their household's) economy. They also did
not recognize nontraditional family models and partnerships beyond
immediate blood relatives. The FSA's limited perspective compromised
their efforts to foster migrants' collective action and reinforced a false
notion of separate spheres that was especially problematic for migrant
workers fighting against more than just poor wages.

Establishing the Migratory Labor Camp Program:
California's Agricultural Labor and Social Crisis

John Steinbeck's depiction of the "Weedpatch Camp" in *The Grapes of
Wrath* provided most Americans with their first understanding of the
government-sponsored migrant camps. In his widely read novel, Steinbeck
depicted California's migrant workers as abject and in need of federal intervention in order to "restore the dignity and decency that had been kicked
out of [them] by their intolerable mode of life." Steinbeck warned readers
that farmworkers would continue to experience some of the worst abuses
imaginable in living and working conditions, and that eventually the "present system of agricultural economics" would be destroyed, unless the federal government intervened.[9] To garner support for the camp program, he
described Weedpatch rather idyllically as a place where the Joad family

found hot showers, indoor privies, and free medical care. The 1940 Hollywood production of Steinbeck's Pulitzer Prize–winning novel further dramatized migrant workers' plight in the minds of most Americans. Consequently, Steinbeck's work resulted in much-needed mainstream publicity for the camp program, which played a critical role in building the political support necessary for the program's expansion in the early 1940s. In a telling statement, Garrett Eckbo, one of the FSA's camp architects, recalled, "*The Grapes of Wrath* was our bible."[10]

Carey McWilliams's *Factories in the Field* was more cautious in celebrating the camp program and federal intervention in farm labor reform, though the study was equally critical to the Popular Front movement hoping to realize the New Deal's social democratic potential.[11] Although he favored the program's development, McWilliams reminded readers that it was merely palliative, reaching only a small percentage of those in need, and not altering the present system of agriculture fueled by what he termed "farm fascism." "The solution of the farm-labor problem," McWilliams contended, "can only be achieved through the organization of farm workers. The chief significance of the migratory camps is that they provide an agency through which organization can be achieved."[12]

Steinbeck supported migrants' self-empowerment, but his approach to realizing better conditions centered on what the government should do on their behalf. He collected the research necessary for his novel while working under the aegis of the RA's Information Division, which partly explains his perspective. In 1936 Steinbeck was hired by editor George West of the *San Francisco News* to publish a series of articles on the Dust Bowl migrants, which appeared as *The Harvest Gypsies* in October. In 1938 they were reprinted by the Simon J. Lubin Society as a pamphlet, *Their Blood Is Strong*. To complete the initial task, RA officials gave Steinbeck access to the agency's files and invited him to stay in the government's newly opened demonstration labor camp in Arvin, California. Steinbeck won the confidence of RA officials as someone who understood farm labor relations mainly through his 1936 publication of *In Dubious Battle*, a novel based on the 1933 Tagus Ranch peach strike and San Joaquin Valley cotton strike in California.

This background helps underscore a significant difference in the approach McWilliams and Steinbeck took to advocate for farm labor reform. In *In Dubious Battle* Steinbeck supports the need for a unified working class to fight the repressive agricultural system, but he portrays all of the striking workers as native-born whites when the reality was that more than 75 percent of the workers engaged in the 1933 strikes were Mexican. He also avoids the more complicated truth that most of the Dust Bowl migrants involved in the strikes actually entered the picture as strikebreakers.[13] In *The Grapes of Wrath* Steinbeck again chooses to call his reader's attention to the plight of the white Dust Bowl migrant. Demographically speaking, his 1939 account was more accurate. By 1936 white migrants accounted for 90 percent of the agricultural workforce in California.[14] Steinbeck's focus was aimed not simply at revealing the transformation under way but at emphasizing how these new migrants were different from the mostly Mexican and Filipino workers in the fields before them. Unlike "the earlier foreign migrants [that] have invariably been drawn from a peon class," he explained, "they are small farmers who have lost their farms, or farm hands who have lived with the family in the old American way."[15]

In contrast, McWilliams's *Factories in the Field* begins by confronting "the violent history of racial exploitation which has long existed" in California to link the Dust Bowl migration to a longer record of capitalist exploitation of foreign farm labor. In this way, McWilliams affirms the new migrants' status as oppressed workers who must organize collectively to achieve agriculture's true social democratic reform.[16] Despite McWilliams's effort to build greater worker solidarity, however, he too positions the Dust Bowl migrants distinctly by stating that they, as white American citizens, are "of an entirely different character." By the time McWilliams publishes *Ill Fares the Land* in 1941, he cements the notion that there are "two types of agricultural migrants: the depression or removal migrants—those who, like the Joads, have been displaced from agriculture and set adrift on the land; and the habitual migrant or migratory worker who, for years, has been following an established migratory route."[17] Although they were both victims of the industrial revolution in agriculture, McWilliams, like Steinbeck, did not view them as equals.

The agricultural economist Paul S. Taylor and photographer Dorothea Lange established a similar claim to McWilliams's by demonstrating in *American Exodus* how the "American white migrants" were simply part of a "long succession of races: Chinese, Japanese, Hindustanis, Mexicans, Filipinos, [and] Negroes" performing "stoop labor" in California.[18] Yet they also contributed to building a national narrative that positioned the Dust Bowl arrivals as "refugees." In narrating the Dust Bowl migrants' "exodus," Lange and Taylor highlight their quintessential Americanness, or "stock," to argue that the migrants represented a long tradition of frontiersmen migrating west for improved opportunity. Taylor first introduced this claim in an article for *Survey Graphic* titled "Again the Covered Wagon" (1935), which Steinbeck built on for *Harvest Gypsies* and *Their Blood Is Strong*, using Lange's photographs. These early camp proponents touted the Dust Bowl migrants as latter-day pioneers to garner support for federal intervention by claiming that more was at stake than the simple well-being of a new wave of harvest hands who happened to be white. The camp program was necessary, they suggested, in order to rescue the American dream that was eroding along with the Dust Bowl people and their land.[19]

Many popular misconceptions about the so-called Dust Bowl migration prevailed when the "migrant hysteria" reached its peak in 1938. For example, only about 6 percent of the migrants actually came from regions most affected by the period's damaging dust storms. Also, many were neither farm owners nor tenants prior to migration. As one FSA official complained in 1940, "tabulators like to lump the whole kit and caboodle under the head of 'migrants'—meaning agricultural workers—when it is known that a good many never saw a farm and have no intention of seeing one if they can help it. Some are mechanics, plumbers, carpenters or anything but farm people."[20] Finally, the wave of newcomers that mostly arrived prior to 1935 was never larger than the number of migrants that entered the state during the 1920s and 1940s.[21] The inaccuracy of the "Dust Bowl" label was surely apparent to those publishing their exposés—particularly Paul Taylor, a well-established expert on California's farm labor conditions. The careful depiction of these migrants as refugees and "displaced Jeffersonian yeomen," however, served as a powerful tool to combat the hostile, racialized perception many Californians maintained about the newcomers and to win approval for the camp program.[22]

The progressive advocates likely did not intend for their Dust Bowl narrative to develop at the expense of the nonwhite and immigrant farmworkers for whom they had sympathy, and they probably imagined that whatever benefits they helped secure on behalf of "removal migrants" would eventually reach "habitual farmworkers." Still, in privileging the Dust Bowl migrants' racial superiority and first-class citizenship, their narrative had a damaging and lasting exclusionary effect. As farm labor advocates and members of the Popular Front, they abandoned a more solidaristic approach demanding federal intervention on behalf of all needy farmworkers and instead embraced a prejudiced discourse that labeled Dust

Bowl refugees as more deserving. Because the advocates accepted the fact that stories and images concerning nonwhite farmworkers would never produce the same compassion necessary to mobilize action, they reinforced the belief that for these families deplorable conditions were ordinary and acceptable. This discourse not only reveals the limits of the advocates' anti-racism, as Linda Gordon argues, but also demonstrates how their popular narratives and cultural representations produced a distorted political response to farmworkers' insecurity during the Great Depression.[23] This response defined not only how the agrarian New Deal addressed farm-workers' poverty but also how we remember these actions historically.

For example, a significant consequence of privileging the popular Dust Bowl narrative is that it further erased nonwhite farmworker families' impor-tant political actions in the years preceding the "Okie crisis." Between 1929 and 1935, mostly Mexican and Filipino migrant families joined together to wage a series of "spectacular strikes" that, according to McWilliams, had never before occurred in such magnitude and with such "far-reaching social significance."[24] In 1933 alone, fifty thousand farmworkers went on strike across California's Central Valley, risking their lives to alert the nation to California's intolerable farm labor conditions. The largest and most violent strike occurred in October in the San Joaquin Valley's cotton fields where more than eighteen thousand mainly Mexican and Mexican American farm-workers joined the communist-led Cannery and Agricultural Workers Indus-trial Union (CAWIU) to demand better housing and wage increases.[25]

The California cotton strike served as an important harbinger for all those concerned with the dramatic changes occurring nationally in agricul-ture during the Great Depression. First, the strike forced federal officials to determine if the 1933 National Industrial Recovery Act (NIRA) applied to migratory farmworkers. Section 7(a) in NIRA eventually allotted only industrial workers the right to bargain collectively, but this was determined by presidential decree three weeks after NIRA passed. Many strikers orga-nized during these early actions assuming that they had federal backing. Moreover, the strike foreshadowed the bitter fight within agriculture soon to erupt across the country as the system of industrial farming expanded and displaced greater numbers of people. Lastly, federal intervention in the strike in the form of direct relief for the evicted workers, an investigation into the growers' abuse of workers' civil liberties, and a final recommenda-tion of a wage increase convinced California growers that they needed to organize politically to protect their interests.[26]

On further investigation, federal inquiries into the early 1930s labor unrest revealed that the majority of the agricultural strikes stemmed from workers' demands for decent housing and sanitary living conditions. According to the RA, in all of the "50-odd strikes in California agriculture" it had been "easy to inflame the laborers by calling attention to the squatter conditions under which they live."[27] The U.S. Special Commission on Agricultural Labor Disturbances, formed out of the National Labor Board, similarly reported in February 1934 that

> Living and Sanitary conditions are a serious and irritating factor in the unrest we found in the Imperial Valley. This report must state that we found filth, squalor, an entire absence of sanitation, and a crowding of human beings into totally inadequate tents or crude structures built of boards, weeds, and anything that was found at hand to give a pitiful semblance of a home at worst. Words cannot describe some of the conditions we saw.[28]

Housing constituted a principal site of struggle because it represented, both physically and symbolically, the authority that growers exerted over migrants' daily lives. Better earnings were critical to improving farmworkers' poor status, but even with better wages migrants could not invest in better housing because of the temporary nature of their employment and the expectation that they would reside in grower-owned property. Migrants' reliance on grower housing limited their bargaining power because farmers could readily evict them as a strikebreaking tool. Even in migrants' own improvised camps, growers held considerable authority over local agencies, which they could pressure to dispose of migrants' housing. Consequently, farmworkers' control over their domestic space was central to their negotiations for improved labor and civil rights.

Plans for the camp program originated in California's Division of Rural Rehabilitation headed by Harry Drobisch. Paul Taylor was hired as a field director for the agency in 1934. Taylor was critical of the New Deal's exclusion of farmworkers from various federal protections since "the rural Depression was deeper, more extensive, and more protracted than the urban." He used his political status in the newly formed agency to advocate for a government camp program to house destitute migrants. Lange, whom Taylor hired and soon married, proved equally instrumental in this campaign. Her photographs focused on migrants' poor living conditions and generated greater public awareness of the real crisis in agriculture.[29]

Together, Lange and Taylor completed five phototextual reports that Drobisch used to try to convince the State Emergency Relief Administration (SERA) to fund the camp project.[30] The reports emphasized two factors in particular: the significance of better living conditions in avoiding a reoccurrence of the violent and costly labor battles plaguing California's fields, and the important transformation occurring as "Americans of the old stock" replaced the mostly foreign nonwhite farmworkers who were the backbone of the industry. Highlighting that these were "native white American" families now laboring in the fields was not simply a means to garner sympathetic support for the program. This realization mattered, Drobisch emphasized, because white citizen workers could not be deported, battered, and denied an American standard of living.[31]

Overzealous efforts to deport Mexican and Filipino farmworker families helped advance the racial shift occurring in California farm labor during the 1930s. According to some estimates, as much as one-third of the U.S. Mexican population left the country during the Depression, though other figures suggest it was closer to one-half. Francisco E. Balderrama and Raymond Rodriguez calculate that approximately one million Mexicans left, either voluntarily or unwillingly, during the 1930s. Many of the labor activists participating in California's farm strikes during the 1920s and early 1930s were among the first targeted.[32] Dr. George Clements of the Agricultural Department of the Los Angeles Chamber of Commerce, a pro-grower organization, explained the implications of the demographic change as follows:

> Of the 175,000 Mexicans who from 1917 to 1930 met the agricultural labor requirements of the whole state, moving from place to place to meet seasonal demands, there were possibly not more than 10% available in 1936. . . . [Mexican workers] were adaptable labor in the agricultural field. They were impossible of unionizing; they were tractable labor. Can we expect these new white transient citizens to fill their place? The white transients are not tractable labor. Being American citizens, they are going to demand the so-called American standard of living.[33]

Although Clements was wrong, both in assuming that all Mexican farmworkers were foreign-born and by claiming that they were "impossible of unionizing," he succeeded in emphasizing how a revolution in agriculture would ensue if Americans continued to displace the more exploitable work-ers. In this way, Clements's argument did not differ much from the warn-ings progressive advocates issued about the new migrants.

When Drobisch presented SERA officials with Taylor and Lange's pro-posal, it was denied for "lack of diversion of funds," but the agency was also heavily influenced by the state's big growers who wanted to keep con-trol over all relief measures and believed that government-run labor camps would encourage further unionization. Consequently, Drobisch took the proposal to the Federal Emergency Relief Administration (FERA) in March 1935, hoping that federal officials would see the need and grant money for the program. In May, Taylor helped secure federal support by inviting the head of FERA in San Francisco, Lowry Nelson, on a tour of migrant work-ers' dreadful living conditions. Although Taylor did not receive the $100,000 he and Drobisch requested, Nelson committed $20,000 (of left-over funds) to construct two demonstration camps. Construction for the first camp at Marysville in Yuba County began in the spring of 1935. Nearly one month after the program began, it was transferred from FERA to the newly created Resettlement Administration headed by Rexford Tugwell.[34]

Tugwell initially objected to the camp program, believing that it fell outside of the RA's mandate and would further subsidize big growers and create additional political tension. RA officials advanced a myopic view for reforming agriculture that led them to focus on aiding dispossessed tenants attempting to farm worn-out lands. They concentrated on rehabilitating landless farmers because many of the New Deal's agrarian reformers were still invested in "the image of the yeoman farmer as the basis for a demo-cratic society."[35] Yet this was a vision that never truly existed in California, as Taylor and McWilliams tried to explain. Consequently, in their initial efforts, RA officials largely ignored the more established nonwhite migra-tory farmworker families who had long suffered from the dislocation, chronic poverty, and racial exploitation characterizing their work.[36]

Not until Tugwell inspected the two demonstration camps (the second at Arvin in Kern County) did he understand the benefits of the program. After visiting with migrant residents in October 1935, Tugwell stated that he was "favorably impressed" and approved plans for the camps' expan-sion.[37] Even still, as the program developed under the RA with four addi-tional facilities in California by 1937—at Winters, Shafter, Coachella, and Brawley—it did so within a narrow vision of rehabilitation. At a conference on "housing of migratory agricultural laborers" in November 1935, for instance, the RA discussed the possibility of building fifteen to twenty additional migrant camps because of their "unique value in serving as reservoirs from which distressed farm people can be filtered upward and selectively re-established on part-time farms, as tenants, and even assisted back to the ranks of farm owners." As the agency's representatives made clear, "for some, the camps will constitute a first rung in a reconstructed agricultural ladder, which they can ascend in traditional American fashion according to their abilities."[38]

Some of the RA's limited rehabilitation discourse resulted from the larger political battles affecting the agency, especially as the RA was transferred to the U.S. Department of Agriculture (USDA) on January 1, 1937, and then transformed into the FSA on September 1, 1937.[39] Federal officials interested in aiding migratory workers were increasingly forced to defend their plans against the more conservative and pro-grower approaches to agricultural policy that traditionally steered the USDA. Moreover, while the RA approved the program in 1935, Congress did not appropriate funds to build the camps until 1939. Consequently, the FSA established the first string of federal camps in California with funds from emergency relief appropriation acts specifically earmarked for "rural rehabilitation," understood mainly as a program for former farmers.[40]

The South's Impact on Rural Reform and the Resettlement Administration's Founding

Tensions plaguing the start of the camp program in California were largely shaped by the New Deal's approach to agrarian reform in the South, where the RA focused most directly on rehabilitating dispossessed sharecroppers and tenants who made up almost half of the farming population. In some states such as Mississippi, the figure was closer to 70 percent.[41] Before mainstream attention centered on the Okie crisis developing in the West, federal officials were consumed by the chronic poverty they "discovered" in the South. When Secretary of Agriculture Henry A. Wallace toured the back roads of the Mississippi delta in mid-November 1936 accompanied by Tugwell, Will Alexander, and Calvin "Beanie" Baldwin of the RA, he found sharecroppers living in unimaginable squalor, weak from disease and malnutrition, and trapped in a cycle of dependency so firmly rooted that they appeared to lack any hope for a better life. On this trip, Wallace carried a copy of Arthur Raper's newly published book, *Preface to Peasantry: A Tale of Two Black Belt Counties* (1936), which called for progressive federal intervention.[42]

Like Paul Taylor, Raper was an activist social scientist (in his case, a sociologist) who believed that the government should introduce socio-economic reforms to help tenants and sharecroppers, especially African Americans, break free from the plantation mentality and planter paternalism keeping them bound to a failing agricultural system.[43] Raper argued that left unaddressed, southern conditions threatened to undermine the nation's recovery from the Great Depression. Wallace and the RA's leading officials understood this full well. As Jonathan Garst, the RA's regional director for California, explained, the migrant and tenant problems were inseparable. When interviewed "about the problems of migratory labor in California," Garst reported, "I have tried in every case to emphasize the fact that this is only a small live eddy shooting off from the dead pool of poverty in the Rural South."[44] By the time Raper's book appeared in 1936, President Roosevelt seemed convinced that "the South presents right now the Nation's No. 1 economic problem."[45] The main issue centered on what approach the government should take to promote rural recovery in the region.

During the first few years of the Depression, southern politicians and their agribusiness supporters resisted federal intervention and the expansion of a welfare state. The gravity of the economic crisis, however, which hastened the collapse of the plantation system and the outmigration of both black and white southerners, created such a calamity that soon many of the region's most prominent planters and politicians demanded "aggressive and imaginative action by the federal government." In 1932 Edward O'Neal, a wealthy plantation owner from Alabama and head of the American Farm Bureau Federation (AFBF), cautioned, "Unless something is done for the American farmer, we will have revolution in the countryside in less than twelve months."[46] O'Neal's assessment helps explain why southerners were among Roosevelt's strongest supporters on the eve of his presidential election in 1932.

Southern elites demanded federal intervention, but on their own terms. While the New Deal proved vital to advancing economic and political democracy in the South, it also exacerbated many of the problems agrarian officials set out to resolve.[47] This contradiction seems especially true of Roosevelt's first policies aimed at providing immediate relief, such as FERA,

NIRA, and the Agricultural Adjustment Act (AAA). During his first presidential campaign, Roosevelt promised "bold, persistent experimentation," and many of the policy makers he staffed on his administration were committed to just that.[48] Yet their creative approaches for rural reform were constrained by deeply influential conservative forces limiting their ability to operate in any way that challenged the status quo.

In assuming the presidency, Roosevelt understood that a more conformist course was necessary to secure congressional support for the New Deal. The southern Democrats who helped vote him into office dominated Congress in 1933, controlling more than half of all committee chairs and most other leadership positions.[49] Consequently, the first legislation enacted to promote rural recovery was, as historian Patricia Sullivan writes, "easily tailored by local southern elites and their powerful representatives in Congress to fit the prevailing economic and political arrangements in the region."[50] Only a few days after his inauguration, on March 10, 1933, Roosevelt invited about fifty rural editors and farm organization leaders, including O'Neal, to meet with Secretary Wallace to design and discuss a program for agricultural relief. O'Neal left the meeting "beaming" and "feeling good," recognizing that the proposal they drafted, which resulted in the AAA, benefited the nation's agricultural establishment.[51] Rather than keeping impoverished farmers on the land, the AAA accelerated their displacement as landlords claimed they needed less labor under the crop-reduction program but actually found it more economical to evict their tenants and sharecroppers instead of paying them the benefits to which they were entitled.[52]

Southern planter influence on the terms of FERA and NIRA resulted in similarly biased policies that produced detrimental effects for farmworkers nationally and reaffirmed large growers' power over existing socioeconomic and race relations across the country. FERA included a Federal Transient Program, which managed millions of dollars for "transient" relief earmarked for "needy persons" who had "no legal settlement in any one state or community." The designation seemed to fit migrant farmworkers' civic and economic status, yet FERA contained specific language excluding farmworkers from its provisions. The reason for this again stems from southern planters' near absolute control over the parameters of federal intervention under the New Deal. Because growers relied on migrants' dependency to keep them in line, they recognized that allowing farmworkers access to an independent source of income would undermine the status quo of exploitation. For this reason, FERA required states to operate with the "utmost vigilance" to guarantee that federal relief funds went to "bona fide transients," not to farmworkers.[53] Such policies help explain why Drobisch and Taylor struggled to secure funds for the migrant camp program from California's SERA.

Southern planters' desire to maintain a cheap, deferential labor force, and to deny African Americans any opportunity to contest their racial subjugation, also resulted in farmworkers' exclusion from NIRA. NIRA allowed the federal government to regulate industry for fair wages, hours, and prices to stimulate economic recovery. In developing codes for each industry, however, the National Recovery Administration established wage differentials based on occupational and geographic classifications that allowed employers to pay some workers less, especially nonwhites relegated to specific jobs such as domestic and agricultural work.[54] Moreover, Section 7(a) of the act gave workers collective bargaining rights. Yet soon after it passed, President Roosevelt barred field workers from these protections. Several reasons were offered to explain the exclusion, including the special problem of protecting perishable crops vital to the nation's recovery, but these reasons masked a more fundamental desire to preserve Jim Crow by denying African American farmworkers any opportunity to secure labor rights. While the southern bloc in Congress supported some economic reforms that would aid the region's chronic poverty, they rejected any policies that might subvert the political structure of white supremacy.

Ira Katznelson argues that we cannot understand the ironies and limitations of the New Deal without placing "the special, often determining role of the Jim Crow South front and center." Although the Solid South encompassed diverse political and economic interests, it was staunchly unified in its fight to maintain the region's racial hierarchy. To keep the South "inside the game of democracy," he writes, "required accommodating the most violent and illiberal part of the political system."[55] The unequivocal racism inherent in the federal government's initial recovery policies extended into the Second New Deal, even as the southern Democratic alliance with Roosevelt grew unstable. The politics of white supremacy shaped the camp program's development, which federal officials promoted as part of their commitment to rural democracy. On the one hand, it served to limit the political power migrant farmworkers could develop on their own by excluding them from key New Deal protections and thus requiring federal intervention through migrant housing. On the other hand, white supremacy became the very discourse progressive advocates engaged in to win political support for the program. Accordingly, camp officials had to balance this incongruity and test the limits between social democratic reform and racial and class suppression throughout the program's duration.

The Second New Deal introduced a more centralized approach and bolder interference in matters of rural poverty concerning race and labor, although agrarian reformers were still largely restricted by conservative congressional power. On April 30, 1935, Roosevelt established the RA by executive order in response to mounting protests organized by the Southern Tenant Farmers' Union (STFU) founded in Arkansas in 1934. The union of mostly black and white tenant farmers and sharecroppers, aided by the Socialist Party, reached more than thirty thousand members at its peak in the late 1930s and spread across the South from Arkansas and Missouri to Mississippi, Oklahoma, and Texas, among other states.[56] In a series of cotton strikes in 1935 and 1936, STFU members successfully drew national attention to the failure of the AAA as a recovery measure and the unwillingness of the federal government to challenge the South's planter paternalism. Additional movements by displaced farmers and farmworkers guaranteed that agricultural officials could no longer ignore their plight. The communist-led Share Croppers Union founded in 1931 among rural blacks in Alabama, for instance, claimed more than ten thousand members by 1936 as it spread into Louisiana and Mississippi.[57] And in February 1935, the National Association for the Advancement of Colored People (NAACP) urged Roosevelt to act on the fact that the AAA had already evicted more than one hundred thousand people from their land.[58]

The USDA officially supported planters against the STFU, much as it had done in response to the CAWIU-led strikes during 1933, by agreeing that radical agitators had riled up ignorant sharecroppers as part of a communist conspiracy.[59] Yet the USDA was deeply divided in 1935, a fact that contributed to Secretary Wallace's "purge" (under conservative pressure) of many of the agency's liberal-minded officials from the AAA in February of that year.[60] The purge of the liberals, combined with sharecroppers' and tenants' continued protests, created the opportunity Tugwell needed to convince Roosevelt to establish the RA, which was committed to rural rehabilitation. Because it emerged outside of the pro-grower USDA, the RA had the room to advance new ideas for socioeconomic transformation. By 1936, however, Tugwell realized that its very independence made the RA an easy target for dissolution. Partly for this reason, he invited Wallace to tour the RA's southern operations in 1936 hoping to convince him of the value of the agency's programs and the need to integrate them into the USDA. One month after their southern tour, in December 1936, Tugwell resigned from the RA trying to protect the agency from conservative backlash and secure its place in the USDA.[61]

Will Alexander, who initially served as the RA's deputy administrator, took over the agency in 1937 as it was transferred to the USDA in January and transformed into the FSA in September. C. B. Baldwin followed Alexander as FSA director from 1940 to 1943. Collectively, the ideological views these administrators held were significantly unconventional in that they took into account the importance of class difference and racial inequality in rural society and supported federal intervention and assistance "for poor people and their oppositional organizations." As Jess Gilbert notes, "Tugwell was the archetypical urban liberal: Ivy League, outspoken, iconoclastic." He was "neither an agrarian individualist nor an advocate of family farming, preferring cooperatives and collectives, the bigger the better." He believed that social justice could be achieved through federal policy managed by rationalistic experts like himself, and carried out democratically in a way that could not be captured by the local power structures he called the "grass-tops."[62] His ideological influence would remain with the FSA's staff long after he resigned from the RA. Critics liked to charge that the FSA's leaders had been "injected with the Tugwell virus."[63]

Unlike Tugwell, Alexander and Baldwin were southerners with agricultural backgrounds, though they too were not necessarily trained agriculturalists. Their liberal politics and concern for social welfare activism inspired many of the agency's most important efforts to expand the boundaries of rural democracy. Alexander was the son of an Ozark farmer in southern Missouri, a former Methodist minister in Tennessee, a former president of Dillard University (a black liberal arts college in New Orleans), and a prominent leader in Atlanta's interracial movement. He continued to head the Commission on Interracial Cooperation, which he established in Atlanta in 1919, when he joined the RA and then became head of the FSA. His activism on behalf of racial equality would earn him, and by extension the FSA, the epithet of "Nigger Lover."[64] When Tugwell recruited Alexander to the RA in 1935, he had just published a coauthored study, titled *The Collapse of Cotton Tenancy*, along with Edwin R. Embree of the Rosenwald Fund and the African American sociologist Charles S. Johnson. The study, mostly drafted by Johnson, presented an outright critique of the AAA's southern cotton program, much to the chagrin of the more conservative USDA leaders. The book essentially supported the STFU's claims that the programs of the AAA "were of the planters, by the planters, and for the planters."[65] In hiring Alexander, Tugwell understood that he represented a challenge to the status quo.

C. B. Baldwin arrived in Washington, D.C., in 1933 recruited by his close friend and mentor Paul H. Appleby (executive assistant to Wallace from 1933 to 1940, and undersecretary of agriculture from 1940 to 1944). Baldwin came of age in the foothills of the Blue Ridge Mountains in Radford, Virginia, where he returned after dropping out of college to get married. By all accounts, he would become one of the FSA's most influential figures. Although not an intellectual like many of the liberals involved in the agrarian New Deal, Baldwin's peers spoke of him as an incredibly apt administrator who deserved much credit for the FSA's success both due to his "managerial skills" and "ideological zeal."[66] Baldwin kept the FSA united under a doctrine that preached "humanity, equality, opportunity, social justice, decency, democracy, potentiality, [and] security."[67] Consequently, Congress frequently attacked Baldwin as a communist trying to "nationalize or socialize the land."[68] His liberal ideologies were so imbued in the FSA's policies and programs, according to members of the farm bloc, that they were practically inseparable. Baldwin resigned from the FSA in 1943 to preserve its credibility and save what little power it still had to effect positive change.

The brief biographies of the RA's/FSA's top administrators provide a better understanding of why southern planters, and the nation's agricultural elite more generally, viewed the agency as a threat to their established order. Initially, not all of the RA's programs were considered controversial, but as the agency increasingly moved away from providing displaced farmers with economic relief and instead supported their broader sociopolitical transformation, it entered into hostile terrain. In 1935 the RA managed four main programs: (1) a land reform program involving purchasing and retiring overused and unproductive land; (2) a rural resettlement program for dislocated farm families in cooperative communities, small garden home projects, and the migratory labor camps; (3) a suburban resettlement program in model communities such as the RA-built Greenbelt towns; and (4) a program to support rural rehabilitation by providing poor families loans and grants to purchase land, equipment, and livestock. Southern planters tolerated the rehabilitation program, which accounted for 60 percent of the RA's expenditures in 1936, so long as it simply helped a few

tenants and sharecroppers move toward farm ownership and did not significantly disturb local arrangements.[69]

The passage of the Bankhead-Jones Farm Tenant Act and the creation
of the FSA in 1937, however, expanded the loan program's reach in the
number of borrowers (including more African American clients) and in the
agency's programmatic scope. As Lee J. Alston and Joseph P. Ferrie estimate, "Spending on rehabilitation loans alone rose from $78 million under
the RA to $125 million under the FSA." The agency also introduced new
rehabilitation methods more disruptive to southern practices, including the
promotion of group services, cooperative associations, neighborhood
action groups, and a debt adjustment and tenure improvement program
aimed at establishing fair agreements between tenants and landlords (mediated through a written contract managed by the FSA).[70] Such actions not
only gave low-income farmers newfound financial and domestic freedom
but also strengthened their bargaining power against planters, local bank-
ers, and merchants. The FSA encouraged clients to know their legal rights
and become self-determining citizens.[71]

Although the FSA was careful not to stir up too much trouble, there
was no denying that FSA programs advocated self-empowerment, social
justice, and collective action, challenging the structure of white supremacy.
Southern planters feared the very thing that former black sharecroppers
such as Sam Brown expressed when asked how he felt about buying his
own farm in Arkansas with the help of the FSA's Tenant Purchase Program.
As Brown stated, "We've got justice now. We've got rights. We can support
our families with food that we raise ourselves. We weren't living before, just
existing. Now I feel I own something, and I've got rights. . . . It's making
us free."[72] Brown not only spoke about what the program had done to
rehabilitate his family but also emphasized the impact it had communally
by speaking in terms of "us" and "we." Though the New Deal was significantly limited in what it did for rural blacks compared to whites, many
African American labor and civil rights groups nonetheless viewed the FSA
as a champion of their rights and its programs as an opportunity to advance
the freedom struggle.[73]

Rather than recognizing the success the FSA achieved in bringing
increased financial, material, and social progress to the South, those who
wished to protect conventional practices only saw impending changes to
their way of life. After 1938, southern politicians were largely united in
attacking the FSA for intervening ways that defied their prescribed role as

an agricultural agency. By the time the AFBF assembled their attack on the FSA in Congress, they were joined by growers' organizations across the country, most notably the Associated Farmers (AF) of California, who felt equally threatened by what the camp program was doing to subvert their business, which was dependent on cheap, deferential, and disenfranchised labor. This farm bloc became further solidified by the fact that "southern farms were becoming 'westernized,' " meaning that they were increasingly mechanized, capital-intensive, absentee-owned, and reliant on migrant labor.[74]

Commercial Growers' Opposition to the FSA's Migrant Labor Camp Program

When the Associated Farmers organized in California in March 1934, they came together as men of big business. The AF's leaders were not "farmers" in any sense but rather representatives of large corporations such as Pacific Gas and Electric, Southern Pacific Railroad, and Bank of America, each with significant investments in agribusiness.[75] They united in response to farmworkers' uprisings across the Central and Imperial Valleys in 1933 and 1934 and their belief that Roosevelt was "coddling Communists" by feeding the strikers who refused to work. Under AF leadership, western growers responded to workers' unrest with violence supported by local community groups and law enforcement, as well as through a powerful political mobilization that, as Kathryn Olmstead argues, proved foundational to the modern conservative movement that later emerged out of California.[76]

The AF generated significant hostility toward the New Deal through their local networks and the clever use of alarmist, anti-red propaganda aimed at weakening organized labor.[77] In their early days, they effectively attacked the CAWIU and its organizers on charges of criminal syndicalism. By 1937 the AF focused their attention on the newly formed United Cannery, Agricultural, Packing, and Allied Workers of America (UCAPAWA) affiliated with the Congress of Industrial Organizations (CIO). UCAPAWA was successful in organizing large numbers of remaining Mexican and Filipino migrants, along with many of the recently arrived white Dust Bowl families in California, with the help of urban progressive organizations such as the Simon J. Lubin Society founded in 1936 and the John Steinbeck Committee to Aid Agricultural Organization established in 1938. Both of these organizations maintained close ties with the FSA and regularly used FSA data to publish information on farmworkers' exploited conditions. The union also received direct support in 1938 from California's new governor, Culbert Olson, who sympathized with migrants' plight and encouraged their organization.[78] Although most of the rank and file in UCAPAWA, as in CAWIU, did not consider themselves communists, many of its leaders were closely affiliated with the Communist Party. Their political radicalism and interracial organizing (which itself was considered communistic in the 1930s) helped the AF arouse considerable opposition against them.[79] When it became apparent that several of the FSA camps served as UCAPAWA headquarters, the AF's union-busting efforts became closely entwined with their anti–New Deal drive aimed at the FSA.

On establishing the camp program in 1935, RA officials hoped that growers would recognize how they stood to benefit from federal housing to "eliminate one potent breeder of unrest" and "as a measure of wise economy, not only of camp costs, but also of the labor supply [available]." Many small farmers did appreciate the FSA's efforts and testified in support of the program's impact.[80] Yet on November 9, 1935, one month after Tugwell visited the RA's demonstration camps, the AF held a special conference in Los Angeles where members voiced their opposition and stipulated their terms should the government continue with its plans. Among other things, the AF wanted the camps managed by a supervisor "under the control of a local committee of growers," for camp facilities to be "as meager as possible so as to emphasize the transient nature of the shelter," and for the camps to be "strictly regulated so as to prevent the spread of subversive ideas." They also insisted that "legal residence in a particular county could not be acquired by transients registered at the camps."[81] Their demands demonstrated the concern at the heart of the battle over federal intervention in national farm labor relations—the fear over a disruption of corporate farming's entrenched dependence on itinerant, noncitizen labor.

Growers were initially unsuccessful in gaining control over the camps' administration, but this continued to be their goal throughout the program's duration. In an article appearing in the *Robstown Record* dated March 27, 1941, for example, the Coastal Bend Group made up of commercial farmers from Corpus Christi, Texas, requested that "a supervisory board of local citizens be set up to govern the administration of the FSA Migratory Labor Camps, correcting policies which at present are having a noticeable effect throughout the region in causing laborers to be indifferent towards securing regular resident employment on farms, and dissatisfied with the wage scale which present commodity prices make necessary upon the farm."[82]

While growers traditionally held the power in negotiating farm wages by threatening workers with eviction if they attempted to organize for better pay, the camps had turned these dynamics around. Workers now had the protection of government housing and economic assistance to pressure growers into better employment conditions. Upset over their loss of authority, growers blamed the FSA for the militancy workers regenerated in the fields in the late 1930s. And with leadership positions in most community-based organizations, farmers' concerns carried considerable weight.

C. B. Baldwin, on recognizing the challenges his staff encountered in Texas, explained in a letter to all regional directors that the concerns the local residents expressed were typical of the complaints the agency heard wherever they established a camp. According to Baldwin:

> Usually as soon as a Labor Relations representative arrives in the area to make a tentative survey, his presence gives rise to a flood of rumors. For example, stories get around that we are planning to set up a kind of concentration camp; that we plan to force all agricultural workers to join a union; that the camp will bring hordes of undesirables who will create major police problems for the local community; that the camp will throw huge burdens on the local education and relief agencies; [and] that the camp will be an eyesore, which will force down the value of property. As a result of such rumors many people have become alarmed, and the groups which always oppose our migrant program have an excellent opportunity to organize an attack upon the proposed camp.[83]

In essence, Baldwin described the very scene that unfolded two months later in Crystal City, Texas. At a public meeting with FSA officials and local community leaders in early May 1941, growers charged that "families accommodated at the camp [were] removed from the labor supply and cannot be depended upon." They insisted that the camps "disturbed labor" by "compel[ling] them to ask for more which will result in sabotage and inefficiency." Additionally, they criticized the FSA's grant budget, which the growers assumed was "established by the government from experience with

Anglo-American families" and believed was "out of proportion for a Latin-American family." This point played into growers' preference for Mexican farmworkers whom they previously controlled by denying public aid. Consequently, the growers added that "camp residents should not be allowed relief if [they] refused to accept labor at any wage." Finally, while they attested to being "accustomed to unionism activity," the growers resented the fact that "the closest organization is on camp premises" because it proved that the "Federal Government, with its housing program, is supporting such activity."[84]

In growers' minds, the FSA desired to position itself as migrants' custodian while indoctrinating them with radical ideas about their rights. By the time the camp program expanded in the early 1940s, southern and western growers joined in providing evidence of the agency's subversive intent. In the Yazoo-Mississippi delta, as Nan Elizabeth Woodruff shows, planters forming the Delta Council protested the FSA's role in removing laborers from the "paternal bonds that sustained them," allowing them to "find common ground with the unions and civil rights groups that pressed for economic and political equality." According to the planters, the presence of communists in the delta, and the STFU and CIO's strength, provided proof of this transformation. Oscar F. Bledsoe, a member of the council, declared that the "perfect harmony" of race relations was "under attack by the New Deal, assisted by the President's wife, the FSA, and the CIO." In his estimation, African Americans "by nature" had "no ambition for social or racial equality."[85] Growers across the country registered similar protests against the FSA's meddling.

For this reason, most growers believed that conditions would be far more satisfactory if the FSA simply left matters alone and allowed them to handle their own business and labor. In a letter to the USDA dated June 9, 1939, for example, thirty farmers from Nueces County, Texas, declared: "We have always handled our labor satisfactory [sic] and peaceably and we believe by locating a camp in this community, it will agitate a feeling of unsatisfaction among the peaceful laborers who have been employed in this community for several years, and for that reason, we consider the locating of a camp here a nuisance to the community."[86]

This claim continued to dominate growers' protests through the early 1940s. In 1943 Mr. W. E. Springer, president of the Agricultural War Commodities, Inc., a corporation established by Arizona farmers to deal with the FSA, testified why the FSA's role in farm labor relations was a problem.

"It is the manner in which they handle or take care of these people or supposed to take care of them," Springer explained. "I don't think they need any care. I think the people who own these farms and have been operating them all their lives are able to take care of them without any outside interference from Government agencies or anyone else."[87] Planters in the Delta Council also claimed that their housing projects, though developed largely in response to federal pressure, were evidence of how "the South can recognize, meet, and solve her own problems, be they housing of agricultural workers or the abstract and greatly exploited 'race relations,' with the leadership, initiative, intelligence, and progressiveness of her own people."[88]

The FSA took a neutral stance when speaking publicly on the matter of farmworker organizing, "being very cautious about any remarks either pro or con," because they realized they stood on "thin ice" politically speaking.[89] In resolving the initial policies of the camp program in 1935 and 1936, RA officials avowed that "persons residing in the camp[s] [were] entitled to the free enjoyment of legal rights, privileges and civil liberties accorded under the Constitution." This included "the right of the camp population to join or to refrain from joining a union for collective bargaining." Therefore, the RA held "no objections to organizers talking with groups of workers in the camps, provided that they [were] invited by the workers."[90] This policy proved critical to UCAPAWA's success in California between 1937 and 1940. UCAPAWA used the protection afforded by the federal camps to mount its most effective organizational campaigns. The union heavily recruited inside the camps, regularly held meetings there, and often used the facilities as strike headquarters.[91]

Migrants' Labor Organizing in the FSA Camps

UCAPAWA had an active local in at least five of the FSA camps in California—Visalia, Arvin, Shafter, Marysville, and Gridley—and participated in union drives in at least three additional camps—Winters, Westley, and Indio.[92] Several camps, such as Arvin and Shafter, also had active Workers Alliance chapters that worked closely with UCAPAWA. The alliance, having formed out of the Communist Party's Unemployed Councils during the early 1930s, functioned mostly as a political pressure group to organize migrants as relief recipients. Camp documents discussing UCAPAWA's activities reveal the significant challenges the union faced in organizing farmworkers despite the state's sympathetic governor, the FSA's progressive intervention, and the heightened public concern for migrants' living conditions thanks to *The Grapes of Wrath* and similar publications.

The contentious situation that unfolded at the Shafter camp in the late 1930s amid a series of cotton strikes exemplifies the trouble that frequently occurred between local growers (supported by the AF), UCAPAWA members, and FSA staff. On March 24, 1939, Charles E. Barry, the Shafter camp manager, warned his supervisors that he had just received a letter from Mr. Phil Ohanneson, a prominent farmer and mayor of the city of Shafter objecting "strenuously" to an article in the Shafter camp paper written by Bud Fisher of the CIO. The letter was also signed by additional growers and shippers, the chief of police, and the city judge. Ohanneson, who followed his letter with a call to Barry's home, told the manager to stop the article "as it was agitating the campers, and also that it is a reflection on the camp, and that the farmers would boycott the campers if it wasn't stopped."[93]

Barry responded that the camp council voted to allow Fisher to write the article and that it was "impossible for [him] to curtail anything that the majority of the people desire." Furthermore, Barry added, "[the migrants] had the same right to publish anything that they wish in that paper, as the farmers had to publish articles regarding the activities of organized labor." Although the last comment showed the manager's hand in sympathizing with the migrants, Barry attempted to absolve the FSA of any responsibility in the matter by stating that "the camp paper did not represent the opinion of the manager, nor the Farm Security Administration" and that the paper was "published by the campers and there wasn't anything [he] could do about it." When Ohanneson demanded that Barry take the issue up with the council, Barry refused and told Ohanneson to do it himself.[94]

Nonetheless, Barry did share Ohanneson's letter with the council at their following meeting, at which time the migrant committee voted to invite Ohanneson to the camp on March 30 to share "his side of the story." The council also agreed to temporarily discontinue publication of the CIO article in the camp paper and to suspend any further CIO meetings held regularly at the camp on Tuesdays. After listening to Ohanneson, the council agreed to vote again on whether to continue with the publication. According to Barry, "the vote for suspension of article, was 16 to 2 for continuance." In the meantime, however, the organized growers complained to higher officials in the USDA, claiming that the FSA staff at the

Shafter camp had "sanctioned, if not fostered, the creation of unrest and class hatred among residents of the camps." The continued pressure was seemingly enough to curtail UCAPAWA's formal organizing activity in the camp. By September 1939, Barry reported that although the Shafter union remained in existence, there appeared no noticeable union activity inside the camp.[95]

The trouble UCAPAWA encountered in the Shafter camp reveals another significant challenge behind farmworker organizing during the late 1930s, which was the union's commitment to interracial, militant collective action among diverse farmworker families. A sizable minority of white Dust Bowl migrants did join and support union activity against many observers' claims that they were too inexperienced and individualistic to organize. James N. Gregory estimates that "one out of every three at least sympathized with [UCAPAWA] and had prior experience with unions or radical causes."[96] UCAPAWA Local No. 42 in Shafter formed its base from the FSA camp of mostly white migrants and the established Mexican community to the south of town. Out of approximately 284 members in the local, more than half were Mexican, black, or Filipino. After UCAPAWA meetings ended at the Shafter camp, in fact, the union base shifted to the Mexican colony.[97] For a moment, the interracial solidarity migrants demonstrated offered hope that they could strike successfully for better wages and working and living conditions. Indeed, UCAPAWA's international vice president, Dorothy Healey, remembered the breakdown of racial bigotry among white migrants, and the climate of solidarity it allowed for, as one of the most rewarding aspects of her career.[98]

Ultimately, however, one of the main reasons that most UCAPAWA strikes failed in California's Central Valley in the late 1930s was because the majority of the Dust Bowl families resisted unionization, believing they had more in common with the growers who touted themselves as patriotic, anticommunist, and opposed to racial equality. The white workers commonly based their distinction on a sense of racial, class, and native superiority over the more traditional migrants, even as their desperate economic condition forced them to undercut the wages their nonwhite counterparts bargained for by serving as strikebreakers. In October 1939, during a massive cotton strike, UCAPAWA was forced to throw a picket line around the Shafter camp "to prevent the Okies from going to the fields."[99] Rather than finding that "the jig was up" with white Americans migrants who would not tolerate the poor standards typically afforded to "foreign peons,"

California's industrial farmers grew emboldened when they discovered that many readily crossed a picket line.

Camp documents offer numerous examples of Dust Bowl migrants' complaints about unions and their impact. On one occasion, James H. Ward, chairman of the Arvin camp council, wrote to the Labor Relations Division in Washington, D.C., worried that several farmers in Bakersfield "spoke about the Camp as a C.I.O. headquarters, and that the Manager of the Camp [Fred Ross] was a strong C.I.O. member himself." Ward felt that they were "about right in a way." As he noted, "The camp has been practically run by the C.I.O. . . . . I don't believe it is a place for us honest and non-Communists to live."[100] At the Marysville camp, "leading citizens of the camp" bragged that "there isn't a red or radical in this camp, and if there were, we'd run them out." Charley Cagle, a migrant from Texas, further explained that organizing "won't do us a bit of good unless it's 100 per cent, and unless all the radicals are killed off. The radicals are so unreasonable, it hurts rather than helps us."[101] Although Cagle seemingly supported labor solidarity of some sort, other white migrants clarified that they opposed the CIO because it was led by "nigger-lovers," and many expressed staunch anti-Mexican and anti-Asian attitudes as well.[102] Accordingly, growers capitalized on such antagonisms to defeat workers' collective bargaining.

Notwithstanding the organizing obstacles UCAPAWA encountered, it remained an important advocate for migrant farmworkers' civil and human rights. In November 1938, for instance, UCAPAWA president Donald Henderson wrote to Secretary Wallace requesting that the FSA consider extending the camp program into the sugar beet regions of Colorado, Nebraska, Wyoming, and Montana. According to Henderson, these were the ideal sites for the FSA to carry out its domestic and health programs because sugar beet workers—of whom 95 percent were of Mexican origin and 65 percent American citizens—constituted one of the lowest income groups in the country. They earned a yearly income of about $300 and were living in colonies "consisting mostly of adobe (mud and straw) houses," he explained.[103] UCAPAWA was also "leading the fight for the transient camp" in several other regions, such as in Yakima, Washington, where in August 1938 it defended the FSA against the AF's local red-baiting campaign aimed at keeping the agency away.[104] Such action demonstrates how UCAPAWA operated as a national CIO union that applied broader political pressure while using a decentralized approach to organizing through autonomous, "worker-centered, worker-controlled" locals.[105]

The socioeconomic context surrounding World War II allowed UCA-PAWA and the FSA to briefly work together to make important gains on farmworkers' behalf using the language of home front democracy and labor maximization. In February 1942, for instance, William G. Carnahan, UCA-PAWA representative of minority groups, approached Joseph Cowen, the FSA camp manager at Sinton, Texas, regarding Mexican farmworkers' deplorable living conditions in and around Mathis. In response, Cowen surveyed the area and found that "between 800–1,000 migrants were living in squalid, depressing conditions and earning poor wages that obviously acted as a safeguard against their possible escape from their miserable plight." One grouping of about 350 people lived in "long metal sheds built in L shape right in town . . . with one outdoor toilet and no bath as far as [he] could see."[106] The FSA responded by pressuring community leaders to develop suitable housing and encouraging some migrants to move into the nearby federal camps. In this way, the FSA and UCAPAWA joined together to highlight the centrality of farmworkers' housing in their fight for dignity.

On another occasion, in October 1942, Donald G. Kobler, UCAPAWA's Texas regional director, wrote to Secretary of Agriculture Claude A. Wickard sharing the words of a Mexican field worker: "Wherever I have been I find a lot of places where the Mexican people is discriminated. . . . Here is the latest example Roy's Café located at North First Street Lamesa Tex bear a sign on the door that says no Mexicans. . . . You know this is dangerous at the present time, because there are a lot of Spanish Speaking people that thinks that don't worth a while to fight for a country where they are not considered as civilized people." In closing his letter, Kobler wrote, "I do not need to labor the ramifications of such abuses as cited, I am sure. We sincerely hope that vigorous action will be taken by the proper federal authorities to eliminate, once and for all, this undemocratic and Nazi-like system of discrimination."[107]

Kobler believed it was the FSA's duty to address the continued incidents of injustice farmworkers encountered in rural communities and at the hands of unscrupulous employers. He frequently visited the Weslaco, Robstown, and Raymondville FSA camps to organize farmworkers who encountered some of the lowest wages and worst conditions in the country. Despite Kobler's efforts, UCAPAWA's union drives proved largely ineffective in South Texas. The region's commercial growers used the threat of deportation and replacement by cheaper and more compliant noncitizen labor to significantly limit the number of agricultural strikes throughout the 1930s and 1940s.[108]

By the early 1940s, the FSA's leading administrators had to pay closer attention to the farm bloc's political opposition mounting in Congress and the pressure to concentrate on wartime exigencies. This resulted in advising the camp managers to further distance the camps from any surrounding labor activism.[109] During one heated occasion at the camp in Tulare, California, in June 1941, Michael P. Bruick, the camp manager, "flatly told a group of [fifty migrant] union members: 'I have been ordered by my bosses to prevent the union from having any headquarters in the camp.'" This prompted a backlash from the camp's UCAPAWA members, who resented that "government union-smashing" had reached the FSA. With the camp council's approval, the union planned to continue to meet at the camp and warned that if they were denied the "right of organization" they would mount a protest along with "union men in all other FSA camps." The organizers were undoubtedly aware that under New Deal labor law farmworkers did not fully possess the "right of organization." In raising the issue, they emphasized how the FSA's intervention was supposed to reverse the consequences of their exclusion. More specifically, the UCAPAWA members pointed to the FSA's hypocrisy in "speaking about democracy and freedom in the camps for a long time," yet denying them the right of self-organization and political action.[110]

Nevertheless, a month earlier, the FSA did intervene rather directly in a dispute concerning Mexican American farmworkers about two hundred miles south of Tulare in Ventura County, California. In April 1941 the Agricultural and Citrus Workers' Union under the American Federation of Labor (AFL) wrote to the FSA concerning a bitter struggle between approximately 3,500 striking workers and various citrus farmers in the county represented by the California Fruit Growers Exchange. The AFL requested that the FSA place a mobile labor camp in the region to aid the strikers—more than seven hundred families, most of whom were "Mexican American permanent residents"—who faced eviction from the grower-supplied camps. The FSA responded by opening the El Rio FSA camp in Oxnard for the duration of the strike, which lasted through May. Approximately 98 migrant families and 569 individuals, of which at least 400 were striking lemon pickers, used the camp as a base from which to organize for improved labor and civil rights. The FSA encountered considerable resentment from the community for its efforts, leading the

AF to petition the local chamber of commerce to have the FSA removed from the county.[111]

The lemon strike became so heated that the Mexican government also intervened. Mexican embassy officials complained that local newspapers were stirring up racial trouble by publishing highly prejudiced statements written by representatives of the AF against Mexican people in an attempt to pressure the strikers to concede. In one such editorial published in the *Port Hueneme Herald*, the author claimed that he witnessed "a group of half white, alien, dirty, obscene, profane half breeds, yelling 'scab' and other Spanish obscenity at attractive, well dressed, clean wholesome American white women and men that were at work." The author suggested, "we need our heads examined if we don't rise en masse and demand the deportation of every one of these aliens at once and clean up this mess right now."[112] In a published response, the Mexican consul, Rodolfo Salazar, strongly protested the editorial's "misrepresentations." Salazar combated the claim that "Mexican reliefer[s]" were draining public aid by noting how a large number of those seeking help were "full fledged citizens of the United States, [whose] ancestors had been living in Ventura County many years before the 'white settlers' arrived there." He also reminded readers that "the workers on strike in Ventura County are exercising the right that the laws of the United States give to its people, regardless of their racial, religious, or political affiliations."[113] In the midst of this controversy, FSA officials kept the El Rio camp operating, acknowledging that the striking workers relied on its provisions to secure an agreement in their favor.

The FSA's earlier intervention in the case of a group of evicted sharecroppers in southeast Missouri, in an area known as the Bootheel, was a much more publicized affair. On January 10, 1939, more than 1,500 men, women, and children (over two-thirds black) set up camp along U.S. Highways 60 and 61 in protest. The "roadside demonstration" was organized by Owen H. Whitfield, an African American STFU-UCAPAWA officer (during their brief merger) and a local Southern Baptist minister. In an astute "politics of representation," as Jarod Roll observes, the refugees scattered their household belongings along the highways for everyone to see as they stood in freezing temperatures demanding that the FSA intervene to ameliorate the crisis that New Deal agricultural policies created. Roosevelt pressured the FSA to respond, which it did initially by providing emergency grants and temporary shelter. Not until January 1941 did the FSA deliver on a more permanent solution by opening Delmo Security Homes—a project providing six new settlements for white families and three for blacks throughout the Bootheel. Although the families hoped to return to their lives as tenants, Delmo was built to accommodate their new status as wage workers. Indeed, the FSA typically counted Delmo among its migratory camp projects.[114]

Delmo, Carey McWilliams found, did not reverse the agrarian transformation under way. "At best it merely cushioned the effect of displacement," he argued, "and temporarily stabilized the labor supply."[115] This was true of the FSA's labor camp program more generally. Agency officials, even the more idealistic among them, never intended for the camp program to offer a permanent solution to migrants' dislocation and poverty. Even though the program began under the RA with rehabilitation as the goal, the FSA recognized that it could not reverse the expansion of the migratory farm labor system under way. Agency officials also understood the powerful political forces they were up against and the reality that it could never reach all of the migrant families who needed aid. For this reason, the FSA largely supported farmworkers' collective organization and often spoke of it as the only real means by which their condition would improve. By touting the virtues of a participatory democracy, providing lessons in self-government, and encouraging cooperative thinking, the FSA advanced this agenda. The camps promoted migrants' rights by providing farmworkers with the economic, material, and domestic security necessary to mobilize and defend themselves.

Migrant farmworkers had always relied on their own informal, spontaneous measures of organization to bargain against their employers and challenge their poor living conditions. This was especially true among the noncitizen and nonwhite farmworkers who were historically excluded from most U.S. labor unions. The farm labor movement that emerged in the Southwest (including within CAWIU and UCAPAWA-CIO) was built on Mexican farmworkers' strong networks of mutual aid societies, community clubs, religious groups, and other socioeconomic and political associations, including Mexican labor unions.[116] The formation of an "association" in the camp in Crystal City, Texas, offers a good example of how this self-organization materialized in the FSA camps.

The Crystal City camp opened in April 1941 to considerable "furor" and "hysteria" in the local community over the revelation of union activity among the Mexican workers in the camp.[117] Paul Freier, the camp manager, admitted that there was a "labor union or a labor association in existence in the camp," but he assured the public that he found "no verification that it is an affiliated movement with the AF of L or the CIO." Moreover, he insisted that "no agitator or organizer" lived in the camp, and that from his best estimation "only about half of the workers in camp [about two hundred people]" were "committed to any 'labor association.'" Although Freier tried to downplay the extent of labor organizing occurring, his report indicated a successful movement by farmworkers against the corrupt practices of individual labor contractors in the area—their main issue of contention, and the reason the laborers were "rebelling." In the end, migrants' self-organizing efforts successfully resulted in the fact that all independent contractors were required to sign a written agreement "stipulating civil treatment of the workers and a safe return to their homes promptly upon the finish of a job."[118]

In writing to his supervisors, Freier praised the migrants' use of the camp as a place from which to better control their own labor potential and bargain for improved conditions. As he stated, "The success in gaining such pledges [from the contractors] depended upon the workers' organized control of their labor." Additionally, Freier contended what many FSA officials believed, which was that "labor must be able to control its supply, and must place its supply into demand before cooperative projects like this [the FSA camps] can prove a showing." Yet by 1941, when Freier reported this case, the FSA walked a fine line in the struggle over farm labor control. The agency clearly supported farmworkers' actions toward self-empowerment and improved rights, yet it found itself increasingly forced to yield to growers' demands to regulate the labor supply necessary for wartime production. The FSA's attempt to manage these conflicting interests led it to operate in contradictory ways that further contributed to the agency's political weakness.

World War II and Migrants' (Re)productive Labor

In late December 1939 Arthur Eggleston, labor editor for the *San Francisco Chronicle*, wrote optimistically about the possibility of "the extension of the wages and hour law and Wagner act to cover agricultural laborers." He reported on the California hearings conducted by Senator Robert M. La Follette's Civil Liberties Committee Investigating Violations of Free Speech and the Rights of Labor. The committee found that during the 1930s agricultural strikes, employers and anti-union officials denied farmworkers and their allies their constitutional rights. Moreover, the committee agreed with labor organizers' assertions that growers used the threat of communism as an excuse to violently attack striking farmworkers and label them dangerously un-American. "As a result of the testimony before the La Follette committee," Eggleston wrote, "the Farm Security Administration, once the center of a vicious fight, may find less heat turned on its program and activities." In Eggleston's estimation, and for the progressive advocates involved in the committee's investigation (including McWilliams and Taylor), the federal hearings legitimized farmworkers' claims against their abusive employers and supported the FSA's migrant program as a critical intervention to provide farmworkers greater security.[119]

By the time the La Follette committee completed its work in 1941, however, the nation was less concerned with the labor and civil rights violations occurring in agriculture and increasingly focused on U.S. involvement in World War II. The political shift appeared especially evident in Washington, D.C., where, for example, in 1941 the House Select Committee to Investigate the Interstate Migration of Destitute Citizens became the House Select Committee Investigating National Defense Migration. With greater numbers of Dust Bowl refugees moving out of the fields and into defense jobs, the farm poverty problem appeared to be solved. World War II allowed the FSA's conservative critics to gain authority in their claim that the New Deal's attention to farmworkers' socioeconomic welfare was unnecessary and any program supporting farmworkers' militant organization was subversive.[120] Rather than finding "less heat turned on its programs and activities," as Eggleston projected, after 1941 the FSA experienced the greatest challenge to its intended project aimed at advancing farmworkers' democratic power.

Nevertheless, the FSA's ability to convince its opponents of its plan to serve agribusiness' interests by facilitating farmworkers efficient migration —that is, moving away from stabilizing farmworker families to controlling their productive movement—saved the camp program from the budgetary cuts and eradication facing most other New Deal agencies and gave the FSA license to expand it dramatically. Whereas in September 1939 the FSA operated thirty-one permanent and mobile labor camps nationwide, accommodating approximately 3,320 families, by February 1942 it had 110 camps in operation or under construction, serving an estimated 20,675 families or nearly 89,000 individuals. In 1942 the FSA also had developed plans to construct 90 additional camps (most of them mobile) serving approximately 140 new locations.[121] These figures underscore why considering the labor camp program mainly within the context of the white Dust Bowl migration in California and Depression-era rehabilitation produces a distorted history of the FSA's migrant intervention.

The FSA's wartime focus on farm labor management did not do away with the agency's more reformist goals to help farmworker families improve their socioeconomic and political status. The FSA continued to highlight the progressive benefits of farmworkers' safe and sanitary housing, improved health and diet, and collective organization. FSA agents, farm labor unions, and migrant farmworkers residing in the camps capitalized on the wartime rhetoric surrounding the virtues of American democracy to promote the ways in which the camp program represented opportunity, equality, and justice for all. Nevertheless, the nation's political mood had shifted from providing relief to fighting the war. This forced FSA officials to emphasize how the camps molded better, more reliable, and stronger workers.

As part of this effort, FSA officials began arguing more assertively and strategically that the camp program was integral to the problem of farm labor supply necessary to reverse crop losses. Agriculture needed, in the words of one official, "an economy of employment that would abolish waste movement and loss to both employer and worker."[122] According to the FSA, the camp program would alleviate this problem by expanding into regions that farmworkers may have avoided for lack of adequate housing, and by serving as sites where labor could be concentrated, recruited, and regulated in a manner previously unaccomplished.[123]

Testifying before Congress in September 1940, C. M. Evans, the FSA's regional director for Texas, claimed that the problem of regularizing the flow of migratory labor

can be solved to a great extent if camp facilities are provided to take care of workers as they move from one harvest area to another. The camp will tend to bring the worker in closer contact with the [farm] placement service and, thereby, with the employer. He can be directed to where there is work available and discouraged from going on a wild chase for a job that results in his losing the little money he might have accumulated from the last harvest. Strategically located camps will likewise help in controlling out-of-State migration, by making it easier for the placement service to keep the workers advised of where to go or where not to go.[124]

As early as 1936, the camp program required "all persons staying at the camps be registered at a public employment office."[125] As the program expanded during the early war years, however, the U.S. Employment Service (USES) maintained a more prominent role in the camps to better regulate migrant hiring.[126] In Texas, for instance, most of the camps had a Texas State Employment Service (TSES) field office located at the entrance. Those camps that did not have an actual employment office still had a TSES agent visit or call the camp every day "for the purpose of registering and replacing labor."[127] The camp managers' monthly reports demonstrate the active presence TSES representatives held in the camps through frequent visits and calls, and in overseeing employer-worker negotiations. The reports also suggest that migrant residents were at an advantage because of the FSA's collaboration with the TSES, since they were often the first to receive employment.

Yet migrant families did not completely benefit from the FSA's expanded labor management efforts. By allowing state agents to more carefully supervise labor negotiations, migrants relinquished some of the autonomy that allowed them to bargain for better working conditions. Mexican workers' mobility was one of the most powerful tools they possessed for self-organization. Growers constantly searched for more efficient measures of labor control, realizing that, as Emilio Zamora writes, "Mexican workers persisted in their attempts to informally bargain improvements in their condition by seeking the highest wage in neighboring farms and towns [or states]." Gunther Peck also found that between 1880 and 1930, Mexican farmworkers in the West were far more successful than other immigrants in maintaining control over their mobility and limiting the amount they relied on exploitive labor contractors. Nevertheless, by 1942 the FSA became "crew leader to the nation," as Cindy Hahamovitch explains. And while they still wished to defend workers' interests, the FSA knew that closely cooperating with the USES meant aiding a traditionally pro-grower and anti-union agency. Indeed, the USES regularly shared information with the AF, among other grower groups, and with the U.S. Immigration Service.[128]

The FSA's camp staff recognized the contradictions this new role created as they were expected to collaborate with the USES to keep workers moving in a rationalized manner "to the satisfaction of the farmers," even if it came at a cost to migrant families. In 1941, for instance, the FSA began enforcing a "one-year residence rule" in the camps.[129] That year, Henry C. Daniels, the manager at the camp in Robstown, Texas, wrote to his regional supervisor, William A. Canon, requesting permission to house a number of Mexican American families beyond their termination date, as the "head of family" migrated to West Texas for cotton picking. Daniels assured Canon that it would not "be a question of turning away eligible farm workers so that these women and children can remain in the community." He also submitted information on several of the families in question to highlight, for reasons of health, economic stability, education, and general domestic safety, why they desired to remain in the camp. Quite revealingly, Daniels lastly explained that the camp staff was "convinced that the cause of these people is one which is very closely tied up with the fundamental reasons for setting up migratory labor camps, and that in order to do the job for which they were established, it is sometimes necessary to change [the] rules."[130]

Canon agreed to allow Daniels and other FSA camp managers to make some exceptions to the application of the one-year rule. However, likely in response to Daniels's plea that "these people look upon this project as their home," he reiterated the FSA's position that the labor camps should function as "temporary shelter communities" for agricultural workers and not places of "permanent residence."[131] By March 1942, Canon proved less lenient on the matter, which stemmed from the continued political pressure the FSA faced to curtail their social reform agenda. In his report to chief administrator C. B. Baldwin that month, Canon explained that "some twenty-five families who had been residing in the [Robstown] camp for about one year, and who were found to be of little value to the community as farm laborers on account of age or physical condition, had been ordered to vacate."[132] The decision reflected what the federal camps would soon become as, in the summer of 1942, the FSA became responsible for managing the Emergency Farm Labor Supply Program involving the recruitment, transportation, and housing of mostly individual male domestic and foreign farmworkers. On April 29, 1943, under Public Law 45, the camp program was transferred to the Office of Labor and the War Food Administration. Many of the camps became labor stations for the nation's food-production soldiers—defined as male, able-bodied, and "valuable" in their productivity—hardly resembling the housing communities for farmworker families they once embodied.

The gendered, familial implications of these developments were significant, yet the FSA's forced attention to migrant laborers' productivity over their social welfare did not create the binary that problematically divided migrants' domestic and work lives. As Alice Kessler-Harris argues, most New Deal policies shared in a set of gendered economic assumptions that reconstituted and perpetuated a manly sense of workers' independence and self-sufficiency, especially in the labor market. Depression-era reform involved protecting the vitality of the male head of household as central to preserving democracy.[133] In an important way, FSA officials subverted the American tradition celebrating individual enterprise by promoting farmworkers' collectivism and providing a more inclusionary access to the benefits of citizenship. Nevertheless, in the camps' dialectical space between home and work, the FSA also failed to challenge the dominant gendered standards on which their project was based. Consequently, the agency reinforced women's dependent status and further contributed to their disenfranchisement, contradicting the social democratic ideals they sought to advance.

Although women's farm labor had always blurred the division between productive and reproductive work, the rise of industrial agriculture gave way to a new agrarian ideology that increasingly relegated women to the domestic sphere as "breeders of a labor supply."[134] Government-sponsored farm policies beginning during the Progressive Era placed a market-based standard of value on farm labor that depreciated the economic contributions of women's agricultural work.[135] Most migrant women occupying the federal camps, however, had long-standing experience as farmers, farmworkers, and packing shed and cannery employees that discredited narrow "producerist conceptions of manhood" also at the heart, according to Neil Foley, of agrarian whiteness. Yet FSA officials repeatedly overlooked the labor performed by migrant women and other family members not defined as breadwinners in the camps. As wives, mothers, or daughters *of* workers, women were characterized as supportive but not pivotal to the family economy. As the United States entered the war, the FSA's home management supervisors further emphasized the wife and mother's foremost job in "rehabilitating her family."[136]

The captions to many of the photographs taken by the FSA's renowned documentary division provide a striking example of how migrants were classified in gendered economic terms. A study of Arthur Rothstein's stunning portraits taken of migrants in the South Texas camps in 1942 demonstrates this point. Repeatedly, Rothstein categorized men as the "Migratory

Worker" while identifying women as the "Migratory Worker's Wife," and if holding a child, the "Migratory Worker's Wife and Child." He also labels older men simply as "Campers" and older women as "Mothers of Migratory Workers." Howard Hollem's image of the "Mexican girl helping to save the cotton crop" further illustrates that when FSA photographers did capture women's labor in and around the camps, it was often recorded as supplemental. Lengthy correspondence between the FSA photographers and their supervisor, Roy Stryker, suggests that such captions were rarely incidental. In obscuring the reality of women's labor this way, it seems likely that Stryker wanted to impose a sense of bourgeois normalcy in the images he knew would reach a wide audience and were vital to maintaining support for the program. Ironically, however, at the same time the government celebrated urban women's labor outside the home, the FSA largely ignored or further domesticated migrant women's contributions to national defense.[137]

The camps' weekly employment reports compiled by the FSA and USES offer further evidence of the agency's limited understanding of who produced essential farmwork. Although the employment form clearly requested that federal officials "be sure to list all members of the household who either worked or were available for employment," the information submitted regularly excluded women's labor and rarely listed their unemployment. In the instances when women's labor was recorded, federal officials still defined the family's condition via the male head of household. When they provided information for a woman or child, it was only in relation to the male worker listed first and typically accompanied by a statement such as "helping husband at . . . " or "accompanied father to. . . ." Unless migrant women were working outside of the labor camp and separate from their male relatives, such as in the local cannery, the FSA rarely made note of their personal impact on the family wage.[138]

Camp officials also did not count the labor women performed on a daily basis for the camp, including picking crops in the community garden, making mattresses for the home shelters, and canning food supplies. Yet the FSA had a policy of compensating men's work in the camps by crediting the hours they contributed toward the amount their family owed in monthly dues or grants. Finally, the employment forms did not account for the way migrant farmworkers, especially the more traditional nonwhite families, labored as part of an extended family economy that was central to their survival. As Chapter 3 illustrates, Mexican migrants commonly

Figure 1. "Migratory Worker, Robstown Camp, Texas." Photograph by Arthur Rothstein, January 1942. Library of Congress, Prints & Photographs Division, FSA/OWI Collection, LC-USF34-024868-D.

Figure 2. "Migratory Worker's Wife and Child. FSA (Farm Security Administration) Camp, Robstown, Texas." Photograph by Arthur Rothstein, January 1942. Library of Congress, Prints & Photographs Division, FSA/OWI Collection, LC-USF34-024847-D.

counted cousins, uncles, aunts, and their married children's spouses, among others, as part of the family unit they provided for.[139]

Acknowledging how the camp program engendered a limited understanding of productive labor is important not only to recover migrant women's essential work but also to further demonstrate how the FSA undermined the collective action and participatory democracy it aspired to generate. Rather than accepting that the FSA's gender constraints were emblematic of dominant ideology at the time, it is necessary to consider how they reconstituted a political framework that kept farmworkers disenfranchised, divided, and bound in their exploited condition by subverting more solidaristic possibilities. The progressive advocates promoting the camp program contributed to this as well by stressing the industrial nature of field work in Fordist terms in order to win farm labor the same legal protections granted to mostly urban men. While the FSA's idealistic visions for agrarian reform included migrant farmworkers' ability to realize their full potential as citizens, the rights discourse they promoted remained limited by their own biases.

The federal labor camps uniquely brought migrants, federal officials, growers, unions, and community leaders together to negotiate the dramatic changes occurring in agriculture during the 1930s and early 1940s. The socioeconomic crisis produced by the vast migration of poor, white, native-born families allowed progressive advocates to finally win political support for a state-sponsored migrant camp program. Individuals such as McWilliams and Taylor understood that the Depression had not created the oppressive labor conditions prevailing in California's factory farms, but it had certainly made them worse and more visible. Capitalizing on the public attention surrounding the Dust Bowl migration, they claimed that these white, American workers would never tolerate employers' exploitive practices. California growers and state representatives initially feared that this was true, but they soon realized that many of these migrants were too desperate or too invested in their privileged class and racial identity to join forces with their nonwhite fellow farmworkers organizing in the fields.

The camp program began in 1935 mainly as an emergency relief measure for destitute white migrants, but local officials also saw it as a way to temper the volatile strikes and political radicalism threatening California agriculture. During the early 1930s, thousands of mostly Mexican and Filipino farmworkers courageously organized massive strikes for improved labor and civil rights in the face of growers' and local authorities' violent suppression. They joined forces with CAWIU and succeeded in bringing federal attention to their plight. In developing the program, however, the RA largely ignored the nonwhite farmworkers who had long suffered from the economic exploitation, racial discrimination, and social marginalization characterizing their work. Instead, the agency focused primarily on rehabilitating the white migrants who they viewed as former farmers.

The RA's emphasis on rehabilitation stemmed from the New Deal's approach to agrarian reform in the South where it focused on resettling and aiding the increasing numbers of dispossessed sharecroppers and tenants. Accordingly, it is impossible to fully grasp how the camp program emerged in the West and developed nationally as part of the Second New Deal without considering the central nature of the South's socioeconomic and racial politics. Southern Democrats dominated Congress, which allowed the region's prominent agriculturalists to lead the charge against farmworkers' expanded rights. The disproportionate influence southerners maintained in Washington also made certain that any reform policies threatening the established order and power of white supremacy would be blocked. Farmworkers throughout the country felt the consequences of this political framework as they were barred from New Deal protections. When white, Asian, Mexican, and African American farmworkers continued to organize throughout the 1930s in civil rights unions such as UCAPAWA and STFU, the nation's farm bloc quickly labeled them dangerous, subversive, and un-American.

The FSA's willingness to protect farmworkers' collective organization and demands for socioeconomic justice guaranteed that the agency would always be subject to considerable opposition from commercial growers, as well as their community allies and sympathetic representatives in Congress. The FSA did its best to tout the camps as places to stabilize the growing numbers of migrant families, offer necessary relief, and help clear migrants from the roadsides. Yet it was quickly apparent that the camps did much more. The FSA sought to advance rural democracy by teaching farmworkers how to become self-determining, politically engaged citizens. Agency officials were rare defenders of farmworkers' expanded rights, and even more notably, by the early 1940s the camps operated as contested spaces where farm labor struggles crossed over and between the domestic, political, and economic terrain. That this occurred was not accidental. The FSA's architects and planners constructed the migrant camps to transform migrants' daily patterns, shift their social orientation in more collectivist terms, and encourage their politicization as citizen workers.

CHAPTER 2

Planning Migrant Communities

The Camps' Built Environment and the Formation
of a New Socioeconomic Order

Reflecting on the Farm Security Administration's (FSA) experience building "highly developed communities," Talbot F. Hamlin, a New York architect and professor at Columbia University, presented the migratory labor problem from the perspective of the planners and architects charged with designing the FSA's farm labor camps.

> In the analysis of what was necessary for such a camp the whole problem of community living had to be grasped. If the people who were to make use of these camps, were to be helped to a sounder, more healthy, more self-respecting life, the communities in which they were to live must be of such a type as to stimulate health, self-respect, and social responsibility.[1]

Hamlin wrote his appraisal of the FSA's projects for an audience of leading architects and designers interested in the impact of modernism on building form, a seemingly odd group among which to highlight new developments in federal farmworker housing. When his piece appeared in *Pencil Points*, the FSA had just completed a boom in camp construction, expanding the program into new areas beyond California—notably the Pacific Northwest, Texas, and Florida—where it was "demonstrating the possibility of improving the conditions of living for the groups at the very lowest level in American agriculture."[2] Whereas in September 1939 the FSA reported operating 29 camp facilities (23 standard and 6 mobile) serving approximately 7,884 families, by the end of 1941 there were a total of 81 camps (55 standard and 26 mobile) in use or under construction.[3]

In Hamlin's mind, the FSA's labor camp projects reflected a dramatic, economic, and inventive response to the migratory problem. According to Hamlin, "the development of one-crop farms demanding enormous picking forces for short harvest periods" had left hundreds of thousands of people wandering about where they might turn to "revolutionary violence" in response to the hardships they endured. Instead, the FSA responded to the crisis by devising a way to make them "self-respecting citizens furnishing the labor necessary to an important part of our productive economy without losing their rights to a decent life."[4] The FSA's housing and community projects for migrant workers and their families went beyond simply attending to their material, domestic, and labor needs. The camps functioned as dynamic spaces in which migrants could maintain their civil rights and build a collective, community-based vision for confronting the challenges they faced as farmworkers.

The Migratory Labor Camp Program offers a valuable lens through which to study the intersections of public housing and citizenship in the United States, especially as it concerns poor communities marginalized by their race and class status. Efforts to link matters of social reform and spatial development did not originate with the FSA, or as part of the New Deal more generally. Progressive reformers involved in the community center and settlement house movements at the turn of the nineteenth century influenced earlier discourses on public housing by demonstrating how neighborhoods and community spaces were essential to the socialization process preparing poor, immigrant residents for American citizenship.[5] Yet a study of the FSA's camp program demonstrates how the ideas progressives advanced about the relationship between domestic space and civic identity came to fruition through large-scale federal action in the rural landscape. The labor camp program helped establish the FSA as a pioneer in low-cost public housing with attention to efficiency in both the scale of what was built and in the socioeconomic regulation of "homeless" migrant families. Considering the FSA's actions in this regard helps us appreciate the role migrant farmworkers had in shaping public policy concerning government-built and subsidized housing for decades to follow.

Despite its long-lasting influence on housing policy and design, FSA agents regularly maintained that their greatest achievements lay "not in architecture, planning or economy, but in the social results of its [housing] program." They reminded observers that the FSA was "not a housing agency, but an agency to rehabilitate farm people."[6] When the FSA was established in 1937, it inherited the migrant camp program from the Resettlement Administration (RA) as part of a series of housing projects, mainly for small farm families. Under the direction of Rexford Tugwell, the RA brought together a team of expert agricultural economists and rural sociologists to attack the problem of chronic rural poverty from a more comprehensive, holistic approach.[7]

As recent studies on the agrarian New Deal have shown, the RA operated under the principle that temporary, direct relief would do little to save impoverished farm families from the economic and ecological crisis of the Great Depression because their problems were deep-rooted in inefficient farming practices. To ameliorate poor farmers' condition, the RA set out to "reshape the rural American landscape" through a range of social, economic, and land-use reforms.[8] More than anything, the RA's rehabilitation efforts sought to transform the cultural characteristics that perpetuated rural poverty. As Jason Manthorne explains, while RA (and later FSA) agents regularly acknowledged the structural forces working against poor farmers, they nevertheless pointed to their habits, customs, and values as the cause of their poverty.[9]

As the labor camp program expanded in the early 1940s, this rehabilitation and reform movement influenced the FSA's agenda concerning migrant farmworkers. Officials leading the camp program believed that farmworkers needed the stability and security that came from decent housing to achieve self-sufficiency and realize the promise of full citizenship. FSA agents claimed that the camps rooted migrants with a sense of place in which to build a collective community and participatory democracy that would produce the most lasting change remedying their impoverished condition.

This chapter begins by examining the FSA engineers', architects', and planners' perspectives as they designed the federal camps to best evaluate how their built environment shaped migrant families. Though one might imagine architects as simply interested in their design ideas for material purposes, this was not the case among those the FSA employed. The FSA's planning team recognized the social and political debates out of which the camp program emerged and designed each building, road, and landscape feature with their broader ramifications in mind. They were "social engineers" in the truest form, something conservative critics would use against them.[10]

To underscore the larger project at work in the camps' material space, I consider the FSA's agrarian planning in a dual sense: that is, from both the perspective of the rural economists who sought to rationalize farm production and the labor migrant stream on which it depended, and from the standpoint of the architects charged with constructing a new social order that promoted migrant citizenship. For farmworker families, the FSA's dual objectives in social and economic planning produced a highly contradictory experience. The FSA's camp program simultaneously aimed to stabilize migrants' domestic condition while supporting the productive necessity of farmworkers' continued migration.

The camps operated in these contradictory terms by working to uplift migrant families through an idealized democracy, even as they structurally reinforced the racial, gendered, and class-based divisions in agribusiness and society that kept farmworkers marginalized. A reading of the camps' spatial geography shows how the FSA planned to resolve the multiple interests and social anxieties that emerged during the camps' formation and as World War II production needs took center stage. The camps were anything but neutral spaces. They were imbued with state forces aiming to reform migrant families to better meet dominant standards of American respectability and model citizenship. And they were spaces to address the nation's labor and military needs while responding to the political pressure mounting against the welfare state.

The Camps' Planned Purpose in Community Building

The persons responsible for planning most of the migrant camps were employed at the FSA's Region IX Engineering Office in San Francisco, California. Garrett Eckbo, one of the FSA's most successful landscape architects, recalled that by the early 1940s the office had "30 engineers, 20 architects, and 3 landscape architects."[11] Herbert Hallsteen, district engineer, was in charge of coordinating the planners' projects, which included the work of Burton Cairns and Vernon DeMars as leading district architects. Nicholas Cirino was the team's regional engineer, and John Donovan was the FSA's chief engineer in charge of overseeing the San Francisco operation from Washington, D.C. Together, the San Francisco team designed camp communities for migrant workers in California, Washington, Oregon, Idaho, Arizona, and Texas, for a total of approximately thirty-one permanent camps.[12] The impact this architectural team had on the camp program was, however, not limited to the U.S. West. As the program expanded dramatically in the early 1940s, the FSA applied the same construction and planning methods (with few variations) to camp locations across the country.

The FSA's regional team of engineers and architects had a considerable amount of freedom to shape the camps' design as they saw fit, although the FSA's central office in Washington reviewed all construction plans and costs before approval. In an interview reflecting back on his experience as a chief architect, Vernon DeMars clarified how unlike construction procedures for the resettlement homes and other RA projects, the FSA's planning team experienced "a remarkable amount of power to make decisions" in their design of the migrant communities. He noted, "In our particular case, our head engineer, Herb Hallsteen, came from Washington, I think, or at least he started from the central office there and then was sent out to run this program." DeMars explained, "I'd overhear him on the phone: look, do you guys want this [done] this year? Okay, then get off our backs. When something's under construction we'll send you some blueprints." Hallsteen's argument, according to DeMars, was "look you guys in Washington don't know anything about this whole migrant problem . . . we know all about it."[13] In truth, most of the architects and engineers working for the FSA came from urban backgrounds and understood little about farmworkers' housing conditions prior to their work for the government.[14] But the job demanded that they quickly immerse themselves in the local environment to better recognize the challenges in alleviating migrants' dislocation.

Despite their unfamiliarity with the problems of rural poverty and farm labor relations, the architects and planners shared a philosophical connection rooted in the belief that architecture could improve social conditions and everyday living, and help resolve inequality. The majority of the team studied at the University of California, Berkeley, earning degrees in landscape architecture and city and regional planning. Most would return to teach there while employed by the FSA, and eventually they established the research and working group Telesis (in 1939) and Berkeley's College of Environmental Design (in 1959).[15] According to Francis Violich—who was responsible for planning the layout of one of the first demonstration camps—the FSA group at Berkeley had deep concerns about the broader implications of their work. As he recalled: "Every lunch would be a seminar. We were planning the whole new world. We were kicking around the ideas in a chapter of [Lewis] Mumford as conceptual material for designing a labor camp in Marysville [California]."[16]

Since the designers applied much of their professional training in high art and modernist architecture in the construction of FSA labor camps, they were often credited by contemporary critics for creating some of the best examples of early American modern design. During the mid-1940s, Elizabeth Mock, curator of architecture and design at the Museum of Modern Art in New York, categorized the "handsome buildings" located at the Woodville, California, migrant camp "[as] the result of careful and economical design." According to Mock, "FSA's San Francisco office has shown that 'bureaucratic architecture' can also be distinguished."[17] Talbot Hamlin similarly acknowledged that "the details of the actual construction of all [the camps'] buildings [were] extraordinarily interesting because they show how the need for economy, creatively conceived, can itself become a means to new and beautiful architectural forms."[18] Such appraisals reinforced the commitment that members of the San Francisco team developed early in their education to value architecture, especially in its most simplified form, as a social art.

As a graduate student at Harvard, for example, Eckbo trained under Walter Gropius and Marcel Breuer, central figures in the establishment of the Bauhaus school in Germany.[19] Eckbo's concern for spatial arrangement and social involvement, and his basic theories about the use of lines, geometric arrangements, and the importance of landscape in breaking up the rigidity of such design forms, factored in his site plans as he imagined them serving farmworker families.[20] The same was true for Corwin Mocine and Francis Violich, Eckbo's classmates at Harvard and eventual colleagues at Berkeley. Though they were designing living spaces for some of the nation's poorest families, the FSA architects regularly expressed a sense of pride that they could bring such modernist elements to the camps' design and in the process alter prevalent conceptions on the role of vernacular architecture. In describing the two-story row houses for migrants in the camps designed by Cairns and DeMars, Eckbo once noted, for example, that they were "like a touch of European modern in the western landscape."[21]

Eckbo's reflection on the European influence was not inaccurate. While employed by the FSA, Vernon DeMars traveled throughout Europe for six months beginning in 1938 studying modern architectural development in places such as Denmark, Sweden, Finland, Latvia, Holland, Germany, Austria, Hungary, and Italy. DeMars brought with him photographs of the

Figure 3. "Multi-family Unit Designed for Permanent Agricultural Workers at the Migratory Labor Camp, Sinton, Texas." Photograph by Russell Lee, March 1940. Library of Congress, Prints & Photographs Division, FSA/OWI Collection, LC-USF34-035766-D.

FSA's Chandler, Arizona, "housing project for seasonal agricultural workers" built in 1936, hoping to impress his European colleagues with the cutting-edge work he had recently produced in the United States. To appreciate the significance of this, it is necessary to recognize how remarkable it is that farmworkers stood at the center of international discourse about modern architecture and public housing. This is not to suggest that the architects' distinguished training did not sometimes result in elitist claims about their design impact, despite their good intentions. DeMars once recalled, for example, while reflecting on the FSA's work in building subsistence homestead projects, that they "were going to bring architecture and good taste to the peasants, in a sense."[22]

The San Francisco team estimated that the work they produced served as a model for a new and improved form of social living that went beyond the material reality of establishing modern rural architecture. As the historian Paul K. Conkin contends:

The many architects of the New Deal communities, despite varying philosophies, were all striving to create, within the conducive environment of their planned villages, a new society, with altered values and new institutions. The new society would, of course, be a "better" society, with "better" necessarily defined by the architects themselves. The communities, always on exhibit, were to demonstrate and advertise the new society to the rest of mankind.[23]

For the housing and community programs developed under the RA and later the FSA, the desire to create a new social order that recognized the value of a more collectivist spirit in America was a top priority. Although much debate occurred among the New Deal planners over how they should carry out their goals, they all understood a "better society" to mean, among other things, a more communal, democratic society.

Rexford Tugwell, head of the RA, believed that "the Great Depression was caused by an inequality in income distribution, leading to a lowered purchasing power on the part of too many people." According to him, uncontrolled capitalism "permitted the 'ganging up' of the unscrupulous few against the many." It was a "system that invited struggle rather than co-operation, divisiveness rather than unity, [and] bitterness rather than tolerance."[24] Tugwell argued that the principles of independence and individualism, on which the nation was founded, must be contested for American society to become more democratic.

The FSA's labor camps set a standard for public housing and community development that future state agencies would aim to model. As part of the New Deal, the camps' development is best understood in relation to parallel projects in community planning that emerged under the USDA. The RA's subsistence homestead communities and greenbelt towns, for example, closely influenced how the federal labor camps were built. While the expenditures allotted to each of these projects were radically different—in general, much less was assigned for the camp program —fundamental aspects of their design scheme were not. The ideological and structural commonalities existing between these housing projects demonstrates the extent to which FSA planners utilized the dynamics of spatial relations as a mechanism of reform.

These communities represented projects in economic and land reform, as well as social and cultural experiments. According to Tugwell, the RA's housing projects were designed in a manner that carefully "place[d] land, houses, and people together" in order "to strengthen the foundations of the whole economic and social structure of society."[25] Regardless of their environment or the socioeconomic position of their inhabitants, a careful examination of the assorted New Deal community projects reveals a strong collectivist philosophy. More than simply constructing a new economic reality for resettled families or industrial and farmworkers, federal officials such as Milburn L. Wilson, director of the Division of Subsistence Homesteads, viewed these communities as the "locale for a new way of life," where "a new improved man with new attitudes and values" would emerge.[26] Wilson believed that neighborliness, cooperation, and group activity would be fostered in an environment where people understood that their well-being and prosperity depended on their ability to work together.

Given their radical disposition, critics viewed these "crackpot utopias" and their idealistic visions for "a new way of life" with much suspicion and distaste.[27] Conservative politicians and local leaders argued that such communities were really socialist-inspired "communes" where federal officials handpicked residents, isolated them from the larger society, encouraged permanent poverty (by placing restrictions on resident eligibility through income level or occupational status), implemented mandatory social programming, and enforced strict rules and extensive supervision. Although the RA worried that dissenting opinion would stifle the housing projects' expansion, they were more concerned that the residents would not recognize the potential of "the community idea" that they sought to inspire. Tugwell supported the idea that "a new era of cooperation and voluntary socialization" was possible, but only so far as individuals were willing to work together and be mutually invested in their future as a community. He was not completely convinced that this could be achieved simply through voluntary cooperation. Instead, he argued, it had to be created or planned.[28]

The need for careful planning was especially true for farmworkers who lacked the autonomy and political power to achieve the kind of rural democracy the New Dealers envisioned. Tugwell recognized that the development of industrial agriculture, especially in the U.S. South and West, produced a starkly divided class system where local communities could not be trusted to practice true grassroots democracy.[29] Instead, he advocated for state-led democratization, which, while more technocratic, was nonetheless more inclusive and collectivist in its vision for reforming rural America. Even though the camp program would not expand under Tugwell's leadership, his approach would distinguish the FSA's efforts from other rural community-building projects that privileged traditional notions of rural life.

Determining Site Selection: Building Community on Contested Land

Although the FSA's planning team described the camps as "new towns" built on "virgin land," the process of site selection required substantial considerations relating to local conditions.[30] These included economic, engineering, and climatic factors, as well as sociopolitical concerns stemming from the surrounding community. In other words, the camps were not established on virgin land, nor were they "self-contained communities" simply because they included all the amenities migrants required. Rather, the surrounding natural and social environment was shaped by historical struggles over land and labor, and it continued to be influenced by the actions and attitudes of growers, city officials, local residents, and farmworkers. The sites on which the labor camps stood were, as a result, highly contested and physically shaped by the politics surrounding migrants' mobility, labor, and social development as American citizens.

FSA engineers faced one of their first challenges in the site selection process when they encountered strong local resistance against the establishment of a camp. They selected potential locations for the camps along heavily traveled migratory routes and, in many cases, in close proximity to major highways. They also gave priority to establishing camps where growers claimed labor shortages existed.[31] The communities in which the camps were built were thus familiar with migrant labor and relied heavily on it to meet agribusiness demands. Even so, the reality of a permanent camp usually generated strong concerns over the placement of "undesirable neighbors." In New Jersey, for example, the FSA acknowledged that one of the main hindrances to establishing the program in the state was "the fear of a permanent camp where migrants might linger on after seasonal work is finished."[32]

While most communities tolerated migrants' presence during labor-intensive agricultural periods, they generally assumed that migrants were temporary workers who should remain largely out of sight. For much of the early twentieth century, communities across the U.S. South and West enforced this attitude with the implementation of regulations such as "vagrancy laws" that forbade migrant farmworkers, especially if they were Mexican and African American, from traveling into certain sections of town.[33] But mainstream society's distance from migrants' domestic conditions perpetuated the problem of rural poverty in a unique way, according to the FSA. As one report on rural housing concluded, "Urban slums had long been recognized, but slums of the open country were undramatic, scattered, not easily visualized. Their social cost was difficult to estimate. Few recognized their threat to community health and welfare."[34] Accordingly, camp officials understood that a major obstacle to ameliorating migrants' living conditions involved making them more visible but also less threatening.

The FSA's decision to place its labor camps near established rural communities fueled organized growers' attacks against the program. Very often opposition was expressed in pejorative terms against the families who would reside in the camps. Mrs. Effie Ball Magurn, for example, drafted a letter to President Franklin D. Roosevelt in April 1940, where she stated her objection to the establishment of a federal camp adjacent to her property in Porterville, California, because "knowing the character of these migrants"—which she described as "utterly devoid of honor and ideals" and shaped by "wanton destructiveness, filth, and dishonesty"—they would "depreciate [her] property" and "loot [her] ranch."[35] V. O. Key, a prominent lawyer in Lamesa, Texas, similarly exclaimed in a letter to Senator Morris Sheppard in May 1941 that "the location of [a camp in Lamesa] will bring a vast number of undesirables to roam our streets, steal our chickens, spread disease and be a general nuisance to our town and community."[36] The concentration of migrants who would surely "increase crime and vice" and "encourage gambling" was also why petitioners in Berrien County, Michigan, hoped to stop camp construction from moving forward.[37]

The conflict that ensued in 1940 over the proposed location of the camp in McAllen, Texas, illustrates how the contention over site selection and the permanent placement of a migrant camp typically unfolded. Residents, businessmen, landowners, and local growers came together to submit a petition complaining about a number of factors they saw as detrimental to their interests if the camp was built. The most notable claims involved the reduction in their property values, the increased competition for employment between residents and local workers, and the economic hardship endured by local school districts and taxpayers who would have to provide public services to migrant families. They also stressed their belief that "such a project would bring into our city and community a class of people that will be undesirable to our present citizenry."[38] This was a remarkable claim given that "both the opposition and the advocates of the camp" generally agreed "that the vicinity of McAllen represented the home base for large numbers of migratory workers rather than a point of influx."[39] Clearly, these farmworkers were not part of the "present citizenry."

FSA officials responded to the petition by inviting McAllen residents to a meeting held in June 1941 to voice their dissent and discuss their fears. C. McNallie, a farmer who owned property on two sides of the proposed camp, expressed his concerns after having already sent letters to Congressman Milton H. West and Will W. Alexander, who headed the FSA. According to Mr. McNallie, the FSA camps at Weslaco and Raymondville had demonstrated, per his own investigation, that "the residents of that community [were] not at all satisfied with the project, and that the inhabitants or tenants in the project [were] very objectionable." This had led him to conclude that the project was "not desirable for next-door neighbors." Moreover, McNallie questioned the procedure and selection of camp personnel, asking if "the manager [would] be a communist or some other sort of radical?"[40] The inquiry reveals how camp opponents used red-baiting tactics to undermine the program even before the camps were built.

C. M. Evans, the FSA regional director, and W. A. Canon, the acting regional director, reassured Alexander that few of the protesters had any real grounds on which to state their grievance. According to Evans, "a check of the names on the petition reveal[ed] that no more than 10 or 12 of them [could] be in any way concerned with the location of the camp at this point, other than the fact that they [were] opposed to the establishment of a migratory labor camp at all." Evans noted that in fact there were "approximately 10 adjoining property owners, and the homes of only some 3 or 4 were close enough to [the] project to be affected by it." He also called attention to the fact that the land selected for the camp "[did] not lie within the City Limits of McAllen, and therefore the protesting taxpayers would not have their taxes increased when the project [was] constructed." To further discredit the protesters' argument, Canon raised questions about the validity of the estimates that they submitted on the value of their various properties. Apparently, Mr. E. A. Smith's "high-class suburban district," for example, was "rendered for tax purposes in the total amount of $1,140.00" but was "composed of 11.2 acres carried in the name of his wife," making it appear well overestimated in value. Similarly, J. W. Bowser's "fine suburban home" was listed at $400, and his ten-acre block at $560, both evidently listed substantially above actual worth.[41]

The McAllen camp opponents were clearly concerned about how their financial interests and suburban ideals would be threatened by the permanent location of undesirable migrants in whom they did not see civic virtue. Highlighting this point, Paul T. Vickers, manager of the McAllen Chamber of Commerce, wrote to W. A. Canon that "none of these men [are] opposed to having the camp at McAllen. . . . Their opposition is based mainly on the fact that your men actually selected probably the choicest residential rural location around McAllen."[42] As an editorial in the *Evening Valley Monitor* further explained, "N. McColl Rd. is one of the more attractive suburban residential areas and hence is not a logical area in which to locate a camp whose residents will be in the extremely low wage group."[43] The candid statement revealed the class and race divide in American agriculture, which troubled the FSA officials invested in community planning and democratic reform.

Mindful of such local grievances, FSA officials built the camps in such a way as to guard migrants from the surrounding community. Yet this often worked against their goals. After a field trip to various existing camps in the winter of 1940, for example, Hallsteen suggested that in Florida "the site selected [for the camps] should be slightly farther away from the town and particularly not backed up against the slum portion of any town."[44] His recommendation was based on improving the "appearance of the project." Heeding Hallsteen's advice when building the Okeechobee camp for black migrants, however, proved to be an obstacle to filling the camp's occupancy goals. As John Beecher, the FSA's chief supervisor in the region, reported: "The absence of a store nearby is perhaps the most real deterrent now operating to prevent more complete occupancy of the camp. Some residents have walked into town and back, a round trip of five miles, to buy a quarter's worth of groceries. It is hoped that some small stores will soon spring up in the vicinity to correct this situation."[45] In seeking to isolate migrants from town tensions, camp administrators created different problems that often proved more of a hardship for the families they sought to assist. Their efforts reveal a central contradiction in the FSA's policy toward community development. As the agency claimed to facilitate migrant workers' inclusion in American society, what they often described as a process of "assimilation," they also sought to contain migrants within the camps' planned communities.

The FSA's promise to keep migrants and their families within the camp space, however, was an important selling point. Migrants residing in the camps would no longer menace or burden surrounding towns by camping out in ditches along the roads, contaminating surroundings with their unsanitary practices and contagious diseases, and absorbing undue public resources. In this way, the labor camp projects offered a reversal of the idyllic promise imbued in the FSA's utopian greenbelt settlements. Rather than providing their residents with a sense of reprieve from the city, the camps helped keep the town free from the migrants who threatened their way of life.

Rural communities' economic dependency on migrant labor, however, made such a distinction in communal space between the camps and their surrounding towns false at best. For instance, Christine Reiser Robbins and Mark W. Robbins found that despite the physical distance between the labor camp in Robstown, Texas, and Robstown's Main Street (approximately two to three miles), former camp residents understood the two sites as "interwoven spaces." While the camp was geographically removed from town, migrant workers traveled to Robstown's Main Street on the weekends where, especially during the busy cotton season, they filled the streets "en masse" and added to the town's vibrant atmosphere. The money farmworkers spent in town allowed Robstown to thrive economically during the 1940s.[46] To appreciate the means that provided for this, however, it is also necessary to consider the agricultural fields as a dominant space that served to interweave the camp and town communities. Ultimately, migrant workers' labor under largely exploitive conditions allowed local towns to prosper. Despite the FSA's efforts to contain social tension, agricultural communities operated at several sites, some more visible than others, that transcended geographic barriers.

The Camps' Built Environment and Social Engineering

A reading of the camps' material space reflects the social tensions that existed between migrant families and the camps' surrounding communities and suggests how FSA officials tried to mediate those relations through a careful choreography of migrants' daily lives. FSA officials used spatial planning to manage migrants' movement and social interactions within the camps by positioning them in different locations depending on their class, gender, and race. This process of social spatialization would promote migrants' cultural assimilation to U.S. middle-class standards for respectable domesticity and citizenship.

By the early 1940s the FSA used what it referred to as a "plan pool," allowing the architects and engineers to apply a highly standardized approach to camp construction.[47] DeMars described the process almost like ordering "a plan for a community" out of a Sears catalog. Some modifications were made to the plans as local resources and natural factors warranted—for example, in the application of adobe to the camp buildings in Arizona and the elevation of buildings above ground in Texas and Florida to avoid flooding. But as the program expanded nationally, the FSA's approach to camp construction was notably uniform. The result was a "camp model" that could be easily replicated anywhere in a rapid and efficient manner.[48]

A bird's-eye view of the migrant camps demonstrates the FSA's interest in a distinctly hierarchical plan with little informality in the arrangement of buildings, plantings, and roads.[49] FSA architects repeatedly acknowledged that the location of buildings was extremely important to maintain a strict spatial order. A typical element of the camps' design, for instance, involved shelters for temporary workers within a hexagonal, octagonal, or circular geometric arrangement. This configuration is evident in the aerial photographs and blueprints for the camps in Yuba City, Westley, and Tulare, California; Lamesa and Raymondville, Texas; Agua Fria, Arizona; and Dayton, Oregon, among others. In the cases where FSA planners did not adopt this design plan, they instead used a simplified linear block pattern, such as row housing, within a similarly rigid orthogonal formation. This approach was influenced by DeMars's trip through Europe from which he returned "filled with some Corbusier ideas" and eager to employ the use of *Zeilenbau* dynamics (a German planning principle that privileged parallel lines of houses).[50]

The FSA architects believed their arrangement of housing and other essential camp facilities encouraged migrants' social interaction and contributed to the process of community formation. It was effective because it placed temporary migrants' shelters close to each other and gave "visual prominence" to a central space where migrants would come together to share public facilities including the toilets and showers, laundry area, community center, playground, and cooperative gardens.[51] Camp architects also argued that the closely integrated arrangement worked well because it "allowed for a continuity of circulation within controlled borders."[52]

Isolation Units
(for serious
medical
conditions)

Labor Homes (a.k.a., Garden Homes)
for Permanent Agricultural Workers

Two-story Apartments for
Permanent Agricultural Workers

Community
Center

Gate House /
Utility
Building

Metal
Shelters for
Temporary
Agricultural
workers

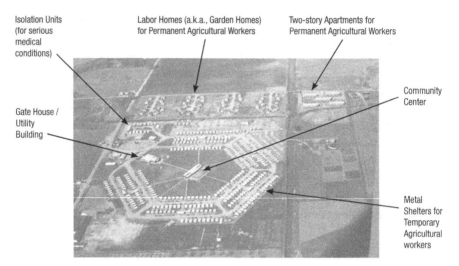

Figure 4. "Air View of the Farm Security Administration Tulare [California] Camp,"
ca. 1942. Library of Congress, FSA-OWI Photographic Collection, LC-US262-
8954.

Regulation of migrants' movement along a main road that circled the camp also allowed FSA officials to pay closer attention to who entered or left the camp. Illustrating this point, Albert K. Short, the camp manager in Raymondville, Texas, reported in 1940 that his staff established a "control chart of the [camp] area," which had made the process of "checking in comparatively easy." Short was referring to the act of directing new residents to their facilities after they registered at the camp. He described a clearly mapped-out arrangement of the camp and recommended that other managers implement similar tools to better facilitate their duties.[53] Placement of the "gatehouse" or "guard unit" at the entrance of the camp typically facilitated this process.[54] The gatehouse accommodated all of the administrative functions of the camp, including the offices of the camp manager and other federal officials, such as agents from the U.S. Employment Service (USES) who made labor arrangements between local farmers and migrant residents. This building also housed the mailroom and, in some cases, the medical clinic.

The location of the administrative building at the entrance of the camp made it difficult for an individual worker, let alone an entire migrant family, to exit or enter the federal camp with impunity. Several documents suggest that FSA officials believed in the importance of supervising who came and went. As one official explained, "While it is desired to have men live in the camps under as normal American conditions as possible, it [is] necessary to develop some arbitrary regulations for our protection with regard to such matters as unrestricted entrance."[55] To help facilitate this regulation, many of the camps had a watchman to patrol the camp and guard the entrance while registering each person in and out and admitting only those that were authorized. Such monitoring discouraged free and undisturbed passage, which to some extent immobilized migrant families residing in the camp. It also complicated an already tenuous relationship between migrant workers and local citizens by creating an explicit buffer between the camp and the surrounding community. Indeed, many of the camps also had a gate, or some other defining marker such as an encircling greenbelt, that further enclosed them.

Several architectural scholars have emphasized the labor camps' "hermetic and controlling order" and the way the rigidity of the camps' schematic layout was intended as a regulatory mechanism to police migrant behavior. According to Diane Ghirardo, "This disposition favored control by the management and the separateness of the community from the neighboring towns." As she concluded, "The objective was to create a community turned in on itself."[56] Labor historians have likewise described the camps as spaces of labor control where government agents closely monitored migrant families to limit their unrest, maximize their full labor potential, and reduce their social threat to nearby communities.[57] After 1943, the camps became increasingly utilized in ways that favored growers' interests over workers' well-being, serving what labor geographer Don Mitchell calls an "architecture of exploitation."[58] Yet the democratizing feature behind the camps' arrangement, and the architects' intention to restore a sense of humanity among those displaced, is significant. By considering both its controlling and democratizing features, the camps' built environment reveals a more complicated history behind what FSA officials intended and what materialized.

In conjunction with the camp buildings, the landscape design reinforced a movement pattern that designated space for interaction, recreation, gardening, and other social activities. FSA designers used plantings and walkways to soften the camps' strict order and provide for a more seemingly fluid spatial arrangement. Eckbo viewed plants and trees as "space-organizing elements rather than as decoration" and as important "conductors for social patterns."[59] As the FSA sought to "anchor migrants to the land" in an effort to stabilize their situation, a tree came to represent more than just a source of climatic relief; it also symbolized the migrants' ability to "take root" in the camp community.[60] Talbot Hamlin explained the camps' landscape objective as such:

> The most careful use has been made of existing trees, and where defi-
> nite groves or stands of timber exist on the property these areas have
> been chosen wherever possible for the community building, the
> schools, and the more permanent houses, so that the migrant driving
> in dusty after a day's work in blazing shadeless fields or a long run
> over sunbeaten and windswept highways may find his relaxation in a
> place dappled with leaf shadows, embowered with trees and with the
> heartening feel of green and growing things around.[61]

While serving to regulate migrants' sociospatial relations, the FSA's plant-ing of trees, hedges, flowers, and other forms of vegetation was also meant to foster a sense of home (not work) in the camps' built environment.

At the heart of this home lay the community building, which was cen-trally located in the camp both physically and figuratively. The building served a number of recreational, educational, and sometimes religious pur-poses. It included the nursery school and elementary school; the library; the auditorium for dances, performances, and movies; the kitchen and craft rooms where federal officials or outside agencies held home demonstration workshops; and meeting spaces for the camp council and other camp-based organizations. The community building allowed migrants to gather and form solidarity through cohabitation and cooperation. The activities con-ducted in the community building resonated with the FSA's reformist efforts to combat migrants' individualistic attitudes.

In the mid-1930s, the FSA constructed the community building near the home and apartment structures for longer-term residents. Yet begin-ning in 1940, FSA architects placed these living quarters away from the center of the camp, hoping that it would improve migrants' self-sufficiency. This left the community building surrounded by housing for more temporary migrants.[62] Camp planners intended for this building to be accessible to both permanent and temporary migrants, yet they placed transient workers and their families in closest proximity to it because, as Hamlin noted, "it was they who [were] the greatest in number and [had]

Figure 5. "Community Building at the Migratory Labor Camp at Sinton,
Texas." Photograph by Russell Lee, March 1940. Library of Congress, Prints &
Photographs Division, FSA/OWI Collection, LC-USF34-035756-D.

the greatest need for intensive community facilities."[63] In this sense, the
camps' structure clearly organized migrant residents within a hierarchical
plan that positioned them at different distances from the center depending on their perceived social and economic condition. The camps' built
environment, in other words, both represented and reinforced social class
divisions among camp residents.

As W. A. Canon explained, those who resided in the "labor homes"
were "families with good reputations for honesty, reliability and sobriety
who have prospects of steady employment for one year or more in vicinity
in agriculture or first processing industries." On the other hand, the "shelter
units" were "provided by the F.S.A. as a home, during seasonal employment
in the locality, for agricultural workers and their families whose migratory
existence isolates them from normal home and community life."[64] Agnes
Meyer of the *Washington Post* similarly explained in a report on the Robstown, Texas, camp that the "labor homes," located farthest from the center

Figure 6. "Interior of Community Building at the Migratory Labor Camp. Sinton, Texas." Photograph by Russell Lee, March 1940. Library of Congress, Prints & Photographs Division, FSA/OWI Collection, LC-USF34-035764-D.

of camp, were for the more permanent families "who have demonstrated superior ability in skills, working capacity, and social behavior." The shelters, centrally situated, on the other hand, were "for the birds of passage," who she later clarified were mostly "Latin American fellow citizens."[65] Despite camp officials' objectives to provide all residents with the same advantages of "normal home and community life," their decision to position permanent families away from the camps' administrative center suggested that these families had earned the right to live outside of its central structure.

Other material elements contributed to reinforcing a distinction between farmworkers residing in the more permanent homes and apartments and migrants living in the temporary shelters. FSA architects initially conceived of the permanent homes as "minimal houses" for agricultural workers employed in year-round occupations that included work in local processing and packing plants, mills, or canneries. By the early 1940s, as more careful consideration went into building permanent housing, most labor homes came equipped with a number of amenities characteristic of contemporary middle-class living.[66] This signaled an important shift in the camp programs' overall objectives. As Greg Hise argues, "The directorate began to focus its attention on transforming agricultural laborers and their families from a seasonal, migrant workforce to a fixed population that supplemented wage work in growers' fields with domestic production, with a view towards self-sufficiency."[67] The distance between the camps' labor homes and temporary shelters also reflected the FSA's distinct aim to shelter some farmworkers who needed to remain transitory as part of the existing industrial agricultural system while facilitating the resettlement and domestic stability of others. In addition to reinforcing class differences, this practice sustained the racialized discourses dividing different workers.

The labor homes at the McAllen, Texas, camp were typical of the housing types provided for permanent single-family residence. Eighty-five fully furnished labor home units rented for approximately eight dollars a month. Each unit consisted of two bedrooms, a bath with shower, a kitchen, a combination living and dining room, and an exterior with a covered porch and designated plot for individual subsistence gardening.[68] FSA designers often incorporated elements such as a terrace, an attached car shelter, or a trellis by the front door as a means of constructing "something more than just the bare bones."[69] The two-story row houses or multifamily dwellings, sometimes referred to as apartments, provided similar conveniences to long-term residents. The prototype apartment was a two-bedroom or four-bedroom unit equipped with a kitchen and dining area, a living room, one bath and shower, and an outdoor laundry porch and children's play porch.

Accordingly, labor home and apartment residents enjoyed a quality of life notably different from that afforded to migrants in the temporary shelters. They had the luxuries of indoor plumbing and electricity, along with the privileges of a private garden, play area, and individual rooms. In 1940 James T. Collins, the camp manager in Yamhill, Oregon, recognized the implications of this disparity when he reported that there was no need for a camp nurse to be stationed at Yamhill because "families in the labor homes are in comfortable quarters with inside flush toilets, shower baths, hot and cold water and are not subjected to health hazards, as are families living in the shelters" who had to make use of shared public facilities.[70]

The camps' multifamily dwellings failed to meet the promise of stable working-class housing. As one report on the FSA's activities found, "Entire families occupy one room, shelter, or tent which is used as a combination kitchen, dining room, and living quarters. The space provided does not permit desired privacy and must, of necessity, result in many embarrassing situations."[71] Because temporary migrants' home space lacked the amenities, privacy, and attributes considered ideal, these families had little opportunity to meet the dominant conceptions of respectable domesticity and personal behavior camp officials expected.

While the FSA celebrated the fact that the federal camps provided migrant housing improvements over what was typically available for seasonal workers and their families, shelter units were rarely more than simple concrete bases with metal or wood structures. Even in the rare case where toilet facilities were provided in the housing units for short-term residents, they were shared among multiple families making use of the building. For example, in Lamesa, Texas, camp engineers constructed twenty-five "Quadruplex Shelters" to house temporary migrants. The design was intended to house four families, two on each side. In the middle, so as to be easily accessible to both sides, the shelter included a separate toilet room for women and men and a designated laundry area.[72] Nevertheless, the standard metal and wood shelters—which were generally provisioned with two iron beds, two iron benches, and a kerosene stove for approximately "a dime a day" or two hours of camp-related work per week—were a marked improvement over the platform-tent units erected during the early stages of the camp program.[73]

In the metal units and row shelters, itinerant families had to contend with many conditions that permanent residents in the labor homes did not. For one, they were exposed to more severe health risks, including dealing with drastic temperatures resulting from poor insulation. In Florida and Texas especially, the hot and humid climate could make the metal shelters unbearable and dangerous. Additionally, temporary residents had less privacy and were susceptible to closer supervision from camp administrators and fellow campers in close proximity. It was not uncommon for the FSA's home management supervisor, for example, to pay short-term residents a home visit "from time to time" to inspect sanitary conditions, workers' employment and grant status, and any other particular needs a family might have.[74] While permanent residents were also monitored in some ways, camp records indicate that short-term residents encountered this as part of day-to-day life. Officials claimed that these workers were less familiar with camp standards and thus required more careful attention.

Figure 7. "Migratory Laborers Sitting in Front of Their Metal Shelter at Okeechobee Migratory Labor Camp. Belle Glade, Florida." Photograph by Marion Post Wolcott, February 1941. Library of Congress, Prints & Photographs Division, FSA/OWI Collection, LC-USF34-057271-E.

Temporary residents were also encouraged to keep an eye out for any violation of camp rules—particularly with regard to inappropriate conduct, such as rowdy behavior, drinking, or gambling—and report it to the camp council or management. This was facilitated by the fact that in most cases the FSA architects located the shelter units facing each other, typically along the main camp road. The planners described their intention in this arrangement in terms of efficiency of building form and community development. Yet in this spatial order, there is evidence of the camps' structure serving to build "a community turned in on itself," though this was not the FSA's objective.[75]

The regulatory element in the camps' temporary section proved significant because it invaded migrants' personal space and undermined family authority within the home. It also complicated the process of community formation by pitting migrant families against each other, despite their design to do the opposite. For example, in an effort to improve migrants' domestic health practices, camp officials not only made "unexpected sanitation inspection[s]" to their homes but also encouraged migrant families to compete for the cleanest living environment, often awarding prizes in the process.[76] Migrants' regulation of social practices was also problematic because it potentially compromised their economic status by linking their behavior as "good citizens" within the camp to their potential as "good workers" in the fields or canneries. By 1942 there was a USES official in every camp, making this a very real concern.

The FSA's decision to house permanent families outside of the camps' inner structure not only served to distinguish their social and class status as people who could afford to occupy the camps' year-round dwellings; it also guaranteed these families more autonomy from everyday camp activities. The permanent dwellings were typically constructed within cul-de-sac arrangements in separate neighborhoods, often with their own entrance and exit to the camp, and with some kind of landscape feature dividing them from the main area. In considering the architects' design elements, in fact, some FSA administrators worried that this arrangement might discourage permanent migrants from developing a cooperative attitude with the short-term families.

In January 1941 Francis T. McSherry, the camp manager in Firebaugh, California, wrote to Harvey M. Coverley, FSA assistant regional director, complaining about "the barbed wire fence across the property, separating the labor home section from the metal shelter section of the project." As he stated, "This sort of thing [is] not only a physical barrier, but also a very bad psychological barrier for the proper cooperative functioning of these two groups, tending to separate them, which, in my opinion, is quite undesirable in this type of project."[77] Before it was removed, permanent migrants at Firebaugh would have to crawl under the fence to attend activities and meetings in the community building. At the Shafter and Coachella camps, this problem was avoided through the construction of separate community center buildings for the labor home and shelter residents. In these cases, the FSA planners appeared to take a more practical approach to providing essential amenities, but in the process they compromised the agency's collectivist intentions.

Permanent and temporary migrants' spatial segregation was further institutionalized through the camps' social programming efforts. For example, camp monthly narrative reports indicate that it was not uncommon for camp meetings and social functions to be divided between labor home and temporary residents. In South Texas, as FSA officials explained, this occurred as the result of a difference in language preference, with labor home residents more likely to participate in English workshops, and temporary migrants preferring Spanish demonstrations. Even so, a clear social distinction appears in much of the rhetoric describing camp activities. For instance, camp managers frequently spoke of labor home residents doing things for migrant families, suggesting that there was some degree of paternalism characterizing their relationship. Although camp officials encouraged permanent residents to cooperate "with the folks in the shelters" and promote the spirit of "the kind of community [the FSA was] trying to build," the site reinforced socioeconomic differences, oftentimes making it difficult for such interactions to occur.[78]

The agency's desire to build a stronger social democracy nevertheless comes across several camp documents. From the program's earliest days, FSA administrators reminded camp managers that "agricultural workers are eligible to admission regardless of race, creed, relief status, etc."[79] When migrants united in the camps to achieve collective self-government, FSA officials proudly boasted about it in their publications. One 1941 newsletter testified to this success at the migratory camp in Indio, California. The report noted that "in many migratory workers' camps, Mexicans and Negroes are severely discriminated against, but in 'Humanity U.S.A' [the name of the Indio camp] all races and religions work together."[80] Similarly, on June 27, 1942, the camp manager in Athena, Oregon, praised the farmworker community, stating, "Nothing has pleased me more than to see the tolerant and friendly feeling among campers here regardless of race, color or creed. . . . Now that we are in a war . . . it is particularly important to remember that 'all men are created equal.' "[81] However, the previous examples notwithstanding, the nation's race and class divide spatially marked the FSA's migratory labor camps.

The camps originated in California in response to the incoming migration of white Dust Bowl refugees who observers warned were American citizens likely to remain in the state permanently. The RA justified the necessity of federal camps by juxtaposing these refugees against a more traditional labor force commonly depicted as foreign, "satisfied with very little," and willing to "stay entirely to themselves."[82] As the camp program began, the racialized characterization of Mexican and Filipino migrant workers as "birds of passage" shaped the decision to construct the camps mainly "for whites." This is clearly evident in the case of the camp in Brawley, California, built by the RA in 1936.

A "social and economic survey" conducted by the RA in October 1936 estimated that Brawley's population in 1930 was about "4,711 American (white), 194 Negro, and 5,534 Foreign (mostly Mexican)."[83] In the agricultural labor force, however, "Mexican Indians" supplied "ninety percent of the stoop labor force."[84] As "the largest city in the Imperial Valley, and the greatest perishable produce shipping center of the United States," the RA understood the importance of establishing a model camp there. In doing so, however, officials positioned "resident workers" (i.e., white Americans) in competition with foreign and nonwhite migrants who lowered their earnings and standard of living. According to the investigators, these supposed foreigners (i.e., "Mexicans") and nonwhites (i.e., "Indians") were "a serious problem," not potential allies in the fight for improved living conditions.

Rather than considering Mexican migrants as ideal inhabitants for the Brawley camp due to their most degraded condition, their serious malnourishment, and their weakened position in the struggle against Imperial Valley growers, all things the RA's social scientists acknowledged in their report, the resettlement agents instead reinforced Mexican families' marginalization by further blaming them for their impoverishment and exclusion from the camp program. The investigators surely understood that many of the Mexican migrants were not "foreign," or at the very least they had resided in the Imperial Valley for a number of years. They had evidence of this as they reported that Brawley was historically divided by the railroads into a white section (on the west) and a Mexican section (on the east), and as they commented on the poor educational opportunities available for Mexican children. Nonetheless, the social scientists concluded that in the Mexican section of town, "the Mexican Indian and the Negro [which they clarified were recent arrivals from the South] reveal the environment for which their social and racial origin has been responsible." They were not only to blame for their poverty, but since it was *they* who remained segregated from the whites "both by volition and custom" and "because there is virtually no racial intermixture," the RA officials concluded that "the camp *in practice* will house exclusively white itinerant field labor" and would not be located near the Mexican quarters of the town.[85]

As this example demonstrates, discriminatory racial practices were imbedded in the migrant camps' built environment even in locations where formal segregationist policies did not exist. In October 1936, the same month RA officials settled on the question of where to build the Brawley camp, Thomas Collins, managing the camp in Arvin, California, wrote to his regional supervisors recommending a solution to the race problem. Since there was "no justification for excluding Negroes, Mexicans, or Filipinos from the camp," he suggested that "they be placed in one unit" (i.e., separately) as was the system followed in Marysville and could be easily replicated elsewhere. The problem could be "easily solved," he stated, "by SUGGESTING to the negro group that they occupy a certain section, and, if necessary, explain to him the advantages of having the colored group to itself." More importantly, he warned federal camp administrators about the political trouble that could occur if they openly violated migrants' civil liberties. As Collins cautioned, "They have in California, a very strong organization dedicated to the rights of the negro and [are] very very strongly opposed to segregation in tax supported camps or communities. For the camp program to 'officially' go on record as having sections for the segregation of the negro, would open us to vicious opposition."[86]

The labor camps that the FSA built along the Atlantic seaboard in places such as Florida, New Jersey, and Maryland were the only locations where the agency officially segregated migrants on the basis of race. Since most of the migrant workers on the East Coast originated in the South, the FSA abided by Jim Crow policies as their mobile camps moved north despite the agency's broader claims toward promoting racial tolerance.[87] Beyond the existing legal systems that reinforced racial segregation in some states, other factors contributed to fostering social divisions in camps across the country. Again, this suggests how the camp communities materialized in ways that were at odds with the social engineering project FSA architects wanted to build as part of a better social order in rural America.

In Texas, for instance, the racial divide existing in the agricultural industry resulted in those occupying the camps' more permanent homes usually being white, because they held more stable and better-paying jobs, while those residing in the temporary shelters were typically Mexican. In several of their monthly narrative reports, the Texas camp managers refer to the temporary section of the camps as "the Mexican quarters." The FSA had no official policy indicating that Mexican migrants could not reside in the permanent labor homes, but very few actually did until the late 1940s. Camp administrators stated that the division existed primarily because Mexican farmworkers could not find stable employment allowing them to stay in the region year-round, and that even when they could, few were able to afford the rent. They refused to acknowledge how Mexican workers' economic situation was fundamentally a racial problem.

Instead of making the labor homes more accessible to Mexican families, especially after acknowledging that most Mexican migrants in Texas originated in the Rio Grande valley, FSA officials took it for granted that Mexican migration was natural and planned the Texas camps accordingly. For example, in 1939, while discussing the site plans for the Princeton camp, FSA social analyst Edward J. Rowell recommended that "it is not believed advisable to build any of the so-called labor homes since very few Mexicans stay in the district through the year."[88] Similarly, in Lamesa, where Mexican migrants predominated, the FSA planning team initially claimed that labor homes were not necessary because "everyone knows [Mexican migrants] do not usually rent places to live." In fact, it was for these reasons that the camps in Princeton, Harlingen, Crystal City, and McAllen, Texas, were originally designed to include only temporary shelters and no permanent housing.[89]

In several instances, FSA officials in Texas had to manage the difficulties arising when concurrently housing Anglo, Mexican, and African American farmworkers as temporary migrants. At Princeton, for example, Rowell reported in June 1942 on the existing "racial trouble" between Mexican and Anglo farmworkers, which likely resulted from a "near riot" that occurred back in 1934 when Princeton onion growers decided to replace white workers with Mexican labor at cheaper wages. Trouble escalated during this incident after Anglo workers returned to the onion fields to "run [the Mexicans] out of the country." Since then, Rowell reported, "there hasn't been a Latin American or Negro that has let the sun set on 'em in Princeton."[90] Perhaps for this reason, C. B. Baldwin, the FSA's assistant administrator, advised in 1940 that plans for the Princeton camp include separate specifications for housing "American" versus "Mexican" temporary migrants.[91] Rowell agreed, recommending that the FSA should revert back to the multiple-unit model originally used in California so that the FSA could provide separate temporary facilities and bath units for "native whites" and for "Mexicans." Oral histories reflecting on the opening of the Robstown camp suggest that this model was followed there, too. Respondents recall that while most of the temporary housing in the camp served Mexican migrant workers, there existed a "separate section" for black migrants.[92]

Commenting on what was "possibly an unconscious segregation of races" in the Texas labor camps, F. V. Meriwether, the FSA's senior medical officer, reported in 1940 that "in the [Raymondville, Robstown, and Sinton] camps the population is dominantly Mexican, while at Weslaco, although the agricultural workers are about 90 percent Mexicans, the population in the camp is 95 percent white."[93] Certainly migrants had a choice in occupying the government's labor camps, and this may have led to a preference of one camp, or one unit in a camp, over another for a variety of reasons. But to suggest that racial segregation was "unconscious" in the FSA camps falsely portrays how the camp planners sanctioned and systematized segregationist practices through the establishment of separate facilities and social spaces for workers and their families.

Another telling factor involves the construction of gender-defined spaces within the camps. Most included a separate workshop facility where boys could get lessons on farm machinery and practice woodwork and other male-dominated crafts, while migrant men worked on improvements for their cars, homes, and the camp project. Conversely, the FSA's documentary photographs demonstrate how the camps' utility building functioned as a distinctly female space. The images richly capture migrant women and girls (usually in groups) canning, weaving, sewing, washing clothes, and ironing.

Not surprisingly, camp administrators abided by normative conceptions of domesticity in the early 1940s, which produced specific and distinct spaces for migrant men and women's socialization in camp. The camps, however, were not traditional homes. They always existed simultaneously as domestic and labor spaces. Consequently, conventional gendered notions of work in the home, in the fields, and for the labor camp were more fluid for migrant men and women occupying the camps than traditional expectations allowed. As FSA planners sought to produce an ideal domestic environment, they created conflicting divisions between home and work, between public and private, and between men and women's labor that migrants may have appreciated but found difficult to uphold.

Community Planning During World War II

The U.S. entry into World War II brought about a dramatic shift in the FSA's focus on migrant housing. The upsurge in labor camp construction

Figure 8. "Community Laundry. FSA (Farm Security Administration) Camp, Robstown, Texas." Photograph by Arthur Rothstein, January 1942. Library of Congress, Prints & Photographs Division, FSA/OWI Collection, LC-USF34-024805-C.

between 1940 and 1942 stemmed from the FSA's ability to convince congressional critics that the camps promoted labor efficiency to win the war. In May 1942 U.S. Secretary of Agriculture Claude R. Wickard stressed the "need for a sizeable expansion of the migratory labor camp program in order to meet the requirements for agricultural workers in the harvesting of crops to be produced under the expanded food program." Nonetheless, other factors effectively prevented the program from expanding as planned. As Wickard's letter to Donald M. Nelson, chair of the War Production Board (WPB), explained, the requirement that the FSA consult with the WPB to obtain permission for the use of various materials in building new camps (related to Conservation Order L-41) put the agency at an impasse. Moreover, the bureaucratic policies requiring WPA approval every time a mobile labor camp was taken down and reassembled at the next site proved contrary to the objective of mobilizing "Migrant Soldiers on the Food Production Front."[94]

Although the FSA encountered significant problems securing the funds and the authority to develop new housing for farm laborers after 1942, the camps expanded in other dramatic ways. The FSA's responsibility in managing the Emergency Farm Labor Supply Program beginning in 1942, and the transfer of the camp program to the War Food Administration in 1943, demonstrate how the FSA mobilized to meet the nation's leading wartime imperatives and in the process altered the camps' site layout, building types, and stated purposes to meet those goals. The FSA's role in designing internment facilities and labor camps for Japanese and Japanese American "enemy aliens," however, best exemplifies the tragic incongruity between the program's intended purpose, the architect's progressive ideologies, and what eventually materialized as part of the FSA's housing intervention.

Almost as soon as President Roosevelt signed Executive Order 9066 on February 19, 1942, authorizing the relocation and internment of approximately 112,500 American citizens and resident aliens of Japanese ancestry (the number of those dislocated by the order was even higher at an estimated 120,300), the FSA was called to assist the U.S. Western Defense and Command and Fourth Army in charge of the operation.[95] Testifying before Congress on March 6, 1942, Laurence I. Hewes, the Region IX FSA director, explained the FSA's role in "handling the movement of aliens" and facilitating their "resettlement." In particular, Hewes acknowledged how the agency was especially well equipped to deal with this problem. As he noted:

> The possible utility of the Farm Security Administration in connection with this problem arises out of our experience with the migration which has come to California within the last 10 years from the West-South-Central States and of persons who have left those States for various reasons and have come to California and become agricultural laborers. The problems of housing, moving people, and trying to establish some form of economic security for dispossessed people, has provided a fund of experience which, if the Army needs it, is available.[96]

Repeatedly, Hewes stressed how the FSA had "been through the fire" gathering information and experimenting with the best practices for resettling migrant families. He drew on numerous examples to make a case for why the farm labor program served as a valuable model for Japanese evacuation and relocation.

Among the points Hewes addressed as evidence was the fact that the FSA had already accomplished the mass resettlement of "uprooted people" (including "tiny babies"). The FSA had also developed construction methods, especially for housing, that were widely acknowledged for their efficiency and economy.[97] He also highlighted the FSA's experience operating a large medical program for agricultural workers, which he used to demonstrate their approach to "a number of affiliated problems, some of which can become very severe and very bothersome in connection with people moved in large numbers from places that they have formerly made their homes." Finally, he talked about the agency's experience in locating suitable land for relocation, "examin[ing] rather exhaustively large tracts of public domain, [making] soil surveys and water surveys, and marketing surveys." These investigations were "fairly complete, fairly scientific and made by pretty well-trained people," Hewes noted.[98]

Congressional members investigating the "Problems of Evacuation of Enemy Aliens and Others from Prohibited Military Zones" appeared readily convinced by Hewes's explanation, even going so far as to ask if the camps for migratory workers were fully occupied, implying that they would make good housing for the evacuees. There was no question that the FSA would play an important role in the operation, and Hewes acknowledged that he had already begun advising U.S. Army general John DeWitt as a member of the Civilian Coordinating Committee. However, it is important to question the seeming fluidity by which federal officials aimed to build Japanese American internment on the experience of displaced and disenfranchised migrant farmworkers. This relational discourse sheds light on the deep contradictions behind the FSA's experiment in democracy as it began under the New Deal and ended shortly after World War II.

The federal camp project spatially constructed race and class on the rural landscape so that it functioned as a place of both promise and despair.[99] Operating under distinct yet overlapping historical contexts, it is clear how the FSA could consider migrant farmworkers and Japanese internees as similarly dislocated populations and FSA camps as ideal housing environments for both. Not only had the labor camps transformed with each new population of migrant residents, but in doing so the camp space manifested different realities and geographies for each inhabitant. For migrant families, the labor camps may have served as a space of containment, but they lived there voluntarily and in exchange for much-needed services, a place they could prosper, and the promise of enhanced citizenship. For Japanese families, the internment camps were similarly supposed to build a participatory democracy and enhance evacuees' sense of citizenship, but they operated foremost as spaces of incarceration where families found their civil rights nullified as they were held against their will, behind barbed wire, with army guns pointed toward them.

Oral histories conducted with FSA architects Eckbo and DeMars, who designed some of the Japanese internment camps, suggest that they recognized the deep ideological contradiction behind their planned projects. This point was brought home in an even more personal manner when two Japanese American FSA architects employed at the San Francisco office were evacuated. As DeMars recalled: "Then we were brought in to do some planning on the Japanese relocation problem. I think we were pretty much emotionally upset at the whole business since we lost two of our young, talented architects, and longtime close friends to it: 'Hachi' and 'Si,' Hachiro Yuasa and Siberius Saito. We thought we ought to make the best of what we felt was a very unfair and unnecessary proposition."[100] DeMars's statement suggests that they had little option but to carry out their task; it was a military command in time of war. Hewes left a similar record showing how, despite his seemingly matter-of-fact congressional testimony, he struggled with this ethical dilemma. As he notes in his memoir:

My first lesson in administrative adversity was forced participation in helping to accomplish the cruel and unnecessary evacuation of all persons of Japanese ancestry from the Pacific Coast. The modicum of justification which military exigencies of the post–Pearl Harbor situation lent this action was more than offset by the highly dangerous precedents it established in violated civil liberties and official acceptance of overt racial prejudice.[101]

Planning for internment ran counter to the political ideology and social reform goals that so deeply influenced the San Francisco office and the architects' working group Telesis (of which Yuasa and other Japanese American architects were a part).

Despite their progressive reasoning about the power of architecture as a democratizing agent, the FSA architects failed to publicly comment on the conflict of architectural practice in advancing racial injustice and the denial of citizenship rights. Instead, in the words of DeMars, they made "the best of it." In material form, this meant that the FSA architects helped design the internment camps with more consideration for what Eckbo termed "the social point of view."[102] In preparing their plans, he and DeMars were determined to provide as many community-based amenities as possible. This stood in sharp contrast to the original plans carried out by the U.S. Army Corps of Engineers.[103] The army's standard plans for the temporary assembly and semipermanent relocation centers demonstrate the goal of efficiency in construction with bare, minimum shelters (typically communal barracks) and the focus on security and detention. As the task of building more permanent internment camps got under way, the War Relocation Authority (WRA) was charged with "relocation, maintenance and supervision" of the evacuees.[104] In this role, WRA officials had some influence over the army's design plans by dictating the internees' spatial management.

In the memorandum of agreement between the War Department and the WRA established on April 17, 1942, General DeWitt distinctly stated that the military's plans for building internment camps were not designed to include "refinements such as schools, churches, and other community planning adjuncts."[105] The specific reference to community planning was intended to distinguish the army's construction of basic amenities for "enemy aliens" from the community structures recently completed by the FSA for migrant and defense workers.[106] DeWitt's concern was not too far off considering that the WRA's director, Milton Eisenhower, and his quick successor, Dillon Myer, hailed from the more liberal branch of the USDA. As committed New Dealers, they brought to the WRA "an obsession with social planning." Like Hewes, DeWitt and Myer were both publicly opposed to Japanese evacuation and sought to use their influence to ameliorate the stringent conditions of internment. "Ever optimistic about the potential of mass social engineering," Mae Ngai explains, "they envisioned the camps as 'planned communities' and 'Americanizing [and moderniz-ing] projects' that would speed the assimilation of Japanese Americans through democratic self-government, schooling, work, and other rehabili-tative activities."[107]

The FSA's architects were well poised to help the WRA achieve these goals. Their design interventions fostered a community environment that sought to contest the punitive forces of internment. Though they could not eliminate the barbed wire fences and the guard towers, "they persisted," as

Ngai explains of the WRA more generally, "in their belief that theirs would be a democratic experiment."[108] Unlike the army's standard plans, the FSA designs "show insistently liberal allocations of recreational facilities occupying entire blocks and significant portions of the firebreaks."[109] According to WRA officials, "The original basic objective was to provide conditions and create an atmosphere that would approximate as nearly as possible, an American community."[110] Despite such utopian goals, critics such as Carey McWilliams (who was an early supporter of the WRA's assimilationist discourse) warned that "the relocation centers are not normal communities. They are institutions and they breed a type of 'prison complex.'"[111]

By 1943, four of the FSA's migrant labor camps also served as temporary internment facilities for Japanese Americans or concentration camps for foreign-born prisoners of war, mainly Latin Americans of German, Italian, and Japanese ancestry. This development further blurred the material reality of the camps as promising communities versus spaces of containment. The Marysville migrant camp in California, for instance, housed approximately 2,465 Japanese American evacuees from Placer and Sacramento Counties from May 8 to June 29, 1942. The Tulare migrant camp also housed approximately 5,061 Japanese American evacuees from Los Angeles and Sacramento Counties and from the southern California coastal area during the period of April 20 to September 4, 1942. The Crystal City labor camp in South Texas represented the largest internment site administered by the Immigration and Naturalization Service and the Department of Justice (DOJ) during World War II. It housed an estimated 3,500 people, the majority of whom were Japanese prisoners from Peru. Some German and Italian POWs from Latin America also lived in the Crystal City facility and were kept in a separate section of the camp. Finally, the Princeton migrant camp located near Dallas was similarly used as an internment facility for a short period in 1945. It incarcerated mostly German POWs captured during the war. As in the Crystal City facility, a ten- to twelve-foothigh fence, guard towers, and floodlights surrounded the Princeton camp. These surveillance features were added to the camps when they were turned over to the DOJ. Only eight months after the internment operation began, however, the Princeton facility housed migratory farmworkers again with the fence and lights remaining.[112]

At least two additional FSA camps in Rupert, Idaho, and Nyssa, Oregon, also housed Japanese internees during the war—although, in this context, they were Japanese American families working under the 1942 Seasonal

Farm Labor Agreement. The Seasonal Leave Program allowed Japanese American internees to work in agriculture as part of a federal effort to "restore loyal citizens and law-abiding aliens to a useful American life."[113] While the evacuees resided in the labor camps, they had access to similar social programming and self-governing committees available to migrant families living in nearby FSA camps. This did not mean, however, that they were free citizens. Residents at the Rupert and Nyssa camps could not leave the migrant camps unsupervised. How could the same space work to build community, foster civic engagement, and promote democracy in one historical context, and serve as a site of discipline, containment, and the nullification of rights in another? To understand this contradiction, it is necessary to view the labor camps' built environment as an instrument reflecting the political intentions and socioeconomic objectives of the state agents that operated it, as well as the reality of daily, lived experience of those who occupied it.

FSA planners shifted their focus when wartime priorities added to the political pressure already mounting against them and required the agency to accommodate different demands. Nevertheless, during the early 1940s the FSA remained ideologically committed to designing collective landscapes that would produce the best conditions for working-class families regardless of the minimum standards and the basic elements that went into their construction. They drew inspiration from modernist architectural theories on the important relationship between spatial order and social development. And they joined with progressive social scientists, economists, and other committed intellectuals to create one of the New Deal's most remarkable social projects—the labor camp program. In their efforts to reform America's rural landscape, to uplift migrant families, and bring order to the nation's agricultural system, these architects and planners left a lasting legacy.

In the more immediate trajectory, the FSA's innovations in standardization, site fabrication, modular planning, and the use of diverse building materials promoted the construction and rapid expansion of new residential towns and industrial "satellite communities" during the postwar period.[114] Because of their experience with building the camps, many of the FSA's architects and engineers went on to assume leadership positions in other government housing agencies where they continued to practice and promote the fundamentals of social planning. The Public Works Administration (PWA) and the Federal Housing Administration (FHA) were among the New Deal agencies that shaped the nature of postwar urban and suburban housing. In this job, federal officials advanced housing policies that likewise sought to "order" American families and systematize new patterns of social relations. Unfortunately, the progressive ideologies promoting collectivism and the civic value of good housing for poor families encountered new challenges by the 1950s.[115] Despite the FSA's influence, public housing authorities often discriminated on racial or class grounds in their provision of federal subsidies and in their guidelines for residential zoning. This maintained segregationist practices that encouraged social division and competition.

The contradictory material reality evident in the FSA's labor camps during the 1930s and 1940s demonstrates the incongruity that exists between the social promise of public housing and its limitations in disrupting poor people's marginalization. Despite FSA planners' intended objective to strengthen migrants' communal and civic identity and enhance social democracy, the camps operated in ways that reinforced the stringent racial, economic, and gendered biases contributing to farmworkers' legal and social exclusion. The camp planners were fundamentally committed to creating a more just and equitable condition for farmworker families, and most families occupying the camps did experience significant improvements in their domestic condition, health, and protection. Yet FSA building and landscape features alone could not reshape migrants' status as disenfranchised workers and citizens. Growers and rural communities demanded that the FSA respect the barriers they created to regulate migrants' rights and acted to counter the democratic structural forces planners imbued in the camps' environment. Migrants themselves also transformed the camps' material space and changed its social meaning. Farmworker families were not simply subjects of the camps' built environment but rather critical actors redefining the camp community in ways that FSA's planners did not necessarily intend or imagine.

CHAPTER 3

Traversing the Boundaries of Camp Life

Migrants' Community Within and Beyond the Federal Camps

On July 19, 2008, I sat down to interview Evaristo Gonzalez, Jr., who resided at the Harlingen, Texas, Farm Security Administration (FSA) camp in the mid-1940s. Pointing to the map he drew, Evaristo explained:

> Okay look, starting from here to there, it's Harlingen [Road]—and Rangerville Road over here in this direction over here. This is the entrance, the main entrance for everyone. Here was the office, here was the workshop, here was the [community] hall with various doors, and here was the cafeteria—because there was a cafeteria here [in the hall]. Here, what I don't remember, well I do remember, you'd enter through here and this was where they gave people shots, where they vaccinated and all of that, here in this part right here. So, everything over here were just small houses. Here there was a wide street—this is where my brother lived, and some cousins and one of my aunts, we lived here as well. And here there were some toilets for this area right here—no showers, the showers were more over here. Then, you continued further ahead toward the other street, and back here is where we had the baseball field, here. This is where I spent most of my time.[1]

Although only a young boy when he lived at the Harlingen camp, Evaristo's memory of the camp remained vivid. He recounted the various material features of the camp space with an assured tone, repeatedly pronouncing the location of certain elements with the word "here." Our conversation revealed how former camp residents maintained a strong conceptual reality of the physical space they lived in. Evaristo was not simply recalling the past in temporal terms; his memories of social relations within the camp were notably shaped by the space itself on and through which these relations occurred.

The most telling representations of the impact the FSA labor camp program had in migrants' lives appears in the "mental maps" they drew in order to explain camp relations. Geographers define mental maps as "model[s] of the environment which [are] built up over time in the individual's brain." Mental maps are "images that speak to the points of contact between people and their environment."[2] In conducting oral history, I was struck by how many of the individuals I spoke to prepared some sort of visual map to illuminate the physical and social space that existed within and beyond the labor camps. Throughout our discussions, people regularly referred to the maps they created so as to frame my understanding of the narratives they described.

In 2015 Israel Longoria Gonzalez (Evaristo's cousin) provided a closer understanding of the familial relations that existed in the Harlingen camp. His parents, Guadalupe and Rosa Gonzalez, moved there with nine of their children in 1941 from a nearby ranch called Los Indios. As he explained, when they discovered the quality housing with running water, electricity, and access to modern toilets and showers, they quickly invited their extended family to live there as well. Between 1941 and 1946, four generations of the Gonzalez family lived in the Harlingen camp. This included Israel's paternal great-grandfather and grandparents; nine paternal uncles and aunts, their spouses, and children; two maternal uncles and one aunt, their spouses, and children; and eight of Israel's siblings, some of whom married individuals they met at the camp and started their own families. The Mexican families he listed in his map with no specific relation were nonetheless *familias conocidas*, families they knew well: they knew them well because his father was a crew leader and had worked with many of them for years.[3]

The FSA regularly portrayed migrants as "farmworkers in a strange land," "adrift on the land," "homeless," and "aimless wanderers" unfamiliar with the labor and social environment forced on them by the Great Depression.[4] This allowed the agency to claim that the camps provided necessary

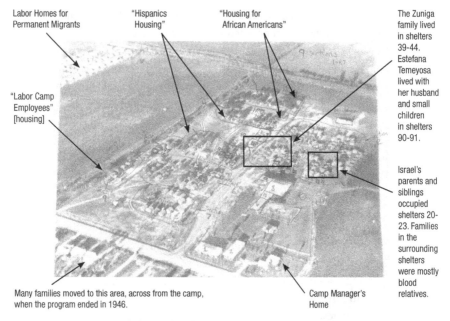

Labor Homes for Permanent Migrants

"Hispanics Housing"

"Housing for African Americans"

The Zuniga family lived in shelters 39-44. Estefana Temeyosa lived with her husband and small children in shelters 90-91.

"Labor Camp Employees" [housing]

Israel's parents and siblings occupied shelters 20-23. Families in the surrounding shelters were mostly blood relatives.

Many families moved to this area, across from the camp, when the program ended in 1946.

Camp Manager's Home

Figure 9. FSA Aerial photo of Harlingen, Texas, Migrant Labor Camp (ca. mid-1940s). Annotated by Israel Longoria Gonzalez. Israel also provided a list to accompany his map. He numbered each of the buildings and shelters to better indicate what they were used for and who lived in the camp. Photo from box 1452, file Braceros generalidades corespondencia, Secretaría de Relaciones Exteriores Archivo Historico, Embajada Mexicana en Estados Unidos de America, 1943-48.

stabilizing environments that would rehabilitate destitute migrants and promote their democratic participation in society. Yet most of the farm-worker families who occupied the camps, especially by the early 1940s when the camp program expanded, had worked as migratory farmworkers for a number of years. Consequently, they were part of a larger network of family migrations or regular work crews. Most migrants also maintained "regional communities," connected to their place of origin and formed along their migratory route.[5] Since South Texas served as a starting point for several interstate farm labor migrations, many of those who resided in the region's FSA camps had well-established communities nearby and could claim ancestral ties to the land. Evaristo and Israel's paternal great-grandmother Maria Balli Gonzalez, for example, was a descendant of Padre José Nicolas Ballí Hinojosa, one of the first Europeans to settle Padre Island (now named after him) along the Gulf of Mexico.[6]

Previous studies examining the FSA's focus on community formation have largely ignored the way migrants defined the labor camps' built environment and constituted their own material and conceptual reality of camp life. They have failed to consider, as Andrew Herod argues more generally about working-class history, the power of workers as geographical actors.[7] The scholarship that does consider migrants' community formation focuses on the white Dust Bowl experience in California where the camp program started. It generally concludes, as Charles J. Shindo writes, that "migrants lacked the power to shape the community beyond the limits placed by the camp manager and the federal government."[8] Building on Walter J. Stein's analysis of Dust Bowl migrants' "rugged individualism," Brian Q. Cannon similarly argues, "Notwithstanding instances of cooperation, camp residents generally failed to identify with one another and to cooperate politically and economically to the extent that administrators had hoped that they would."[9] These claims deny migrants any agency in shaping camp relations and the camps' economic and political geography in their own terms. They also too readily dismiss migrants' willingness to work collectively by stressing how they valued their independence.[10]

The approach historians have taken reflects what the agrarian scholar James C. Scott theorized about state processes of sedentarization. Scott argues that while planned state-based communities have rarely materialized as anticipated, "the effect of these schemes . . . lies as much in what they replace as in the degree to which they live up to their own rhetoric." As Scott contends:

> The concentration of population in planned settlements may not create what state planners had in mind, but it has almost always disrupted or destroyed prior communities whose cohesion derived mostly from nonstate sources. . . . Virtually by definition, the state-designed settlement must start from the beginning to build its own sources of cohesion and joint action. A new community is thus, also by definition, a community demobilized, and hence a community more amenable to control from above and outside.[11]

While it is necessary to acknowledge how the camps' bureaucratic and physical structure regulated migrant families, residents nevertheless continuously reconstituted their own reality of camp life. Through their personal and collective efforts, migrants ascribed meaning to the camps' built environment in ways that supported and challenged how FSA officials understood the process of community formation. This perspective is significant because it illuminates the role that migrant families played in shaping the program's social reform efforts and in ensuring their own self-reproduction. Contrary to Scott's assertion about the power dynamics in state-planned communities, migrants occupying the federal camps were not ineffective in contesting the aspects of camp life they disliked, and many were not "starting from the beginning" when building communal bonds that extended across and beyond the camps' space.[12]

To best demonstrate how migrant families perceived, encountered, and remade the labor camp communities they occupied, this chapter considers migrants' decisions to participate in the camp program and evaluates the actions they took to build community bonds in ways that tested the FSA's project. While some migrants understood the camps as limiting, others chose to view them as a mechanism by which to improve their lives. The majority of migrants likely understood the camps in both these terms, neither totally supporting the camp project nor completely rejecting it. Acknowledging this duality provides a fuller account of how migrants experienced and shaped the camps' built environment. For example, while close living quarters contributed to the FSA's surveillance structure and fueled disputes between migrant neighbors, they also encouraged families to establish essential and enduring relationships that rendered important resources for negotiating their status as migrant farmworkers.

This chapter evaluates migrants' experiences across the camp program nationally but pays particular attention to the seven federal camps located in South Texas. FSA agents identified important regional community patterns in other states as well, such as in the "origin islands" of African American farmworkers traveling from Georgia to Florida and up the Atlantic Coast. Yet South Texas offers an especially important site in which to carry out this analysis. Many of the families who once lived in the camps continue to reside in the area immediately surrounding the site where the former camp existed, a matter that greatly facilitated my oral history research. Their decision to remain near the camps after they closed was influenced by the fact that most had previously lived nearby. As FSA agents discovered during the early 1930s, Texas was unusual because it was both the starting and ending point of a large-scale migration. According to farm labor expert Carey McWilliams, the migrant problem in Texas was especially problematic because "unlike other states, Texas cannot send its migrants elsewhere at the end of the season for Texas is their home." Despite this realization, government officials and local communities usually viewed Mexican farmworkers as "nomadic and outside American civilization."[13] If FSA officials were truly committed to enhancing Mexican farmworkers' democratic rights, they needed to acknowledge migrants' long-standing community, civic, and spatial claims in their own terms.

Migrants' Views of Camp Life: Deciding to Live in a Federal Camp

Although few archival documents record migrants' decisions to live in an FSA camp, the information available suggests that it was a choice made with careful consideration of the benefits and pressures associated with living there. FSA reports and migrants' own testimonies demonstrate both the apprehension and confidence migrants held in their estimation of what the camp program offered. Ultimately, for the migrant families that chose to participate, the advantages the camps provided in terms of safe and sanitary housing, medical care, a steady diet, and childcare outweighed the burdens.

The camps' first migrant residents, the Dust Bowl families arriving in California in the mid-1930s, significantly tested the FSA's cooperative, democratic experiment with their stubborn independence, according to historian Walter Stein. As Stein explained, "The Okie liked to think of himself as 'beholden to no one,' an individual making his way alone with neither aid from, nor gratitude to, the government or anyone else." This outlook stemmed from their Great Plains personality, he concluded. "Because he was white, isolated on his farm, and free from the restraints imposed upon dwellers in more populated areas," the Dust Bowl migrant lacked experience subordinating individual interests for the betterment of the group.[14] Both Stein and James N. Gregory focus on Dust Bowl migrants' resistance to farm labor unionization as an example of how their values and disposition prevented them from identifying with a broader class-based, collective movement as migrant workers.[15] Gregory, however, determines that this stemmed not from the Dust Bowl migrants' "rugged individualism" but rather from their identification as farm owners, not workers. Indeed, he contends that cooperation was "certainly nothing new" for these migrants, and he cautions that the "individualist" label was "another one of the mistaken stereotypes generated by a society that was uncomfortable with its rural shadow."[16]

If Dust Bowl families did abide by the FSA's collective project, Stein argues that they did so only initially and because of their desperate condition that landed them in the FSA camps. "It is possible," Stein writes, "that in the early days of the camp program, the migrants were so demoralized, so apathetic, that, told to *be* democratic, they were democratic."[17] Indeed, most subsequent studies on the Dust Bowl migration draw similar conclusions. Cannon, for example, asserts that when faced with serious illness or death, "camp residents rallied around each other, identifying with one another as administrators had hoped they would," but this was mostly incidental and subsided "as time wore on and the novelty of the camp and its organizations diminished."[18] Yet the very trauma that Stein and Cannon point to provides possible counterevidence to Dust Bowl refugees' experiences of community formation within the camps.

A series of interviews, song recordings, and audio documentation of meetings in the California camps produced by ethnographers Charles L. Todd and Robert Sonkin in 1940 and 1941 demonstrate how Dust Bowl families' troubled lives prior to migration, and then in California, shaped their view of the camps in positive terms. In their "migracious" songs and poems describing their displacement and subsequent experiences, many conveyed arriving at the camps disoriented as newcomers and significantly in distress from their time on the road.[19] This evidence shows how the hunger, poor health, frustration, and homesickness they faced tested their values and produced a vulnerability from which they welcomed the idea that they were not in it alone. Although many migrants commented on the tension that existed in the camps over shared responsibilities, they still spoke of the camps' value in social and democratic as well as economic terms.[20]

On August 16, 1940, for instance, J. W. Becker and his wife sat before Todd and Sonkin's Presto disc recorder at the Shafter camp and explained how it was "a poor man's paradise" where "whether you have money or no [sic], you will always find a place to eat and sleep." As Mr. Becker recounted:

I have heard much said concerning the federal camps as being a very undesirable place, but my experience has proven to be quite the

contrary. We have lived in various private camps and found conditions very unsatisfactory with much more rent to pay. So, finally,
[my] family and I decided to move into the migratory camp at Shafter, California. . . . We find various people here of different rearing.
And, some are educated, some uneducated. Some are good, and
some are indifferent. But, nevertheless, it teaches one a good lesson
to try to get along with the various classes of people. It's a good
experience. It's something that we all need. In fact, I believe the
more we get of this the better we will become. The better citizens.
And, when we get the better things of life, we will appreciate them
more.[21]

Mrs. Becker continued the interview discussing how when they arrived at
the camp, they fumbled with the hot water system and sewing and laundry
machines, but that in each case they learned quickly because their fellow
migrants were there to say, "Well, is there something we can do for you?"
Possibly the Beckers aimed to please the ethnographers in telling these stories, perhaps viewing them as affiliated with the FSA. Todd and Sonkin,
however, recorded numerous accounts that exemplify similar sentiments.

Two days before they sat with the Beckers, they recorded Wayne "Gene"
Dinwiddie at the Visalia camp where he performed a song he composed
titled "Home in the Government Camp." He sang:

How often we've traveled the low road with that big cause and heavy
    load.
How often we've traveled along with nothing to do but sing some
    old lazy song.
Home, give us a home, so we won't have to roam. A place to call
    our own.
For something overhead, and something for a bed, and something
    to call our own.
Home, home, in a government camp, so we won't have to be called
    a tramp.[22]

The song expressed a clear desire to settle down in the camp and faith in
the idea that this would help migrants improve their material condition
and social standing as citizens. Other migrants similarly reminded fellow

campers of their circumstances prior to arriving at the camp and emphasized the significance of mutual understanding in making the camp an ideal
home. At the Arvin camp, for example, Rosetta Spainhard recorded her
poem, "The Government Camp":

> Hear all, hear all from the government camp.
> We all came here, fled broken land . . .
> If we would only think it over right.
> To live in this world is a pretty hard fight.
> But we can all be thankful for this place to stay.
> And put all of those foolish ideas away.
> We can make this camp a beautiful town.
> If we only give a smile instead of a frown.
> And there's only one way this thing could do.
> Do onto others as you'd have them do onto you.[23]

Spainhard's poem called on her fellow neighbors to acknowledge their
shared responsibility in building the camp community and in ensuring the
program's success.

These migrant testimonies do not obscure the fact that significant tensions existed, or that personal values sometimes conflicted with the project
of community formation taking place. Indeed, Spainhard's poem was
inspired by her feeling that some migrants expected to receive government
aid without doing their share of work in the camps. Nevertheless, many Dust
Bowl migrants proved eager to work collectively because they understood the
advantages it had to offer. By failing to give enough attention to the traumatic
conditions that influenced the Dust Bowl migrants' decision to enter and
remain in the camps, previous studies have minimized the power they had to
define the camp experience for themselves. They also elide the possibility that
migrants did not have to relinquish all of their individual autonomy to
embrace a cooperative attitude inside the camps. As Todd observed, "For
many 'Okies' this government camp is the first taste of real democracy. Theirs
is a collective life, with plenty of outlets for individualism."[24]

While some Dust Bowl families were probably reluctant to enter the
FSA camps when they arrived in California, there is little evidence documenting their unwillingness to do so. By the early 1940s, however, FSA
officials reported numerous cases of Mexican and African American farmworkers avoiding the camp program in California, Texas, and Florida. As

traditional migrants, it is possible that their apprehension stemmed from a closer understanding of the industrial farm labor system, and a reluctance to disrupt the established resources and practices they developed to manage their migration. Economic conditions had not drastically improved for Mexican and African American farmworkers by the early 1940s, so the shift from the Great Depression to World War II did not necessarily influence their decision to reside in the camps. Instead, FSA officials suspected that traditional migrants refused to live in the camps because they feared federal intervention would bring increased control over their labor, mobility, and domestic practices.

In January 1941, for instance, L. Burkett Arnold, the camp manager in Sinton, Texas, reported that Mexican families "from this immediate vicinity" were finally moving into the camp, which, he pronounced, "indicates a breakdown in resistance to [the] program among the Spanish-speaking people, or at least the lessening of their fears and suspicions concerning us."[25] Although Arnold did not indicate why these families avoided the camp, Russell Lee, who spent considerable time photographing migrants in South Texas, noted that local migrants were "very suspicious of governmental activity, due to local newspapers' use of the term 'concentration camps' [when] referring to the FSA camps."[26] In 1940 James Moore, the camp manager in Robstown, also found that "ordinarily well-informed people [had] the conviction that the camps [were] . . . training centers for the military," internment camps for "all persons of Nazi - Fascist - Communist - convictions," or "concentration camps for transients in general."[27] John Fisher, the FSA's director of information, acknowledged this problem and suggested the use of "some other terms such as an 'overnight camp' or 'placement center camps'" so as to avoid "misinterpretation."[28] Yet the issue was not a matter of simple misunderstanding.

Migrant families may not have understood the FSA's intentions, but they had enough experience with state officials managing farm labor conditions to know that government agents rarely intervened in their favor. Consequently, even when they better understood the program's intentions, they worried about having to answer to federal administrators and relinquishing some degree of autonomy. In March 1941, for instance, camp manager Albert K. Short reported his frustration in trying to convince several migrants occupying nearby makeshift settlements to move into the Raymondville, Texas, camp. As he noted: "They offer various and sundry excuses for not moving in. One has said that he had lived in that manner for 8 or 10 years, and it is more desirable than living anywhere else. Another told me that he desired to have his personal liberties and exercise them to the fullest extent, and he recognizes that they could not be done in camp, and he prefers to live out in the brush."[29] Despite pressure by local citizens that the FSA obligate these migrants to move to the camp, Short believed that he could go no further than to contact them and explain the benefits of the program.

In many instances, fellow migrants and farmworkers attempted to convince others to move into the camps. The effort camp residents made to clarify popular perceptions demonstrates how not all migrants viewed living there in regulatory terms. For example, in June 1941 Gloria Castro, representative of the "*Juvenil* Club" (for ages sixteen to twenty-five), published an article in *El Eco*, the local Mexican paper, that attempted to "debunk the rumors among Santa Paula Mexicans" that the El Rio, California, FSA camp was a "concentration camp." Castro wrote:

> The idea of this explanation is to show the residents of this Ventura County the truth of the life and happiness we lead in this camp. And that it is not true that visitors are not allowed. That it is not true that residents cannot go out at night. No sir, this camp is not a prison . . . we are happy here and we accept the laws that we have set on ourselves, which have been misinterpreted by outsiders. The laws here are for our own benefit. About cleanliness, good order, and the welfare of all.[30]

Emphasizing what Castro believed to be the egalitarian nature of camps' self-governing system, she further exclaimed, "don't think that we are under the yoke of persons superior to us." In this way, Castro placed migrant residents in control over their own welfare and in doing so sought to redefine the camps' built environment in the eyes of distrusting outsiders as a positive place where fellow Mexicans could realize their full potential.

Alton R. F. Williams, a prominent African American businessman in West Palm Beach, Florida, and editor in chief of the "Negro Section" devoted to African American news in the *Belle Glade Herald*, attempted to do the same for black migrants. In a feature titled "Why Not Live Better" published on December 12, 1941, Williams questioned why the shelters in the FSA's "negro camps" stood empty given the condemned one-room shacks scattered across Belle Glade "literally overflowing with humanity."

These shacks lacked running water, lights, and sanitary facilities, and yet migrants seemed to favor them over the FSA's modern camps. Williams also addressed the apparent concern over the camps' regulations:

> It is true that the elected council of the people have made camp rules of order that are enforced by the people themselves. This is as it should be. Where people live together there must be discipline of a lasting sort. [It] must be self-imposed and this can be achieved only through education. If this type of discipline in the migratory labor camps influences the Negroe's [sic] choice of a place to live, it should bring the families to the camp and not turn them away from it.[31]

The Negro Section also included news about the FSA's Okeechobee camp and its recreational programs, nursery school, and medical clinic. The newspaper highlighted the way more "disciplined" black farmworkers had organized to make the federal camp a place of opportunity, economic security, and social stability.

The hardships most migrant families encountered to make ends meet usually influenced their decision to move into an FSA camp, even if they maintained ambivalent feelings concerning the program's management. Alcario Samudio's account of how his family arrived at the Weslaco, Texas, camp in 1944 offers a dramatic example of the conditions affecting migrants' consideration. As he explained:

> My family had been working for the Carters for a while, but in 1943 my father was killed and my mother was six or seven months pregnant from my little brother. So, the big landowner, Mr. Carter, had no use for our family because my mother was pregnant and my oldest brother was about 7 or 8. I mean, we were pretty young and [had] no way to help out in the farm. So, they kicked us out. And we had no place to go. We went to a *comadre*'s house for a while. From there we moved to the labor camp.[32]

While not everything Alcario recalled about the Weslaco camp was positive, the affordable rent and social services available in the camps played a big part in guaranteeing that the Samudio family would survive. He credited the strength of the camp community for his family's well-being. Speaking of one particular couple at the camp, which he described as "the ones really in charge," Alcario recalled, "[Mr. and Mrs. Atilano and Chata Suárez] did a lot of favors for us. A lot of the time my mother couldn't afford the rent and they helped out."[33]

The camps' potential as places of community and opportunity was reinforced when relatives and close acquaintances already lived there. Several interviewees spoke of this factor, in addition to the camps' valuable amenities, as the principle cause influencing their family's decision to move into an FSA camp. Their explanation demonstrates how migrants' practices of community formation were often based on bonds they, not necessarily the FSA, had created and maintained.[34] The social and familial ties that existed at the Harlingen camp are particularly remarkable. In the early to mid-1940s, nearly all of Israel Longoria Gonzalez's family lived there. The exact number of individuals, including aunts, uncles, their spouses, and their children, is difficult for Israel to recall. Yet based on his family chart it is possible that as many as 130 of Israel's relatives lived in the Harlingen camp at some point. Additionally, many of the families that were not blood relatives were nevertheless closely tied to the Longoria Gonzalez family because they worked with Israel's father, a crew leader. In other words, they were members of the regional community the Gonzalezes formed as migrant workers prior to arriving at the camp.

According to Israel and his cousin, Evaristo, Israel's father, Guadalupe Gonzalez, was responsible for moving "his people" to the Harlingen camp, or *el campito*. As Israel recalls:

> My father was the first one who discovered the camp. He brought all of his people [there] because it was really beautiful compared to the ranches where they were living. My mother's people moved there, too. Other people my father worked with followed him as well. We were all big families. They knew they would be more comfortable there than where they lived. The ranches where they lived didn't have indoor toilets, electricity, running water, and people had to go to the canals to get water to drink and cook and do laundry by hand.[35]

Evaristo also emphasized that those who moved to the Harlingen camp were "old acquaintances and cousins that were coming from the same ranch, not a number of different places." Evaristo's sister, Maria Guadalupe

Figure 10. McAllen, Texas, Migrant Labor Camp (ca. mid-1940s). As drawn by Herón Ramírez.

Barrera, added that the homes were really nice, but they were also afford-able and made "for people like us, who lived working in the fields."[36] These points reiterate the practical matters, not just familial connections, that also influenced their participation in the camp program.

Herón Ramírez and Victor M. Ramírez (first cousins once removed) lived at the McAllen, Texas, camp from 1942 through about 1947 and simi-larly recalled that most of the people who lived there hailed from neighbor-ing Starr County. Consequently, although they were not related, they still knew each other from working together in the local fields and packing sheds. By the mid-1940s Herón's father, Secundino Ramírez, and three of his siblings—Fortunato (Victor's grandfather), Ubaldo, and Goya—lived in one corner of the McAllen camp along with their families.[37] These family ties strengthened the camps' collective efforts by creating an environment where migrant families trusted one another and readily cooperated to create the best possible living conditions.

Even in cases where migrant residents had not known each other prior to arriving at the camp, various individuals recall camp relations in strongly communal and familial terms. As Maria Guadalupe explained:

We lived among acquaintances. Everyone was very fraternal—we shared seeds, food, and other things—it was very beautiful. In other words, we saw each other as if we were all the same people [and] came from the same place; all of the people. There were never any gossiping people; you never saw that some would say, "Look, this one thinks she's so great, or this one this or that," no, no, no, everyone equal.[38]

It is likely that Maria Guadalupe's idyllic memories of the camps' social relations were influenced by her position as a young child. This may have shielded her from the greater tensions that existed among camp residents, even family members. Yet the way she and others described daily exchanges in the camp provides greater insight on the willing interdependence migrants fostered based on their mutual status as farmworkers.[39]

For Alcario's and Israel's families who had lived on grower-owned properties prior to moving to the Weslaco and Harlingen camps, the FSA camps became their central home. "Nobody had property," Israel explained, "because they lived in the ranches with their bosses for whom they worked in the fields." As a result, Israel conjectured, "I don't think [my family] ever went back or continued to work for the same grower."[40] According to the FSA's population reports, Israel's family moved to the Harlingen camp in October 1941 from property owned by the Landrum family.[41] Israel explained that prior to settling at the Harlingen camp his family lived in shacks very close to Landrum's fields and across from the historic house. Despite believing they never went back to work or live there, he noted that they continue to bury family members in a plot the Landrum family provided on their property.

Migrants residing at the McAllen camp also developed close bonds that strengthened the communal environment in the camp; however, their understanding of home was simultaneously shaped by the connection many sustained with their place of origin. Herón Ramírez described how it was customary for McAllen camp families to travel back to Starr County almost every weekend to visit extended relatives. He recalled that come Saturday morning everyone packed up for the weekend and piled into a couple of trucks headed for ranches and homes in Starr County. For Mrs. Ofilia Ramírez, Victor's mother, the weekend trip was especially meaningful because her mother, Beatriz Cantu, lived at their ranch in Fronton (then known as La Hacha) with her younger siblings. Like her nephew Herón, she recalled that there were a number of families in the McAllen camp who lived their lives divided by keeping one home in the camp and another elsewhere.

Recognizing the relationships migrants maintained with people and places outside of the camp is critical for understanding how they imagined their community relative to federal official's claims. The FSA generally assumed that migrants lacked a sense of community based on the fact that they were constantly on the road. Consequently, the camps were designed to engage in a project of community building by establishing settlements that would teach migrants to cooperate while providing necessary shelter and aid. Although certainly many experienced a transient lifestyle for the first time during the Great Depression, the majority of farmworkers who occupied the camps built in the early 1940s had long lived and worked as migrants. They belonged to well-established communities, most often located in multiple places.

An FSA study of migratory labor conditions in Florida, conducted in the winter of 1936–37, revealed early on the significant organization and interdependence involved in black farmworkers' regional communities. The study found an important and prevalent pattern where "the folks from home stick together." The "origin islands" were such that "entire sections of a town, or even single small towns, originate in a certain locality in another state." According to the FSA, this pattern complicated previous studies on migrant workers in Florida, which claimed that it involved more single workers versus whole families as compared to the West Coast. As the FSA's labor officials explained, most Florida migrants had family members who remained at home. Nevertheless, they traveled in "car groups" or large trucks with friends or relatives, "pooling expenses, and living together in Florida."[42] Camp documents for Bridgeton, New Jersey, confirm that African Americans' "origin islands" often followed the harvest from Florida up the Atlantic Coast. FSA photographers captured various images of "truckloads of Florida migrants" arriving at the Bridgeton camp after "three days and three nights" traveling in the rain.[43] The camp's migrant newspaper, *Weekly Migrant Worker*, also frequently reported on migrants' collective return to Florida when jobs were available.[44]

In South Texas the FSA encountered an especially difficult problem defining the boundaries of the camp communities they established. Federal inquiries into migratory labor conditions in 1940 suggested that approximately 65 percent of all migratory workers in Texas (85 percent of whom were Mexican) claimed South Texas as their home.[45] As a result, FSA agents questioned the labor camp program's role in the region, since its intended purpose was to house migratory workers en route.[46] Agency officials unanimously agreed that the "present housing conditions" for Mexican farmworkers were "simply scandalous."[47] Yet they debated over the best response to ameliorate the situation.

For example, N. Gregory Silvermaster, in charge of the FSA's labor division, observed the following situation in Willacy County:

> Most of these people are old residents in the county; in fact, descendants of former land owners under the Spanish regime. They are all American citizens. Our subsistence cottage program would be greatly instrumental in arresting the further physical and social disintegration of these people. It is clear to me that there are many such communities throughout the Lower Valley which need assistance of similar nature.[48]

In researching the migrant problem in South Texas, Silvermaster could not ignore the fact that most of the migrants were "legal aliens," as he put it. Although other FSA agents also recommended "an emphasis on permanent housing rather than temporary shelter," the FSA did not alter the camp model in the region. The agency, therefore, acknowledged Mexican farmworkers' entitlement to civic resources as legal residents and pointed to the strong regional community sustaining Mexican farmworkers from South Texas, but they nevertheless developed the camp program as if Mexican migrants were inherently transitory.[49]

Community Solidarity and Conflict Within the Camps

Although many migrants entered the camps with a strong sense of community, cohabitating in the camps' close environment reinforced these bonds. Everyday struggles affected the camp community like any other, but the precarious nature of migrant work meant that the community relationships formed in the camps were especially critical to a family's welfare. Migrants had less secure resources available to them and were typically denied public assistance, so they greatly depended on one another to get by. Though the federal camps granted migrants added security, families trusted and relied on their collective strategies as much as they did the government's helping hand.

Herón Ramírez recalled an incident exemplifying the specific group identity migrants created in McAllen, which united them as camp residents. As he explained:

> There was this one time where [the camp staff] gave us this material to make curtains. And it was kind of a broadcloth type of thing, so we didn't like it. Mom didn't like it, so she started making shirts for us and dresses and skirts for my sister out of that material. Pretty soon, the whole labor camp were dressed like curtains! So people would see you in town, and they'd go, "You're from the labor camp!" Or, actually, we called it "El Campo." You didn't have to ask why, you were either wearing a shirt or skirt made out of that material, and only camp people would have it—it was a kind of a grayish, bluish type of color.[50]

While few markers so clearly identified camp residents outside of the camps' terrain, Herón's story reveals the strong feeling of commonality camp occupants experienced as a result of participating in the program. To wear a shirt or dress made from camp material represented more than just the fact that one lived there. It also expressed a shared experience in broader socioeconomic and cultural terms as low-wage, mainly nonwhite farm laborers. That families occupying the camps saw each other, as Maria Guadalupe described it, "as if we were all the same people/came from the same place" indicates how an understanding of their shared status worked to reinforce a sense of community among them, one that was further cultivated by the FSA's social programing inside the camps.

Oral histories, the FSA's monthly narrative reports, and migrants' weekly camp newspapers testify to the diverse ways that migrants participated in the process of community formation. An analysis of these documents shows how families used the camps as a site to build peer networks and promote organizations based on social, cultural, political, and work-related matters that not only improved their personal condition but also strengthened their extended communities. Several sources, for instance, reference the development of mutual aid committees and other voluntary self-help efforts. A "welfare committee," whose main purpose was to help new families with any food or clothing necessities, existed in most FSA camps.

Yet migrants regularly worked outside of these more formal and carefully supervised systems to help each other out. The day-to-day actions migrants took to provide one another economic and moral sustenance proved fundamental to nurturing a community environment within the camp space.

When a fellow camper fell ill, as was the situation with Andrea Allala from Harlingen, Texas, who suffered from a severe case of tuberculosis, campers frequently stepped in to raise funds for treatment. In Ms. Allala's case, "the women and girls" in the camp organized a shower to boost her spirits before she was sent away for hospital care.[51] On a similar occasion, a "Latin American woman" with two small children found herself in desperate measures due to a husband who was suffering from stomach cancer. Her friends and neighbors at the Crystal City camp cooperated in helping her make a mattress and in guaranteeing that she received a loan for food from the camp council, as well as certification for surplus commodities. The assistance the camp community provided this woman—especially in ensuring that her husband would be well cared for at a local hospital—was absolutely indispensable because economic necessity forced her to travel with her father to the midwestern beet fields, leaving her husband behind.[52]

Accidents and deaths among the camp population also considerably strengthened community relationships as families consoled each other through tragic circumstances. Such was the case after the night of December 22, 1941, when a truck full of "Latin-American laborers" returning from work cutting spinach collided with a car and caught on fire and burned. Seven of the laborers were from the Crystal City camp, but camp residents also knew many of the other workers who lost their lives. For the next few weeks, social activities in the camp were limited, and Christmas festivities were cancelled as residents mourned the deaths of their close friends and relatives.[53] A couple of months later, the Crystal City camp also grieved the loss of Mr. and Mrs. Eulalio Villareal's six-month-old baby, whose heartbreaking death was "caused by a foreign body logged in the trachea." Fellow migrants "worked wholeheartedly with the parents of the deceased" to offer the family whatever form of support they needed.[54]

According to monthly camp reports, it was not uncommon for migrant women and infants to die during childbirth. Indeed, it occurred enough that camp administrators often reported it without much comment. However, when "Señora Estephana [Estefana] Temeyosa," age forty-two, passed on June 28, 1942, due to a postpartum hemorrhage that lasted six hours, Harlingen camp residents were profoundly upset. As Dell Caver, the FSA home management supervisor who reported her death, affirmed, she was one of the first and most beloved residents of the Harlingen camp, "admired by both the Latin-Americans and Anglo-Americans." As Caver explained: "[Estefana] had won a name for herself as a lover of flowers. She had many beautiful flowers around her cabin and took great interest in planting them around the Community Center. She was a good wife and mother and was active in camp activities; she, as well as her family, was an ideal camper."[55] Caver reported that Estefana left behind four children— two girls, ages 13 and 9, and two boys, a 4-year-old and an infant to whom she died giving birth. Israel Gonzalez, however, provided greater insight on the family's loss. One of Estefana's older sons, not accounted for by Caver, Zeferino, Jr., married Israel's sister, Elisa Gonzalez, five years after his mother died.[56] Israel explained that Estefana was indeed one of the first to move to the Harlingen camp. She also had a large family residing there, including her elder parents-in-law Don "Goyito" and Doña Anita Zuniga. That Israel could recall, the Zunigas and Temeyosas occupied at least eight shelters in the camp.

FSA administrators also commented regularly on instances where children had been "left abandoned in the care of the camp at large," which failed to recognize the way migrants entrusted the camp community with childcare responsibilities. When 18-year-old Andrew Mitchell, from the Princeton, Texas, camp was found fighting with his 14-year-old sister during the time his father was "gone to West Texas" (his mother was deceased), fellow campers "show[ed] him wherein he was falling short of a good citizen."[57] The assumption that children were "left abandoned" also discounted the difficult decision families made in needing to migrate for work but wanting to keep their children safe. Mr. Tanis Garza's situation at the Robstown camp exemplifies this common factor. As the camp manager, Henry C. Daniels, reported:

[Mr. Garza] does not want to take his four children out of school and drag them off to the West Texas cotton fields to live under the conditions under which the migrant families on the move must exist. He states that he would like very much to leave his wife and children here because he knows that nothing would happen to them while they were here, and that if anything did happen to them we would be here to help them.[58]

Figure 11. Estefana Temeyosa's in-laws, Don Gregorio "Goyito" and Doña Anita Zuniga. Original photo caption reads, "Camper and Wife, FSA (Farm Security Administration) Camp, Harlingen, Texas." Photograph by Arthur Rothstein, January 1942. Library of Congress, Prints & Photographs Division, FSA/OWI Collection, LC-USF3301-003622-M1.

According to Israel, migrants wanted to take advantage of the stable camp community they formed in the federal camps, which was not a resource generally available to them in growers' seasonal housing. Contrary to the FSA's reports suggesting that it was typically "the head of household" who migrated out, Israel also clarified that some years his mother traveled to West Texas for cotton and his father stayed behind in the camp.

Migrant residents also frequently relieved a family's poor condition by collectively caring for children in need of assistance, even when their parents were present. At the Crystal City camp, for instance, residents quickly secured food, clothing, a mattress, and a few household articles for the family of "an old man with two small girls, one quite deaf," who arrived at the camp severely destitute.[59] Migrants at the Harlingen camp also acted on behalf of Rafael Ontiveros, who moved there with ten children under the age of fourteen, each with "no shoes and only a few clothes." His twenty-seven-year-old wife had died giving birth to their eleventh child prior to moving to the camp. As Dell Caver reported, "The family of pretty, bright, and attractive children, [had] won the favor of the whole camp." The Ontiveros family lived in shelters 29 and 30, according to Israel's mental map.[60]

While migrants' social interactions often occurred in ways federal officials intended, they nevertheless existed as a result of migrants' own efforts and willingness to foster cooperative relations. In Bridgeton, New Jersey, for example, John Collier, Jr., documented (in at least sixteen photographs) African American migrants' collective efforts to erect their own prefabricated labor homes. FSA camp officials clearly benefited from migrants' labor in this way, but this does not diminish the self-determination and pride migrants felt in their ability to establish better conditions for themselves and for each other.

Migrants also successfully utilized the camps' buildings, amenities, and social programming to form community ties as they saw fit. The community center building represented an especially important site for migrants' joint activities, particularly the regular Friday or Saturday night dance. In Texas, migrants recall some of their fondest memories moving to the tunes provided by camp musicians such as members of the Longoria Gonzalez family who formed the Orchestra Cuellar. Fernando Longoria, related to Israel's paternal grandfather, was one of the orchestra's accordionists. Evaristo and Israel's uncles, Pablo Fuentes and Marcelo Perez, played the bajo sexto and other guitars. Fermin Leal, another uncle, also played the accordion. Evaristo remembers that many acquaintances from all over the surrounding region came to the weekend dance. Several people, including his sister Maria Guadalupe, eventually married someone they met there. Her husband, Ramon Barrera, came from Colonia Alta, a nearby community. She recalled that he came to the dances with his uncle, Cesario Barrera, who

Figure 12. Some of the Ontiveros children in front of their shelter. The nurse and girls in the photo are carrying Meliton Ontiveros, who, according to Israel, broke his leg while riding a bike. Original photo caption reads, "Harlingen, Texas. FSA (Farm Security Administration) Camp. Nurse Taking a Boy with a Fractured Leg Out for Air." Photograph by Arthur Rothstein, January 1942. Library of Congress, Prints & Photographs Division, FSA/OWI Collection, LC-USF34-024934-D.

played in a *conjunto* with "El Ruco" Raul Martínez and his uncle Narciso Martínez—now widely recognized as the "father of Texas-Mexican conjunto music." "El Huracán del Valle" (the hurricane of the Valley), Narciso Martínez, was known for his fast-paced polkas and *huapangos*, popular at the camp. The FSA's "weekly activities" reports suggest that anywhere between one and two hundred people attended the camp dances, which typically lasted about three hours.[61]

The community center building, which was nearly identical in FSA camps across the country, was structurally ideal for this occasion. The folding doors used to divide the center into smaller rooms during the day were easily retracted, leaving a wide cement floor that allowed dancers to sway across the room with little interruption. Because of its auditorium-like architecture, musicians could set up on one side of the room (typically on

Figure 13. "Saturday Night Dance. Community Center. Robstown Camp, Texas."
Photograph by Arthur Rothstein, January 1942. Library of Congress, Prints &
Photographs Division, FSA/OWI Collection, LC-USF34-024883-D.

a stage), dancers could move about the middle, and there was still enough
space for tables, chairs, and benches along the ends for spectators socializing. Other building features—such as the overhead lights, insulated structure, and access to bathrooms and a kitchen that provided hot and cold
running water—likewise contributed to making the community center a
great place to entertain. Indeed, local high schools and civic organizations
inquired regularly about using the building to host their events.[62] Camp
managers typically allowed this to happen, recognizing that it bolstered
local support for the FSA's camp program.

The documentary images FSA photographers captured of camp dances, which include at least forty photographs nationwide, provide an important glimpse into migrants' joyful times socializing in the federal camps. These pictures suggest that even in the FSA's temporary camps where a "big recreation tent" served as the community center building, migrants valued the respite that came from singing and dancing together into the night. John Collier, Jr., for instance, took several photographs of black farmworkers dancing at the mobile camp in Bridgeton, New Jersey, where "every night is dance night."[63] His photographs, along with those of his colleagues, suggest that the dances were typically family affairs, with people of all ages in attendance. In their oral histories, many of the people who were children when they resided at the camps emphasized the happy feeling that came from watching their hardworking parents have a good time. Perhaps more than any other aspect of camp life, their memories of the communal dances mark that period as the "good old days."[64]

At times, the dances also offered young men and women a rare opportunity to fraternize without their parents. Both Maria Guadalupe and Guadalupe Mena stated that the dances provided a valuable space for them as teenage women to socialize with fewer restrictions.[65] Because chaperonage of Mexican daughters was a prevalent custom in the early 1940s, these women acknowledged that their parents would likely not have allowed them to attend the dances had they not occurred inside the camps where other community members could supervise their actions. Others who were younger in age at the time recall that children were not always welcomed at the dances for fear that they might misbehave. Alcario Samudio remembered going with his friends to watch the dancers at the Weslaco camp, his widowed mother preferring to stay home. When those at the dance would refuse to let them in, Alcario and his buddies would climb onto the roof of the community building, or up the side windows, to take a peek inside. On several occasions Chata Suárez, "one of the other mothers at the camp," caught them on the roof. "She would throw rocks at us to get us down," Alcario laughingly recalled.[66] Indeed, some camps actually created incentives to keep the children away. At the camp in Firebaugh, California, those ages five to twelve who "agree[d] to remain away from the overcrowded, Saturday night dances" were rewarded with a weekly "[movie] theatre party" in town.[67]

The FSA staff monitored some of what went on at the camp dances, mostly because outside visitors attended, but many former migrants do not recall the staff's presence in regulatory terms. Instead, they privilege memories of the camp dances as times when their community bonds were further strengthened. Zora Mildred Bennett, who worked in the nursery school at the Harlingen camp, remembers that the dances were extremely popular and included raffles, prizes, or some form of competition, "like a cakewalk or something." She also stated that although she herself did not attend, staff members would go to "watch out and make sure bad things didn't happen."[68] The fact that no liquor was allowed in the camp, according to Mrs. Bennett, prevented problems from occurring at the dances. She also believed the camps' watchman or manager discouraged any trouble by positioning himself at the entrance of the camp to observe those coming in and out. Although the dances were held after hours, most camps registered all nonresidents on arrival. Despite Mrs. Bennett's claim, however, Evaristo and his sister Maria Guadalupe did not recall any of the staff acting as guards at the Harlingen dances. Both stated that Cyril Laffoon, the camp manager, never attended, and that Jack Reagan, the camps' maintenance man, was indeed always there, but only because "he really enjoyed the music and loved to dance."[69]

The community center also hosted weekly movies that were especially popular since migrants could not usually afford the films shown in nearby towns. The labor camps that did not have their own movie projector typically invited an "itinerant movie operator" who charged a five-cent admission fee for his picture shows. Most films were screened for entertainment value—such as Tex Ritter's *Song of the Buckaroo* (1938) or Alan Ladd and Robert Warwick's *Meat and Romance* (1940). Now and again, however, the camp staff selected travel, health, and other educational films to screen, including *She Saves Who Sews for Victory* (1942).[70] Regardless of the movie, migrants appreciated the diversion and time spent together. At the Weslaco camp, Minerva ("Minnie") Suárez Capello recalled that during the summertime, movies were shown every Tuesday night, and it was standard for families to bring a covered dish to share while they watched the film.[71]

The community center provided a central space for migrant families to come together, socialize, and foster a sense of camaraderie, but it was not the only place where such relations occurred. Musicians, for example, did not wait until the weekend to perform their songs. According to Aida Hinojosa, who also lived at the Weslaco camp, her next-door neighbors, the Drakes, would frequently sit out in front of their shelter and play music. In the evenings, "they'd have little concerts for us," she remembered. FSA photographer Arthur Rothstein documented some of the Drakes' spontaneous performances for their migrant neighbors.[72] Guadalupe Mena, from the Weslaco camp, similarly recalled that although they would come home tired from a long day of work in the fields, people would sit around and talk in front of their shelters while someone played the drums on a small washtub turned facedown. She also remembered that men and women would get together in the evenings, either in someone's home or outside in the common area, to play *chalupa*, a card game much like bingo. Sometimes prizes would be raffled off at these gatherings, with proceeds going to the communal camp fund.[73]

Most labor camps were surrounded by nothing but rural farmland, consisting mainly of vegetation, brush, or agricultural fields and orchards. This landscape reinforced migrants' communal relations inside and around the camps' space. In Weslaco, camp inhabitants recall being encircled by nothing but cotton fields. As a result, Aida remembers running around the camp as kids with the DDT dusters flying overhead.[74] The distance from town encouraged the Weslaco children to find clever ways to entertain themselves. Charles Lee ("Chalk") Thomas liked passing time playing marbles, especially an odds-or-evens game he and his friends called "cachoosee." Minnie Suárez Capello agreed, remembering that her brother Tito would take her along to make their holes with the heels of her bare feet. FSA photographers captured approximately forty images of camp children across the country huddled together playing marbles. Such photographs serve as a powerful reminder of the camps' domestic and familial space, reminding us that these were more than just labor camps.

The large canal system that irrigated most farms in the Lower Rio Grande Valley also remains a vivid place in migrants' memories of their childhood. Chalk remembers that the canals, where he learned to swim, provided probably the most popular form of summertime diversion for the Weslaco camp kids. One of his favorite spots to swim was in a section under the main road that provided an entrance to the camp. "When the water would go down and there would be about that much air in there [he measured with his hands], we'd swim under that road like a pool. . . . There was catfish in there bigger than I am," he exclaimed, "big catfish!"[75] At the Harlingen camp, Mr. Laffoon, the camp manager, noticed that the kids liked swimming in the canals so much that, according to Evaristo, twice a summer he took them in his truck to Boca Chica on the Gulf Coast.[76] Israel also remembered that the adults would sometimes swim in the canals, too. He specifically noted that his uncle Evaristo (Evaristo, Jr.'s father) would take a dip in the canal surrounding the Harlingen camp every year on June 24, El Día de San Juan (the Catholic celebration of Saint John the Baptist), as part of a common ritual to wash away one's sins.[77]

Migrants' memories of swimming in the canals as children are significant considering that most public pools in the Rio Grande Valley during the early 1940s would have only admitted Mexican families on certain occasions, if at all.[78] Herón Ramírez recalled a time when one of the Anglo families in the camp invited him to the Cascade swimming pool in McAllen, Texas. The Anglo family lived in a single-unit shelter near Herón's family (fig. 10, housing #6). Robert, Jr., one of the children in this family, known in the camp as Pancho, was Herón's best friend. Although, according to Herón, the Anglo family "saw no color," racial restrictions as they existed outside the camp community reminded him of their difference. Speaking of his experience at the Cascade pool, Herón remembered, "I had to wait for them outside the fence, while their family had their fun jumping around, because I couldn't go in."[79] Despite the fact that the Anglo family was from the labor camp, Herón stated that it was "unheard of" to see families like those at the Cascade pool swimming around in the canals. In this way, Herón pointed to a social distinction he witnessed between camp residents and the surrounding community in both class and racial terms. He also indicated how the social pressures and norms that existed outside of the labor camp space challenged the community relations shaped within it.

Community Conflict Within the Camps

Despite the advantages of labor camp life, migrants did not view all communal relations within the camps in positive terms. While close proximity in the camps' domestic space fostered important social networks and collaborative efforts, it also produced conflicts. Scholars writing about the Dust Bowl experience in California have demonstrated how many of the migrants residing in the FSA camps resented its "goldfish bowl atmosphere," as Anne Loftis described it. Brian Cannon also provides convincing evidence of how, despite their shared experience, Dust Bowl families viewed themselves as different from one another in religious terms and in their lifestyles more generally.[80] Yet even in the FSA camps across South Texas, where migrant residents were more familiar with each other and had more established communal practices, tensions existed. The labor camps were never as idyllic as either the FSA's reformers or some migrants portrayed them.

Ironically, since camp officials were so invested in strengthening migrants' cooperation, the camps' social programming and built environment often reinforced migrants' miscommunication. For example, monthly narrative reports from various camps indicate that it was common for camp meetings and social functions to be divided between the more permanent families living in the labor homes and camp residents occupying the temporary shelters. In Texas, where this practice separated the camp in racial terms—with the labor homes typically occupied by Anglo families, and the shelters housing mostly Mexican and (to a lesser extent) African American families—FSA officials stated rather passively that the division resulted from language differences. In her monthly narrative report dated May 8, 1942, Dell Caver of the Harlingen camp explained how:

> The Mothers' meetings on Friday afternoons did not work out satisfactorily, and they have decided to work in two separate groups—Latin-Americans meet on the second and fourth Mondays and Anglo-Americans on the first and third Mondays; they are meeting in the homes; this arrangement seems to wkr [sic] better as the Anglo-Americans became tired while someone interpreted to the Latin-Americans—and vice versa.[81]

Although migrant residents may have believed in the camps' collectivist ideology, in practice this ideology was challenged by the ethnoracial and cultural distinctions that existed among them.

Israel Gonzalez's mental map of the Harlingen camp provides further evidence of the social divide that existed in Texas's racially "integrated" labor camps. Although the FSA did not build separate camps based on race in Texas as it did in Florida, Israel's map reveals how the temporary-worker section of the camp included designated "housing for African Americans," some of which was located among the "Hispanics housing" (fig. 9). That Israel could remember, "there were not problems between any of the races," but he also emphasized that they did not interact very much. This distance was influenced by the FSA's spatial segregation of farmworkers' housing but also upheld by camp residents' social practices. Israel recalled, for example, that the black teenagers liked to have their own dances in the community center where they would play music from the jukebox. "The Hispanic teens would go to see them dance," Israel stated, "but they never joined them. . . . They would just stand to one corner to see them dance," he indicated, "because they liked the way they danced." Israel speculated that the lack of social interaction, which he believed extended to the camps' migrant committees, was also probably due to the African American families' temporary residence, usually only during the cotton season.[82]

Herón Ramírez also pointed to the camp's racial divisions in describing the case of several families who lived near him at the McAllen camp. Referencing his mental map, Herón explained:

> These ladies were Anglos [points to #13 on his map where the Anglo family lived]. They were completely anti-Mexicans. It was all girls. They were very aloof. They didn't want anything to do with us. It was the thing to do. It wasn't anything with us. They just didn't mess around with us. They didn't even talk to us. But a very crazy family lived here [points to #14 on his map where a Mexican family lived]. She [the matriarch] didn't like gringos.[83]

Herón's description purposely emphasized how racial tensions in the camp were often motivated by societal norms, rather than personal feelings. He also clarified, especially in using the term "gringo," how Mexicans likewise held feelings of racial prejudice. Minnie Suárez Capello recalled a similar situation at the Weslaco camp: "You know, I remember some tension. Because we associated with the Thomases [Chalk's family] and the Reynolds—we knew no discrimination. But there were people in the camp that saw us as traitors. You know, they would see us as, 'oh se juntan con los Ang- [stops herself from saying Anglo] los gringos. Se cree que es gringa.'"[84] Like Herón, Minnie's choice of the term "gringo" instead of "Anglo," and her use of the Spanish language in narrating part of the story, demonstrates her intent to highlight the racialized nature of this conflict. Yet Aida Hinojosa responded to Minnie's comment interjecting, "Yes, but I don't think that's terribly important. I think what's important here is that there was a racism here [in the Lower Rio Grande Valley] that just wouldn't quit."[85] Aida's remark sought to refocus the source of tension and racial antagonism to forces outside of the camp space. She went on, for instance, to describe the harsh racism she experienced in the segregated "Mexican school" she and Minnie attended outside of the Weslaco camp.

Beyond reinforcing migrants' existing racial biases, the camps' built environment also produced contentious relations by visibly marking the economic differences existing among various farmworkers. Alcario Samudio of the Weslaco camp, for example, spoke somewhat humorously of the two-story multifamily apartments for more permanent migrants as the "high-rises." "What few Anglos lived in the camp," he explained, "lived in the high-rises." Alcario and his family lived in the one-unit shelters for temporary migrants more centrally located inside the labor camp. Other migrants similarly viewed a distinction between the various Weslaco housing structures. Minnie received a good bit of teasing from Chalk and Aida when she described "moving up" to the apartments after her father was hired as the camp's foreman. Aida also recalled that they referred to the manager's home as "the mansion." Such memories suggest that migrants recognized class differences in the camps and participated in giving meaning to this distinction in their daily interactions.

Although migrants made the most of their condition and enjoyed the friendly relations they nurtured in the FSA camps, they were clearly shaped by the personal compromises that came with living there. One of the most significant issues regularly discussed by camp officials and migrant residents concerned the issue of privacy. According to Herón, the lack of privacy at the McAllen camp ultimately convinced his parents to send his younger sister (their only daughter) to live with her grandparents in Fronton, Texas. The topic of privacy also most upset Alcario Samudio when recalling domestic conditions in the Weslaco camp. As he emphasized:

> I didn't like the bathrooms because they were shared and there was
> no privacy. I hated that! Even in the showers, no privacy—*nada*
> [nothing]! There were washing facilities in between the men and
> women's showers, but everybody had to go to those showers from all
> the single dwellings. Except for the high-rises, they had their own
> individual showers [and toilets]. The toilets were also shared; they
> were in the middle of the quadrant. There was something like eight
> seats for men and eight for women, but there were no doors or any-
> thing! Now that I'm all grown up and very smart [he says this while
> laughing], I remember how inhumane that could have been, or was.[86]

Alcario ended his statement with the following comment, perhaps seek-ing to redefine his painful experience in positive terms: "I remember the showers were like maybe fifty feet or maybe even seventy-five feet long. [The area] where all the showers would be. As boys, we would wet the floor and we'd go sliding on our bellies. The cement was that smooth! I remember that like it was yesterday." The memory shows how camp life involved a constant negotiation where migrants simultaneously experienced moments of shared joy and hardship.

Oftentimes, camp practices abetted the migrants' close monitoring of each other, further compromising migrants' privacy. Camp newspapers, produced by camp residents, reveal how migrants' personal affairs became public because of the camps' close living quarters and activities encouraging "self-government."[87] Gossip columns—such as "The Snooper Speaks," "Among Our Campers," "Dirt," "Snoop or Stupe," and "All Around the Camp"—printed intimate details about migrants' domestic lives and warned fellow campers about any residents who might "bear watching." In the camp paper one could find out, for instance, who was dating whom; who was sick and with what; who was going out of town and where; who was a good or bad dancer; who owed money to the camp fund and how much; who failed to attend a camp meeting; who had been out drinking too much and too late; who was fighting with their spouse; and who needed to clean up around their home. While the extent to which camp officials encouraged migrants to report on one another's actions is unclear, there is no doubt the FSA benefited from migrants' self-policing.

Camp staff did, however, sometimes express frustration with migrants' attention to the more unflattering aspects of each other's lives, especially when it caused trouble. The October 3, 1941, edition of *Spotlight*, the Weslaco camp paper, included the following complaint from camp manager G. Travis Melton:

One thing in the camp I have never been able to understand is what appears to me a lot of needless flannel mouthing. Various stories reach my office about trivial matters pertaining to individuals and groups in the camp. It would seem that a lot of this gossip would be ignored and that a lot more of it would never be started. If you have facts to base up your assertions it is all right to talk. It would be a lot better if you would do your talking at the Council and court meetings instead of out under the trees to individuals who you figure might listen. As John Mundy says, you can hear anything in this camp except money rattling and meat frying.

Melton scolded migrants for having more interest in their frivolous gossip than in governing the camps. In doing so, he admonished migrants for their inability to see the bigger picture in needing to cooperate.

Several months earlier, Guy Griset, manager of the camp in Indio, California, wrote to his regional supervisors inquiring about the limits of "freedom of the press" as it applied to the camp papers. Although the camp staff was "not pleased" with many of the articles published in the *Happy Valley*, including the appearance of "the likeness of the Nazi symbol," they did not take immediate action, waiting instead for the Indio camp community to address the matter themselves. The situation finally reached a boiling point concerning the April 11, 1941, publication of the paper that included "scurrilous allusions regarding individuals and in certain instances introduced obscene and profane ideas." Although the migrant editors argued that camp residents supported their ideas, the camp council and about twenty other migrant residents proceeded to burn the papers publicly and clean out the printing room to express their indignation.[88]

By suppressing the publication of offensive material and malicious information concerning fellow migrants and the camp staff, FSA officials and the council called on migrants to exercise greater responsibility in how they depicted the camp program to outsiders. "The contents can create either good or bad impressions of community life," warned Harvey M. Coverley, the FSA's assistant regional director for California. Coverley recommended that camp officials remind all editors of the "community papers" that the newspapers circulated among a wide audience beyond the camps. They reached those that are "interested in and sympathetic to our efforts to help provide better approaches to solving the so-called migrant problem," he explained, but also critics who want "tangible evidence with which to 'smear' them."[89] Although it was understandable that migrants sometimes lacked mutual respect, FSA officials believed they needed to reflect a more stable version of community relations if they wanted to secure better working and living conditions.

Migrants' Understanding of Community Beyond the Camps

FSA officials were very concerned with public perception of the camp program because of the strong local and national pushback. Consequently, they took great measures to establish good relations with local communities. In addition to renting out the community center hall for local events, they placed camp photographs and positive stories in local "friendly papers" and hosted regular "open house" gatherings where outsiders could tour the camp and participate in the camps' recreational programing.[90] Camp managers also frequently participated in the town's civic affairs as a way to foster better relations with local leaders. In Crystal City, Texas, for example, camp manager Robert L. Elliott also served as a member of the Rotary Club and director of the chamber of commerce.[91] Despite the FSA's efforts to integrate the camp program into local affairs, the agency constructed the camps to function as "self-contained communities" where migrant farmworkers would not burden the surrounding town.

Migrants residing in the camps, however, frequently conveyed how they imagined their community in terms that transcended the camps' boundaries. They contested the limits the FSA's notion of community imposed when they invited their friends, relatives, and interested parties from the surrounding area to participate in a host of activities and celebrations at the camp. They also did this when they utilized the camps to organize for more extensive political, economic, and cultural purposes that affected their broader regional communities. In Texas, camp reports describe sizable gatherings, most often in the community center building, for the occasion of *piñatas* and *quinceañeras* (birthdays), "Latin American weddings," "Latin American dances," "Mexican dinners," Cinco de Mayo, Diez y Seis de Septiembre, Día de Guadalupe, and Día de San Juan.[92] These events strengthened community bonds within the camps, but they also reinforced migrants' deep connection to their transregional and transnational communities. Migrants' efforts to define community in their own terms compelled FSA officials to broaden their understanding of their collective project.

FSA administrators, for example, hoped that migrants could learn about the usefulness of cooperative farming and gardening while residing in the camps and frequently spoke about the importance of developing cooperative enterprises as a means of reinforcing American democratic principles. Migrants at the Crystal City camp aimed to uphold these ideals when in May 1941 they petitioned the FSA for a loan to establish a large-scale subsistence farming project—complete with a poultry plant, dairy, citrus project, and truck garden. As they stated in their appeal:

The products of these projects, together with what little we earn on the outside, would fit us to meet our conditions better, and so many of us would be getting things really good for us. Our wives and our children would help us at this too. It would mean much to a family thousand miles away picking beets to know that somewhere there is a little house, and a milk goat of their choice, and fresh eggs, and meat, and other things waiting for them when they come. . . . [The additional aid such an enterprise would bring is necessary] if a family is to meet modern commercial needs like cars, picture shows, and clothing.[93]

The migrants' proposal embodied the American ideals to which the camp program aspired by asserting their desire to have land that through hard work could produce the fruits of prosperity, allowing a man to properly care for his family. Rather than simply defining their endeavor by normative American standards, however, the Crystal City camp council—consisting of Andres de Santiago (chair), Matilde Cardenas, Elvin A. Parker, Antonio de Leon, and Samuel Abiles—was careful to emphasize the camp population's experience with collective farming through the Mexican "ejido system." In other words, they firmly situated their knowledge of cooperative land use within Mexican, not simply U.S., terms.[94]

William A. Canon, FSA assistant regional director, responded to the council's request stating that "in the past cooperative associations, through a lack of educational planning, have sometimes assumed obligations which later proved to be very burdensome." For this reason, "small beginnings are preferred to large initial outlays."[95] Implying they did not fully understand their proposal, nor that they had the proficiency by which to carry it out (despite their stating otherwise), Canon recommended that the migrants first develop a "workable plan." He believed the migrants needed better organization and should get better acquainted with the details of such an operation before the FSA would consider it further. Canon's decision to dismiss the petition is especially troubling considering the ideological and practical exchange occurring at the same time between agrarian federal officials in Mexico and the United States. As Tore C. Olsson's work demonstrates, much of the FSA's leadership was closely following Mexico's agrarian experiment as it unfolded in the mid-1930s under President Lázaro Cárdenas, viewing it as a model for rural reform in the U.S. South. In a visit to Mexico in 1942, C. B. Baldwin, the FSA's chief administrator, acknowledged that "we could also learn much from their experience with ejidos."[96] On the ground, however, camp officials failed to recognize the particular knowledge Mexican migrants brought to the FSA's camp project in transnational terms.

Migrants' activities and camp-related networks also took on added meaning when they appropriated the camp space to mobilize around broader social concerns, including health, diplomacy, and racial discrimination. The *Willacy County News* in Raymondville, Texas, for instance, reported extensively on the June 11, 1943, occasion of a *gran baile*, or large dance, held in the community center at the Raymondville camp. The League of United Latin American Citizens (LULAC), the most prominent Mexican American civil rights organization at the time, sponsored the event in order to raise funds for the Tubercular Association. An orchestra, Johnny Barry y Sus Díez Músicos, entertained the group as men and women danced in formal attire. A class distinction almost certainly existed as LULAC was a middle-class organization composed mainly of well-educated and influential political or business figures in the Mexican American community. Nevertheless, the event united LULAC members and the camp's farmworker families around an important cause affecting a large percentage of the Mexican community in the region.[97]

The Second World War brought an added dimension to migrants' efforts on behalf of their wider community by calling on the FSA's promise of American democracy. Activities at the Yuma camp in Somerton, Arizona, provide an especially revealing insight on the significance of community integration, public relations, and migrants' democratic commitment. In 1942 the Yuma camp population consisted of Mexican and Filipino American families, Mexican braceros, Filipino nationals, and white Dust Bowl families. Due to the camp's diversity, camp officials frequently advised residents to observe "the American ideal of Christian Charity without bias or race hatred." In a section of the Yuma camp paper titled "The Manager Speaks," Tom Montgomery admonished the camp because "word ha[d] gotten around camp that the Sat. night dance was for 'white people only.'" "In the first place," Montgomery wrote, "the word 'white people' is hardly a fair word to use in a camp such as this where there are so many races."[98]

Montgomery's concern extended beyond interracial harmony. He, like his FSA colleagues nationally, believed the camps demonstrated the virtues of American democracy based on, among other things, equal opportunity and popular consent through self-government. Montgomery reminded migrants of the broader political implications of their actions when stating:

Many of us tend to be prejudiced towards other people simply because they seem strange and foreign compared with the people we have known all of our lives. This happens not only between people of different color and language—but also between people from different areas. . . . The lesson from this experience is pretty simple. Prejudice against different racial groups is Un-American! It is especially harmful to our democratic unity at a time when we are fighting against the forces of fascism who make racial hatred and religious bigotry their creed.[99]

In the spirit of "democratic unity," the Yuma camp sponsored a number of recreational activities—namely, baseball tournaments, boxing matches, rodeos, and dances—to strengthen cooperation among migrant farmworkers and develop closer ties with nearby communities, including across the U.S. national border. The camps' interracial baseball team, for instance, organized tournaments with nearby grower-owned and FSA-run farm labor camps, U.S. Army camps, the "Yuma Indians," and Mexican players from "San Luis across the border in Old Mexico."[100]

The Second Annual Field Day, held on Sunday, March 6, 1942, was one of the biggest and most publicized events at the Yuma farmworkers' camp, attracting an estimated three thousand people. According to an FSA report, the affair was attended by "Mexicans, Spaniards, Indians, Negroes, Gypsies, and Americans from various states." Most people came from two nearby U.S. Army camps and six other FSA labor camps. As Montgomery explained, "Contenders of different nationality took part in the contests, which included baseball, boxing matches, basketball, volleyball, horseshoe pitching, foot races, and such milder sports as croquet, checkers, dominoes, marbles and top spinning." The athletic events were followed by a free barbecue dinner, which the Yuma camp community served to more than four hundred people, and an awards ceremony where the "Queen for the day" (a Yuma camp girl) presented trophies, medals, and ribbons to the various winners. The evening ended with a dance that included a jitterbug contest. The first-place prize was "won by a man who is half Alaskan Indian and half Filipino and his partner, a full-blooded Cherokee girl." Second place went to "a local Mexican couple" and third place to "a soldier from one of the Army camps and his American partner." Migrants residing at the Yuma camp hosted the day, and Montgomery gave particular credit to the "reception committee" composed of "fifteen attractive girls, Mexican,

Figure 14. "Baseball Game at the Annual Field Day at the FSA (Farm Security Administration) Farmworkers Community. Yuma, Arizona." Photograph by Russell Lee, March 1942. FSA/OWI Photographic Collection, LC-USF33-013267-M2.

Spanish and Americans." For the occasion they sewed their own uniforms that consisted of matching white dresses with a red sash, and they did all the work of showing visitors about the camp, answering questions, and "generally [making] everyone feel at home."[101]

Local community members, other FSA camps, and FSA officials in Washington, D.C., celebrated the Yuma camp residents for the fine work they did in bringing everyone together for the field day. Helene Louise Ritchie, secretary of the Holtville FSA mobile camp in California, wrote to thank the Yuma community and underscored that "the manner in which the whites, Mexicans and Filipinos mingled in good fellowship is certainly proof that Democracy still works and exists at least in part of the world."[102] Federal agency officials in D.C. also appreciated how the event helped publicize the "successful work [the FSA was accomplishing] in promoting interracial relations."[103] FSA photographer Russell Lee captured more than sixty photographs of the day's activities, which the agency's Information Division used to illustrate the camp program's contributions to wartime unity. This was especially important in 1942 as the FSA faced increasing congressional

Figure 15. "Girls of the Reception Committee at the Annual Field Day of the FSA (Farm Security Administration) Farmworkers Community. Yuma, Arizona." Photograph by Russell Lee, March 1942. Library of Congress, Prints & Photographs Division, FSA/OWI Collection, LC-USF33-013274-M5.

pressure questioning the utility of its social programing efforts. As Montgomery acknowledged, "It must be remembered that [these] are Agricultural workers putting in 10 to 12 hours a day in the fields."[104] He reminded outsiders that migrants' contributions to the war were not simply based on their labor but also found in the deep commitment they demonstrated to advancing America's democratic ideals.

A series of migrant poems titled "I Am an American," printed in the Yuma camp paper *Migrant Mike*, reveal how wartime conditions strengthened migrants' patriotic association to the United States as their home. One anonymous entry read: " 'See,' said my father pointing to the flag that fluttered near, 'that flag of stars and stripes is yours; It is the emblem of the promised land. It means, my son, the hope of humanity. Live for it—die for it!' Under the open sky of my new country I swore to do so. And every drop of blood in me will keep that vow. I am proud of my future. I AM AN AMERICAN."[105] Yet even as migrants affirmed this commitment, the war urged many to act on behalf of other national communities of which they were also a part. On January 2, 1942, for instance, Filipino migrants at the Yuma camp organized "a mass meeting of Filipinos"—including individuals from the surrounding localities—in an effort to "help their country in an hour of need."[106] The appeal for Filipino unity came a few short days before the Battle of Bataan, an unsuccessful attempt by American and Filipino military forces to liberate the Philippines from Japanese rule. At their meeting, the migrants passed a resolution to hold fund-raising events and collect money from voluntary contributions that would be sent to the Philippines as a measure of wartime aid. In a call to action posted in the camp's newspaper, A. S. Baptista, committee secretary for this Filipino association, wrote: "Members appeal to all true, loyal citizens of the Philippines to give a hand to this noble venture. We cannot just sit around and let our folks—parents, brothers, sisters and friends—suffer. 'We'll fight to the last man,' is the word from our folks back home! Have we anything to offer to that? Most emphatically *YES*, so let's give, give till it hurts! It's *Action* there! Let's show Action here, too."[107] By mobilizing around issues affecting their homeland, Filipino migrants clearly situated their community beyond the labor camp space and demonstrated a more complicated transnational identity politics.

Migrants' actions to organize in support of the Philippines must be understood within the volatile politics surrounding national identity, citizenship, and American democracy during World War II. As colonial subjects of the United States, Filipinos were considered U.S. nationals but not U.S. citizens. As nationals they could freely migrate to the United States for work or to settle permanently if they wished. The Tydings-McDuffie Act of 1935, however, established the Philippines as a commonwealth (rather than an "unincorporated territory") of the United States and declared for the purposes of immigration that "the Philippines shall be considered a foreign country." Under the new law, Filipinos who migrated before 1934 became "aliens" subject to deportation. The Filipino Repatriation Act of 1935 subsequently targeted Filipino aliens for removal. Between April 1936 and July 1941, the United States deported more than two thousand Filipinos and explicitly barred them from returning to the United States.[108] Filipinos' status as "Americans" was, therefore, a precarious condition, notwithstanding their allied position in the Pacific war against Japan. Although by 1942 U.S. wartime labor needs may have changed public opinion about the value of Filipino farm labor, it was a dangerous time to declare anything but 100 percent loyalty to the United States. The May 1942 opening of the Poston

Japanese internment camp in Yuma County, about 130 miles north of the Yuma FSA camp, was a stark reminder of this reality.

Through their collaborative efforts, organizational initiatives, and varied uses of the camps' material space, migrants appropriated the camps' built environment and reshaped its spatial dynamics. The social networks migrants maintained within and outside the camps played a central role in manipulating the structural forces the camp space produced to best serve migrants' needs. Analyzing how migrants imagined and utilized the camp space demonstrates how the camps functioned as places where domestic relations rendered important resources for mediating migrants' daily struggles as exploited workers, impoverished families, and second-class citizens. Moreover, migrants' participatory experience in establishing the camps as domestic spaces of collective action empowered them to organize around larger socioeconomic and political objectives, some of which transcended national boundaries. These efforts to broaden the program's understanding of civic and community identity demonstrate migrants' authority in defining the labor, political, and social geography in which the camps operated.

By depicting migrant farmworkers as dislocated people in need of stable environments that fostered mutual understanding and cooperation, the FSA negated migrants' deep connection to the regional communities they maintained in their place of origin, along their migratory routes, and in the sites where they lived and labored. Camp officials assumed that migrants' sense of belonging or feeling of rootedness was linked to a specific territorial identity. This ignored the social labor involved in farmworkers' established strategies to maintain communal relations and form kin networks across space, and in light of the constant economic pressure to keep moving. These very strategies supported the camp program's success in sociospatial terms. As migrants' mental maps illustrate, migrants built on their communal and familial networks and the knowledge they had of the landscape surrounding the camps to forge a camp community. Rather than viewing the camps simply as regulatory spaces where FSA planners and camp officials practiced complete influence over migrants' daily practices, it is necessary to consider migrants' power in shaping the camp community and its intended political purpose. Sometimes migrants' practices worked in line with the FSA's social reform goals by bringing workers together and strengthening their sense of self-determination. But at other times, migrants' behavior defied the FSA's expectations and frustrated the federal agents who believed they acted in farmworkers' best interests.

Migrants' testimonies remind us that these camps were not utopian spaces. Farmworkers recognized that participating in the program and cohabitating in the camps' close shelters involved compromises. Yet they valued the services the program provided and found strength in the camaraderie they created in the camp community, which included children and elders. Labor camp life, no matter how difficult, promised migrants a sense of security and better opportunity for advancement compared to the ditchbank settlements or grower-owned housing on which they were typically forced to rely. Migrant families understood that the FSA's provisions and protections could be lifesaving. The lack of privacy or required participation in camp activities was a small tradeoff for access to the basic rights the FSA guaranteed. One of the most far-reaching examples of this involved the FSA's medical program for agricultural workers and their families, which is the subject of the next chapter.

CHAPTER 4

"A Chance to Live"

The Fight for Migrant Health and Medical Reform Under the Farm Security Administration

The same migrant families that petitioned President Franklin D. Roosevelt in July 1941 (discussed in the introduction) ended their appeal against vacating the Farm Security Administration's (FSA) labor camp in Weslaco, Texas, by demanding "a chance to live." In addition to the economic claims they made as "qualified citizens" and "good Americans," they forced federal officials to consider how the lack of protections they encountered as migrant farmworkers affected their personal and family's well-being. While their more humanistic plea may have seemed overly raw and dramatic, it made explicit what was at stake. The FSA camps provided sanitary housing, access to subsidized and professional medical care, and a regular nutritious diet. Life on the road, in makeshift camps or grower-supplied housing, rarely guaranteed the same security. For petitioners Atilano and Matilde Suárez with a newborn son and a daughter who was only about a year and a half old, the stress of caring for their family on the road was very real.[1]

In response to the petitioners' plea, FSA officials in Washington, D.C., recommended that the camp manager handle the Weslaco migrants' request on a case-by-case basis, particularly since a bad cotton harvest beset the Coastal Bend region, threatening their livelihood. The response mirrored a concerted effort by the FSA nationally to safeguard agricultural migrants against the socioeconomic forces that predisposed them to poor health. In 1936 the Resettlement Administration (RA), the FSA predecessor agency, launched one of the largest, most far-reaching experiments in health care delivery undertaken by the federal government when it established the Medical Care Program under its Public Health Section.[2]

As the FSA took over the RA's responsibilities in 1937, it expanded the medical program to include more preventive care, hospitalization, and dental services. More notably, the FSA widened the scope of rural aid to directly tend to migrant farmworkers' medical needs. The FSA's medical program was positively one of the most significant ways the agency realized its effort to give farmworkers the same basic protections afforded to most other laborers under the New Deal. Through the formation of various state-based Agricultural Workers Health Associations (AWHA), first developed in California and Arizona in 1938, the FSA offered migrants critical aid to combat the alarming rates of disease, malnourishment, and infant mortality that plagued their lives. In an unprecedented, extraordinary manner, the FSA's health plans forced the nation to recognize migrants' abysmal health. The plans also substantiated migrants' claims about the impact their status as racialized farmworkers had on their inability to receive medical care. Even as conservative critics increasingly attacked the FSA by the early 1940s, the agency fought to preserve its intervention in migrant health, allocating substantial resources to enhance farmworkers' prospects for a healthier future.

In the process of conducting this promising effort, however, the FSA's migrant medical program also reinforced problematic cultural biases that further exploited and racialized rural poor people across the United States. In California, Texas, and Florida, the FSA celebrated the rationality and modernity of European American culture over the ignorance and backwardness of "off white" Dust Bowlers, Mexicans, and African Americans to promote the medical program's contributions to social reform. For instance, FSA officials spoke critically of migrants' "granny remedies" and "quack healers" when explaining why they were in such poor health. The agency also blamed migrants' promiscuity and ignorant fecundity for the birth of too many babies (relative to the family's limited resources) and the spread of venereal disease. Finally, the FSA called attention to migrants' poor knowledge of healthy foods and an adequate diet, even as it emphasized that high levels of disease and infant mortality stemmed from malnutrition and poverty.

This chapter highlights the broader socioeconomic context from which the camp program emerged to reveal the logic behind the federal government's concern for migrants' health on the one hand, and migrants' desires to protect their families on the other. The FSA's need to maintain support for the camp program required that they remain flexible in the way they promoted their medical objectives. Although most FSA officials believed that access to medical care was a fundamental right that should be granted to all Americans, they nevertheless emphasized how migrants' improved health was central to their economic rehabilitation. Their intervention was also necessary, they claimed, to check the spread of contagions and enhance migrants' efficiency as workers. Ultimately, the FSA sympathetically portrayed migrant families in need of curing, alongside claims that their improved health would produce stronger bodies that were less menacing and more productive for industrial farming.

In highlighting the important way that migrants' bodies represented a critical site on which the FSA sought to enforce dominant notions of appropriate domestic behavior, mold healthier workers, and serve the interests of agribusiness and civil society, I avoid an oversimplified framework that emphasizes discipline and control and limits our understanding of state intervention in poor people's lives.[3] The FSA's medical program did not simply operate in regulatory terms. Nor were migrants' experiences in relation to this intervention limited by what Susan M. Reverby describes as common "binaries of suffering and resistance." As she and Jeffrey Ferguson argue, one should consider the historical contingencies that muddy the waters of health care and race to imagine alternative experiences.[4] Close analysis of the FSA's migrant medical program suggests more complicated decisions involving expressions of negotiation and contestation, rather than only discipline and resistance. In this narrative, state medical officials were not simply benevolent or perfidious, and migrant families not merely tragic victims. Instead, as the opening anecdote suggests, they made calculated choices resolving to acquire the resources necessary to feed their babies and care for their loved ones. In this process, migrants embraced, even as they questioned and oftentimes disrupted, the FSA's medicalization.

A central component of this analysis, therefore, involves examining the tension between public health care and medical racialization, particularly as it intersected with migrants' civil rights during the 1930s and 1940s. Racial discourses of degeneracy and deficiency continued to shape how the FSA framed its medical intervention and how the broader public received it despite growing research in the biology of disease, the emergence of new treatments, and the recognition of environmental factors as most influential to infection. Characterizing migrant families as "unfit" fueled the logic existing among many communities positioning migrants outside the realm of social membership and American citizenship.[5] As the FSA and public health officials worked to "clean up" and modernize migrants' bodies and daily cultural practices, they claimed to restore migrants' civic virtue. Camp officials also reminded migrants, especially women, of their civic duty to break the "chain of disease" by modifying their family's unhealthy domestic practices.[6] As World War II began, the FSA relied even more dramatically on the link between health and productivity as essential to the growth of a vibrant democratic body individually and nationally.

The debates within the U.S. medical profession concerning third-party intervention and government involvement in health care delivery help frame the discourse through which the FSA's medical program ended in 1946. Although rural doctors benefited from the government's health subsidy, and the FSA cautiously enlisted various medical leaders in formulating and executing its health plans, the agency could not curtail the eventual charges of advancing "socialized medicine." By the mid-1940s the FSA's intervention in developing a comprehensive national health care program for farmworkers became the center of significant criticism by the American Medical Association (AMA), who, in conjunction with the nation's farm bloc, complained about losing the right to manage their businesses. The alliance between organized medicine and agribusiness proved pivotal to destroying one of the most remarkable efforts in migrant aid to date.

The Camps as a "Public Barrier to the Spread of Disease"

Although conservative critics attacked the FSA for engaging in matters beyond their domain, agency officials argued that medical care was central to the rehabilitation of rural families. As they explained, while some growers furnished adequate housing for their workers, migrants had to "pitch their tents on the road-side, on ditch-banks, or in vacant lots on the outskirts of small towns" where crowded and makeshift conditions created a "constant danger of small-pox, typhoid, and scarlet fever epidemics."[7] These conditions were exacerbated by the fact that migrants did not typically qualify for local public relief because of strict state residency requirements. Inadequate medical care also resulted from migrants' inability to pay for medical expenses and from their constant mobility, which did not allow for prolonged medical attention.

The FSA used national surveys conducted by the U.S. Public Health Service (USPHS) and other medical organizations to highlight migrants' health deficiencies. For instance, in the border area of Hidalgo County, Texas, where Mexican migrant families accounted for a significant portion of the population, studies found that tuberculosis rates were approximately eight times higher than the national median during the 1930s, "averaging nearly 400 cases per 1,000 residents compared with 51 cases per 1,000 nationally." In general, migrants' mortality rate from tuberculosis was almost two hundred times higher than among the total U.S. population.[8] Similarly, the county health officer in West Palm Beach County, Florida, a booming truck-crop region, reported that "more than fifty percent, and in some sections [as many as] eighty percent, of the migrants [were] syphilitics."[9]

These statistics allowed FSA officials to build on local citizens' fears by insisting that migrant farmworkers carried dangerous contagions as they traveled, creating a serious health hazard and burden. Baird Snyder, the FSA's chief engineer, aimed to make this claim clear when in 1939 he requested that his team of public health engineers collect "additional data on pathogenic disease along the streams of migration, with special emphasis on those loci at which [the FSA had] erected these public barriers [the migrant camps] to the spread of disease." According to Snyder, this particular enterprise would allow the FSA to "evaluate, as time wears on, the actual public health value of a migratory camp against pathogenic disease." Snyder had confidence that over time the FSA could prove that the federal camps were "worth to the public health alone all that they cost."[10]

The engineers' preliminary findings in Texas demonstrated how closely pathogenic diseases and agricultural labor migration were tied together. As Karl Buster, District 5 engineer, noted:

The geographical lines of incidence of typhoid closely follow the geographical lines of migration of casual farm labor. . . . Disease does follow the lines of communication. Typhus fever has been followed across the state from the western portion to the eastern portion. The dreadful influenza epidemic followed transportation lines through the state. Dysentery and typhoid epidemics follow the cotton pickers in their migration to new fields. We know the line of migration of cotton pickers originates in the southern portion of the state and extends north through the central and eastern portion, thence northwest and terminating in the area around Lubbock.[11]

The proof of widespread disease among migrant farmworkers allowed the FSA to argue that the camps were an asset to local communities, and not a social and economic liability as many contended.

Ernest Wilson, the FSA's field supervisor, for instance, garnered support for the establishment of the camp program in South Texas by telling the Kiwanis Club in Sinton: "Children will go to your schools free of communicable diseases and with clean bodies." Moreover, "workers having better living conditions and medical care will be able to render a much better service to the farmers for whom they work."[12] Although FSA officials were genuinely interested in helping migrants by providing sanitary housing, clean water, toilets, and a steady diet, they still claimed communities needed protection from migrants' poor health. Dr. William P. Shepard, president of the Western Branch of the American Public Health Association, testified to such benefits in Congress before the Committee on the Interstate Migration of Destitute Citizens in 1940. "Contagious diseases are no respecters of social class or geographic boundary," he warned. The FSA camps, Shepard argued, presented the only exception where migrants' health needs were improved.[13]

While communities did risk exposure to the communicable diseases migrants carried, the public discourse concerning menacing farmworkers had damaging consequences. As FSA officials drew on standard public health ideologies that pathologized migrants, they advanced existing narratives linking cultural deficiency to transgression in race and citizenship terms. By the late nineteenth century, health and hygiene were increasingly accepted as fundamental characteristics of American identity. Health officials commonly claimed that unless individuals could learn to adopt modern health practices and maintain a higher standard of living, they represented a threat to the nation's prosperity. For this reason, those unable or unwilling to meet the nations' developing health standards were not "fit" for social membership. As Natalia Molina and Alexandra Minna Stern, among others, have shown, the discourse of foreigners as undesirable, inassimilable germ carriers has long worked to justify U.S. immigration restriction and exclusion. But as this case shows, the association of foreignness and disease has also served to marginalize native-born Americans, marking them as outsiders and compromising their legal citizenship.[14]

Ignorance and Disease: Migrants' Public Health Threat

The FSA relied heavily on narratives that depicted migrants as dangerously ignorant to highlight the tragedy that migrants' illnesses were often preventable. This ignorance, they argued, stemmed from migrants' rural backgrounds, religion, race, culture, and lack of education. For the Dust Bowl refugees, their refusal of treatment, denial of diagnosis, and decision to practice their own folk remedies called into question their "real American" heritage as native-born white Protestants. Their medical ignorance, in other words, facilitated the mounting social stigma against them in California as antimodern, uneducated, poor southern whites. The Okies' social stigma, combined with their economic status as farmworkers, subjected them to prejudices "traditionally addressed to foreigners."[15] Indeed, local residents claimed that Dust Bowl refugees' malnourished bodies made them look racially other. By identifying them as separate and alien, local communities justified their unwillingness to provide Dust Bowl families aid as entitled fellow citizens.[16]

The FSA contributed to Dust Bowl migrants' negative depiction by portraying them as incautiously ignorant to gain support for their medical intervention. In 1938, for example, the California State Department of Public Health published a report reflecting on the first couple of years of the camp program. The report stated:

> There can be no denial of the difficulties encountered. Here is a group of people, 75% of them American . . . often from rural areas remote from public health contact or consciousness. . . . They usually have neither knowledge of simplest health and hygienic measures nor money to get the food or care which they need. Little contact with the "outside world" has made them "sot" in their ways, still relying on superstitions and "granny remedies" to raise their children.[17]

Although the report concluded that the camps' health education program was helping the Dust Bowl families recognize the value of the health advice they received and suggested that they were appreciative of learning how to "use their meager incomes and limited resources to a better advantage," it nonetheless promulgated a view of these families as primitive. Despite this, the report contributed to the FSA's success in establishing the AWHA in

California, which provided these families much-needed aid as it further stigmatized their actions.

Esther A. Canter presented a similar portrayal of the ignorant migrant in her story, "California 'Renovates' the Dust-Bowler," published in May 1940 in the AMA's popular health magazine, *Hygeia*. The article featured the experiences of FSA camp nurse Judy Forbes, who attended to the constant challenge of caring for these backward Okie families. In the article we meet Mrs. White, who would rather spend her grant check at the "beauty shoppy" than show up for typhoid shots; Mr. and Mrs. Woods, who refuse to acknowledge that their tenth child is blind, instead insisting "she's goin' to be a prophet when she grows up"; and Jenny Martin, the "self-appointed camp nurse," who explains that "everything woulda been oaky-doaky" with Mrs. Simpson if she "coulda found a black hen" with which to cure her childbed fever. Although it is impossible to determine if Canter's article was fictionalized, readers would assume that the social and medical plague these migrants presented was undoubtedly real.[18]

For New Deal progressives seeking to "renovate" the Dust Bowl migrant, the process clearly involved teaching them to have faith in modern doctors and accept the FSA's medical program, even if it meant changing their long-held customs, diets, and personal beliefs. Yet the trope of the "ignorant migrant" distorts the serious health crisis that prompted many migrants to seek the government's help. It negates the fact that many families understood their desperate condition and wanted aid even as they maintained traditional practices. The FSA's individual medical reports, for instance, narrate a disturbing account of human suffering that illuminates why the Dust Bowl refugees accepted medical intervention. The reports also serve as a rich medical biography of the first families that sought the camps' clinic services.

For example, in 1938 Lucy, age 36, wife of Louis, age 41, had four daughters and two sons ranging from the age of 15 to 2. She suffered from "fissures and ulcerations of skin" due to pellagra, "a decayed tooth," "a middle ear infection," and "uterine bleeding due to miscarriage." According to the FSA's medical staff, Louis and Lucy represented "typical dust bowl refugees." They were people who had always worked and made their own way, but the desolation brought about by the continuous droughts in the Southwest had "swept away" all their earnings. They had not arrived in California with "visions of easy relief. . . . It was only after their economic condition became so desperate that they were slowly starving—having no shelter but their truck and what few bed covers they owned—their plight taking its toll in what was already poor health—that they applied for relief." The report concluded: "Had not the government means of caring for this family, such as was done through Farm Security Administration, there is no doubt but that some members of the family would have perished and the remaining ones a county responsibility as they would eventually have become totally unemployable."[19] Ultimately, Louis and Lucy regained some of their health. This meant that he was able to "give a good day's work," she was able to "take over the management of her family," and the children could return to school, promising the family a better future.

The FSA's individual medical reports humanize the families in need of medical attention and helped label them deserving of the government's intervention. The alarming statistics revealing migrants' poor health, and the more personal reports describing their distress, justified the FSA's intervention. Ultimately, the FSA insisted that these families could be rehabilitated, educated, and vaccinated toward better health and a more productive future as contributing citizens. As the medical reports testified, these were once self-supporting families who found themselves in desperate straits due to the unnatural outcome brought about by hard times.

Pathologizing Dust Bowl refugees in this way created a significant problem in cases where the FSA could not rely on similar narratives to garner sympathy for sick migrants, or to defend its intervention. Not surprisingly, similar medical reports do not exist for the African American or Mexican American migrant families that participated in the camp program in the U.S. South and Southwest. Their visits to the FSA's clinics were usually recorded in more statistical terms, without the personal narratives explaining the circumstances that displaced them or tracking their long-term progress. Given that the camp program did not expand into regions where black and Mexican farmworkers predominated until the early 1940s, the FSA could not blame the Great Depression for their ill condition. More importantly, however, the focus on rehabilitation, while still rooted in a concern over productivity, did not work the same way for families who traditionally followed the crops. The conditions Americans found intolerable for the Dust Bowl refugees were considered normal for Mexican and black "habitual migrants." As a 1941 FSA report for the camp in Robstown, Texas, explained, "The residents of this camp [of which approximately 95 percent are Mexican American] . . . have never been land owners, tenants, or even share croppers but have followed day labor the most of their lives. This means that their health has been neglected for generations. They are very susceptible to disease and infections. This presents a health and sanitation problem of extreme magnitude."[20]

FSA officials relied on prejudiced discourses to support the continued need for a medical program in the 1940s, despite their recognition that racial and class barriers limited Mexican and African Americans' socio-economic opportunities. These discourses further racialized struggling farmworkers and compromised their fight for civil rights. Quite ironically, then, the same efforts the FSA made to draw public attention to the severe socioeconomic plight Mexican and African American migrant families encountered "for generations" perpetuated existing fears concerning diseased brown and black bodies by making them more visible.

Several photographs taken by the FSA's documentary division in Texas and Florida demonstrate the extent to which migrants' domestic and cultural practices served as the focal point for the agency's health reform efforts. Unlike the FSA's more iconic imagery of the Dust Bowl refugees—which worked to depict white migrants as victims of their social circumstances—the migrants in these images were clearly at fault for their condition.[21] For example, Russell Lee's images of Mexican farmworkers' living conditions in Crystal City, Texas, taken in 1939, included a photograph with the following caption: "Mexican mother and child in home. This woman had given birth to baby on bed while she had an advanced case of gonorrhea. The baby at time picture was taken was ten days old. The baby slept in the same bed with the mother and she was caring for both it and the small child by her side."[22] In his series of photographs, Lee observed that Mexicans were unaware of the health risks they posed to their families and communities and thus partially responsible for the health-related problems in their lives. Other image captions read: "Mexican mother and child in their home. Note flies which are prevalent in all these Mexican homes"; "Mexican with advanced case of tuberculosis. He was in bed at home with other members of the family sleeping and living in the same room"; "Tubercular Mexican in bed at home. Windows are tightly closed."[23] Lee's photographs draw the viewer's attention (through the explicit caption) to the subject's unhealthy practices and the dangers they presented.

Lee also captured, however, several photographs that show how Mexican families in Crystal City consciously negotiated the structural poverty and racial degradation they encountered by creating order in their lives despite their substandard housing. Though the FSA may not have considered these photographs as useful to support the claim that they urgently needed to intervene, Lee also documented Mexican farmworkers' elaborate home altars, neatly folded clothes in wooden baskets, belongings organized in stacked cardboard boxes, and clever decorative elements such as a curtain made from bottle caps and a baby mobile made from Christmas garland.[24] These photographs suggest that Mexican farmworkers were mindful agents creating habitable environments for their families as best they could within their limited means, and not simply oblivious or indifferent transmitters of disease.

FSA photographs of southern black sharecroppers and farmworkers captured similar practices, evidently demonstrating their ignorance about disease and medical treatment. In 1939, for instance, Lee also took a photograph near Marshall, Texas, of, as he described: a "Negro boy drinking 'milk' made of flour and water. The boy was sick and his mother had given him this as a delicacy." In another image taken near Jefferson, Texas, Lee captured "two negro men passing a young baby through a hoop to cure the 'stretches' which are caused according to Negro superstition by a woman who is menstruating picking up a young baby."[25] Such photographs, though ostensibly harmless on their own, collectively worked to reinforce the notion that external conditions and poverty were not the only causes of poor health. Again, the images suggested that individuals' cultural practices and social behavior determined their (and their children's) prospects for a healthy life.[26]

While scientifically most research on germ theory had moved beyond such conclusions by the early twentieth century, evidence of the transmission of bacteria fueled concerns over prevention that led medical professionals and public health advocates to focus on modifying individual and collective behavior. The FSA's focus on migrants' domestic and cultural practices allowed for old racial predisposition theories to thrive, linking racialized farmworkers to disease both scientifically and socially.[27] Ultimately, the FSA's approach to migrant health teetered between the more personal and biological determinants explaining migrants' illness.

A problematic example of this involves the FSA's concern over the spread of venereal disease, particularly syphilis, among African American farmworkers in the Lake Okeechobee region of Florida during the late 1930s and early 1940s. Public health officials in Palm Beach County considered venereal disease to be "the greatest scourge of the area" and estimated that one-half of the black migrant population was afflicted with syphilis.

The syphilis death rate in Palm Beach County was twice the state average in 1941, the highest in the country.[28] FSA officials reporting on the problem linked the situation to two important factors beyond slum housing: "the care the Negroes receive[d] [as] usually supplied by quacks and healers, midwives, and Indian herb doctors" and "the night life of the Negroes."[29]

Although John Beecher, the FSA's supervisor for the Florida migrant camps, estimated that about 80 percent of the migrants in Florida "live[d] under unsanitary, dangerous, and subhuman conditions of housing," and highlighted the fact that "preventative and curative health provisions in the area [were] inadequate," he also reinforced the belief local residents maintained about "the Negroes' [need for] good times" and the danger this presented in community health terms. FSA photographer Marion Post Wolcott captured several images of "negro juke joints" in the vegetable section of south central Florida, which the FSA used to demonstrate the "lack of healthful recreational and social facilities in the lake area" that bred "all kinds of license and crime," according to Beecher. The images revealed couples closely jitterbugging, men drinking and playing table games, and black migrants spending their hard-earned money, underscoring the racial logic growers in the region maintained about why African American farm-workers did not merit better wages.[30]

FSA studies found that there were vast areas in the South without any doctors, especially those willing to serve African Americans even if they could afford it. As one FSA report attested, the state of Florida allowed for free medicine for venereal disease (VD) control, but local practitioners had to donate their services. The result, according to agency officials, was that "there is virtually no treatment for negroes in the state." Indeed, the Osce-ola and Okeechobee FSA migrant camps were opened in response to the Florida State Board of Health condemning a considerable number of tent colonies and shelters in the Belle Glade area.[31] The FSA's willingness to intervene to care for black farmworkers who could not otherwise access medical aid demonstrates their democratic commitment to extend services to marginalized farmworkers and advance racial justice. Yet the agency did not justify their actions to ameliorate black migrants' poor health simply on account of their being the victims of poor housing and labor conditions. They also argued that black farmworkers were the agents of personal men-ace that threatened communities.[32]

Dr. William Weems, the Palm Beach County physician, solidified this point when testifying before Congress in 1940. As Dr. Weems explained, "I know that with the Negroes, due to their promiscuous nature, it is impossible to investigate each and every case that comes to us to determine the source of the disease and such things as that. We are assuming the responsibility of these migrants, and it is important to us to see that they get the best health conditions possible." It was essential that the government do what it could to make it mandatory for syphilitic migrants to have blood tests, health cards, and treatment, because they were handling our food, according to Weems, and because "with syphilis spreading as it is today among the lower class of people, unless something drastic is done in the very near future, institutions in every state in the United States will be filled with inmates from complications of this disease."[33] In this way, Dr. Weems succeeded in both bringing attention to the medical crisis affecting black migrants and further pathologizing African Americans' personal behavior by claiming, for example, that "Negro promiscuity" was not only the root of the problem but also so prevalent as to be incalculable.

The concern over migrant syphilis reflected the larger national debate leading Congress to pass the National Venereal Disease Control Act in 1938. As Allan M. Brandt explains, the act represented a broader shift from VD as "a problem of personal willfulness and individual turpitude" to a "social problem, worthy of government intervention."[34] Yet even with Dr. Weems's claim that the high levels of VD merited government action, the FSA perpetuated familiar racist discourses marking blacks as a "syphilis-soaked race" that demanded careful monitoring. On closer consideration, for instance, it is clear that while a medical concern over the rise of VD existed in Florida, social forces specifically constructed the health problem in race terms. In his testimony, FSA supervisor Beecher confessed that county health authorities such as Weems were "not sure about [the] percentage of syphilis among the Negro migrant population" but calculated it "on the basis of such experience as they have had." Testing had only been done in the FSA's "Negro camps," and it was through this index, Beecher stated, that "we can only guess" the rate of infection.[35] This recognition underscores how the FSA's medical program engaged in racializing a fundamentally structural and socioeconomic problem, even as it claimed to "break down prejudice and superstition" to "create a desire for medical attention" among blacks.[36]

The FSA's medical reports and correspondence concerning migrant care leave no doubt of the agency's devotion to ameliorating farmworkers' poor health. The FSA understood that without adequate amenities, state and local resources for medical attention and public welfare, and growers sympathetic to their condition, migrants were the victims of "much needless suffering and many preventable deaths."[37] However, the FSA's role in perpetuating biased views that maintained cultural, racial, and moral reasoning for migrants' susceptibility to disease had a great cost to migrants' condition beyond their physical state. For African and Mexican Americans, especially, such narratives compromised their fight for civil rights by subjecting them to common discourses of degeneracy and dependency that were deeply racialized. Such narratives challenged migrants' efforts to navigate their personhood and political power, which impeded the FSA's democratizing goals.[38]

The FSA's Migrant Health Plans: Federal Medical Aid in Action

The FSA's agricultural workers' health plans emerged from agency officials' realization that farmworkers would never achieve "economic security" without the establishment of "health security" first.[39] Ralph C. Williams, the FSA's first chief medical officer, insisted that for those not convinced by the agency's compassion for migrants' human rights, a migrant health plan also made sense "from a purely economic point of view." Based on the FSA's estimates, 50 percent of rural families failed to pay back their rehabilitation loans because of "bad health." FSA agents believed that if rural families, including farmworkers, were ever to recover a sense of self-reliance, something had to be done to improve their health.[40]

Prior to the mid-1930s, the AMA, by far the most powerful organization of medical professionals, opposed the idea of government involvement in health care delivery. In general, organized medicine was wary of "third-party intervention" in traditional patient-doctor relations and feared the possibility of a compulsory national health insurance plan where they would have little control over its application.[41] During the Depression, however, the AMA increasingly accepted the FSA's medical programs as part of a broader emergency measure to improve migrants' health conditions and contribute to rural doctors' economic stability.[42] The FSA's willingness to accommodate local medical leaders' concerns and suggestions by enlisting their close participation in the formulation and execution of the government's health plans appeased physicians' fears of state medicine and convinced them that they stood to benefit from the program's legitimization of their profession.[43]

The FSA's precautions in preparation for the health program serving the camps in South Texas provides a case in point. FSA representatives and local physicians held several meetings in different locations before finalizing how the medical plan would work. They also met with the president and secretary of the local county medical society during several organized conferences and consulted different regional health specialists. These meetings went a long way in addressing medical leaders' concerns over the federal program and garnering their support. As R. C. Williams reported, "On previous occasions [Dr. Holman Taylor, secretary of the Texas State Medical Association] has been inclined to scold us in a good natured way about what he termed 'socialized medicine.' At a conference in the spring of 1940, however, he was quite friendly." Williams believed that the success of the medical care programs had "convinced [Taylor] that our program was working in a manner that satisfied the physicians as well as the families."[44]

Each of the AWHAs was headed by a board of directors consisting of four FSA officials and three medical professionals—one from the state medical association, another from the state health department, and the third from the area where the labor camps were located. Although local variations existed among the seven AWHAs the FSA eventually developed, the agency's health care program remained fairly consistent throughout the country.[45] Its principal objective was to serve low-income agricultural workers who could not obtain medical assistance from welfare agencies because of residency requirements or lack of funds. The FSA encouraged migrants to visit one of the associations' participating clinics where they could receive "on the spot treatment" and secure a referral to a participating local physician for additional care.[46] The program entitled migrants to full medical, surgical, hospital, and dental care, including coverage for medications and any "special diet requirements" prescribed by the doctor.[47] Patients were expected to pay as much as they could, but for the most part all expenses were billed to the corresponding AWHA, which the FSA subsidized.[48] The FSA's medical records suggest that the most common conditions for which migrants sought treatment included problems associated with malnutrition, the respiratory and digestive systems, general infections, and obstetrical care.

The FSA's sincere effort to improve farmworkers' health and provide them care they were denied under the New Deal is evident in the fact that

AWHA services covered all farmworkers, not just migrants residing in the camps. Nurses on staff in the federal camps regularly visited surrounding grower-owned and independent migrant settlements to conduct immunization campaigns and encourage farmworkers to visit the camp clinic for medical treatment. Conservative figures suggest that the FSA covered anywhere between 75,000 and 200,000 migrants in its plans at any one time.[49] The shifting nature of migrant work made it difficult for the FSA to estimate the final cost per person for the plan, but they calculated that it cost "between $1.50 and $2 per person per month."[50] While not all of the migrant families that qualified made use of the services, the FSA's readiness to extend such aid was unprecedented. The health plans challenged the racist and conservative practices local communities used to deny farmworkers any protections that might improve their ability to bargain for better wages and conditions.

By the early 1940s the FSA set up migrant health clinics in about 250 key areas of labor concentration throughout the country, mostly as part of the camp program. A few large growers allowed the FSA to open clinics on their private property, and clinics also existed in public locations.[51] The medical staff running the clinics offered migrants the best care available in modern medicine. A panel of local physicians served the camps in their region on a rotating basis providing therapeutic services. The doctors arranged to work on either alternate days (for about one hour, but often for more if needed) for one week or one month at a time. They earned approximately ten to twelve dollars per day plus additional compensation for home visits or special cases.[52] Dental care was usually offered either in a clinic or by referral to the offices of local dentists. Additionally, several full-time dentists served the AWHAs in operating mobile dental clinics to bring regular care to a maximum number of those needing it.[53]

The FSA also extended hospital care to migrant farmworkers for more acute problems and "the amelioration of chronic and disabling conditions affecting health and working efficiency."[54] FSA medical officials contended that a high proportion of migrant health cases required hospitalization because of farmworkers' "generally meager living conditions." Existing racial bias, however, also factored into the FSA's reasoning and its remarkable decision to purchase two hospitals.[55] Frederick D. Mott, who replaced R. C. Williams in 1942, explained that "hospital costs often tend[ed] to be high because in areas where ward accommodations [were] not available to Negroes or Latin-Americans, it [was] necessary to engage private rooms for

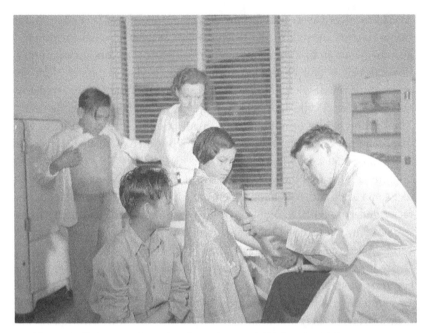

Figure 16. "Robstown, Texas. FSA (Farm Security Administration) Migratory Workers Camp. Family in Clinic for Treatment." Photograph by Arthur Rothstein, January 1942. Library of Congress, Prints & Photographs Division, FSA/OWI Collection, LC-USF34-024917-D.

such persons."[56] The lack of hospital facilities or doctors willing to serve black and brown farmworkers in the South and Southwest influenced the FSA's 1941 decision to purchase the Burton Cairns General Hospital in the Eleven-Mile Corner area of Arizona and to build the Belle Glade General Hospital in south central Florida.[57] This extraordinary action underscores the FSA's efforts to advance farmworkers' civil rights. Each hospital had about sixty beds—separated in a "white and negro wing" in Belle Glade— and was equipped with modern medical equipment "far better than in the average rural hospital."[58]

According to the FSA's medical leaders, the public health nurse was undoubtedly "the keystone of the preventive as well as the therapeutic medical care program."[59] The FSA's migrant nurses typically came from the USPHS or through local referrals, and were responsible for most immediate medical cases, daily health services, and preventive educational efforts. Earning an annual salary of about $1,440, the nurses not only staffed and managed the camp clinic almost daily but also lived on-site to ensure migrants' good health. By the early 1940s the nurses typically occupied one of the migrant camps' labor homes, but an early article by R. C. Williams suggests that they initially lived inside the clinic building. Such conditions express the type of dedication expected from the FSA nurse to carry out her work. More than any other requirement, according to Williams, a nurse willing to work in the camps had to have "an interest in serving distressed people." It was up to her, he explained, "to restore the migrants' confidence in themselves by showing them the way to health and cleanliness, to instill in them a desire to keep it up, even after they have left the camp."[60]

Academic and popular articles written by camp nurses point to the commitment they felt in providing migrant families much-needed medical care.[61] Adela Ballard, writing in 1935, explained how, for the first camp nurses recruited in California, the job was a religious service. As she noted, "As I read my Bible Jesus Christ said, 'Go out and do something.' Some of us have to preach by our acts, and I'll bet those people get more of a Christian message out of a nurse rolling up her sleeves and helping them when they have a sick baby or a burned kid, than from a preacher coming in once a month to preach a sermon!"[62]

The Council of Women for Home Missions (CWHM), under which Ballard and other early nurses served, continued to play an important role in the public health and educational component of the FSA camp program throughout its duration.[63] Yet by the early 1940s, as the medical plans expanded nationally, nurses expressed more of a professionalized role in their work even as some of the broader social responsibilities characteristic of the Progressive Era still informed their approach. In 1942 Mary Lee Brown, for example, published an article in the *American Journal of Nursing* explaining how when the FSA interviewed her for a position as labor camp nurse, she "barely knew what the word 'migrant' meant." After years of traveling with migrant families in California and Florida, she recognized that nursing in a migratory labor camp "offer[ed] qualified nurses an opportunity to do a really creative piece of work in a significant and pioneering program undertaken by the United States government."[64]

For African American nurses especially, the FSA's medical program constituted a valuable avenue to gain professional legitimacy and assist their communities in accessing modern services. Nurses such as Mary Alsop, serving the labor camp in Bridgeton, New Jersey, and Juanita Williams, serving the Okeechobee camp in Florida, had to be understanding, resourceful, and smart intermediaries between the mostly white health professional staff serving the regional AWHA and the black migrant community largely suspect of the FSA's intentions when the program began.[65] From 1940 to 1942, African American nurses treated at least 19,263 migrants in the Okeechobee, Everglades, and Pompano camps for black farmworkers in Florida. This represented a significant accomplishment considering the lack of medical aid in the region prior to the camp program and the larger political forces of white supremacy that denied blacks enhanced civil rights.[66]

In addition to acting as a "confidante to the workers," FSA nurses practiced considerable clinical and administrative authority over day-to-day medical decisions in the camps.[67] Their responsibilities included, for instance, conducting thorough health examinations of each migrant seeking residence at the camp; deciding whether migrants required isolation, hospitalization, or a referral to an outside doctor; and providing minor medical or surgical treatments or, in emergency cases, triage care. Nurses also prescribed treatment plans and, with the doctor's approval, dispensed medications. Furthermore, they followed up with sick patients, sometimes visiting their homes daily, and also organized regular inoculation campaigns for the camp and surrounding region. Additionally, they planned and facilitated nutrition classes and well-baby clinics. On top of this, FSA nurses were expected to maintain a detailed record of all health-related activities in order to submit a monthly medical report to the corresponding AWHA and FSA regional office. Finally, with what little energy she might have left, the nurse was expected to promote the FSA's medical program by meeting with outside agencies and organizations concerned with migrant health.[68]

Perhaps because of the nurses' obvious devotion and hard work, their daily relations with camp inhabitants and surrounding farmworker families often resulted in mutual feelings of trust and admiration. Migrant families frequently expressed their appreciation for the nurses in camp newspapers and reports to the camp manager. Despite the pressure and burden the nurses exerted in migrants' daily lives by visiting their homes regularly to inspect for sanitary conditions, appropriate nutrition, and child-rearing, migrants recognized their beneficial service.

"An Ounce of Preventive Is Worth a Pound of Cure":
FSA Public Health Education

In his monthly narrative report for September 1941, James Martin, the camp manager at the camp in Princeton, Texas, celebrated the nurse for doing an excellent job at keeping medical needs down. "She believes that, 'an ounce of preventive is worth a pound of cure.' "[69] In carrying out this motto, the nurse applied the most important approach FSA health officials had toward ameliorating migrants' serious needs with long-term results. Direct and immediate attention was necessary, the FSA claimed, but a lasting improvement in migrant health could not be achieved without a program of prevention. To this end, the camp program incorporated elaborate measures in health education to teach migrant families about nutrition, sanitation, personal hygiene, prenatal and postnatal care, and the more general aspects of "healthy" home management and self-conduct. In the process, FSA medical representatives diagnosed migrants' transgressive health practices as a leading cause in their predisposition to illness.

A study of the workshops, lessons, and committees facilitated by the camps' nurses and home management supervisors (HMSs) reveals how federal officials sought to impose new practices of domestic behavior, institute new standards for proper medical care, and transform migrants' cultural and traditional values to better meet their notion of good health and citizenship.[70] In this process, the FSA aimed to acculturate migrant families to satisfy modern, American standards of health, hygiene, diet, and personal care. Although most of the migrants who initially occupied the labor camps were U.S.-born, their socioeconomic status and identity as racialized, non-white farmworkers made them susceptible to a process of Americanization touted in both class and racial terms of rehabilitation and progress. By maintaining beliefs about migrants' culture as deficient, the FSA failed to incorporate migrants' knowledge about nutrition and health care into their lessons.

Like earlier progressive reformers, the HMSs believed that migrant women, particularly those that were mothers, had the ability to change their family's traditional practices by instituting changes toward "better health." In this sense, migrant women became key mediators in negotiating the pressures associated with the FSA's medical program and critical actors in shaping the government's health measures. Migrant women attended lessons and engaged in discussions on numerous topics, including "Questions

About Your Teeth," "Typhoid and the Fly," "Home, Hygiene and Care of the Sick," "Keep[ing] Fitness with the Right Foods," and "Diets to Fit the Family Income." In these classes they learned how to make soaps, shampoos, and toothpaste, to can foods and make budgeted grocery lists, to prepare recipes for "a well-balanced diet," and to keep dangerous pests and disease carriers out of their homes.[71]

According to an FSA guide compiled by the HMS staff in Texas, the educational program's principal aims included teaching migrants about the fundamental relationship between personal health and "cleanliness habits." This would help build a basic understanding of the principles of prevention and control of disease, the staff argued, and lessen their transmission and ill effects. The FSA also wanted migrants to develop practical knowledge of how best (both safely and efficiently) to handle simple illness, and even medical emergencies, at home. In the realm of nutrition and food preparation, the HMSs claimed that regular lessons and demonstrations would go a long way toward building "stronger, healthier, and happier American farm workers."[72]

To further inculcate the ideas introduced in the home management workshops, camp officials encouraged migrant women to participate in various "women's committees" responsible for instituting appropriate measures of health and sanitation within the camp. The FSA also supported the formation of "girls' clubs," which functioned partially for recreational purposes but also allowed the FSA's nurses and HMSs to teach early lessons on domestic responsibility and female morality. At the camp in Sinton, Texas, for example, Miss Charlotte M. Tompkins, the HMS, instructed Mexican American teenage girls on how to spend money wisely, choose good companions and friends, develop appropriate boy-girl relationships, maintain a neat and attractive appearance, and share in the responsibility of keeping a clean and happy home.[73]

The migrants that made up the women's committees in Texas were primarily white, not because of any apparent racial bias by the HMSs but because they represented the more permanent residents with year-round employment. Mexican families typically lived in shelters closer to the camps' administrative center where they could be more easily supervised in their adoption of camp policies. In the Crystal City camp, for instance, an Inspection Committee regularly accompanied the camp nurse, Miss Chandler, in making a weekly, unexpected examination of the more temporary residents' living environment. In an ironic outcome, the camp section or district having the cleanest shelters, comfort stations, and shared grounds received one bar of soap for each family in that section.[74]

In addition to holding lessons on matters of hygiene, nutrition, and childcare, nurses and the HMSs frequently instructed the camps' women on matters related to sex education and family planning. The FSA staff distributed information on such topics as "Preparation for Pregnancy," "The Question of Sexual Relations," "Step by Step in Sex Education," and "Preparing for Marriage" (in Spanish when necessary) as part of this effort. They also required that all migrant mothers attend prenatal and postpartum clinics. To make sure they complied, the camps' health personnel carefully monitored women's attendance, going so far as to publicize a list of names expected at the "baby clinic" in the camp newspaper.[75] According to the FSA, "constant supervision" by the nurses and doctors was necessary for a "well baby."[76]

Although camp administrators commonly depicted Dust Bowl women as foolish in their views toward childbearing, FSA nurse reports suggest that they were eager to learn about "baby spacing" and often chose to live in the camps to ensure good prenatal care and hospitalization if necessary.[77] In the late 1930s nurse Mildred Delp considered the need for birth control education so grave among the migrant families she worked with in California—with mothers " 'all frailed out' from having too many children in quick succession"—that she wrote to the Birth Control Federation of America in New York pleading for help.[78] Margaret Sanger, founder of the organization, flew out to California in 1938 to establish a plan whereby Delp would work to teach migrant mothers a simple contraceptive technique. FSA officials in Washington, D.C., fully supported this work but made it very clear such efforts were to remain unpublicized.[79]

As a field consultant for the federation, Delp worked closely with FSA nurses to teach sex education to as many migrant families as were willing to listen. In the six-month period from March to August 1940, for example, Delp's reports suggest that as many as 858 migrant women were interviewed about their use of contraceptives and their number of pregnancies.[80] Most often the FSA nurse or the camp council invited Delp to speak at the camp. Delp described the Dust Bowl families she worked with as "fiercely proud of their fecundity and their babies." This outlook required her to "explain with the greatest of tact what was meant by planned children." Indeed, she was careful to use the term "baby spacing" and not "birth control" when she spoke. On one occasion, under a tent in 105-degree heat, she met with a group of about thirty migrant women. On a Gynaeplaque—"a soft rubber reconstruction of the external and internal female genital organs"—she demonstrated how to insert the contraceptive device. Delp explained that the sponge and foam jelly method could be used easily in camp living conditions, and, she clarified, it was better than the "useless [and] often harmful" strategies based on "old wives' tales and word-of-mouth."[81]

While this meeting ended with several migrant women "deluging" Nurse Delp with questions, showing considerable interest in birth control, not all Dust Bowl families were open to the FSA's education on contraceptive use. At the camp in Brawley, California, for example, "some of the fathers and mothers exhibited an overweening modesty" regarding an educational film shown on prenatal care. According to the manager, "Quite a few felt their Victorian sensibilities outraged."[82] According to Delp, this is why the agency's sponsoring doctors should lead regular meetings on the topic of birth control for fathers in the FSA camps. "Most of these men," Delp explained, "do not understand the real purpose of our program. . . . At times," she concluded, "one feels feeble and disarmed before such a sea of ignorance."[83]

While the methods and virtues of family planning may have confused Dust Bowl families, and likely most people at the time, what could not escape their notice was the number of babies and children dying around them. This factor alone motivated migrants to seek the FSA's medical care. Congressional investigations in 1940 and 1941 revealed disturbing trends in infant mortality among migratory families. In one county in the San Joaquin Valley of California, during a single picking season in 1937, migratory workers lost fifty babies due to diarrhea and enteritis. That same year, Tulare County in California's Central Valley reported children dying at the rate of two a day, with 90 percent of the mortality occurring among migrant families.[84] Although the Depression had seriously worsened existing conditions, most reports suggested that migrant farmworkers had long suffered higher infant mortality rates (IMRs) because of their meager, unsteady income, their unsanitary domestic environment, and lack of medical attention. A public health study conducted in Colorado from 1920 to 1930, for instance, found that IMRs were "shockingly high" among Mexican sugar beet workers. In 1930 alone a group of 140 Mexican families had lost 308 children.[85] These conditions had not improved by the early 1940s. Health officials in Hidalgo County, Texas, reported that the average mortality rate per live births was "98.3 per thousand, nearly two and a half times that of the national average."[86]

Although public health officials working with the FSA understood that migrants' poor labor conditions, income, and housing contributed to their varied maladies, they believed that many infant deaths were preventable if migrant women had access to prenatal and postpartum care and, more importantly, if they delivered their babies in a hospital under the supervision of a modern physician.[87] Even as USPHS studies indicated that migrant women were delivering their babies without the help of a doctor primarily because of a lack of access, the FSA's health reformers insisted on migrant mothers' responsibility to care for themselves and their babies as a way to improve the problem of infant mortality. An FSA pamphlet on "keeping the baby well," handed to migrant mothers in the South, reinforced this point. According to R. C. Williams, "some infants die during the first few weeks of life from causes over which the mother has no control; but after this period, if an infant fails to do well, the fault is almost invariably on the part of those who care for him."[88]

The FSA's insistence that a physician be present when migrant women gave birth was one of the agency's most intrusive measures.[89] The agency's medical program, however, reflected broader public health attitudes seeking to transform obstetric care into a practice exclusive to licensed physicians (or professionally trained midwives) and confined to modern clinics or hospitals and services. A USPHS study for 1935–36 revealed that in small southern cities, "about one-sixth of the deliveries to white women and one-half of the deliveries to negro women in families with income under $1,000 took place without medical supervision."[90] A few years later, in 1940, public health inquiries found that 71 percent of nonwhite women in the United States still delivered their babies with the help of a midwife.[91] The FSA medical staff believed that considerable gains to combat infant and maternal mortality were possible if they intervened to alter this trend.

A tragic case involving a Mexican family from the camp in Robstown, Texas, illuminates why migrants' home births represented such a problem. The incident was described by Agnes E. Meyer in the *Washington Post*, in a story titled "Camps Aid to Valley Workers: Projects at Robstown Are Transformation for Migrants."

She could have had her baby delivered without charge through the camp arrangements with the local physicians. But this poor creature had more confidence in the mid-wives to which she had always been accustomed. She slipped out of camp when she felt the baby coming, to an old hag who acts not only as midwife but as *curandera* or curer of all ills, natural [and] supernatural. As the woman's placenta would not separate from the uterus, the midwife pulled at it until she had turned it inside out. When the distracted husband summoned help, rigor mortis had already set in but the midwife still had the bloody mess in her hands.[92]

On investigating the case, Meyer concluded that the *curandera*'s practices were primitive, unsanitary, and basically inferior, especially in light of the camp's "first-rate medical facilities." "The dirty hovel's rickety cabin was a litter of rags, unmade beds, holy pictures," she noted, "which are used for unholy purposes, and tawdry junk of every description." Meyer—who was undoubtedly influenced by Dr. Lee Janice, the FSA field medical officer whom she accompanied in the inquiry—concluded that this explained why the Mexican town in Robstown had such a "staggering infant maternity death rate, whereas the camps where housing [was] clean and medical facilities first-rate [had] conquered even the all-prevalent intestinal afflictions to a point where not a single infant [had] succumbed to them."

As camp residents, the Robstown woman and her husband understood the choice they made by "slipping out" to acquire the birthing services of a midwife and healer, or *partera*.[93] Even though the FSA taught migrant women about the benefits of delivering their babies with doctors in medical facilities, and despite the fact that the FSA's health plan in the state would have covered all costs associated with the birth, the couple decided to pay thirty-five dollars for the *partera*'s services. Given the circumstances, why did they make such a costly decision?

Although it is impossible to know for sure what influenced the family's choice, a few important possibilities are worth considering. One explanation involves a language barrier that might have existed between the medical staff and the migrant woman and her family. By the early 1940s, FSA officials understood that this barrier was a serious matter affecting migrants' willingness to participate in the medical program, particularly in regions such as South Texas where a majority of the migrants spoke Spanish. For this reason, Williams noted that "a working knowledge of Spanish as spoken by the average Mexican [was] important for the camp nurses. . . . Should they not have a working knowledge of Mexican-Spanish [at the time of employment]," he recommended that they be "required to begin a study of this language at once."[94] FSA officials reasoned that if the medical staff spoke some Spanish, they would seem more "sympathetic to Mexican migrants," making migrants more likely to trust in their health services.[95]

Another reason could have been that the Robstown couple preferred the assistance of a female Mexican *partera*, whose birthing practices were likely more familiar and comforting, than a male physician and clinic, where parturition was treated solely as a medical practice. Unlike the male physician, *parteras* customarily provided both emotional and physical care, including abdominal massages and various herbal tea remedies pre- and postdelivery. In most cases, *parteras* also allowed the woman's relatives to assist in the birth, possibly explaining the presence of the "distracted husband" in Meyer's account, and engaged in traditional rituals such as saving the placenta and umbilical cord for special treatment according to custom.[96] It appears that these are not things Meyer understood or cared to acknowledge.

Although any or all of these factors may have influenced the Robstown couple's decision, what is most suggestive of their choice to deliver their baby as they preferred, and not as FSA officials saw fit, is that it demonstrates how migrants found ways to challenge the pressure to conform to the standards federal officials imposed. In other words, although migrants may have chosen to participate in the camps' social welfare reforms in exchange for housing and other amenities, they continued to practice their own approaches to family management and health care based on their personal convictions. Racialized depictions such as Meyer's discredited the medical knowledge and skill of Mexican midwives to link superstitious "old hags" and senseless Mexican families in a narrative of tragic outcomes. By subverting, altering, or even evading the FSA's health reform measures, migrant families questioned to what extent a visit to the doctor would truly improve their status as poor, racialized farmworkers.[97]

Yet migrant families were willing to manage the cultural racism imbued in the FSA's practices to bring about more lasting improvements to their condition. Although camp documents (mostly written from the FSA's point of view) make it difficult to evaluate to what extent migrant families genuinely appreciated the FSA's health program, their engagement suggests that many recognized it offered a valuable service, source of relief, and the potential for improved living. Given the high rate of disease, malnutrition, and infant mortality, it is not surprising that many families appreciated the practical lessons in health and hygiene, the medical attention, financial assistance, and even female camaraderie the camps afforded. Although some migrants may have resented the FSA's paternalistic approach, they also understood that these services provided a basic right to improve their lives.

Many migrant women, for instance, expressed how the FSA's nursery school program allowed them to better balance their work in the fields with their labor and responsibilities at home. The nursery school provided migrant children with nourishing meals, educational and recreational programs, clothes, and professional supervision by trained teachers and the FSA nurse or HMS. Although camp reports suggest that some parents needed convincing that their children would be better off in the nursery school than at home or in the fields, most women understood that the program afforded an invaluable service, freeing them to work to supplement their family income. Indeed, the contribution the nursery program made to "relieve the mothers completely of parental responsibility during working hours" was an element much promulgated by FSA staff, especially as World War II got under way. The nursery school program represented the FSA's intervention in reproductive health as a means to both secure a healthier future for migrant women and children and guarantee women's labor as productive farmworkers for the nation's welfare.

Various FSA studies describe the common deprivation found among migrant children nationally during the late 1930s.[98] Katharine F. Lenroot, head of the Children's Bureau of the Department of Labor, exclaimed, "You don't know what a starvation diet is until you make a complete survey of one of the [FSA labor] camps." Among the top five counties with migrant populations in California in 1937, the Children's Bureau found that "only 10.5 percent of school-age children were getting 1.5 pints of milk daily—the amount considered optimum for growth and development—while 16 percent were getting no milk."[99] FSA field investigators in Belle Glade, Florida, similarly observed that "whiskey bottles are encountered with more frequency than milk bottles" in the "negro quarters." The finding, while seemingly anecdotal, condemned African American families even as it aimed to highlight their malnourishment.[100]

In calling attention to the situation in Belle Glade, FSA supervisor John Beecher hoped to highlight the irony in the fact that "[in] one of the greatest vegetable producing sections in the country," black vegetable workers consumed deeply inadequate diets while their "children play[ed] aimlessly

Figure 17. "Robstown, Texas. FSA (Farm Security Administration) Migratory Workers' Camp. Members of Mothers' Committee Serving Lunch in Nursery School." Photograph by Marion Post Wolcott, January 1942. Library of Congress, Prints & Photographs Division, FSA/OWI Collection, LC-USF34-024740-D.

around the muck." Beecher described migrant children "dabbling in the filthy, uncovered pits of last year's community toilets," with little or no supervision. In one "negro quarter" where a "rudimentary nursery school existed . . . , a former insane asylum attendant was taking care of a group of pre-school children for a fee of 25 cents a day each." According to Beecher, "When interviewed, she was feeding a six-months old baby left in her care canned meat and spaghetti and simultaneously trying to teach her other charges how to march in the garbage-littered court. Their attention was soon distracted, however, by the appearance of a drunken woman, in whose reeling wake traveled a crowd of laughing children."[101] Such accounts aimed to highlight the urgency in creating a well-established, government-funded nursery school program that, much like the AWHAs, coordinated services with other agencies to bring migrant children everywhere greatly needed care.

Each FSA camp eventually maintained a formal nursery school program available to any migrant family wanting to enroll their children for a small fee and volunteer hours. Paul Vander Schouw, supervisor for the labor camps in West Palm Beach, boasted that "the nursery school set up in [his] region [was] physically the best in the country." In truth, there was a largely standard process concerning how the program functioned nationally, resulting in "first-class services," according to the FSA. The Work Projects Administration (WPA) supplied trained teachers (usually three), a maid, and a cook to run the nursery. Additional help came from the camp nurse, HMS, and paid or volunteer migrant mothers as "assistant teachers."[102] Accommodations usually allowed for up to a hundred children at any time, and most programs were open for about seven or eight hours a day, beginning between six and seven in the morning.

Typically, WPA staff worked only six hours, so camp members and staff had to pick up the extra work. In Florida's white migrant camps, for example, where migrants typically labored in the packing sheds through the early morning, the nursery school was open twenty-four hours a day, seven days a week. White migrants paid twenty-five cents a day for these services, while black migrants in the same region paid ten cents for more limited hours corresponding with their work in the fields. Migrant mothers (not fathers) were also required to volunteer about four hours a week at the school or as part of parent-education meetings.[103]

The FSA's nursery school photographs demonstrate the agency's deep engagement and close attention to childcare matters inside the camps. The images document, for instance, the well-planned curriculum used to instruct migrant children through music, painting, puzzles, reading, and crafting. They show WPA nursery staff spoon-feeding children healthy meals paid for by the local AWHA, which included things like "fresh vegetables, adequate protein, fresh milk, and cod-liver oil." Other photographs show staff washing the children's feet before naptime on their individual cots (not shared family beds) where "uninterrupted rest and sleep [was] made possible." One group of images shows migrant children brushing their teeth as part of their "morning routine" in front of modern sinks, "where warm running water, soap, and individual toilet articles, all within easy reach, make cleanliness practicable and enjoyable." Finally, the photographs point to the great collaborative effort necessary to run such a program. This included interagency cooperation between the WPA, FSA, and sometimes volunteers from the CWHM or the National Youth Administration. But it also included intracamp collaboration among staff, migrant mothers, and migrant youth. The FSA staff especially praised the adolescent girls who showed great interest through their camp clubs, such as the "junior campers' league" or "sunshine health club," in learning domestic and teaching skills.[104]

To be sure, the nursery school program's success depended greatly on the work migrant families invested by volunteering to care for and instruct migrant children, can extra food for their meals, and donate camp funds to purchase necessary supplies or pay additional staff. A notable example of this occurred at the Okeechobee camp for black migrants in Florida. There, "the people themselves" voted to donate the profits made at the camp cooperative store to pay for nursery school staff and meals not provided by the health program. This represented a sizable contribution. For example, in December 1942 the store's gross business was $3,960, a remarkable amount for a cooperative enterprise that started with a fifteen-dollar loan from the migrant camp fund.[105]

Such actions provide an important counternarrative to the FSA's more paternalistic depictions of migrant families, which suggested that migrants were either ignorant of the medical program's benefits or, in more racist terms, too uncivilized in their habits and requiring additional care. In Belle Glade, for example, the FSA's regional educational and community activities adviser, Katharine Deitz, warned Edith Lowry, executive secretary for the CWHM, that the "negro worker" sent from the CWHM to work with black migrants should have nursery school experience and understand "the type of negroes we are working with—almost primitive." As she further explained, "They will have to realize that changes move slowly with these people, and getting their good will, and understanding is the first step toward this."[106] Yet in acting to secure extended aid for the nursery school, the migrant families at the Okeechobee camp showed that they in fact were critical agents in advancing the health program and not unwilling migrants coerced into participating.

Beecher's reports for Florida also provide ample evidence that migrant families recognized the benefits of the government's medical program. As he explained, "Both whites and Negroes, we find, are highly appreciative of the opportunities which the camps afford to live decently and to assume community responsibilities. Our experience with them is conclusive proof that migrants in Florida, as well as in California, show themselves to be good Americans when they are given a fair chance."[107] Similarly, in Robstown, Texas, Agnes Meyer, even while disparaging one migrant mother for seeking the services of a *partera*, nevertheless acknowledged, "The opportunity to keep their families clean was one of the features most appreciated by these hard-working women." It had resulted, in Meyer's estimation, in the "amazing improvement in morale and behavior" among the mostly Mexican migrant population, and had produced "a general sense of well-being, self-confidence, and stability."[108] In a significant way, migrant families' participation in the FSA's health program reinforced their claims to full citizenship by demanding standards and amenities worthy of "good Americans." Their claims supported the FSA's democratizing promise to include farmworkers in the national polity and expand their labor and civil rights.

Oral histories with former camp residents in Texas reveal the important negotiations involved in deciding how best to use the FSA's health services. Mrs. Ofilia Ramírez, for example, described how life at the labor camp in McAllen had made things easier for her and her family. She stated, "The homes were well built. There was running water and electricity for ironing. Everything was modern, not like at our ranch. That's why we liked it." Mrs. Ramírez was careful to assert, however, that it was the migrants' responsibility to keep camp accommodations well maintained. As she noted, "We had to keep everything very clean. In case there was an inspection or something, we would be ready."[109]

Herón Ramírez (Ofilia's nephew) also remembered his mother as fairly receptive to the ideas and lessons promoted by the HMS at the McAllen camp. About matters related to cooking and nutrition, for example, he exclaimed, "When it came to the food, we experimented! My family would eat spinach and artichoke, and roast turkey and things we had never had before because they told Mom it was good for us. If the nurse or those lessons told you it was good for your brain and that sort of thing, we ate it."[110] Herón's mother was eager to treat her family to a healthful diet that did not include Mexican food because she trusted the camp staff. Though they were not as nutritious, Herón most fondly remembered the cookies his mother made with the camp's food supply. He stated, "You know those peanut-butter cookies, the ones with the fork marks on top? Ooh, my mother made the best ones!" Herón's memory of eating his mother's cookies serves as a powerful indication of the camp's domestic importance. For most migrant families on the road, such a simple family treat was rarely available.

The Ramírezes' use of less favored commodities further demonstrates how they negotiated the programs' acculturation efforts. Herón also amusingly recalled, on describing his family's regular weekend trips to visit relatives in neighboring Starr County, "We'd go see Grandma and Grandpa and the house where we were born and raised. My mother would take powdered milk and eggs [supplied through the camp program] that nobody liked to eat, and give them to Grandpa so that he could mix it with the slop to feed his pigs." Such accounts, while lighthearted, express the important way migrants embraced the FSA's health reforms while adapting the resources the program offered. The Ramírezes' use of the FSA's food distribution presumably went beyond what program officials intended, but for this migrant family, it still provided a source of sustenance. In this way, we see again that migrant families were rather mindful agents who were molding, and perhaps even outsmarting, the FSA's medical program to attend to their needs.

Migrant children, not unlike their parents, also weighed the pressure FSA officials exerted to comply with the health program against the rewards it promised to deliver. Alcario Samudio, who resided at the Weslaco camp, remembered lining up one day to have his tonsils removed. As he described it, "There was this one day that there was a whole line over there [by the clinic], and I went to check why that line was there. I thought they were giving something away. But no, they were taking tonsils out! And they were gonna give free ice cream and comic books, so my brother and I both got in line. There was a whole line of kids! We had no problem."[111]

Aida Hinojosa, Minerva Suárez Capello, and Charles Lee Thomas, also from the Weslaco camp, recalled less amusing times, such as the itchy and burning sensation from regularly having DDT (an insecticide) sprinkled over their head. At this time, DDT was commonly used for public health purposes to control body lice and other contagions. Zora Mildred Bennett, who helped run the nursery school at the Harlingen camp, confirmed that they kept a saltshaker with DDT in the school. Before the kids went home each evening, she or another staff person would sprinkle the top of their heads. Their hope, as she explained, was that the children would then go home and some of the DDT would sprinkle there as well.[112]

Aida also described how she and several children dreaded lining up for a frequent dose of cod-liver oil and painful typhoid shots. The sentiment was common enough that on one occasion, Dell Caver, the HMS for the Harlingen camp, complained about the problem of several "Latin American" families not wanting to send their children to the nursery school. According to her report, the children refused to go because they did not want to take the daily dose of cod-liver oil. Their mothers agreed the oil was unnecessary and kept their children home.[113] These mothers assumed a real risk in failing to conform to the medical program's standards. Usually, the nurse and HMS took active measures to try to change their minds, or, if the situation was serious, they requested that the manager evict these families from the camp because they threatened the health of the rest of the camp community.

FSA officials went to great lengths to ensure that migrant families maintained a healthy standard of living, as the home economics and health education classes reflect. On entering the camp, the FSA required each family to pass a thorough health examination at the medical clinic and take a series of vaccinations, primarily for typhoid, smallpox, diphtheria, and whooping cough. During peak season, it was not uncommon for the camp nurse and doctor to conduct well over a hundred medical examinations in one week.[114] According to the program's health administrators, incoming residents were subjected to medical screenings in order to identify any illness "likely to endanger the health of other camp occupants, or chronic conditions likely to render the applicants ineligible for camp residence."[115] Even after residing in the camp for a period of time, migrants were required to have regular examinations and keep up with the required immunizations.[116]

That the FSA's medical program chose not to concentrate its efforts on those migrants with serious medical conditions illustrates how it functioned mostly as a preventive measure that attempted to control the spread of communicable diseases among migrants who were mostly healthy. By the early 1940s hostile congressional investigations and subsequent budgetary cuts pressured the FSA to reformulate its health objectives to better reflect the nations' wartime agenda. To do so, the agency had to prove that their foremost concern was not ensuring migrants' social welfare and physical well-being but erasing any obstacles to increased farm labor production. In this way, the FSA's migrant medical program increasingly existed within the camps not simply to keep migrants healthy but to keep them working.[117]

"Weapons Against Sickness and Disease": Migrant Health and Defense Labor

Situating the FSA's camp program within a broader objective of national defense during World War II, home economics specialists from the Texas camps, along with representatives from the Texas Farm Laborers Health

Association and Community and Family Services (a social welfare agency), published a sixty-page "educational program" in July 1942 to use in the production of "healthier happy families who could make a greater contribution to the democratic way of life." The principle objective of "War Weapons for War Workers," according to its authors, was to "develop an awareness among low-income farm worker families of the need for good health habits, sanitary environment, and adequate personal skills and weapons against sickness and disease." Camp officials and their allies argued that the "practical skills" or "weapons" farmworkers would gain from these educational programs could be used to "attack the mental and physical disabilities which may prevent his attaining maximum usefulness as a producer and processor of essential war materials."[118]

For FSA officials committed to maintaining support for the migrant camp program, transforming its social welfare rhetoric to better reflect migrants' contribution to the war in democratic and labor terms became critical. Agency officials claimed that inasmuch as food production was central to the war effort, and migrants were central to food production, then migrants' improved health was vital to national defense. As one FSA report explained, "It was a peacetime plan that fit wartime needs."[119] Moreover, the FSA insisted that the migrant camps addressed escalating concerns over farm labor shortages by providing growers a site from which to recruit readily available and healthy workers. In this sense, the FSA focused less on depicting migrants as a population in dire need of medical attention and more on promoting migrants as a workforce whose well-being was indispensable to their "maximum usefulness as producers and processors."

In speeches and radio shows, and especially as part of congressional hearings to investigate national defense, camp representatives justified the agency's devotion to migrant health as part of an effort to make America strong both in its physical, individual capacity producing "food for freedom," and in its moral, national defense of democracy. "Long before there was any talk of defense," R. C. Williams explained in 1940, "the Farm Security Administration was carrying out a program which is basic to our defense efforts." Highlighting the implications of the FSA's actions in democratic, not simply economic terms, chief medical officer Williams stated, "Now that danger threatens us, we are taking stock of what this country of ours means in terms of freedom and welfare of the people. We are realizing, as we never did before, that we are all in the same boat. And we are beginning to enlarge the implications of security and health to include all the people."[120] The camp program's expansion between 1940 and 1942, with more than forty camp locations built during this time, suggests that the FSA was rather successful in defending the government's role in aiding farmworkers as "an army of soldiers without uniforms."[121]

An FSA radio talk on December 18, 1941, days after the Japanese bombing of Pearl Harbor, exemplifies how camp officials understood their project in productive and democratic terms and hoped to convince others of the same. On air, Mrs. Davidson, the HMS for the camp in Brawley, California, stressed the following: "It is building the health, the physical fitness, the social well-being of our people, and doing it in the democratic way. Hungry people, under-nourished people, ill people do not make for strong defense. . . . Let us make every American strong, stronger than ever before, sturdier in body, steadier in nerves, surer in living."[122] Mr. Engstrand, the Brawley camp manager, added that beyond "helping farmers by keeping up a sufficient supply of labor," the farm labor camps promoted democracy by advancing "unity." As he explained:

> We don't expect industrial workers to work well unless they are
> rewarded; unless their wages keep up with the rising cost of living.
> We don't expect farmers to raise more food unless prices are kept
> up. . . . The same conditions apply to the migrant farm workers. At
> the very least, they certainly must have decent shelter, health, and
> facilities for education and recreation. Our Community program
> offers such opportunities because it is convinced that Americans are
> entitled to an American way of life.

Engstrand emphasized that "where conditions like this exist, people know they are sharing in a democracy they are being called on to help defend." In a final point, Mrs. Fleming, the camp nurse, added that "if we are not to repeat the mistakes which are proving costly today," after the war was over, efforts needed to continue to keep these families healthy and strong.[123]

The FSA also advanced more pressing claims concerning its wartime impact when pointing to the nation's commitment to democracy failed to convince others of the camps' importance in providing medical care. For example, in 1943 the FSA collaborated with the USPHS and the U.S. Army to carry out a venereal disease control program within the Florida labor camps where again they identified notable syphilis outbreaks. The health officials claimed that male recruits isolated in army camps throughout the

South were "going to the same whore" as the men in the labor camps and thus were "pick[ing] up the organism and spread[ing] it around." The program, they contended, would go a long way in protecting the health of both essential war workers and servicemen.[124] Such actions demonstrate how the FSA's health services took on an added rationale as part of wartime national defense.

Perhaps the most notable example of this involves the FSA's role in administering the Emergency Farm Labor Supply Program to employ contract workers from Mexico and the Caribbean beginning in 1942 and 1943, respectively. In this capacity, the FSA's medical personnel, most often affiliated with the USPHS, gained responsibility for conducting thorough medical examinations of all contracted workers both at labor recruitment stations abroad and in the U.S. labor camps. These examinations were critical for growers dependent on "able-bodied workers" since the individuals recruited were inspected for signs of dangerous pathogens, inhibiting ailments, or a weakened condition (including mental illness) that might affect their ability to work.[125] The screenings resulted in "eliminating workers who [were] unfit," according to Dr. Frederick Mott, who became the FSA's chief medical officer in 1942, and in "rejecting workers who [could not] stand the 'gaff.'"[126]

The health requisites outlined in the binational agreements guaranteed adequate public health services and emergency medical care at no cost to the foreign worker.[127] Consequently, all laborers recruited under U.S. contract were admitted to the corresponding AWHA in the region where they worked. The medical needs created by this sector of defense labor resulted in an important upsurge in activity for the FSA's Health Services Branch at a time when the FSA faced increased scrutiny and pressure to curtail its social welfare measures. Indeed, the FSA's medical program was one of the only progressive services the agency maintained until 1946 when it was terminated. Nevertheless, domestic workers found it more challenging after 1943, with the FSA's transfer to the War Food Administration (WFA), to attain the health care they needed. The WFA prioritized "workers who had a contractual relationship with the Federal Government for agricultural work." These measures limited the camps' medical staff's ability to serve migrant families who arrived at the clinics on their own. As one 1944 report explained, "Services to domestics were only optional, whereas adequate care for the Mexican nationals was required by their individual contracts with the government."[128] Although domestic farmworkers' medical needs had not lessened, they would progressively struggle to find the "health security" FSA officials once provided.

An "Unholy Alliance" and the End of the FSA's Migrant Medical Program

By 1943, growing criticism by conservative politicians, professional medical organizations, and commercial farm groups intent on eliminating federal intervention forced the FSA to defend its medical program against insurmountable forces. While commercial growers opposed the FSA's actions all along, the war strengthened their political attacks and required the FSA to function with declining resources and authority.[129] The role that physicians participating in the migrant medical program played in precipitating these controversies proved particularly detrimental to the FSA's Health Services Branch. FSA medical officials had prided themselves in their ability to convince local doctors and county medical societies of the value of the FSA's health plans. Losing their support represented a powerful blow to the fight for migrant health care.

In 1943, for example, the surgical panel servicing the camp in Sinton, Texas, wrote to Congressman Harold D. Cooley, chair of the Select Committee to Investigate the Activities of the Farm Security Administration, an investigation intent on eliminating the FSA. In their letter, the doctors declared:

> We, the signers of this letter . . . feel as though this [the medical clinic] is another form of socialized medicine that some of the socialist-minded bigwigs are trying to cram down our throats. . . . There may have been a time when these people should have had their medical services paid for and it may come again, but for the past 2 years it has been a crying shame that these people have been cared for by the Government on a free basis, like charity, when they all made good money and always have money in their pockets, when they will work.[130]

The Sinton doctors were resentful of the benefits the FSA clinic made available to the camp population, which they explained was "inhabited mostly by peon Mexicans" who were "just like children [in that] the more you do for them the less they are willing to do for themselves." According to their letter, "Mexicans can lay around camp, complain of illness or inability to get work, and get the Government grants to live on." In suggesting that "these people"—that is, Mexican Americans, since Texas growers could not contract bracero guest workers until 1947—did not merit the FSA's liberal medical provisions, the doctors posed a larger question concerning the government's responsibility to protect one of the nation's most impoverished populations. Instead of raising awareness of Mexican American farmworkers' serious medical needs, the doctors found it more important to stress in their letter how these migrants took advantage of government welfare and used their illnesses as an excuse not to work.

In their protest, the doctors represented a broader critique emerging from the political alliance between the AMA and powerful growers' associations, such as the Grange and Farm Bureau. The AMA feared the possibility of a compulsory national health insurance plan, which the FSA soon publicly supported despite a clear opposition by leading medical groups, some rural physicians, and most county medical societies. The nation's farm bloc, on the other hand, was arguably the FSA's most formidable adversary throughout the agency's existence. Commercial growers claimed the FSA's programs undermined their authority by encouraging workers' self-determination and civil rights. United around the mutual values of "individualism and freedom" over what they perceived to be the FSA's "collectivism and regulation," this "unholy alliance," as Dr. Mott declared it, threatened to end the FSA's medical care programs.[131]

The Cooley hearings, however, also included a report submitted by the AMA's Board of Trustees that suggested most participating doctors were actually quite pleased with the FSA's rural health plans. Based on a 1942 survey, the findings indicated that they were satisfied by "a vote of nearly 4 to 1." As the report further attested:

Twenty-one out of twenty-eight states reported that the families included were receiving more or better, or at least earlier medical care than they had received before introduction of the plan. There was almost equal unanimity of opinion that the physicians as a whole received more money under the Farm Security Administration plan than they had been able to collect from the same body of patients previously.[132]

Such conclusions forced members of the Cooley committee, as well as the AMA, to acknowledge that some aspects of the FSA's medical plans had merit despite what individual doctors such as those from Sinton indicated.

The AMA's support for the FSA's health programs was always contingent on the fact that the agency served needy farmers and farmworkers at a time of crisis. Also, the plans supported struggling rural doctors and did not disrupt traditional medical relations such as voluntary participation and free choice of physician.[133] Once the FSA began testing these limits by extending coverage and services, and as the wartime economy brought greater economic stability, the AMA became more critical of the FSA's role. Nothing cemented their opposition more than the FSA's public support, beginning in 1943, for the Wagner-Murray-Dingell bill to establish a national health insurance.[134] This proved what the AMA and others concerned with "socialized medicine" feared all along—that the FSA health plans were a "rehearsal" for universal health care.[135]

Testifying before Congress on the merits of the Wagner-Murray-Dingell bill, Dr. Mott clarified that the FSA entered into health care for economic, not ideological reasons, but their experience had undoubtedly provided important lessons from which those considering a national health plan could benefit.[136] By this time—when the bill was first introduced in 1943 to when it was reintroduced in 1945—several factors influenced the chief medical officer's support for the bill. For one, the FSA was barely alive after the Cooley hearings in 1943. Many of the agency's most progressive leaders had already been ousted when the FSA was transferred to the WFA, and those few remaining recognized that their foothold was weakening. When the bill came before Congress a second time, officials such as Mott testified as if they had little to lose. The immediate postwar political atmosphere created minimal hope for an expansion of the federal government in health care.[137]

Another factor greatly undermining the FSA's power to defend its medical services, and the value of national health insurance more broadly, emerged from the growth of private and physician-sponsored group plans after World War II. In March 1946, as Congress still debated the Wagner-Murray-Dingell bill, the AMA's Committee on Rural Medical Service sponsored a National Conference on Rural Health Care in which they, along with the Farm Bureau, attacked compulsory health insurance as "socialized medicine and misguided government paternalism."[138] Their mutual interest against federal regulation resulted in support for private, nonprofit Blue

Cross hospitalization and medical society physician service plans. In rural communities across America, plans sponsored by the Farm Bureau, the Grange, and sometimes the Farmers Union (even though they supported national health insurance) multiplied as an alternative to state medicine.[139] These plans, as Michael Grey explains, "offered hospital coverage, but few covered ordinary physicians' visits and none incorporated the broad range of nursing, prevention, health education, nutrition, and sanitation services typically available to FSA families."[140] In other words, they advanced a much more limited view of "medical service." Most small farmer and farm-worker families could not afford the grower-sponsored plans anyway, which was the problem that brought the FSA into health care delivery in the first place.

When Congress terminated the FSA in 1946, the agency was forced to dissolve any support for the various AWHAs, and most migrant medical clinics closed. In a last-ditch effort to support farmworkers' health, the FSA sold the majority of the equipment in the migrant clinics to growers' organizations taking over management of the labor camps "in the hopes that medical care could be continued under other arrangements."[141] In most cases, though, growers showed little interest in investing in migrants' well-being, and conditions reverted to those that existed prior to the FSA's involvement. Sadly, in some situations, conditions actually worsened, par-ticularly as domestic farmworker families were pitted against foreign guest workers for limited resources in ever more exploitive jobs.[142]

The loss migrant farmworkers experienced as a result of the FSA's defeat cannot be measured by statistics alone. At best, the migrant medical pro-gram reached fewer than a quarter of all agricultural workers. But the promise it sought to offer in health security was far greater. In the immedi-ate sense it could mean "the chance to live," as the residents petitioning to stay in the Weslaco camp made clear. In a more lasting manner, the FSA's intervention produced a feeling among the nation's most marginalized workers that they mattered and deserved an opportunity to better them-selves as contributing citizens. As L. L. McAlister, a black tenant farmer from Greensboro, North Carolina, testified in 1943, "It seems to me perti-nent that in any appraisal of the work of the Farm Security Administration, evaluation should not only be in terms of dollars and cents, but also in terms of the health, and happiness, and human and citizenship rights of people."[143] Indeed, it was this larger transformation beyond farmworkers' economic condition that troubled the FSA's most conservative critics.

Migrant families across the country took advantage of the FSA's idealistic efforts to improve their lives. The gains they could acquire with federal support outweighed the costs associated with the FSA's pathologizing discourses. For migrant women who were the primary target of the camps' health education efforts, mediating these pressures was often complex. But migrant families participated in the workshops to learn how to better care for their loved ones, they attended vaccination clinics wanting protection against further illness, and they came together to advocate for better living and laboring conditions, to protect their families' well-being. They did this while defending their personal health choices and bodily autonomy against the state-generated medical ideologies and practices that sought to determine their care.

The negotiations evident in migrants' encounters with the FSA's health reform measures reveal the value of analyzing the intersections of citizenship and the medicalization of race, gender, and work in more complicated terms. The tension between public health care and medical racialization is clear in the FSA's unprecedented efforts to allocate medical resources to families urgently in need of them, even as it fueled an official discourse of migrants as irresponsible and deficient. All migrants who sought the FSA's care and believed themselves entitled as "good Americans" subjected themselves to the discourses that labeled them transgressive. For Mexican and African American farmworkers, the decision to accept federal aid was especially risky because it reinforced dangerous claims about their dependency and inability to act as responsible citizens. Yet migrants' willingness to participate in the camp program, beyond demonstrating their own determination to improve their lives, advanced their struggle for national belonging and representation. As marginalized farmworkers, racialized others, and excluded Americans for whom ordinary avenues of medical care were closed, this fight was most meaningful.

The medical program was a radical manifestation of what was possible—from the perspective of both migrant families who needed government aid to alleviate their suffering and FSA officials who saw disadvantaged farmworkers as deserving of these protections. To eradicate the human suffering created by poverty wages, substandard housing, and social alienation, the FSA understood that farmworkers' civil and labor rights had to succeed as a priority. To this end, the FSA directly challenged the power structure governing agricultural communities that benefited from farmworkers' status as racialized noncitizens by politicizing migrant workers.

CHAPTER 5

The Contested Meaning of Migrant Citizenship

Farmworkers' Education, Politicization, and Civil Rights Claims

In 1941 farmworkers Jose Flores and Augustus Martinez sat with two ethnographers from the City College of New York to address the problem of racial discrimination against Mexicans in the United States. Charles Todd and Robert Sonkin were conducting field research on migrants' lives inside California's Farm Security Administration (FSA) camps. Whereas most of their interviews featured the experiences of Dust Bowl refugees, the situation in El Rio's "FSA camp for Mexicans" in Ventura County, California, disclosed a different reality. Martinez explained that nearly all of the families in the camp had worked as migrant farmworkers in the region for, on average, at least fifteen years. They also knew each other well before arriving at the camp. Most of them had moved to the camp together from a nearby grower-owned settlement where the employer had evicted them because of a strike. In a revealing exchange, Flores and the ethnographers discussed the specific topic of civil rights and the FSA's role in promoting full citizenship:

> [Todd:] Do you think [Mexican Americans in the camp] are getting
>   all the benefits that Americans are supposed to get?
> [Flores:] No . . . and the only way I feel they could make good
>   citizens out of Mexican people, [is by] treating them like
>   American citizens.
> [Todd:] Do you think they'd make good citizens?

[Flores:] Oh absolutely, they sure will. I know they will make good
   citizens, if they're just treated the right way.
[Todd:] Do you think a project like this camp that we're in can be
   any help in training people to be good citizens?
[Flores:] I feel that . . . a camp like this will do a lot of good to
   become good citizens. . . . This camp the good that it's doing
   is through education mostly, and showing the people that by
   getting together they can get somewhere.
[Sonkin:] Have they ever been in a council like this before, in self-
   government?
[Flores:] No. They've never had a self-government council like this
   before.
[Todd:] Do you think the democratic process is good in educating
   them?
[Flores:] There is one good thing in educating, it gives the
   democratic point of view at least, because everyone has the
   right to vote and make decisions.[1]

The conversation illuminates several important aspects of the FSA's
camp program as it concerned migrant citizenship. Although Martinez
and Flores explained that most of the farmworkers in the camp were
American-born, the ethnographers nevertheless inferred that the migrants' citizenship status was still in process—asking, for instance, "Do
you think they'd make good citizens?" Moreover, in their inquiry as to
whether the Mexican American migrants had any previous experience
with self-government, Todd and Sonkin offered a perspective typical
among FSA officials. They assumed that migrants in the camps remained
ignorant of the "democratic process" and, as one administrator put it,
the "advantages that should be theirs under a democratic form of self
government."[2] In other words, while the FSA understood that migrant
farmworkers' class status contributed to their disenfranchisement, they
nevertheless defended the camp program in racialized terms as a way to
socialize and Americanize farmworkers.

The FSA's democratizing rhetoric was troubling for farmworkers such
as Flores and Martinez who expressed a clear understanding of the forces
contributing to their marginalization as nonwhite, long-term migrants.
Martinez carefully emphasized in his interview, for example, the historic

practice of racial subjugation in the region. He specifically noted how Mexicans were segregated in public facilities and "treated like peons" by their bosses. The farmworkers' strike for better wages in lemon picking currently under way also pointed to El Rio migrants' collectivity and self-organization, characteristics FSA officials had defined as essential to "good citizenship." Todd and Sonkin therefore failed to recognize the irony in alluding to the camps' "lessons in democracy." But as Todd would soon come to find out (after becoming manager of the FSA camp in Tulare, California), the camps' democratic experiment also involved educating mainstream society on their duty to uphold America's values and honor migrants' civil rights.

From its inception, the camp program aimed to do more than simply solve the temporary crisis brought on by the Great Depression. It sought to transform farmworkers' everyday lives as a way to improve their political power and promote the virtues of a participatory democracy. Even as the FSA increasingly intervened in the 1940s to solve work shortages, facilitate hiring, and regulate wages and working conditions, the camps were never simply labor stations or palliative measures to aid needy families. By teaching migrants what FSA officials believed were core democratic principles, such as self-discipline and communal responsibility, the camps' self-governing system planned to convert migrants into full citizens. Through these actions, the FSA directly challenged the race-based exclusion of farmworkers in the New Deal's labor and social welfare policies. In effect, the FSA's practice of encouraging disenfranchised farmworkers' political participation undermined the electoral and economic hegemony the agricultural establishment held in most rural communities.

According to the FSA reformers, migrants' participation in the camp council and other formal committees provided them valuable "lessons in democracy" that prepared them for participating as citizens in local and national affairs. In part, the democratic script the FSA advanced reflected a classic liberal understanding of democracy based on the principle that all citizens were equal before the law and had the right to equal access of political power and representation. Democracy also granted individuals the right to certain freedoms, privileges, and liberties protected by the U.S. Constitution. Ultimately, however, the FSA envisioned a democracy far more substantive and participatory than merely formal and representative —one tied to a broader, everyday civic engagement through which all migrants could voice their ideas and enact full citizenship. FSA officials held that democracy resulted not only from migrants' enfranchisement but also from their daily participation as citizens in a political community characterized by collective responsibility and behavior.

This chapter evaluates the FSA's democratic intentions in relational terms—among diverse farmworker families, in different regions, and across the shifting economic and political terrain introduced by the end of the Great Depression and the onset of World War II—to reveal the agency's important commitment to empowering migrant citizenship and advancing farmworkers' civil rights. A wider view of the camps' experiment in democracy shows how despite the FSA's efforts, migrants' realization of full citizenship proved largely elusive. Migrant farmworkers' varied experiences of racialization and legal status compelled FSA officials to acknowledge the reality that not all U.S. citizens were equal, and that real and prolonged access to democratic rights was conditional.

In the process of negotiating the FSA's democratizing project, migrant families embraced the FSA's conception of American identity by participating enthusiastically in the camps' self-governing system and recognizing, as Flores put it, "that by getting together we can get somewhere." Yet migrants also significantly challenged the FSA's assumptions positioning them as naive to the principles of American democracy and the advantages it afforded. They did so by articulating their own kind of political identity and critiquing the broader structural forces that kept them marginalized. To best exemplify how migrants maneuvered between competing understandings of national and local citizenship, this chapter examines migrants' struggle to access public relief and education. Although the FSA worked to strengthen migrants' political claims as deserving citizens, local communities commonly restricted migrants' access to social membership and public entitlements. Such challenges forced the FSA and local state representatives to determine the boundaries of migrant citizenship and consider how farmworkers' exclusion disrupted the principles of U.S. democracy.

The Problem of the "Federal Homeless" and the Promise of Restored Dignity

During the mid-1930s the careful depiction of Dust Bowl families as white American "refugees," forced for lack of opportunity to engage in migrant farmwork, served to temporarily redefine the occupation of seasonal farm labor in race, class, and civil rights terms. Because these were not "habitual migrants," described by John Steinbeck as "foreign 'cheap labor'" from a "peon class," the camps would help "restore the dignity and decency that had been kicked out of them by their intolerable mode of life." Restored "dignity," Steinbeck argued, went beyond an attitude of self-importance. It spoke to a broader notion of redeemed citizenship that strengthened the migrants' democratic duty. As Steinbeck explained:

> A man herded about, surrounded by armed guards, starved and forced to live in filth loses his dignity; that is he loses his valid position in regard to society, and consequently his whole ethics toward society. . . . We [speaking for the Resettlement Administration] regard this destruction of dignity, then, as one of the most regrettable results of the migrant's life, since it does reduce his responsibility and does make him a sullen outcast who will strike at our Government in any way that occurs to him.[3]

Although Mexican, Asian, and African American farmworkers suffered from poverty wages, hostile and dangerous work conditions, and unsanitary housing in California's industrial farms, they were largely excluded from these early narratives concerning those deserving enhanced citizenship.

Carey McWilliams and Paul S. Taylor, however, understood how the Dust Bowl migrants' displacement symbolized a much bigger problem. The Depression refugees, they argued, were "merely the first major army of the dispossessed," illuminating in California what likely would result elsewhere in America as "the farmers of today find themselves the migrants of tomorrow."[4] For this reason, Taylor warned that the migrant problem should not be considered isolated or local. As he saw it, "The situation in the state provides a 'pre-view' of what will occur in varying degrees and in modified forms on a national scale," particularly as the specialized, highly mechanized, and intensive form of industrial farming that met California newcomers prevailed throughout the country.[5]

If the migrant problem was increasingly a federal problem, as the camp advocates argued, FSA officials believed that local and state residency requirements for farmworkers seeking public relief were largely to blame. Such policies contributed to migrants' displacement and ensured that they were "not only homeless, but stateless, and townless—sans everything but American citizenship."[6] The problem stemmed from the fact that there no uniform settlement statutes, not only between states but also within states and counties, and across townships. While residency guidelines restricting public assistance had always posed a problem for migrant farmworkers, Depression-era conditions and rising interstate migration led many states to further tighten their policies. California's state law varied on local practice but generally required three years of continuous residence to qualify for relief.[7] This condition of statelessness had significant practical implications, according to McWilliams, in that it produced a special category of distressed persons—the "federal homeless" or "alien Americans"—who despite their status as U.S. citizens were without legal settlement, political representation, and public welfare.[8]

Exemplifying this point, one "helpless" case worker at a local social agency in California explained the following to Adela J. Ballard, an FSA migrant nurse, in 1935: "I know all you say is true. The family has worked. They came in response to agricultural need. The work has not paid a living wage, to say nothing of providing for the period between the harvests. But you know my hands are tied. These people are neither residents nor are they citizens." But as Ballard made clear for readers of *Missionary Review of the World*, "in order to obtain citizenship there must be residence within a community for a period of years! This is generally impossible for the agricultural worker." Consequently, the nurse cautioned readers about what could happen without reform: "The fact that the state and the county in which the work has been done repudiates responsibility leaves hearts seething with bitterness, a ready prey to the agitator advising strikes, hunger marches, and violence."[9]

Federal efforts to stabilize migrant farmworkers and control public relief, however, significantly threatened the power relations historically defining California agriculture. This became apparent in 1933 when Congress passed the Federal Emergency Relief Act (FERA) to help alleviate the hardship caused by unemployment during the Great Depression. To qualify for federal relief, recipients had to establish and maintain permanent local residence. Immediately, growers complained about how the law discouraged farmworkers' mobility, essential to their farm system. They also understood that a permanent or semipermanent labor supply, with federal aid at hand, was more amenable to collective bargaining.

As FERA went into effect, the consequences of federal relief were soon evident. In the context of the well-publicized San Joaquin Valley cotton strike in 1933, for instance, McWilliams argued that "the workers had been able to win a partial victory largely because they were able to obtain some assistance from the local relief agencies [through federal aid] during the strike." Due to such intervention, "a bitter fight was launched to wrest control of the relief agencies from the federal government and to place this control in the hands of county officials and State agencies directly under the dominance of the shipper growers." Historically, state relief worked hand in hand with labor supply demands. Relief officials in California "boasted of the efficiency with which they 'co-operated' with farm industrialists," mainly by cutting relief right as harvest hands were needed in the fields. Federal intervention aimed at stabilization therefore disrupted an important form of labor control. It also presented a political danger by conferring not only eligibility for local relief and protection from deportation but also the right to vote.[10]

Growers feared that worker empowerment could lead to larger socio-economic reforms. For this reason, when FSA agents spoke of restoring migrants' sense of belonging, self-worth, and political voice, they deemed the agency's intervention as outright subversive. In a public speech on October 22, 1941, Calvin B. Baldwin, the FSA's chief administrator, explained that while many of the FSA's jobs seemed pretty unrelated, "there [was] one common denominator."

> This denominator is not simply increasing the incomes of these families. . . . It isn't even to help them cooperate and help themselves by helping each other. . . . The fundamental job that we're doing is to help people regain a sense of personal worth—a self assurance that they are needed and useful workers in a democracy—a human dignity that has been all but squeezed out of them by the pressure of poverty they have had to endure.[11]

Baldwin went on further to emphasize that restored dignity and a sense of belonging would encourage low-income farmers and farmworkers to "have a voice in the life of their community. . . . From there," Baldwin claimed, "it is not such a big step into county affairs, then to an interest and participation in State and national Government. . . . By this means," he argued, "the voice of the disadvantaged in agriculture [was] being trained to speak in public." The FSA's efforts to protect farmworkers' voice in the exercise of their civil rights demonstrates the wider expanse the agency viewed as essential to ameliorating the migrant problem and, indirectly, to reforming California agriculture.

Several leading agricultural experts and prominent community representatives supported the FSA project aimed at migrants' rehabilitation in social and political terms. For instance, in 1939 Dr. Stanley B. Freeborn, the assistant dean of the College of Agriculture at Berkeley, affirmed that he and his colleagues agreed unanimously that

> the only real and lasting solution [to the migrant problem] will be one that enables the migrant to make a place for himself in the social and economic pattern of this state or elsewhere. These people, many of whom once owned their farms and lost them through unavoidable circumstances, can become industrious and useful citizens once again if only they can be given the opportunity. They come of as good stock as any other portion of our population. All they really need is a chance to prove their worth.[12]

To give Dust Bowl refugees that chance, the FSA camps offered them safe, sanitary housing, health care, and regular employment (or relief). Although most of the FSA's conservative critics preferred that the agency limit its commitment to migrant rehabilitation in simple economic terms, camp officials argued that full recovery would only occur with migrants' ascendance in a broader, democratic capacity as fully engaged citizens in their communities and country.

In 1940 Pastor Clarence Wagner, chair of the Ministerial Migrants Committee in Los Angeles, testified before Congress in support of the FSA's effort to strengthen social democracy, stating:

> Agriculture is the main industry of California. By numerical count, the migratory agricultural worker makes up the largest group employed in the maintenance of that industry. That this group should have no voice in the democratic processes of the State and Federal Government we consider as representing a very real danger to the democracy of our State and Nation as a whole. Therefore, we feel that it is incumbent upon the Federal Government, interested in the preservation of democracy, to make available through the suggested extension of their housing, medical and relief program,

conditions under which these migratory workers can sustain themselves until they are legally entitled to voting privileges and an equitable voice in government.[13]

Wagner feared the social cost associated with a large class of disenfranchised
Americans. He recognized that without the stability provided by the FSA's
intervention, migrant farmworkers could never realize the full privileges of
citizenship.

Due to the FSA's public defense of its clients' democratic rights, the
agency's critics in the American Farm Bureau regularly charged that its
rehabilitation program represented a sinister effort to politically organize
the rural poor and "create a group of voters subservient to their orders."[14]
Leading FSA administrators did their best to contest these assertions, but
they could not control what some of the FSA staff said on the ground to
ignite such charges. In October 1940, for example, C. M. Evans, the FSA
regional director covering Texas, wrote to C. B. Baldwin about an incident
that had stirred up some trouble at a conference for FSA personnel and
other government agencies in Robstown. Clay Cochran, the manager for
the camp in Weslaco, read a paper at the conference that recommended the
FSA "should make a definite fight to have the state constitutional amendment with reference to [the] poll tax suspended and should also encourage
migratory people to become a pressure group demanding of the government more and better service in the way of jobs, wages, grants, etc." Evans,
known to favor a more conservative approach, suggested that Baldwin fire
Cochran or remind him that this department was not a "propaganda
agency." In response, Baldwin agreed that perhaps Cochran should have
demonstrated better judgment, but he supported the idea that "democracy
can best be served through free discussion of important public issues,"
which the FSA should encourage among its employees.[15]

The FSA's decision to include migrant farmworkers in their reformist
vision demonstrates the agency's far-reaching intent to promote agrarian
social justice. The Cochran controversy showed how the FSA's critics claiming that the agency promoted subversive ideas were not entirely wrong. As
the farm bloc feared, many FSA employees did believe that the camp program provided an opportunity to educate migrants about the "real causes
of his being driven from the land," as Cochran put it, and to encourage
their understanding that, regardless of race, "they are all in the same
swim."[16]

The Camp Council and the FSA's Lessons
in Self-Government

To facilitate migrants' political assimilation, the FSA trained families in the camps in the principles of American democracy and reminded them of their responsibilities as participatory citizens. Camp officials touted a broader notion of citizenship wherein migrants learned self-discipline, good moral character, and a greater sense of social responsibility. Practicing a personal and collective understanding of citizenship, FSA officials believed, reinforced migrants' entitlement to the civil and political rights bestowed by the state. Migrant citizens, then, had the obligation to utilize these rights to practice their political power in a way that served the larger community. Thus, for FSA officials guiding migrants in the virtues of self-government, citizenship was at once a legal status protected by the American Constitution, a system of rights and privileges to be valued and shared equally, a form of political activity to be exercised with social responsibility, and a basis of identity from which to define one's sense of membership and allegiance.

The camp council best modeled the FSA's democratic doctrine and granted migrants the opportunity to develop into more engaged citizens. Camp documents offer an important insight into the significant role the council played in maintaining order and in managing daily relations between migrants and the FSA. The council's most important job was to make sure that residents abided by the camp constitution, which they received on arrival. Modeled on the U.S. Constitution, it set up the guidelines for living in the camp "republic." The constitution was drafted collectively with input from migrants and the camp manager, and it explained the rules concerning general conduct, curfews, and other matters of responsibility such as contributing to the camp fund. It also outlined the process of self-government, including the number of representatives on the council, the frequency of elections, and how to appeal council decisions. The FSA strongly encouraged all migrant families residing in the camps to participate in the regularly scheduled town hall–style council meetings.

In most cases, the camp constitution called for a new council election every three months to allow for a fluctuation in the camp population. Although all men and women over the age of twenty-one were eligible to serve on the council, few women actually did. Camp records indicate that migrant women generally served on domestic committees addressing camp sanitation, welfare, and recreation.[17] Before elections, the FSA encouraged campers to meet with members of their "district" (section of the camp) and discuss who they wanted to nominate and what ordinances they wished to see on the ballot. The camp staff then provided each voter with a secret ballot that listed candidates and a variety of camp issues.[18] Nominees made public speeches to promote their candidacy and published their platforms in the camp newspaper. Any resident over the age of twenty-one, or person who was married, had the right to cast a ballot on election day. At least one delegate from each district was elected to serve on the council. This allowed for equal representation in the camps' governing body, ensuring that all migrants regardless of length of residency, race, or language proficiency had the opportunity to participate in the camps' administration.

In addition to passing resolutions concerning the expenditure of camp funds or forming subcommittees to address the camps' needs, the council served an important juridical role guaranteeing migrants' model citizenship. For instance, the council acted as a court, complete with judge and jury, trying cases involving any violation of the camp constitution, mediating camp disputes, and imposing consequences for improper conduct. Typical cases brought before the court included matters of public intoxication, quarreling, and destruction of property. Sometimes, however, the more ambiguous reasons of not having "the right attitude" or of being an "undesirable citizen" and an "unsanitary housewife" could also land migrants under investigation and subject to eviction.[19] These cases clearly indicated how normative American values of respectable domesticity and gendered morality, reinforced through the FSA's home management education, influenced the council's decisions.

The FSA camp managers held the "executive power" to veto any ordinances or court decisions, but the council did not represent a "sandbox democracy," as several scholars have concluded.[20] Camp documents show that managers rarely intervened in any coercive manner against migrants' wishes. When they did get involved, it was commonly at the request of the council members themselves. This hands-off policy was a clear directive from the FSA office in Washington, D.C., reinforced with each camp manager's training. For instance, after some time at the camp in Arvin, California, under the tutelage of Tom Collins (the FSA's first camp manager), one trainee reported that he learned that "the manager should make himself felt, rather than seen and heard. . . . Campers make their own camp rules. The only interposition by the manager is that the law be upheld, and that nothing be done to interfere with the rights of others. Other than this instance, the manager should never use shall, will or shall not."[21] This policy existed to encourage migrants' confidence that they could solve their own problems.

The trainee's report also spoke of the seriousness with which council members ran the democratic meetings at Arvin, revealing the importance migrants placed on their self-governing system. After the council subjected the trainee to intense questioning to determine his fitness for the manager's job, the trainee commented on how impressed he was with the camps' effectiveness in "restoring human beings to reliable citizens." As he declared:

> When I left that room . . . I felt as though I had been through an inquisition, which indeed I had. I felt as weak and as starchless as if I had run a two mile race. The men and the emotions that I had seen, and the emotions I had personally experienced that night were more real, more dynamic than any painting; more moving than any story. The very men who had asked me those questions, and who had sat so righteously and rightfully to judge me in respect of them had come into camp with little pride and ambition. Beaten and kicked by society, they could not answer to the term "decent citizens." And yet, in that committee meeting they evidenced to me the qualities and the character which is the life blood of any functioning democracy. These were men, not derelicts![22]

Overwhelmed with emotion, the trainee ended his report by quoting a migrant father who had just discovered that he could register to vote: "Isn't it wonderful to be an American citizen!" Such sentiment epitomized the FSA's underlying goal of strengthening migrants' political voice and civic power outside of the camps.

FSA Democracy as Civil Rights: The Fight for Educational Equity in Texas and Florida

U.S. involvement in World War II presented significant challenges to the FSA's democratic script. On the one hand, the war strengthened the camps' democratic promise. On the other hand, it fueled growers' criticism of the camps' social reform efforts and bolstered their claim that labor productivity was more vital to the nation's stability. That the camp program expanded most notably during the war demonstrates the FSA's strategic ability to justify its utility in labor supply terms. In working for labor and democracy, however, the FSA continued to highlight the centrality of migrants' civic lives to their role as essential war workers.

Speaking before the National Farmers' Educational and Cooperative Union of America (NFU) on November 17, 1941, in a talk titled "Our Ultimate Defense," C. B. Baldwin explained why the FSA would continue fighting rural poverty and supporting farmworker civil rights in light of the more present "danger to our democracy."

> We feel the peril to our way of life more sharply than we did a year ago—but we also see our goal more clearly. That goal might be stated as: Opportunity and freedom shared by all. Those two words, "opportunity" and "freedom" add up to "democracy." More than ever before we Americans know now that democracy cannot be fragmentary. Democracy is not democracy until it's passed around. To perfect our defense calls for a full sharing of benefits as well as a sharing of the duties of these critical times.[23]

Baldwin continued by arguing that an essential element in the battle against Nazism involved recognizing how the democratic system in the United States "ostracizes" and "isolates" low-income people from full citizenship and the "joyous participation in the normal affairs of their communities." For Baldwin, our ultimate defense in wartime rested not only on the increased production of essential war goods, especially crops, but also on the continued dedication to promoting opportunity, freedom, and democracy for all. The foundation on which America stood in fighting the war abroad, he emphasized, depended on the sharing of benefits and duties related to citizenship.

Baldwin's use of inclusive language emphasizing political and economic democracy reinforced his claim, against mounting congressional opposition, that the FSA's actions toward migrant reform were deeply patriotic. With the nation's global commitment as "the great arsenal of democracy," this language sharply countered growers' accusations that the FSA was full of communist officials "promoting socialistic and impractical farming projects." Baldwin skillfully emphasized how the FSA was not only "not 'un-American,'" but was actually attempting to make the American dream a reality for hundreds of thousands of neglected low-income farm families."[24] He directly challenged the nation's farm bloc by making farmworkers' civil rights, especially their battle against economic and racial injustice, part of the U.S. fight against totalitarianism. As Baldwin understood, farmworkers could not remain an excluded class barred from the nation's labor and social welfare protections if America truly embodied a democratic ideal. The FSA's willingness to defend farmworkers' rights was especially critical as the demand for more labor allowed the FSA to expand the camp program during the 1940s. As the program grew, the FSA reached thousands of farmworker families who had long suffered from their lack of political representation and socioeconomic equality.

Mexican Americans and the Struggle for Educational Rights in Texas

Despite the FSA's remarkable effort to embrace more established migrants in their advance of farmworkers' democratic power, many found it difficult to trust the federal government's intervention. Mexican migrants undoubtedly recalled the recent government-sponsored mass deportation campaigns between 1929 and 1935, when at least one-third of the Mexican-origin population (two-thirds of them American citizens) left the United States.[25] And in the early 1940s, African Americans were still grappling with the "raw deal" they received as part of the New Deal's intervention in the U.S. South. After federal agricultural reforms forced many black tenant farmers and sharecroppers to turn to wage work, they were denied protection under the National Labor Relations Act, restricted from employment in public works programs, and threatened with violence at public relief centers.[26] Unlike the Dust Bowl families who drew national attention, few Americans sympathized with the destitute and depoliticized status of non-white and noncitizen migrants.

Labor leader Luisa Moreno dramatized this point in a speech she made at the panel of Deportation and the Right of Asylum of the Fourth Annual Conference of the American Committee for the Protection of the Foreign Born, held in Washington, D.C., on March 3, 1940. Moreno was at the conference representing the views of El Congreso de Pueblos de Habla Español (the Spanish Speaking People's Congress), a labor, civil rights, and community-based organization founded in 1939, which she largely led.[27] As part of her speech, Moreno declared:

Long before the "grapes of wrath" had ripened in California's vine-yards a people lived on highways, under trees or tents, in shacks or railroad sections, picking crops—cotton, fruits, vegetables—cultivating sugar beets, building railroads and dams, making a barren land fertile for new crops and greater riches. . . . Their story lies unpublicized in university libraries, files of government, welfare and social agencies—a story grimly titled the "Caravans of Sorrow."[28]

In describing Mexican migrants' exclusion, regardless if they were "descendants of the first white settlers in America or noncitizens," Moreno revealed how they encountered the nation's "undemocratic practice" of discrimination in multiple forms. Why would they seek naturalization, she asked rhetorically, if they experienced "unequal wages, unequal opportunities, unequal schooling," and the "denial of the use of public spaces in certain towns?" For this reason, El Congreso recommended a concerted action to integrate all Spanish-speaking people "into the American nation." According to Moreno, this would transform the nation's "Caravans of Sorrow" to "Caravans of Hope."

A closer analysis of the camp program in Texas provides a useful lens by which to examine how the FSA's democratic script developed in the early 1940s in significant, if limited, ways to offer Mexican migrants greater "hope." The camp program began in Texas in 1939, and by 1941 the FSA had built nine permanent camps throughout the state—in Lamesa, Crystal City, McAllen, Weslaco, Harlingen, Raymondville, Robstown, Sinton, and Princeton. FSA officials constructed these camps while Congress eliminated many New Deal programs and questioned the agency's role in wartime defense mobilization. Despite the shift away from Depression-era concerns over relief and recovery, FSA officials in Texas remained dedicated to their broader social welfare objectives and committed to developing migrants' full citizenship. In contesting firmly established social boundaries, FSA officials boldly defied the existing order even as they sometimes reinforced the biased discourses on which different farmworkers were racialized.

In South Texas, where seven out of the nine camps were located, local communities rarely considered Mexican farmworkers beyond their role as laborers, even though most were citizens (either U.S. born or longtime residents) from the surrounding area. Federal regulations on immigration, repatriation campaigns, and the increasing number of white farmers entering the migrant stream did not alter the racial composition of migrant labor in Texas as dramatically as it did in California.[29] This reality produced different implications for the FSA's actions in South Texas where their investment in migrant democracy meant intervening in a racially stratified social and economic milieu. In this context, the FSA clearly defied farmworkers' legal and social exclusion from the standard labor and civil rights protections afforded to other workers.

The FSA's involvement in the "Mexican educational problem," as local school representatives dubbed it, offers a notable example of how the agency linked migrants' poverty to matters beyond their workplace experience. In a monthly report dated December 12, 1941, FSA officials at the Robstown camp explained their trouble with local school administrators:

> We know that the Farm Security Administration was not set up to build schools and school systems. All we can hope, I suppose, is that the school district will realize their error and do something to correct it. There is a tendency among Latin American children to quit school long before they have even begun to get any benefit from their study. This is largely due to the economic pressure under which these families live. However, we know of no segment of our American people who have a greater need for the opportunities offered by education. If we are ever to amalgamate the Latin-Americans among us and teach them the democratic way of living, we must begin with decent educational opportunities for these children.[30]

FSA agents were frustrated by the clear racial bias underlying the school district's decision not to accommodate Mexican farmworkers' children. Accordingly, they reminded local school authorities that these children were citizens entitled to the rights and privileges of public schooling. Indeed, in using the ethnic identifier "Latin American" versus "Mexican," FSA officials demonstrated their awareness of the political implications of these terms as they related specifically to rights claims.

In defending the Mexican migrant families, FSA administrators also directly challenged the school district's claim that the federal camp had created the problem by bringing these children into the region. In a letter to J. W. O'Banion, assistant state superintendent, H. H. Bashford, FSA acting assistant regional director, argued: "It is our feeling that the Robstown Independent School District is not providing equal educational opportunity for all school-age children who reside within the district. The Bullard Elementary School which is designated as the Latin-American school is extremely over crowded, which condition it appears, has existed for some time."[31] Bashford's letter criticized the racially segregated school system in place in South Texas by exposing how the Robstown school district had long evaded their responsibility for providing Mexican American children a quality education.

The FSA's public acknowledgment of the barriers Mexican migrants faced to exercise their rights, and its willingness to intervene to correct such abuses at a time when their political legitimacy was on the line, is a remarkable testament to how far the agency's social democratic commitment extended. Yet even as the FSA acted in an unprecedented way to fight existing racial prejudice, camp agents limited their democratic promise by depicting Mexican migrants as alien citizens unfamiliar with the principles of democracy and their rights under the law.[32] This differed from the democratic script they applied to the Dust Bowl refugees who needed the camps' democratic lessons to *restore* their dignity and self-worth.

For example, writing about what he observed at the Robstown camp, Arthur E. Scott, the FSA assistant regional director for Texas, remarked:

> The population of this camp is approximately 95% Latin-American who have never known the advantages that should be theirs under a democratic form of government. The educational process with this group of people is slow and tedious. They are very appreciative once they understand the purpose of the migratory labor camp program. This was clearly demonstrated recently after six or eight months of training in this camp when approximately 80% of the qualified persons voted in a community council election.

Under FSA guidance, and with some "training," Scott explained, Mexican American migrants could make important gains to secure their rights as U.S. citizens. As he further noted: "While they are legal citizens of this state, they have seldom exercised the privileges of franchise due largely to the fact that they have been a subdued people for generations and are not aware of their privileges under our Constitution."[33] Although FSA agents acknowledged how local officials disenfranchised Mexican Americans, they still emphasized political ignorance in identifying the root of the problem. This perspective best supported their claim that Mexican American migrants needed the FSA's lessons in democracy to *realize* (not restore) their full citizenship.

The battles over educating Mexican farmworker children often came down to the question of who was responsible for incorporating migrants into the realm of U.S. citizenship. Much of the controversy surrounding efforts to grant camp children access to public schooling occurred because compulsory school attendance laws depended primarily on whether migratory children were considered "residents" in the community in which they lived. Laws varied because in most cases states authorized local school officials to determine the residency status of children in their district. Such flexibility in the law made migrants' educational rights subject to local prejudice, further exemplifying what McWilliams described as the problem of "alien Americans." Even if the migrant children were U.S. citizens, local school districts could determine that they were not legal residents eligible for public education.

Although residency restrictions affected all migrant farmworkers, the struggle Mexican migrants faced in Texas was inherently different than the experience Dust Bowl refugees encountered in California. Mexicans' unequal treatment was not a temporary problem caused by the Depression or their status as migrant farmworkers. Rather, Mexicans' inequality and exclusion from full citizenship germinated from a historical legacy of displacement, injustice, and racial bigotry. Unlike the Dust Bowl migrants who were "white beneath the grime" and could "literally scrub off the badge of their inferiority," federal rehabilitation alone could not recover for Mexican families the dignity and decency they deserved.[34] For this reason, Mexican farmworkers needed the FSA to help them engage in the much more challenging fight for civil rights on not just class but also racial terms.

During the 1930s, the League of United Latin American Citizens (LULAC), the largest Mexican American civil rights organization at the time, identified educational inequity as a key political issue in their struggle against racial discrimination. Similar to the stance FSA officials would later express, LULAC believed that unless children of "Mexican extraction" received equal educational opportunities (compared to that of whites), they would never be able to "measure up to the requirement of American standards."[35] By the early 1940s, however, LULAC had failed in advancing federal legislation to prevent unequal schooling through the courts. Consequently, the FSA's intervention against local practices of racial discrimination in Texas, and its efforts to fund the expansion of public schools or construct their own private schools in the migrant camps (which, contrary to local custom, were racially integrated), underscores how importantly this "farm agency" acted to alter existing relations.[36]

The FSA's actions to advance Mexican Americans' educational rights also proved meaningful for foreign policy interests at the onset of World War II. In 1940 President Roosevelt established the Office of Inter-American Affairs (OIAA) to advance the Good Neighbor Policy and promote improved economic, political, and cultural relations between the United States and Latin America, especially Mexico. The U.S. State Department was concerned that Latin American nations could fall under Axis influence if convinced by propaganda that discredited the U.S. claims of good will, hemispheric unity, and the fight for democracy worldwide. OIAA officials believed that correcting discriminatory practices within public education was vital to incorporating Mexicans politically into "broader U.S. interests."[37] In Texas the OIAA funded the Good Neighbor Commission (GNC) and passed the so-called Caucasian Race–Equal Privileges Resolution in 1943 to combat racial discrimination against Mexicans. Beyond labeling Mexicans white in name, however, the GNC did little to guarantee Mexicans equal rights. The commission hardly enforced the resolution and employed few penalties for noncompliance.[38]

The FSA's involvement in the Mexican school problem demonstrated an unprecedented federal concern for Mexican civil rights when it was increasingly meaningful to foreign policy negotiations with Mexico. Yet the FSA's actions were also limited. While the agency highlighted the problems inherent in Mexican migrants' poor schooling, in the end it did little to disrupt the larger pattern of racial segregation that prevailed throughout the state. The FSA focused on providing equal access to education, not on redefining the racial parameters of separate schooling. Agency officials, in other words, expanded the limits of their authority within the boundaries of racial exclusion affecting Mexican farmworkers' civil rights in the early 1940s. Although the FSA was genuinely concerned about how such discriminatory practices reinforced Mexican's depoliticized status, they could not compel local communities to accept their democratizing efforts to correct these conditions. The fact that their own primary schools, built within the labor camps, were racially integrated (except for in Florida) suggests that the FSA likely supported desegregation but was too politically vulnerable to get involved in such a fraught arena.

African Americans and the Struggle for Educational Rights in
Florida

The FSA's experience in Florida dramatically exemplifies the political mine-
field the agency maneuvered when it came to matters of race, citizenship,
and social reform. In much the same way that the FSA's concern with
migrant stabilization threatened California's system of industrial agriculture, actions to free southern sharecroppers and tenants from landlord and
merchant dependency threatened the planter paternalism that dominated
southern agriculture. More specifically, the FSA subverted the South's existing order by granting tenants rural rehabilitation loans, resettling former
sharecroppers on collective farms, and offering migrant workers relief
through temporary services.[39]

The economic implications of federal welfare were one thing, but the
FSA's dangerous tendency to advocate for social reform that could lead
to political transformation was quite another. As Sidney Baldwin concludes, "[In demonstrating] the relationship between chronic rural poverty, ignorance, social isolation, racial discrimination, and political
impotence," the FSA went beyond simple farm issues in the South to
"preach a philosophy of life." John Fischer, the FSA's director of information, conceded that the southerners who were opposed to the FSA "were
opposed for understandable reasons." As he attested, "We were in many
ways subversive of the *status quo*. Our efforts to improve farming techniques were not the ends, but rather the means by which poor farmers of
the South—many whites but especially Negroes—might be made more
effective politically and socially."[40] Yet even as the FSA recognized the way
its actions seemed to "promote class conflict" and "stir up the races," as
leading southern congressmen contended, they carefully abided by local
practices and "southern sensibilities" concerning race. By no means were
the FSA's New Dealers indifferent to the pervasive inequality they found
in the region, but they were considerably restricted in the actions they
took to correct it.

All of the labor camps the FSA established in the U.S. South (with the
exception of Texas) were officially segregated by race. Florida had the biggest concentration of camps with eight locations built between 1940 and
1941. The first camps built were the Osceola camp for white migrants and
the Okeechobee camp for black migrants in the Belle Glade area. Pahokee,
near Lake Okeechobee, also had two FSA camps by the summer of 1940,

one each for white and black workers. At that time, the FSA was also constructing a camp for black workers in Pompano, southeast of the first four camps. And in 1941 the agency built three additional camps, two in Homestead (even farther south) for black and white workers separately, and the Canal Point camp near Pahokee for black workers.[41] The Jim Crow system extended beyond the camp inhabitants as even the camp managers, medical staff, and home management supervisors were assigned to a location based on their race.

Unlike the Mexican migrants who lived in the Texas camps, the majority of African American farmworkers in South Florida were not originally from the area. According to a 1937 FSA study, they came from Georgia, Alabama, Tennessee, Arkansas, and Mississippi, in that order.[42] As Cindy Hahamovitch explains, various forces came together between 1920 and 1940 to create the migrant labor system that dominated in South Florida by the time the federal camp program intervened. The first involved the costly impact of the Depression on cotton production in the South, especially Georgia and Alabama. The second was rooted in a simultaneous rise in industrial agriculture in Florida, particularly as local officials voted to drain the Everglades in the early 1920s and clear the land for large-scale commercial farming. Finally, the third force concerned the rise of the "permanent transient," what Hahamovitch describes as "the migrant farmworker who had no sharecrop arrangement to return to, no state of residence, and no home to speak of."[43] In McWilliams's terms this was yet another rank of the "federal homeless"—a consequence, as he and Taylor warned, of factory farming.

Contemporaries writing about the FSA's concern for migrants in Florida warned that the agency had its work cut out for it in "the muck" among the most "wretched people living in filth and squalor." According to the Associated Press (AP), the camp program marked "a new phase in the development of one of America's last frontiers—the Florida Everglades."[44] As AP reporter Larry Rollins explained, the rapid development of the winter crop industry in "what was hardly more than a swamp not many years ago" had created some of the worst living and working conditions for farmworkers nationally. Testifying before Congress in 1940, John Beecher, FSA supervisor for the Florida camps, reported that indeed while "here and there a grower or packing house operator [built] relatively decent quarters for his more permanent workers, this activity fail[ed] by a wide margin to keep pace with the ever-increasing influx of seasonal workers."[45] By placing blame for the lack of adequate housing on the general forces of agricultural development, the FSA skirted the more critical claim that growers failed to responsibly provide for migrants' domestic needs.

The FSA was not concerned with the housing crisis exemplified in the rapid growth of migrant shantytowns and tent settlements for reasons of basic labor standards alone. The agency's greater worry centered on the impact such destitute conditions had on matters of everyday citizenship. Beecher posed the following more fundamental questions immediately following his statement on the effects of the agricultural boom: "If housing of the Lake Okeechobee migrants constitutes the worst rural slum in the country, what of the large social environment? To what extent do migrants participate in general community life, what educational opportunities are presented to their children, what recreational outlets exist for the different age groups, what facilities for the care of their health?"[46] The "wretched" state of affairs did not surprise Beecher and his FSA colleagues. They understood the interrelated problems caused by crude and unsanitary housing, lack of educational opportunities, and poor wages combined with restrictive relief policies.

Local growers and community representatives nevertheless argued that the problem concerning migrants was essentially more cultural than structural and economic. Growers' letters to the FSA claimed that all black farmworkers wanted was to earn a day's wage to spend at the local juke joints in order to gamble, drink, and chase women, rather than to think responsibly about their family's welfare.[47] Without challenging these racial biases directly, FSA officials contended that the federal camps would demonstrate how "migratory Negroes respond when they achieve reasonable economic security, are given decent living places, adequate medical care, and wholesome recreational outlets." The camps, Beecher testified, "should throw a good deal of light on whether the people are living as they do because they prefer filth, ignorance, vice and general wretchedness, or because nothing better is offered them." If given a fair chance, Beecher believed the migrants in Florida would "show themselves to be good Americans."[48]

In a notable way, Beecher's claim was similar to the argument FSA officials made on behalf of Dust Bowl refugees and Mexican American migrants concerning their democratic potential. This inclusive promise of full citizenship was, however, complicated by a different reality for southern African American farmworkers. Like the white Dust Bowl refugees, many black migrants in the FSA camps understood how it felt to be uprooted during the Great Depression. Black farmers were also "in exodus" and experiencing for the first time the life of a "permanent transient." African American migrants could also lay claim to being "American," despite not possessing the full rights of citizenship, in a way that Mexican American migrants as alien citizens could not. Yet because they did not possess the privileges of whiteness—as most Dust Bowl refugees did, and as Mexican Americans could aspire to politically (albeit in a limited sense)—African American farmworkers further tested the FSA's commitment to expanding democracy, particularly the right of all migrants to maintain the "normal standards of American life" regardless of race.

The FSA identified the prevailing problem of poor schooling as a central issue contributing to black migrants' poverty and disenfranchisement, much like they had for Mexican Americans in Texas. In 1942, at a southern conference for FSA county supervisors and field personnel in Little Rock, Arkansas, leading agency officials explained that

> in the long run the most fundamental approach to a solution of the problems of low income families is through the educational system and the breaking down of traditional social and political barriers which have been established. These barriers have usurped the rights of low income farm families. In fact, they have been disfranchised through actual practice. . . . In the educational approach it will be necessary to break away from traditional procedures. . . . Thence remains a job of liberalizing these institutions to get them to do the job.[49]

Southerners who were fearful of the FSA's actions viewed this rhetoric as dangerous, even though the agency refrained from any direct language advocating racial equality and social justice. Their concerns likely stemmed from the fact that the FSA did at times openly defy southern norms by insisting that "equal services be given to Negro and white children." According to one contemporary article, the FSA was also "working toward wiping out the salary differential that commonly . . . discriminates against the Negro teacher."[50]

In South Florida specifically, growers worried that the FSA's studies on migrant education disclosed such alarming findings that the agency could ignite reform. An FSA interview with the Palm Beach County superintendent in 1940, for example, revealed that "education [was] in competition with beans in this country, and beans [were] winning out." The interview captured the situation in the Lake Okeechobee area, where, as Beecher concluded, "education apparently [was] not trying to give beans much competition." At the time FSA officials met with the superintendent, there was only one truant officer for all of Palm Beach County, and she focused her attention solely on white children. Like school authorities elsewhere, education officials in the county argued that the migrant children constituted a serious problem in that there were simply not enough facilities to accommodate them, plus the children were "badly retarded, and difficult to adjust to the school discipline."[51]

While the situation was also dire for the children of white packing house workers, who on average did not advance beyond the fourth grade, black migrant children had even less hope for an education. Studies for enrollment in the Belle Glade Negro School demonstrated how dramatically field work affected school attendance. In the winter of 1940, for example, many black farmworkers put their children in school for the first time following a disastrous freeze that destroyed the bean crop. Enrollment at the "negro school" quickly skyrocketed to 503 students. After some months, however, when the beans came in again, local FSA agents found that the enrollment dropped to only twenty in attendance. As they reported, "Ninety-five percent of the children were [back] in the bean fields. They had to be."[52]

FSA studies conducted at a nearby lakeside town similarly disclosed a distressing educational pattern for African American children that correlated with the farm season. Although the negro school in this area was established in 1920, twenty years later only six students had successfully graduated. Three-fourths of the students repeated grades 1, 2, and 3, and the average first grader was ten years old. Monthly figures for 1940 showed that while many black children attended regularly during the off-season, most dropped out once bean picking commenced. For instance, about fifty boys and girls had attended the school from late August, when classes began, until early October, after which only a couple returned sporadically.[53]

The FSA contended that irregular schooling limited black children from attaining the knowledge and skills necessary to improve their job opportunities, much less engage with civic life as adults. The educational adversity black farmworkers experienced was even more dramatic when one considers that the majority of black migrant children never received any schooling at all. As Beecher recounted in his congressional testimony, "Even if the bean pickers decided to give their children the benefits of education, it would be impossible for the working-mothers to get them washed, dressed, fed, and sent off to school in the morning, as the parents go to the hiring yard at dawn."[54] The insecure nature of farmworker hiring in the region, which consisted of a grower recruiting workers on a daily basis through "broadcasters" or contractors "barking" available jobs and wages, compromised the stability necessary for parents to keep their children enrolled in school. FSA officials recognized the alarming impact this farm labor system had in broader social democratic terms, particularly on the next generation of African Americans.

FSA Actions to Secure Migrant Education Inside the Labor Camps

Camp officials acted in remarkable ways to secure migrants' access to quality schooling and to encourage regular attendance. According to George Hay, manager of the camp in Raymondville, Texas, "There was a constant effort on the part of the camp personnel to keep children in public school."[55] FSA directors expected all managers to maintain a thorough record of migrant children's school enrollment and attendance. When a child did not attend regularly, the camp's home economist visited the family and made inquiries into the matter. At the camp in Harlingen, Texas, the manager went so far as to request that "a good reason be given to him every time a child missed [class]." Such a policy demonstrates how camp officials maintained a stricter attendance policy than local schools.[56]

The FSA also found ways to mediate some of the socioeconomic factors limiting migrants' educational attainment. They allotted "school clothing grants," used their association with other government agencies to find donations for school lunches, and provided transportation when school buses refused to pick up the camp children. Hay, for instance, proclaimed that he and his staff at Raymondville had "stimulated school attendance" by setting up an agreement with the school district where the camp would use its "facilities and labor" to can food for the school lunch program in exchange for the children's noontime meal.[57] At the Robstown camp, the manager reported that "on days during inclement weather the [FSA] project truck" along with "two trucks owned by the campers and three cars cooperate[d] in getting the children to school."[58] Such measures, combined with migrants' collective efforts to improve conditions—such as organizing sewing workshops to make school clothes and volunteering to cook and can food for the school cafeteria—helped substantially improve migrant children's educational access.

Although these efforts did not guarantee that the quality of education available to migrants outside the camps would improve, the FSA's added attention to educational access demonstrated an important commitment to advancing migrants' civil rights. This practice was particularly meaningful considering that the U.S. Federal Fair Labor Standards Act (1938) failed to protect farmworker children in the areas of wages, hours, and safety regulations to the same extent that it governed child labor standards in urban industries. The FSA placed careful attention on migrant schooling in the midst of political debates over child labor regulations because it recognized that education represented a core site on which to extend the promise of American democracy. Public education was an equalizing force that while not guaranteeing equal outcomes, promised everyone a fair shot at improving their lives. Letters from FSA administrators to school representatives stress the responsibility communities had "to provide equal educational opportunity to all school-age children who reside within their district."[59] In exposing the problem of migrant schooling, the FSA underscored how "deplorable" it was that migrant children were "looked upon as outsiders" and were thus unable to achieve the privileges of American citizenship to which they were entitled.[60]

The FSA directly funded the expansion of numerous public schools and constructed separate educational facilities for migrant children within most of its labor camps to ensure migrants' access to quality education. FSA officials typically established classrooms in the camps' community center building, where hired teachers and the camp staff did their best to reproduce a formal school setting. In some cases, however, the camp schools were much more elaborate than typically available in rural communities. The racially integrated elementary school at the camp in Weslaco, Texas, for instance, was one of the largest schools built by the FSA. The school consisted of "a four-classroom building complete with lockers, heating and lighting, toilet facilities, lavatories, drinking fountains, blackboards and window shades." The Weslaco Independent School District agreed to operate the school as a unit of the district, to furnish all instructional materials and classroom supplies, and also to provide regular maintenance.[61]

Limited reference to the camps' school curriculum suggests that the FSA's approach to migrant education did not differ significantly from what local

Figure 18. "Third Grade Elementary School [Students], FSA (Farm Security Administration) Camp, Weslaco, Texas." Photograph by Arthur Rothstein, February 1942. Library of Congress, Prints & Photographs Division, FSA/OWI Collection, LC-USF33-003655-M4.

schools offered.[62] Typically, the closest school district provided the teachers, which likely meant that they brought a standard curriculum from the district to the camps. Several references concerning the experience of Mexican and African American children, however, do point to the FSA's support for "emphasizing vocational training and guidance" to offer a more "practical education."[63] Providing vocational education to nonwhite and immigrant students was a common practice in the 1940s.[64] High school–age girls at the Okeechobee camp for blacks, for example, were preparing in 1941 "to be competent household employees." The home economics course, which required that students first "undergo a thorough physical examination at the clinic before they could enroll," taught various phases of sewing and working with new appliances such as an electric mixer.[65] Such efforts, while often embraced by the camp population at large, reinforced the racial biases that tracked nonwhite, poor children into low-level and gendered occupations.

The FSA's educational efforts aimed at migrant adults speaks more directly to the way the agency sought to assimilate migrants into mainstream U.S. society. By the early 1940s, the Work Projects Administration

Figure 19. "Third Grade Elementary School [Classroom], FSA (Farm Security Administration) Camp, Weslaco, Texas." Photograph by Arthur Rothstein, February 1942. Library of Congress, Prints & Photographs Division, FSA/OWI Collection, LC-USF33-003656-M2.

(WPA) assisted the FSA in offering adult classes in most of the labor camps. At the Sinton and Crystal City camps in South Texas, for instance, the WPA sponsored bilingual classes in reading, writing, arithmetic, and government.[66] Camp officials believed that these classes would improve migrants' overall competence. They also specifically noted how they would help Mexican migrants "to qualify better in passing their examinations for citizenship." Camp statistics for 1941 and 1942, however, show that most of the Mexican migrants residing in the Texas camps were American-born. Rather than simply reinforcing Mexican Americans' status as foreigners, the FSA likely equipped Mexican immigrants (especially those who arrived at an early age) with the necessary knowledge to successfully naturalize.

Camp administrators also suggested that the adult education classes were specifically contributing to the war effort by encouraging young men to join the military. In Sinton, for example, the FSA noted that the camp had approximately 335 residents who were ineligible for military service "because of their inability to read and write the English language." W. A.

Canon, the FSA's assistant regional director, believed that if the migrants "could be prepared for enlistment," the FSA might be able to secure additional assistance from local agencies in funding the adult education program. Through its various uses, the FSA's adult education program offers another remarkable example of how the agency sought to advance migrant citizenship and participatory democracy beyond the fields.[67]

Migrants' Self-determined Efforts to Achieve Educational Opportunity and Full Citizenship

The few records that directly represent migrants' perspectives on the school issue suggest that farmworkers embraced the FSA's efforts to improve their education as a way to ameliorate their impoverished conditions. Still, migrant families often took initiative over their own educational opportunities rather than relying on the FSA, or another public agency, to provide resources on their behalf. The adult education classes sponsored by the WPA, for example, were made possible largely through school supplies provided by the migrants' cooperative fund administered by the camp council. In some cases, migrants also organized their own classrooms for the camp children instead of waiting for local school officials to comply with the FSA's demands. In Crystal City, Texas, for instance, Andres de Santiago and another migrant organized daily classes in English and arithmetic. Most of the Mexican students who attended had never been to school. According to a camp report, the school was highly successful, "flourishing with practically 100% attendance." As a result, the FSA received "numerous requests that the Latin-American children from town be given the opportunity to obtain their schooling" at the Crystal City camp.[68]

In Florida, African American families also came together to improve migrant children's education. The home economics course training girls for domestic work, for instance, was sponsored by the Okeechobee camp council, which purchased a mixer, refrigerator, and "countless numbers of other articles" to ensure the program's success. This action received much praise from the "colored section" of the *Belle Glade Herald*, a local newspaper.[69] In 1941 C. B. Baldwin also wrote to U.S. senator Claude Pepper (D-FL) boasting about the "remarkable extent" to which black farmworkers in Florida were demonstrating "self-help" in education. He highlighted in particular how the migrant council in one of the "Negro camps" had recently sent a boy and girl to Florida A&M College in Tallahassee with the money for their tuition coming out of the collective camp fund.[70]

Migrants' actions to utilize the camps' commitment to democracy as a tool for advancing their education exemplifies the important political role they played in molding public understanding of migrant citizenship and in altering the racialized narratives that defined them as ignorant and apolitical. In 1941 Augustus Martinez from the El Rio camp captured this commitment in the following statement:

> Here in Ventura, County, we're trying to . . . get the young folks united and trying to be respected, you know. At the same time [as] trying to be respected, why get 'em together. Show 'em what American citizens' privileges are and how he can use them. And at the same time, it gives us a more powerful arm so we can defend ourselves. United together. Because that way we can show 'em, if we get together and vote, we can show them that we got something to talk about. Because the government of the United States is something that respects everybody. And, if you work hard, according to the laws, why there's no difference in the government and in [what] race you are.[71]

"United together," the Mexican migrants in El Rio believed they had the power to defend themselves against the discriminatory practices they experienced on account of their race and status as "alien Americans." In a manner that exemplified what Luisa Moreno contended about Spanish-speaking people's civil rights struggle, Martinez and other council members framed their lemon strike beyond achieving "better wages." Instead, the migrants underscored how their strike was "about trying to be respected" and "to have a decent feeling." For this reason, they believed that organizing a "kind of Americanization classes" to train the camp youth in exercising their privileges as American citizens was critical to voicing their demands for dignity and long-term equality.[72]

Migrants in El Rio also stressed the need for greater public education on racial discrimination against Mexican American farmworkers and their families. This was the flip side of the assimilation process FSA officials described as necessary. In a more direct way than the FSA was typically willing to express, Martinez emphasized the importance of voting to "show [other Americans] we have something to talk about." Exercising a political voice was critical not simply for enhanced rights and opportunities, he argued, but also to change the biased public opinion working against them. As Jose Flores explained, migrants in El Rio reached out to "American clubs" throughout the county to "tell them about the discrimination against Mexican people." "Because it's really the public who makes this discrimination against Mexican people," he clarified, "it's not the government particularly; it's the public itself who does it." In this way, both Flores and Martinez emphasized their belief in the federal government as a democratizing agent. It was "a government that respects everybody" with "no difference . . . in what race you are," as long as "you work hard." The camp program afforded migrant families a space where they could test these ideals.[73]

Mexican migrants' actions to further develop their political identity illuminate the complicated ways in which migrant families negotiated their sense of national belonging from within the camp program. Camp records suggest that migrants employed varied strategies that must be understood as complementary (rather than competing) claims to Mexican American citizenship. In Crystal City, Texas, for example, camp manager Paul Freier reported in April 1941 that the "leaders of the population proposed a working democracy in their own language and in their own style."[74] Freier noted that the Mexican American migrants had not only adopted resolutions from other camp locations in establishing the camp's constitution but were also influenced by the 1857 Mexican Constitution as promulgated by Benito Juárez, a copy of which they had in their possession.

While Freier's report does not elaborate on how specifically the camp council adopted measures taken from the "Juárez Constitution," several factors concerning the document suggest why it was inspirational. The policies outlined in the Juárez Constitution advanced the principles of the Enlightenment, and a more general moralistic, humanist philosophy. For instance, the 1857 Constitution guaranteed Mexican citizens basic civil liberties and equal rights, including freedom of speech, equal access to education, and protection of their land and labor from both the government and the Catholic Church. Juárez, a Zapotec Indian from Oaxaca who became president of Mexico in 1858, was a heroic figure both for his *indio* and peasant origins and for carrying out La Reforma, one of Mexico's most progressive, liberal political and social revolutions. In the United States, the Mexican working class remained inspired by his ideals well into the twentieth century, as evidenced in the numerous mutual aid societies, fraternal organizations, and other community-based associations named after Juárez. These forms of self-organization and mutual aid were well established among Mexican farmworkers by the 1930s and proved critical to their survival, advancement, and collective action against the poverty and discrimination they encountered in the United States.[75]

In some instances, migrants' actions defining their political development reflected the principles of *mutualismo*—a collectivism and liberalism rooted in a more "Mexicanist" tradition. Concurrently, though, Mexican American farmworkers appropriated the camps' Americanizing rhetoric to assert their status as white Americans deserving the full benefits of U.S. citizenship. In 1940, for example, migrants residing at the camp in Raymondville, Texas, insisted that the camp personnel refer to them as "Latin-Americans" rather than "Mexicans." As Albert Short, the camp manager, explained:

> Throughout all of this section [in the Lower Rio Grande Valley] the Mexican is recognized mainly as one whose citizenship is still in Mexico. We have Latin-Americans in this section whose complexion is as white as any of us and who somewhat resent the classification Mexican. We also have people from other Latin-American countries. It seems to me that it would be preferable for us to indicate what is called Mexican population on this registration sheet as Latin-American. This term is preferable to the majority of this class of population because many of them are truly loyal American citizens.[76]

By embracing a term that was at once hemispheric and an assertion of U.S. citizenship, migrants' claims to "Latin-American" identity demonstrated their awareness of the broader political implications involved in defining themselves apart from Mexican immigrants. While they surely related to Mexican nationals' exploited condition as U.S. farmworkers and remained culturally and ideologically connected to their roots in Mexico, the Mexican American migrants at the Raymondville camp nevertheless recognized the great significance of calling attention to their political status as "loyal American citizens" deserving of full and equal civil rights.

During World War II, when civil rights activists increasingly questioned the value of American democracy, the Raymondville migrants' claims to being "Latin-American" revealed a profound understanding of their subjugated and disenfranchised condition. Such expressions, emanating from migrants' own understandings of an American identity, which they some-times articulated in cross-border terms, further demonstrates how Mexican American farmworkers did not arrive at the FSA camps destitute of political ideas and democratic values like some FSA officials assumed.

Japanese American "Evacuees" and FSA's Contested Democracy

As agricultural production needs expanded during World War II, the FSA's struggle to preserve democratic "opportunity and freedom . . . shared by all" met considerable challenges. The Seasonal Leave Program (SLP) that FSA officials coordinated to utilize Japanese American evacuee labor offers a powerful example of how the agency hoped to manage growers' rising labor demands and continue the fight for improved farmworker civil rights. Almost immediately after President Roosevelt signed Executive Order No. 9066, growers in the northwestern states of Oregon, Idaho, Utah, Wyo-ming, Colorado, and Montana began clamoring for the use of Japanese farm labor. Milton Eisenhower, director of the War Relocation Authority (WRA), had plans for establishing a work corps program "to avoid a sizable reserve of workers sitting idle in relocation centers," but he initially received some backlash from state representatives fearful of hosting "enemy aliens."[77] The continued pressure exerted by sugar beet growers in the Inter-mountain Region, however, could hardly be ignored, and on May 13, 1942, the WRA and the Wartime Civil Control Administration established the SLP, whereby Japanese American evacuees could be released from reloca-tion centers for farm work.[78]

The stipulations of the SLP required that the participating state gover-nors and local law enforcement officials sign a pledge testifying to a labor shortage in their region and guaranteeing the evacuee workers' safety. The agreement clearly specified that the employers must pay prevailing wages and pay the workers' housing and transportation costs to and from the assembly centers or internment camps. Finally, the plan insisted that the evacuees were "forbidden to leave the designated areas to which they were assigned."[79] This rule existed supposedly for the evacuees' own protection, but it clearly conformed to the broader national security concerns warrant-ing Japanese surveillance at the time. By mid-October 1942, an estimated ten thousand Japanese American men and women were on seasonal leave while growers continued to demand more. In total, between 1942 and 1944, approximately 33,000 Japanese Americans left U.S. internment camps (mainly Minidoka, Heart Mountain, and Granada) to engage in farm labor.[80]

Initially, FSA officials insisted that Japanese evacuees fell outside of the terms of the Emergency Farm Labor Supply Program, in that they were neither Mexican braceros nor domestic laborers freely available for employment. Growers, however, insisted on the FSA's help to save their crops vital to the war. They used a familiar refrain stressing an emergency labor shortage, and they exaggerated their labor needs. Ultimately, the growers demanded that the FSA include Japanese evacuees under the "same plan" paying for the transportation of Mexican braceros.[81] They claimed, quite ironically, that Japanese evacuees were needed to replace "the Mexican labor that was used in the sugar beet areas [which was] now largely employed in California, replacing the Japanese labor that was removed from that area."[82]

In collaborating with the WRA, the FSA maintained primary responsibility for transporting, placing, and protecting the Japanese American workers and their families. Companies employing the evacuees were expected to help subsidize the costs, but WRA officials concurred that the FSA needed to maintain a close watch over the program in order to guarantee that essential services were provided and that labor conditions were favorable to the workers. In the early stages of the program, evacuees complained about the need for more adequate heating facilities, community kitchens and dining areas, and improved medical attention.[83] They also demanded that federal officials do something to address the problem of local harassment and guarantee that public services such as schooling were available to them on relocation.[84]

As the SLP got under way, the FSA used it to demonstrate their contribution to the war in labor supply terms. Unlike in California, growers in the Northwest and Intermountain Region stated frankly that "it would have been impossible for them to have harvested their crops had the Farm Security Administration not established a labor camp in [their] community." The Utah-Idaho Sugar Company reported, for instance, that the camp program had "played a very essential part in providing for the Japanese workers who harvested the crops in that area."[85] Although only three of the twenty-eight FSA camps in the region specifically housed Japanese evacuee labor—one in Nyssa, Oregon, and the others in Caldwell and Rupert, Idaho—the

FSA also cooperated with local agencies to offer housing and services for seasonal leave workers in other facilities.[86]

The SLP was vital to meeting emergency wartime labor demands, as repeated telegrams from growers made clear. But an equally critical aspect of the program concurrently involved a problematic advance of the welfare state and the FSA's democratic script. FSA officials justified Japanese internment as an Americanizing and democratizing opportunity much as they touted their New Deal commitment to progressive, social reform for migrant workers. In general, the FSA contended that "all persons residing in the labor camps [were] entitled to free enjoyment of legal rights, privileges, and civil liberties."[87] Although Japanese Americans were essentially citizens whose rights had been nullified, the FSA made no specific mention of the contradiction that their participation in the camp program exposed. Despite their legal status as "enemy aliens," the FSA expected Japanese families to participate in the camps' assimilationist efforts and act like ideal citizens of a democratic republic. Ironically, since in the case of internment it was the federal government voiding Japanese Americans' civil liberties, this was another way the FSA accounted for a population of "alien Americans."

In a featured story written by the FSA's Information Division titled "Calling Dachau—Little Nyssa Speaks!" FSA officials explained that Japanese evacuees were entitled to "elect [their] council and plan for [their] welfare and camp government" just like any other group residing in the federal labor camps. The article underscored how the U.S. government empowered Japanese Americans by providing them the opportunity to "get back to work, earn some money, and help the war effort." FSA officials also used the article to underscore how unlike the concentration camps of Nazi Germany, FSA labor camps were models of democracy through self-government and cooperation. For example, the story stated how on arrival at the Nyssa camp, the FSA manager, Ormond Thomas, told Japanese American families, "This is your camp and your community. America is a democracy. This FSA camp is a segment of that Democracy."[88]

FSA officials believed that the evacuees could practice the tenets of democracy by organizing camp councils, managing cooperative stores, and maintaining other community-based activities. In their view, the SLP afforded a critical opportunity for Japanese Americans to combat the prejudiced attitudes they faced as racialized enemies and prove their loyalty and commitment to the United States. Consequently, the FSA claimed the camp program was successful as an Americanizing project in convincing local communities of Japanese Americans' worthiness in labor and civic terms. As the Nyssa experience demonstrated, according to the FSA, "folks grew accustomed" to the presence of Japanese families in their vicinity because "they worked well—they worked hard. They were orderly, quiet, and unbelievably clean. . . . They aren't like the Japanese of the Imperial army of the Son-of Heaven. They know what democracy is about. This is their war, too."[89] Although there was "a no more hated group in the United States than the Japanese in the months after Pearl Harbor," several districts in the Pacific Northwest had to change their biased views, according to George Renan, an FSA labor relations specialist, on realizing that "the Japanese saved the beets and everybody knew it."[90] In 1942 the Caldwell chamber of commerce passed a resolution thanking them for their important role in the sugar beet harvest.

FSA officials were confident that the change in attitude toward Japanese Americans in Idaho was valuable for altering the reception other nonwhite migrants might receive in the area. As Renan reported, "Under the impact of the war if the attitudes could change towards the Japanese in Idaho, it is not too much to expect attitudes to change toward the Negroes in the Northwest." Most blacks, according to Renan, avoided the area where prior employment resulted in substandard wages, discrimination in public facilities, and a refusal by white migrants to work alongside them. Gregory Silvermaster, the FSA's labor division director, concurred with Renan that "attitudes shown by citizens of the northwest toward Negroes" might change "as it becomes more evident to them that we must use all of our labor resources on a fair basis in order to hasten the day of victory." In this way, the Japanese evacuee experience provided FSA officials an avenue by which to advocate for African American migrants' civil rights. As Silvermaster contended, local leaders had to understand that "Negro [workers] can be expected to be of maximum aid only if they are treated on an equal basis with their white fellow citizens."[91]

Not all agreed, however, that the SLP represented a voluntary opportunity based on the promise of U.S. democracy. In an editorial published in the *Christian Century* on August 12, 1942, for example, one critic pointedly asked: "Are Evacuees to Become Peons?" The author noted that while enlistment in essential war work was "accepted as a clear indication of the [evacuee's] patriotism and loyalty to the United States," in truth, "lacking other opportunities of employment, the evacuee had actually little choice in the matter."⁹² Even as residents in the FSA camps where agents celebrated the value of American citizenship, the evacuees lived circumscribed lives. For instance, Japanese families at the Nyssa camp were not allowed to go into town except for a few hours once a week and only under strict supervision.

Despite these restrictions, the camp program represented an important alternative to Japanese internment. Japanese American evacuees understood the power in earning wages as emergency farmworkers. Mathias Uchiyama's family grew strawberries on their truck farm in Cornelius, Oregon, before the evacuation. He recalls that his father attended a meeting while at the assembly center in Portland where various families discussed moving to the FSA camp in Nyssa as part of the SLP. As Mathias remembered, it was a collective decision made among several families originally from the Fukuoka Prefecture in Japan. "There was kind of a loose knit clan type of think, and they were kind of looking out for each other," he clarified. Mathias believes that his family's financial stability was his father's foremost concern. He recalls his father stating, "We just can't stay in camp here, in the center because we've got mortgages to pay. . . . We just can't afford to, we'll lose everything."⁹³

Evacuees also recognized that their labor helped them affirm their identity as Americans committed to the war effort and provided "a chance to get a breath of fresh air," as Mack Mayeda recalled. "[I] took a gamble" on farm work, Mack emphasized, because it was "better than suffering a slow death in camp."⁹⁴ Although it was impossible for evacuees to completely escape their feeling of imprisonment, their daily activities as labor camp residents blurred the boundaries of their legal status as "enemy aliens." In Wilder, Idaho, for example, FSA agents reported in June 1943 that twenty male Japanese evacuees were living and working alongside "200 male Jamaica negroes [foreign contract workers], 10 American negro families, and 15 American white families (southerners)." This aspect of the report aimed to show how "different races [were] living together without strife." Yet the report ignored how the evacuees' legal condition as "enemy aliens" under internment set them apart from other domestic workers.⁹⁵

Similarly, in Nyssa, Oregon, FSA photographer Russell Lee recorded several images of Japanese American evacuees shopping and eating in town as well as dancing at the home of a local Japanese farmer with other Japanese Americans from the surrounding area. Since the Japanese in Oregon were not forced to evacuate, the individuals at the dance were not under

Figure 20. "Nyssa, Oregon. Japanese-Americans who were evacuated from a coastal area and who now live at the FSA (Farm Security Administration) camp attending a dance given by a local Japanese farmer. There are some Japanese-Americans who are permanent residents of this section of Oregon; they were not subject to evacuation orders. These permanent residents naturally have retained complete freedom, while the Japanese-Americans living at the FSA camp are under certain restrictions." Photograph by Russell Lee, July 1942. Library of Congress, Prints & Photographs Division, FSA/OWI Collection, LC-USF34-073596-D.

the same legal restrictions as the evacuees, despite their shared racial identity. The migrant camp newspaper, the *Rupert Laborer*, similarly offers an important glimpse into evacuee life at the camp in Rupert, Idaho. There, Japanese American families established cooperative gardens, camp committees, and their own "special police force," and organized recreational activities in the surrounding area.[96] In this way, Japanese families experienced some degree of autonomy that offered a respite from the duress of internment. It was an "opportunity," as Harley Ito recalled, "to get on the opposite side of barbed wire."[97]

This sentiment was clearly expressed in October 1942 when 214 residents at the Nyssa camp petitioned federal officials for permission to "remain at the migratory labor camp rather than to return to a Relocation

Center." They did so with the recognition that "there would be no work available for them in the area during the winter months," thus requiring them to subsist on very little. They also requested to stay regardless of the fact that conditions in the tents "would not furnish sufficient protection from the cold . . . inasmuch as they [were] from a warm climate."[98] Despite these circumstances, the Japanese American families viewed the FSA camp program as an opportunity to live with greater self-determination. By choosing to reside in the FSA's care, they tested the agency's devotion and inclusion of those deserving democratic power and complete civil liberties.

FSA officials recognized that what was at stake in the SLP went beyond simple matters concerning farm labor supply and increased production. Notwithstanding the conservative pressure to scale back on their reform agenda, the FSA continued to maneuver the political terrain for expanded farmworker rights. For instance, during the first year of the program in Idaho, R. T. Magleby, FSA assistant regional director, took advantage of a meeting he had with Governor Chase A. Clark on the topic of the "Japanese labor problem" to pressure him on the trouble the FSA had "in connection with the present Idaho school law."[99] After receiving confirmation that the FSA had "made a very distinct contribution to the agricultural welfare of the state through the use of [the] camp programs," Magleby insisted that Clark act against the present state law "prohibiting any school district from furnishing school services to children of such camp residents unless and until the Government undertakes to pay the cost thereof." The FSA used the opportunity presented by the state's labor shortage to pressure the governor into supporting a "new law acceptable to us," as Magleby described it. The FSA's continued effort to get local authorities to accept responsibility for migrant children's education reflected the agency's enduring mandate for democratic reform.

The FSA's actions in other matters related to Japanese internment also point to the way the agency and its officials wrestled with their democratic mission under wartime order. For instance, after being removed from his role as the FSA's chief administrator coordinating the bracero program (due to grower pressure), Laurence Hewes went on to serve as the federal official in charge of locating qualified operators to manage the California farmlands "abandoned" by Japanese evacuees. In a letter to Dr. Ramson Bird, president of Occidental College, dated May 23, 1942, Hewes registered his lament concerning the matter. As he remarked, "The tremendous difficulties implicit in this job are obvious. It is not the American way to throw groups heedlessly into concentration camps. Most of the evacuees are

American citizens with all the rights afforded members of this democracy."
However, "guided and sheltered by the government," Hewes believed that
the Japanese farmers could at least rest assured that they had sold or leased
their lands "in complete fairness" and "without loss to any substantial portion of their crops."[100] In truth, much evidence exists revealing the hasty,
inefficient manner in which temporary operators managed Japanese farmlands. In many cases, they were turned over to collective operators, more
readily able to handle the Japanese style of farming, but typically connected
with local growers' and shippers' organizations such as the California Fruit
Exchange, which had long opposed the FSA.[101]

As the FSA gained responsibility for brokering Japanese internment by
managing Japanese evacuees' housing, labor, education, and farmlands, the
agency pushed the boundaries of social democracy beyond the fight against
rural poverty, farm dispossession, and the damaging effects of commercial
farming. The FSA succeeded, to some extent, in granting Japanese families
greater autonomy at a time when repressive measures against them were
justified by other state mechanisms. The FSA's interactions with Japanese
evacuees, however, also expose how the camp program's democratic script
failed to consider the harsh reality of legal noncitizenship and enemy status.
Not only did the Japanese experience affirm the fact that not all citizens
were equal before the law; it also undermined the idea that practicing and
learning normative American systems and doctrines would lead to
migrants' assimilation, acceptance, and civic empowerment.

In working to tether the ties between migrants and the state through an
expanded democratic right, the FSA acted in a remarkable manner contrary
to key New Deal policy in the mid-1930s. As southern congressmen
ensured that farmworkers were excluded from Social Security benefits, collective bargaining rights, and other workplace guarantees, the FSA fought
to include all migrant farmworkers in the national polity as citizens worthy
of protection. In doing so, the agency directly challenged the established
economic and political order in the nation's most important agricultural
states. The camp program not only offered migrants safe housing and economic stability against most growers' wishes; it also advanced farmworkers'
struggles for economic citizenship and racial justice. Such actions, though
ultimately undermined by conservative congressional pressure and the
FSA's need to accommodate growers' labor supply demands, nevertheless
provide powerful evidence of how far the agency went to advocate for those
most disenfranchised in rural society.

A broader relational view of the FSA's actions among diverse farm-worker families, however, also illuminates how the agency's democratic promise resulted in varied experiences of self-government and conflicted forms of citizenship. For the Dust Bowl refugees, FSA democracy promised rehabilitation in terms that would restore the dignity, decency, and social status they lost in migration and in their racialized position as farmworkers. For Mexican "alien citizens," FSA democracy promised access to a previously unknown institution and the privileges it afforded. In particular, it promised, as it did for African American farmworkers, educational equity and better living conditions to combat the discriminatory forces they encountered as second-class citizens. Finally, for Japanese American evacuees and "enemy aliens," FSA democracy promised the opportunity to prove their loyalty and commitment to the United States through farm labor. It also stood as a way to distinguish American war policy against the more brutal example witnessed in German concentration camps. In this way, the FSA's democracy reinforced problematic nationalist claims on the back of Japanese American farmworkers devoid of civil liberties.

The experiment in democracy FSA officials advanced through the camp program—and the interrelated, if uneven, way migrants experienced it—reveals the extraordinary action the agency took to test the boundaries of national belonging in the late 1930s and 1940s. That they did so, even if only momentarily, is extraordinary. The FSA's efforts allowed migrant families to mediate the pressures associated with their noncitizen status as transients, farmworkers, nonwhites, and war enemies. It also provided the support and stability migrants needed to combat their status as "alien Americans" in their own terms. While migrants enthusiastically embraced the FSA's self-governing system, as evident in their camp council actions, they also relied on their own resources for civic advancement and socio-economic justice. Most migrants understood that the battle against the racist, exploitive forces of industrial agriculture extended far beyond the FSA's reach. Consequently, they continued to nurture their own forms of collective action to further claim recognition, social membership, and political participation in meaningful ways. Mexican migrants such as those in El Rio, California, also reminded FSA agents that while they benefited from the camps' democratic tutelage, it was mainstream society that needed to educate itself on the discriminatory conditions farmworkers faced. To uphold the nation's democratic ideals, U.S. society needed to recognize farmworkers' civil rights.

However, the political empowerment and socioeconomic stability migrant families found in the camp program was significantly compromised after 1942. The bracero agreement FSA officials negotiated with Mexican government officials, along with the Caribbean guest worker program launched in 1943, increasingly undermined the democratic voice domestic farmworkers achieved with the FSA's support. By 1943 the structure the FSA established under the New Deal to strengthen migrants' economic citizenship mostly crumbled. As industrial workers in U.S. defense manufacturing plants celebrated good wages and new work opportunities brought about by the war and their union drives, American farmworkers across the country were left increasingly vulnerable to exploitive work conditions, declining wages, dilapidated housing, and little hope for redress through state-backed collective bargaining.

CHAPTER 6

The Demise of the Camp Program

Industrial Farming and the Embattled Welfare State

On May 11, 1943, Irving Abkin, the manager for the FSA camp in Wood-ville, California, wrote to the agency's assistant regional director, Myer Cohen, reporting on the trouble he encountered "since the coming of Mexican Nationals." The arrival of Mexican farmworkers as part of the Emergency Farm Labor Supply Program had created tense conditions among camp residents. As Abkin explained:

> The first reaction on the part of the permanent residents here was to thoroughly resent the coming of the Mexicans. The prejudice is understood in terms of their southwestern background where contact with other than anglo-saxon groups on a common basis was unheard of. . . . Frankly, it has made the job of working in the community a lot more difficult. There is a sort of mass surliness within the community and they are always on their toes to see that the management does not extend itself when it comes to the Mexicans. Understand, of course, that these attitudes cannot be separated from the economic question. Most of the American residents now identify the management with the interest of the Growers. This is not an easy impression to dispel.[1]

Abkin and his staff did what they could to assure the American residents, the former Dust Bowl refugees, that they still sought to protect their interests despite the arrival of foreign workers whom they viewed as competition. Notwithstanding his efforts at "community integration," Abkin concluded that the practical problem of facilitating relations between the two groups had created "a real headache."

The tension caused by the arrival of Mexican braceros was rooted in a more fundamental problem for the FSA that stemmed from competing labor systems and varying understandings of race and citizenship in the United States. One labor system, which most clearly influenced the FSA officials who first launched the camp program in 1935, sought to reinforce farmworkers' reproductive power. It promoted migrant security, stability, good health, nutrition, and education as a way to maintain farmworkers' labor capacity while reaffirming their role as citizens to enhance social democracy. In this system, farmworkers' claims to American citizenship, and, in some cases, to whiteness, were central to the FSA's defense of their full labor and civil rights.

The bracero program and the Caribbean guest worker program reintroduced an agricultural labor system that stood in far contrast to this ideal.[2] Reminiscent of earlier racialized indentured labor arrangements, the guest worker programs of World War II increasingly centered on extracting labor productivity without any of the costs of reproduction. Mexican and Caribbean workers' "disposability," especially as deportable noncitizen and nonwhite workers, was an essential part of what made them desirable to commercial farmers.[3] This system dominated industrial farming by the mid-1940s, after which domestic farmworker families found themselves unable to compete and secure any of the benefits the FSA once afforded them. If the Woodville families doubted the FSA's commitment to defending their socioeconomic welfare, it was because by 1943 the agency had lost considerable political power to exercise any meaningful action in their favor.

This chapter examines the FSA's role in managing the terms of the Emergency Farm Labor Supply Program to consider how the agency's liberal officials attempted to protect both domestic and foreign farmworkers' interests in the process. I argue that the FSA's administrators recognized how the labor importation programs would undermine many of the gains they had accomplished through the camp program. Thus, rather than viewing their actions as evidence of a shift toward prioritizing growers' interests, I illuminate the political battle the FSA underwent to maintain the power to regulate farm labor wages, housing, and working conditions in farmworkers' favor. The FSA's struggle to protect the labor camp program and the welfare services it afforded all farmworker families proved central to its political fight to remain active in the way the agency's reformers first envisioned.

Despite their efforts, or perhaps more accurately because of them, various growers' associations and their congressional allies intensified their attack on the agency. In 1943 they succeeded in passing a bill transferring the FSA's farm labor programs to "safe hands." President Roosevelt signed Public Law (PL) 45 on April 29, 1943. The law shifted administrative control of all guest worker programs, the transportation of domestic farmworkers, and the migratory labor camp program to the far more conservative, pro-grower War Food Administration (WFA). At this point, the FSA remained alive as an agency, but its social reform programs became severely compromised.

The political battle that followed PL 45 in many ways signaled the end for the FSA. In March 1943 hearings to investigate the FSA's activities had already begun, with Congressman Harold Cooley of North Carolina, who had long opposed the FSA, chairing the committee. In May 1943 separate congressional hearings to determine the FSA's appropriations for the 1944 fiscal year resulted in a 43 percent cut to the FSA's rural rehabilitation program. Not all of the FSA's opponents wanted the agency abolished; some believed that certain programs outside of the agency's dangerous "social experiments," such as the tenant purchase program, were worth saving. Nevertheless, the FSA's critics were united in their belief that the agency should be "cleansed of its sins," which primarily involved ridding it of its more progressive—some argued, communist-leaning—leadership under FSA administrator Calvin B. Baldwin.[4] By the end of 1943, Baldwin, and many of the FSA supervisors at the national and regional levels who shared his ideologies, had left the FSA. Their departure opened the door for Cooley and the farm bloc to advance a bill to eradicate the FSA and create a new, more conformist administration in its place. U.S. president Harry S. Truman signed the Farmers Home Administration Act terminating the FSA on August 14, 1946.

The camps manifested a key battleground on which farmworkers, growers, local communities, and the government negotiated migrants' right to access the opportunities promised under the doctrine of U.S. democracy. Accordingly, the FSA's political demise after 1943 produced considerable material and ideological changes to the camp program that distinctly marked the camps' transformation into extractive spaces with little consideration for farmworkers' political power and welfare. To evaluate the implications of this development, this chapter ends by considering the camps' legacy, particularly concerning migrants' continued fight for expanded labor and civil rights. It also explains the important role some of the FSA's agrarian reformers went on to play, after the camp program ended, in working for social justice in the United States and informing rural development efforts abroad.

The FSA's Role in the Emergency Farm Labor Supply Program

In May 1942 Laurence I. Hewes, the FSA's region IX director (covering California, Arizona, Utah, and Nevada), began meeting with various U.S. Department of Agriculture (USDA) and immigration officials to discuss plans for the importation of Mexican farmworkers.[5] The officials were responding to commercial growers' escalating demands that the government supply the additional labor force necessary to meet increased wartime production requirements. U.S. secretary of agriculture Claude Wickard traveled to Mexico in the early summer of 1942 to begin negotiations for a new labor importation program. When a binational agreement was reached on August 4, 1942, Wickard appointed the FSA the central agency responsible for the recruitment, transportation, and housing of Mexican contract workers, or braceros. Hewes left for Mexico City in early September 1942 as the federal representative charged with finalizing arrangements and launching the program.

It is useful to know a bit about Hewes's background to understand why his appointment was significant and controversial. Hewes personified the progressive politics characteristic of the FSA's early New Dealers. Rexford Tugwell recruited him to serve as an assistant when the Resettlement Administration (RA) was formed in 1935. After Tugwell resigned from the RA a year later, Hewes remained in the agency headed by Will Alexander, which became the FSA in 1937. In 1939 Hewes left Washington, D.C., to serve as the FSA's region IX director. In this role, he became an integral adviser in the expansion of the camp program nationally. His experience in resettling migrants in California resulted in army orders to help carry out the evacuation of Japanese Americans from the West Coast, including dispersing of their farmlands, which he administered during the spring of 1942.[6] In May 1942, the same month Hewes met with U.S. officials to discuss the Mexican labor program, the War Relocation Authority also assigned him the task of managing the Seasonal Leave Program allowing Japanese Americans to depart U.S. internment camps for work on farms primarily in the Northwest. Hewes was thus a central player in the exploitive racialized labor landscape unfolding throughout the rural West.

Hewes's memoir, *Boxcar in the Sand*, reveals how he felt in carrying out these tasks, which he describes as "repugnant both to belief and judgment." In particular, Hewes explains the irony in his assignment to coordinate the bracero program. "I had publicly discounted grower claims for more labor and had particularly opposed their demands for importation of labor from Mexico. I was already in the bad graces of growers because of my earlier conduct of migratory agricultural-labor camps and so, according to wartime logic I was selected to work up an arrangement with the Mexican Government creating machinery to important thousands of Mexican field workers."[7] Hewes was very vocal about the fact that "with better management, better wages, [and] improved living standards" there existed an adequate supply of domestic labor available. Studies conducted by the Bureau of Agricultural Economics (BAE) supported his claim, estimating in early 1941 that even if the United States entered into the war, "more than a million and a half farm workers could leave agriculture without impairing the nation's agricultural production."[8] Nonetheless, Hewes had to respond to growers' "imperious demands," as he described them, to recruit foreign workers knowing that the effort was partly aimed at reducing domestic farmworkers' collective labor power. As the labor organizer and scholar Ernesto Galarza clarified, it was the advantageous position farmworkers maintained to bargain for better conditions that truly presented the "crisis" for growers.[9]

Consequently, Hewes committed himself to making the most of his authority to determine key aspects of the bracero agreement. According to Hewes, "As in the case of the Japanese evacuation, I had to have other than official reasons for participating in this unpleasant work. I found a reason in a determination to obtain maximum protection for Mexican workers."[10] Commercial growers already suspected his motives. In the fall of 1942, during hearings conducted by the House Agriculture Committee, various growers' associations—including the American Farm Bureau Federation (AFBF), the National Grange, the National Cotton Council (NCC), and the Associated Farmers of California (AF)—protested vehemently that Wickard had "appointed the wrong agency" to administer the program. C. C. Teague, speaking for the citrus industry in California, argued that the FSA was "deliberately creating unsettled conditions which made it difficult for employers to get along with their braceros."[11] Other growers similarly complained that the FSA sought to secure bracero wage and labor protections that were "completely impractical and unnecessary."[12] For instance, Oscar Johnston, president of the NCC, explained Arizona growers' position as follows:

> The contract submitted by the Farm Security Administration to the cotton farmers . . . contains certain regulations with respect to "imported" labor which would require the farmer to guarantee to the picker a minimum number of hours' or days' employment a week and a minimum compensation. [This presents] a radical departure from the regular piece-work basis which has been accepted as a basis of pay for almost 100 years.[13]

The cotton farmers charged FSA officials with dangerously undermining the farm labor system that growers knew and relied on to successfully harvest their crops.

Even more disturbing, growers insisted, was the FSA's expectation that they provide foreign workers amenities beyond basic standards, what they considered "costly pampering" or "socialistic provisions," such as a special diet of familiar foods and regular medical care.[14] Harvey L. Hansen, assistant secretary of the Farm Labor Subcommittee of the Santa Clara County USDA War Board, wrote to Hewes directly to inquire about such expectations:

> We are wondering if you would be kind enough to give us a full outline as to the provisions and the rules that are laid down for farmers obtaining the help of these Mexicans. We have in mind one case where the distance from the living quarters to the fields is some four hundred yards and the farmer has been instructed that he must haul them to the field in the morning and haul them back at night. It is also our understanding that he was instructed that he had to take them to night school three nights a week.
>
> While it may be necessary to educate these people, we feel that our primary object is getting sugar beets harvested. The farmers are extremely busy and we are wondering just how far they can go in the fulfillment of all of these regulations and still get their crops harvested.[15]

Other growers were less diplomatic in their protests, claiming that the FSA's "crackpots" and "lamebrains" were "placing every conceivable hindrance in the path of getting help."[16]

In Pinal County, Arizona, Senator Carl Hayden tried to impress on the discontented farmers that "the Mexican Govt. didn't want anybody to come up at all, but insisted in the Agreement on certain housing conditions, wages, etc." As the senator explained to the FSA, however, "those people in Arizona don't believe that. They think [the] FSA is using [the] Mexican agreement as a means not of taking care of Mexicans, but [of] raising housing standards of all labor in this country."[17] Rather than viewing the FSA as simply ignorant or unsympathetic, commercial growers believed the agency was guilefully working to win for domestic laborers "forms of protection which had never been conceded."[18] They were not mistaken. As Cindy Hahamovitch argues, by requiring that growers offer domestic labor the same guarantees the Mexican and British colonial governments demanded for their workers—including a minimum wage, a 75 percent employment guarantee, free transportation, subsidized housing, and protection against racial discrimination—the FSA tried to ensure that the guest workers improved, not worsened, domestic farmworkers' condition.[19]

When Sr. Rafael Arredondo from Mexico's Department of Labor visited various California farms in November 1942, shortly after the program began, he expressed concern that growers "want to continue employing workers from Mexico, but they desire to deal with each worker individually." Arredondo believed Hewes should know that the growers aimed "to deprive the Mexican workers of what might be termed collective bargaining and also the assistance and direction of the F.S.A."[20] Hewes understood that most growers resented the FSA's control over the program. Accordingly, getting farmers to follow the agreed terms became increasingly challenging. In a letter to C. B. Baldwin dated February 20, 1943, he confessed: "The present arrangement with the Mexican government requires that the FSA undertake to use and enforce certain minimum standards of health, welfare, housing and in general other fair labor practices and we are finding it extremely difficult to get compliance in areas distant to the border and almost impossible near the border." Hewes recommended that the FSA maintain "the very strictest enforcement of the program." He feared that if the FSA did not uphold the guarantees it made, the agency was "in danger of . . . finally losing every principle for which we have stood and on the basis of which the Mexican Government placed its faith in the Farm Security Administration."[21]

Although the growers blamed Wickard for the FSA's appointment as the contracting agency, Mexican commissioners insisted that the FSA perform this role. They were impressed with the FSA's work, "particularly in the operation of migratory camps in California," as one FSA official explained, which convinced them that the progressive agency would protect Mexican nationals from mistreatment.[22] The FSA tried to do so, as Hewes's efforts attest, but it lacked the political power to effectively regulate recalcitrant growers both in the fields and in Congress. Only two months after Hewes wrote to Baldwin, the growers succeeded in wresting control of the farm labor supply program from the FSA.

The Beginning of the End: Public Law 45 and the Departure of the FSA's Reformers

The nation's most influential growers in the AFBF and the AF disagreed on how best to rid the FSA of its authority to regulate farm labor employment, but they remained fiercely united in their commitment to regain control over the right to manage their workers. On April 29, 1943, President Roosevelt signed PL 45, which the AFBF and the AF had drafted. The law transferred administrative control of the bracero program and the newly established Caribbean program to the Office of Labor in the WFA, an agency dominated by officials from the rural South and essentially led by the nation's agricultural establishment.[23] Paul Vander Schouw, the FSA's southeastern regional director, had just signed an agreement (based on the Mexican program) with British colonial officials on March 16, 1943, to employ Bahamian farmworkers in Florida.[24] The FSA's transfer to the WFA helped industrial growers across the country accomplish exactly what they wanted. Carey McWilliams described this as "the impossible: stabilization without its consequences; a regular labor supply, without responsibility of its maintenance; privately controlled camps operated at public expense."[25]

Despite the FSA's assurance in 1942 that they were "trying in many ways to raise the standard of life for all farmworkers," PL 45 eliminated any hope domestic laborers held that growers' preference for foreign workers would not further deteriorate existing conditions. Before the law was signed, Father Luigi G. Ligutti, the executive secretary of Catholic Rural Life Conference (CRLC), telegraphed Secretary Wickard, warning him of

the "impending danger" behind growers' intent and its costs in greater
political terms for the United States at war. As Ligutti argued:

> Wages of imported Mexican and other farm labor human beings
> deserve and must have adequate compensation, living family wage.
> If democracy is to continue and prosper by having peons, wage
> slaves, rural slums, child labor let us cast aside our boasted pretense
> at justice and humanitarianism. [CRLC] advocates just and demo-
> cratic treatment of all labor including farm labor no matter what
> the cost and consequences. Why should commercial mass produc-
> tion farmers call themselves efficient and boast they are contributing
> to high standard of American living when by their wage scale they
> debase a portion of our American population? If we are fighting for
> something worthwhile economic democracy should exist in our own
> household.[26]

Ligutti's message powerfully articulated what many opponents of PL 45
felt, that the farm labor system commercial growers wanted was inherently
antidemocratic. In early April, during Senate hearings on House Joint Resolution 96 (to become PL 45), spokesmen for the National Farmers Union
(NFU), CRLC, Southern Tenant Farmers' Union (STFU), Congress of
Industrial Organizations (CIO), and other labor, church, veteran, and civil
rights groups testified adamantly that it represented a "peonage law" reminiscent of earlier indentured labor arrangements where workers held few
rights if any to protect themselves.[27]

The most significant stipulations in PL 45 specified that any federal
agency involved in recruiting, transporting, and placing agricultural workers could not use their resources "directly or indirectly to fix, regulate, or
impose minimum wages or housing standards, to regulate hours of work
or to impose or enforce collective-bargaining requirements or union membership." Exceptions applied for imported workers, but "only to the extent
required to comply" by the agreement reached with foreign officials.[28] This
did not guarantee guest workers much because the law also eliminated the
FSA's power to regulate such standards, leaving it in the hands of agencies
such as the U.S. Extension Service, who were more favorable to the growers.

Furthermore, the Pace Amendment, attached to PL 45, stated that federal funds could not be used to transport domestic farmworkers "from the
county where he resides or is working to a place of employment outside of

such county without the prior consent in writing of the county extension agent," who was likely a local farmer.[29] The law, in other words, deprived domestic farmworkers of the right to find better work, "a right which had been the cornerstone of labor law for free workers since the early nineteenth century," as Hahamovitch argues, and one of the few bargaining tools farmworkers possessed as laborers excluded from the National Labor Relations Act.[30]

In early June 1943 C. B. Baldwin protested vehemently to Chester Davis, war food administrator, that the FSA was not afforded the due respect and opportunity to defend its interests against PL 45, and he pleaded that at the very least the migratory labor camps remain under the FSA's sole control.[31] It was too late, however. In addition to stripping the FSA of the guest worker programs and the power to improve domestic workers' employment, the law also placed the camp program under the WFA's authority. In the WFA, all FSA labor camps were officially renamed "farm labor supply centers" from their previous designation as "farm workers' communities." The change clearly reflected the profound ideological shift that accompanied the program's reorganization. It is important to acknowledge, however, that the proposal to change the camps' name actually originated in the FSA. This recognition matters because it exemplifies how, even before PL 45 passed, FSA officials fought to maintain their role in the farm labor program by responding to growers and restructuring the camps' intended purpose as sites to promote efficient agricultural production.

N. Gregory Silvermaster, director of the FSA's labor division, outlined the agency's plans in a paper prepared for the FSA Administrator's Staff Conference in November 1942. As he explained, "a fully developed system of farm labor supply centers" was needed to emphasize the camps' role as "a clearing house for farm manpower supply and demand." Adding five hundred additional camps to the existing program would "serve as a link in a nationwide chain, replacing with minimum standards of healthful housing and positive placement information the old ditchbank dwellings and rumor-ridden job-hunting, so wasteful of time and energy of the seasonal worker." Ironically, Silvermaster suggested that the new name reflected how "a residential and placement center for farm workers must be more than just a 'camp.'" What he envisioned maintained important provisions for "habitual farmworkers and their family members," such as "decent and healthful lodging, supervised recreation for young people, and instruction in farm labor skills supplied at no cost to either farm workers or employers."[32] Although he placed the camp program within the productionist discourse necessary to prove the agency's commitment to the war, he demonstrated the FSA's intent to preserve its original promise to aid American farmworkers and their families.

The conflict these goals produced was immediately obvious as foreign workers began arriving in the camps in the early fall of 1942, and it only worsened as PL 45 went into effect in the spring of 1943. For instance, Warren M. Engstrand, the community manager for the camp in Brawley, California, wrote in his monthly progress report for November 1942 about the arrival of more than two hundred Mexican nationals, acknowledging that this forced him to "refuse admission" to domestic families. Engstrand hoped for a better solution:

> We believe that a third or half of the tent homes ought to be reserved for domestic labor. Rents are high in Brawley and it does not seem to us that our contractual obligations would be violated by preserving a portion of our original mission to provide housing for domestic agricultural workers. . . . If we reserve our project exclusively for Mexican labor not only a hardship will be inflected on American workers but in addition an unpleasant feeling of being discriminated against will likely develop. In a very practical sense on the other hand we must calculate the problems that would inevitably arise from close association of single Mexicans and American families.[33]

Engstrand predicted what would soon unfold across several camps, as the opening story concerning Woodville reveals. There, the manager Irving Abkin added, part of the problem was "the physical layout of the camp. . . . It was built with the admirable purpose of community integration and convenience," he acknowledged. Yet "the result is a sort of boomerang since the advent of the [Mexican] Nationals." Trying to find a way for both sets of workers to "live as brothers in one happy family" was practically impossible. By December 1942, Glen Trimble, who replaced Engstrand as manager, reported that Brawley contained "two largely separate communities" under the organization of separate camp councils for domestic and foreign workers.[34]

An even greater concern for Trimble involved the camp's physical deterioration. It started with the FSA's budgetary cuts and worsened with the arrival of the Mexican workers. According to Trimble, he approached the local growers about possibly providing a maintenance man to help repair the damaged buildings, since they bore the responsibility of providing for the guest workers. Yet they insisted that the FSA handle all matters related to the camps' care. One month later, the question of who should pay for the camps' upkeep was settled, but Trimble doubted anything would come from it. As he reported in January 1943:

> Negotiations between the state office and Mr. Hewes have finally placed the responsibility for caring for this on the growers—in theory. In practice we have not to date, two and a half months after the arrival of the Mexican Nationals, received any help whatsoever from the growers in meeting this problem. I cannot insist too strongly that this failure has created and continues to create a serious and mounting health menace in the tent house section of our camp.[35]

Although FSA officials tried to keep the camps operating in a manner that would secure migrants' socioeconomic welfare, growers insisted this was not a priority. Their lack of concern for farmworkers' lives transformed the camps' built environment soon after the labor supply program began. Before long, the camps themselves personified the disposability of the system.

Increasingly, as the WFA became concerned with housing braceros in the West and Caribbean guest workers in the East, officials did away with housing for nuclear families and facilities for community organizing, instruction, and recreation. Most of the existing camps began the transformation by designating a separate unit or section of the camp for housing foreign workers.[36] But others constructed after the importation programs began were built with this intention from the start. For example, in California the Lamont, Patterson, So. Shafter, Soledad, Wasco, and Woodland camps were built in 1943, one year after braceros began arriving in the state. With slight variation among them, each of these projects had minimal provisions in comparison to the FSA camps previously built. The camps built in 1943 typically included only frame row shelters or barracks to house workers, a manager's apartment or house, a foreman's apartment, an isolation unit or some trailer space, and a mess hall.[37]

In restructuring the camps' built environment, the WFA not only veered away from offering housing and amenities that served entire migrant families; they also increasingly abandoned any intention toward fostering broader socioeconomic reform and civic engagement. When asked in early June 1943 about existing recreational facilities in the camps, Hewes acknowledged that "with the onset of the war, the manpower shortage and one thing or another, that has pretty well dwindled off."[38] By the mid-1940s few camps still had nursery school programs, home demonstration workshops, and the various camp committees sponsoring different activities. Yet camp statistics suggest that migrant families continued to occupy the camps in ample numbers so as to require such services. For example, from July 1, 1943, to June 1, 1944, the Farm Labor Supply Centers housed approximately 150,000 people. Of these, 51,000 were "foreign born," 48,000 were "interstate workers and their families," and 50,000 were "intrastate workers and their families."[39]

The structural transformation the camps underwent privileged male workers migrating without families and discriminated against farmworking men and women who traditionally labored together and with extended family members. Prioritizing single male workers was not mere practice based on growers' preference; it was a mandated priority under PL 45. The Office of Labor ranked shelter use in the camps as follows:

1. Foreign agricultural workers brought in under the transportation program.
2. Interstate domestic workers brought in under the transportation program.
3. Domestic migratory workers who are normally engaged in crop harvesting and who have been eligible for camp occupancy in the past.
4. Intrastate workers in cases where facilities are not already occupied or are not needed by any of the preceding classifications.[40]

This policy extracted from farm labor the domestic power essential to keep migrants thriving. Maximizing the "manpower" available to pick crops meant making the fullest utilization of masculinist labor, not social welfare services gendered female. Paul Vander Schouw reflected this new attitude when he recommended in his narrative report for August 1943 that the WFA convert the camp for white migrants in Pahokee, Florida, to housing for Bahamian guest workers. As he explained, "During the previous year's peak season, the camp had housed only 213 workers old enough to work, although it was filled to capacity." But he went on, "If the camp was used for Bahamians only, it could house at least 800 easily."[41]

In cases where this transformation was not as rapid, such as in Texas where growers could not officially contract braceros until 1947, the FSA's compromised political power was nevertheless obvious. In each effort to expand its social welfare mission for American-born workers—for example, contesting segregated education, enlarging the medical insurance program, and providing stable, more permanent farmworker housing—camp officials met strong resistance from growers and their community allies who refused to see migrants beyond their role as exploitable workers. Indeed, the rampant evidence of racial discrimination in Texas caused both Mexican and Jamaican government officials to insist that their nationals not be permitted to work in the state. Consequently, Jesse Gilmer, the FSA regional director in Texas, felt the agency was caught in the middle. As he explained in June 1943, if the FSA pushed for guest worker contracts under such conditions, they would be "accused of fostering racial discrimination." Yet if they refused to cater to growers' demands, they would be "accused of discrimination against the state of Texas."[42]

For the FSA's reform-minded officials who "closely identified with the proscribed programs," abandoning the FSA's experiment in democracy proved too difficult to bear. By the end of 1943, most leading FSA agents in Washington, D.C., and across the various regional offices who supported the agency's original mandate were gone.[43] The political hostility they endured left little choice in the matter. From its inception, the FSA encountered significant opposition that constantly forced FSA officials to divide their time between politically defending their agency and actually carrying out its programs.[44] The political battle intensified in 1941 with the formation of the Joint Committee on Reduction of Nonessential Federal Expenditures, led by Harry F. Byrd, the Democratic senator from Virginia. Other than Robert M. La Follette, Jr., the progressive senator from Wisconsin, no committee member defended the FSA or Baldwin from communist charges, among other indictments. In his final report, Byrd recommended that the FSA and any other "New Deal experimentation" be abolished.[45] The agency lived on only because of its central role in coordinating the farm labor supply program necessary to meet wartime production.

Nevertheless, the attacks from the farm bloc continued with each subsequent consideration of the FSA's budget in Congress. In 1943 the combined forces of the House and Senate Appropriations Committee hearings, the work of the Cooley Committee to Investigate the Activities of the FSA, and the passage of PL 45 largely destroyed the agency. As Sidney Baldwin explains, what emerged from this battle was hardly the same organization, even if it continued to bear the same name.[46] The FSA's congressional critics made it clear that for the agency to survive in any form, C. B. Baldwin and those closest to him had to resign. The *Commercial Appeal* out of Memphis, Tennessee, captured the general sentiment among many of the FSA's opponents: the "idea" of the FSA was fine, but it had been "impregnated with ideologies and causes." If the agency continued, the editorial asserted, "it must have its top leadership overhauled [and] the Tugwells and Baldwins must be removed from positions of influence."[47] The agency's original agrarian New Dealers were considered too socially conscious, too justice-minded, and, quite notably, also too un-American to have any say in U.S. farm labor relations.

Most in Washington understood that the proposal to remove Baldwin as head of the FSA was the price the agency had to pay for congressional appropriations moving forward.[48] In a letter to President Roosevelt dated June 14, 1943, Roosevelt's administrative assistant, Jonathan Daniels, wrote:

> The move to get rid of Baldwin is an effort to remove a man who has become almost a symbol of the New Deal so far as it relates to agriculture. I am afraid that the substitution of any other man now would be a blow to the morale of many of those in the government who have been the most loyal and consistent supporters of the administration. I doubt that any appeasement of the reactionary farm bloc will work. If they "get" Baldwin first, they will get Farm Security by other means later.[49]

Despite Daniels' apprehension, which Eleanor Roosevelt shared, there was little the president could do to reverse the unfolding situation. At the end of August 1943 Baldwin officially resigned. Hewes reflects on this moment in his memoir, as follows:

> In my own mind too, there was little doubt that the game was finished; so along with several of the original group, I handed in my resignation, which was promptly accepted. . . . Several of us planned to join Baldwin on his next assignment. . . . [However,] when I left for the new job, Baldwin had already left Government service and Washington. . . . My state of mind was bad. The shock of final separation from Farm Security still numbed me.[50]

Despite the agency's reorganization under more conservative and limited terms, the FSA's congressional opponents would not rest until the FSA was no more.

The End of the Federal Camp Program, 1946

Beginning in March 1944, the Cooley Committee—or "Coolie Committee," as liberal critics called it—introduced a bill to finally abolish the FSA.[51] This bill, and a subsequent one introduced in February 1945, did not pass, mainly because Congress felt the legislation was not urgent. The agricultural establishment, even more closely aligned with banking interests by this time, felt otherwise. In April 1946 Cooley introduced a third bill, the Farmers Home Administration (FmHA) Act, which successfully terminated the FSA and created the FmHA in its place. The following year, after lengthy debate over what would happen to the FSA's projects, the labor camp program officially ended. On July 31, 1947, Congress approved PL 298, which allowed the secretary of agriculture to

> dispose of any labor supply center, labor home, labor camp or facility . . . and any equipment pertaining thereto or used in the Farm Labor Supply Program . . . for such prices and under such terms and conditions the Secretary may determine reasonable, after taking into consideration the responsibilities to be assumed by the purchaser, to any public or semipublic agency or any nonprofit association of farmers in the community who will agree to operate and maintain such facilities for the principal purpose of housing persons engaged in agricultural work and to relieve the Government of all responsibility in connection therein.[52]

Careful wording in the bill guaranteed growers, either independently or through their associations, the right to buy the camps while simultaneously denying labor and social welfare groups the opportunity to do so. This arrangement is what California's AF and other grower organizations had demanded from the start.

To be sure, not all growers favored this development. For much of the FSA's political fight, small farmers nationally defended the camp program. Members of the NFU regularly testified before Congress in the FSA's defense. After the AFBF, the NFU was the second-largest farm organization. As family farmers, they understood the threat industrial agriculture represented to their way of life. The FSA had not only defended their interests against the market forces dictated by big growers but also provided them with loans to maintain their farms during the Depression. And the camps had offered small farmers a convenient place from which to recruit a few farmworkers when necessary.[53] Members of the California Grange similarly testified that they were gravely concerned with "the moves to turn the federally-operated camps into vast company-housing schemes." As they saw it, "sooner or later, most large-scale company-housing turns out to be an instrument for supplying cheap labor. And the ultimate end of that, is the end also of the operator of the family farm."[54]

For this reason, both organizations supported a counter bill (HR 3856) introduced by Congresswoman Helen Gahagan Douglas (D-CA). The Douglas bill would have put the FSA's farm labor programs under the U.S. Department of Labor and required growers to pay prevailing wages set by the secretary of labor, provide employment for at least 75 percent of the work days in the period of employment, and provide housing and subsistence conforming to minimum standards set by the secretary.[55] Most importantly, the bill would have allowed the camps to continue running with federal funding and regulation.

Instead, as Don Mitchell shows, "By September 30, 1947, nonprofit growers associations had received control of twenty-six of the twenty-eight labor supply camps in California."[56] Under full grower management, the former FSA camps began deteriorating as rapidly as farmworkers' hope that the federal government would protect their interests. In a survey for the BAE conducted in November 1948, Carl C. Taylor, head of the Division of Farm Population and Rural Life, reported that he was "quite distressed at the changes . . . taking place." As he explained:

> The stench in some parts of [the] camps was so offensive that a
> person hated to go into them at all. Some of the families called on
> were so dirty that it was quite obvious that the group control meth-
> ods, through the camp councils, sanitation committees, etc., were
> no longer operating. Broken windows in some camps had been
> replaced by dirty blankets, odd bits of clothing and the like, indicat-
> ing that the camp administration might not be functioning. . . .

I had seen nothing like this when the government was operating the camps. The people had taken pride in their camps and particularly in their garden homes, they had felt responsibility for keeping them in good condition. Their councils and committees had in fact, been schools in responsible citizenship, order, cleanliness, and good behavior.[57]

Taylor's report was sympathetic to the hardship he witnessed among the people residing in the camps. Nevertheless, he also contributed to a familiar culture of poverty discourse by blaming migrants for their lack of "administration" of the camp and the "destructive attitude" developing among them. In this way, he supported what several camp managers had to say in defense of the pitiful situation unfolding. As one manager's assistant put it, "the fear of the government" had previously made residents respect the camp property and behave better. It was not entirely the growers' fault, in other words, that the camps were falling apart. In fact, quite ironically, some growers contended that the camps were already "very badly run down" when they took over, and they were the ones investing to fix them up.[58]

However, Taylor's report also found that all of the growers' associations running the camps had drastically cut the camps' staff and eliminated most of the services necessary to maintain them, even as they raised rents by exorbitant amounts. In most cases only two individuals operated the camps, and usually with very little oversight from the association in charge. One migrant resident who had lived in the camp for more than eight years complained, "One man cannot possibly do all of the maintenance work, and the man now in charge has completely given up trying. He spends most of his time keeping out of sight so that he won't be plagued to deal with hundreds of calls for repairs, replacements, etc. . . . [or] he spends a great deal of time on his own farm." Despite the fact that "practically nothing [was] being spent to keep the place in repair," the man noted that the grower association had raised the rental rates twice, more than doubling the cost of the apartments since government ownership. "It looks as though somebody is making a lot of money off of us," he concluded. Most tragically, however, he and other longtime residents lamented the fact that although they once believed they were going to make a "nice community out of this camp," now they realized it was becoming a place "hardly fit to live in." The sadness with which they expressed such observations left

Taylor with the impression that "the deterioration of the [camp] occupants [was] probably more significant than the destruction of the physical property."⁵⁹

Many progressives hoped to communicate this cost to wider audiences through newspaper coverage of the camps' closing shortly before PL 298 passed. In general, the stories urged public action by encouraging readers to quickly "register their opinions" with their representatives in Washington that "a serious governmental mistake [was] being made." In a series of stories for the *San Francisco News*, for example, reporter Vernon O'Reilly captured what would happen to California's migrants with the liquidation of the camps. One article titled "Lonesome Road Again?" published on June 26, 1947, featured the Garcia family (mother, father, and nine children) residing at the Woodland Farm Labor Supply Center. According to O'Reilly, the camp was "no paradise." As he explained, "It was originally built as a barracks for guayule labor" (Mexican braceros). The work involved in making it habitable for a family was challenging. "Raising a few stocks of corn, a few hills of beans and some onions, or prettying up the place a little with a few flowers requires a back-breaking struggle, but people like the Garcia's do it," O'Reilly asserted, "because they want to call the place home." Yet the Woodland camp would not serve as a "home" any longer. Consequently, O'Reilly reported, the Garcias would "have to break up the family." According to Mrs. Garcia, "she and the younger children probably will go to live with relatives in New Mexico, [while] Mr. Garcia and the oldest boy will stay in Woodland where they have work."⁶⁰

O'Reilly's article ended by discussing conditions at the camp in Yuba City, California, almost fifty miles north of Woodland. There, the resident nurse had just received her notice of termination. O'Reilly explained that the nurse would temporarily continue serving Mexican nationals, but she could only "advise" American farmworkers "from Missouri, Indiana, Montana, [and] Tennessee." In this way, he emphasized the injustice at hand, clarifying that it was native-born, and presumably white, migrant families who would face discrimination under the new law. Indeed, O'Reilly stressed how now the nurse could only tell migrant parents to take their sick child to the county hospital where they must "hope the authorities there will wink at the fact that the baby is not a resident of California, and therefore not entitled to public care." Among those soon to be left homeless and disenfranchised in the state, the article explained, "are more than 6,900 children under 16 years of age."⁶¹

To exemplify what would occur to these migrant children, O'Reilly wrote another article on migrant families in Santa Clara County, which appeared on July 7, 1947, titled "Insanitary Camps: Is This U.S. Way of Life?" In it, he described the children already living in the ditch-bank camps running "ragged and dirty, without supervision or guidance." The article was accompanied by photographs illustrating migrants' abysmal conditions. One image showed makeshift tents and dilapidated privies. Another displayed a large group of children, including toddlers, working in an apricot processing plant. The accompanying caption explained that "these children[,] . . . lacking recreational facilities, are permitted to work in an apricot processing plant to keep out of trouble while their mothers and fathers are away from home." O'Reilly hoped to alarm readers by demonstrating how the majority of migrant children old enough to work labored in the fields, with the youngest left in the care of their slightly older siblings, or wandering aimlessly in and around unsanitary camps.[62]

In Texas, camp advocates published similar appeals, hoping that the camps might somehow remain outside of growers' control. Agnes E. Meyer of the *Washington Post* also circulated a series of three articles, reprinted in the *Texas Spectator*, featuring several federal camps in the Rio Grande Valley. As the article for June 30, 1947, explained, the camps represented "more than just stop-over shacks for traveling migrants." They were "real homes," Meyer argued, where migrants had established a community and benefited from the amenities federal agents provided. For this reason, Meyer warned that unless Congress did something about it, "one of the only serious efforts ever put forth to help ease the plight of the Latin American migrant worker will be headed for the ash can." With no federal agency left in place to protect migrant workers, Meyer feared that conditions for these American families would deteriorate quickly.[63]

The Unitarian Service Committee (USC) working out of the Farm Labor Supply Centers in McAllen and Harlingen, Texas, also wrote to friendly supporters concerned about the eviction of migrant families occupying the camps. In particular, they outlined what the termination of the camp program meant for improved labor and race relations in the U.S. Southwest. The USC explained that the current camp residents were "U.S. citizens" and that the Valley Farm Bureau looking to purchase the camps was "primarily interested in using the camps as centers for alien contract labor." In 1947 the Mexican government was gradually lifting the ban on bracero labor in Texas.[64] The USC worried that there was no plan in place to relocate the evicted citizen residents or to provide them with the necessary services they received in the camps. Beginning in May 1947 the USC offered an extensive social service program for farmworker families in both camps. It included childcare, recreational activities, home demonstration workshops, vocational education, English language instruction, preventive health services, and community organization. More importantly, according to the USC, they were making significant contributions to the "sociological study" and direct improvement of "relations [between] Anglo and Latin peoples." In private hands, it was unlikely that the camps would afford domestic farmworkers the same security and opportunity to improve their socioeconomic condition and civil rights.[65]

The Camps' Historical Legacy

Despite significant protests from farmworkers' unions, social welfare organizations, and sympathetic state officials, the foreign labor importation programs dominated industrial farming by the late 1940s, as did the conservative, antilabor coalition in Congress. Subsequently, domestic farmworker families experienced a succession of "adverse effects," despite the supposed protections written into the foreign labor agreements guarding against it. In addition to a deterioration in the quality of farmworker housing available, especially for families, the effects included a dramatic drop in wages as the "prevailing wage" became the minimum that braceros, not domestics, were willing to work for. It also included domestic workers' displacement from specific jobs they had long held and a "reclassification downward to less productive work at lower wages." Additionally, domestic workers encountered frequent harassment from growers and "the weakening of organization and the use of braceros in strikes."[66]

In 1947 Ernesto Galarza, who worked endlessly to document these changes, was hired as the research and education director for the National Farm Labor Union (NFLU), affiliated with the American Federation of Labor. The NFLU formed in August 1946 out of the STFU, which realized that it needed to reorganize its strategy of helping sharecroppers and tenants now that most were migratory farmworkers. As Donald Grubbs describes it, NFLU president H. L. Mitchell essentially followed his members west to California.[67] Indeed, the union first focused its organizing drives on the Dust Bowl migrants who remained in agriculture. On October

1, 1947, the NFLU launched a strike against the DiGiorgio Fruit Company "with profound implication for our democratic way of life," according to Mitchell. DiGiorgio was the world's largest fruit-producing company based in the San Joaquin Valley. When the 130 braceros, and approximately 70 undocumented workers, refused to cross the picket line, DiGiorgio management arranged it so that a USDA representative arrived on the scene and forced the Mexican workers back to work under threat of deportation. Mitchell understood that "the use of foreign nationals as strikebreakers," despite the fact that it violated the binational labor agreement, "set a serious precedent."[68] Commercial growers could operate with immunity from state sanctions at the expense of American citizen families.

As Andrew Hazelton explains, from 1947 to 1951 growers directly recruited braceros with "minimal oversight or enforcement of the program safeguards that were part of the wartime program."[69] After 1949, this included making labor arrangements at recruitment centers closer to the border, even as both U.S. and Mexican officials knew this would fuel the problem of unauthorized entry by "wetback labor," as it was commonly termed. Throughout this time, Galarza was busy recording the damaging effect the bracero program's poor management was having on domestic labor. In one anonymous letter from Arvin, California, dated March 1950, a farmworker wrote:

> I am writing this few lines to said hello and ask you just a simply question. How could we win a strike with so many wetbacks . . . working every day while we citizens are starving[?] . . . Dear Mr. Galarza, I am one of the striker at the DiGiorgio over two years ago. I lost my friend. I spent what little money I have save, now here I am in the worse situation in my life. If this is what we call democracy I don't want any part of it; if our union don't do something for us citizen and our citizen tomorrow our childrens of today; something serious may happen.[70]

Galarza and the NFLU continued organizing on behalf of domestic farmworkers, arguing that the grower-dominated agricultural system discriminated against American farmworkers in guaranteeing (mostly on paper) guest workers entitlements that U.S. workers lacked. It was not until 1964, however, that the controversies surrounding such facts helped terminate the bracero program.

For a moment in June 1950 it appeared domestic farmworkers might again have the federal government on their side. President Truman launched a commission to investigate "the problems and conditions of migratory farmworkers both alien and domestic." The president's Commission on Migratory Labor held twelve hearings around the country examining the impact of both the Mexican and Caribbean guest worker programs. In an unprecedented decision, the commission affirmed U.S. farmworkers and their unions' claims about their displacement and the violations they witnessed in guest worker hiring. The committee's final report, issued on March 26, 1951, acknowledged that "we have used the institutions of government to procure alien labor willing to work under obsolete and backward conditions and thus to perpetuate those very conditions. This not only entrenches a bad system, it expands it."[71] Remarkably, the report also recommended that Congress extend coverage of the National Labor Relations Act of 1947 to American farmworkers. Its findings notwithstanding, the committee concluded that the guest worker programs should continue with federal oversight restored. By this time, Congress was already debating the terms of a new law to authorize the bracero program. PL 78, signed on July 12, 1951, responded to renewed grower pressure concerning labor shortages related to the Korean War. The law required growers to pay for workers' transportation and care, and the federal government would subsidize the cost of administration and compliance.[72] However, PL 78 further entrenched the exploitative farm labor system the committee uncovered.

While debating the new terms of the bracero program, Congress passed PL 475 on June 19, 1950, transferring the remaining permanent federal labor camps that were not previously sold (thirty-nine in total) from the USDA to the Federal Housing Authority (FHA). Subsequently, the FHA was to hand over the camps to local public housing administrations (PHAs) so they could "be rehabilitated and brought up to safe and sanitary standards." Indeed, the USDA granted about $2 million to the FHA for this purpose. The PHAs were then required to operate the camps as "low-rent housing for the principal purpose of housing agricultural workers . . . with rents not higher than such tenants can afford." This was not what labor and progressive groups favored, since in most rural communities the PHA was grower-controlled.[73] Yet under various county housing authorities, the camps did continue for an extended period to service farmworker families across the country, and several still operate in this form today.

For instance, in South Texas, Hidalgo County currently operates the former Weslaco camp as the Northside Apartments and the former McAllen camp as the Memorial Apartments for farmworkers.[74] In Lamesa, Texas, the Dawson County Farm Labor Association managed the old FSA camp until 1980 when Israel and Maria (Mary) Ybanez purchased it to provide low-income farmworker housing. Most of the original buildings and trees planted by the FSA in 1941 are still visible when driving along the oval road that continues to define the community. In 1991 the site was designated a historical landmark with 43 of the original 53 FSA buildings still standing.[75] In California the former Tulare (Linnell), Woodville, Arvin, and Shafter camps still operate as county-run "farm labor centers." At both Linnell and Woodville, the Tulare County Housing Authority "provide[s] classrooms for Headstart programs [and] daycare facilities . . . for children while their parents are at work."[76] Kern County operates the farm labor centers at Arvin and Shafter, with each site offering more than eighty units with two to four bedrooms. The former camp in Caldwell, Idaho, also operates as the Caldwell Housing Authority, which describes itself as "a modern town with 243 units of housing and several amenities."[77] Except for the city of "Los Ybanez," each of these sites currently operates with support from the Office of Fair Housing and Equal Opportunity established in 1968 as part of the War on Poverty.

In their oral histories and collective records, former migrants recall the camps as spaces that continued to function in an important, if conflicted, way to promote community development and self-mobilization. That is, they remained important sites for advancing their labor and civil rights struggles.[78] In June 1965, for instance, the Linnell and Woodville camps—which were grower-operated through the 1950s and county-owned by the early 1960s—became the site of an intense labor struggle over "poor management" and "unjust rent increases on [the camps'] substandard shelters." The striking Mexican American farmworkers were also protesting the fact that the Tulare County Housing Authority demanded a payment of fifty cents per month from each family for the "camp council dues." Yet the council had not been active for at least seven years. In response, the farmworkers declared, "the Councils will again act for the people," directly acknowledging the origins of the camp council model in the 1930s and 1940s.[79]

The Tulare rent strike was one of the first labor actions organized by the National Farm Workers Association (NFWA) headed by Cesar Chavez and Dolores Huerta. Incidentally, Chavez and Huerta arrived in the San Joaquin Valley in 1962 after leaving the Community Service Organization (CSO) where they were trained as organizers by Fred Ross, Sr., a former FSA camp manager. Ross managed the labor camp at Arvin from 1939 to 1941. After a brief position as an FSA regional adviser, he joined the War Relocation Authority in September 1942 to coordinate community services (based directly on his migrant camp experience) for Japanese families interned at Minidoka in Idaho. Ross would cofound the CSO, along with Antonio Rios and Edward Roybal, in 1947. In 1966 he rejoined Chavez and Huerta as a full-time organizing director for the United Farm Workers Union (UFW) where he trained thousands of farmworker activists for the next ten years. Ross's experience represents the legacy inspired by the FSA's democratic experiment.[80]

UFW members, however, did not need Ross to understand the long civil rights struggle of which they were a part. In 1965 the Tulare strikers not only recognized that they stemmed from "a long line of brave men who through the years, have sacrificed themselves so that others could live better," but they also criticized the government for acting "against the people." "The people have no voice in the government," declared one farmworker. "In this country they are supposed to have a voice."[81] Ultimately, UFW members succeeded in winning support for *la causa* because they built on a civil rights unionism with historical roots in the 1930s. They took advantage of the liberal, political climate reintroduced by the War on Poverty to demand "a voice" as citizens in a supposed democracy. They pressured the federal government to "live up to what it claims it is."[82]

The 1960 CBS News landmark documentary *Harvest of Shame* proved an important tool for mobilizing popular support for farmworkers' basic rights. In its closing scene, broadcast journalist Edward R. Murrow reminds viewers that migrant workers "do not have the strength to influence legislation. Maybe we do." Murrow describes migrant farmworkers as part of "the excluded Americans" and features their experiences as the "1960s Grapes of Wrath." In one of the documentary's most dramatic scenes, we meet a nine-year-old African American boy named Jerome. He is caring for his three infant sisters in one of the migrant shelters located at the old FSA camp in Okeechobee, Florida. The camp is in a squalid state. The scene shows Jerome nursing his badly injured foot on a bed partly eaten by rats, while flies swarm around a bowl of baked beans likely serving as their next meal. When Jerome's mother, Allean King, is asked why her children were not in a nursery school, she replies, "I don't make enough to pay for it." The film exposed how migrant farmworkers remained shockingly underpaid, undernourished, and underprotected, according to Murrow.[83]

In Texas, the Robstown camp also stood as a powerful symbol linking the camp's New Deal past to its more recent struggle for socioeconomic justice during the 1960s and 1970s. Christine Reiser Robbins and Mark W. Robbins's oral history research on the Robstown camp, collected as part of an effort to acquire a historical marker for the location, demonstrates the value of considering the camp program's history within a longer framework. After federal liquidation of the camp in 1948, the Robstown facility became low-income farmworker housing run by Nueces County. Although the camp was already in poor shape when the county acquired it, its material condition deteriorated rapidly through the 1950s and 1960s. Sam Keach and brothers Solomon and Oscar Ortiz described housing conditions during this time as "one light bulb, dirt floors, and out-houses." They also recalled the school, which notably remained open at the camp, as "uncomfortable and cold." Most of the individuals Robbins and Robbins interviewed remembered the labor camp in dual domestic and labor terms—in this case, associating the camps' deterioration with the exploitive agricultural economy in South Texas and their "lack of freedom" as workers.[84]

In 1968 South Texas emerged as an important center of political activism with locally founded national civil rights groups such as the League of United Latin American Citizens (LULAC) and the American G.I. Forum mobilizing the Mexican American community to demand their rights. Former LULAC president and lawyer Tony Bonilla situates the Robstown camp's closing within this emerging political consciousness. As Robbins and Robbins explain, in 1968 Bonilla, then chair of LULAC's civil rights committee, wrote a public letter to the Nueces County Commissioners' Court describing the camp's unfit condition with "trash accumulation, lack of maintenance, flooding, and leaking roofs." Although he proposed that LULAC help refurbish the camp, the county decided it made more economic sense to close it.

The camp was revived in other ways, however. In 1970 the American G.I. Forum leased the south end of the camp, which had housed the more permanent migrant families in the 1940s, to build a "village" of low-income housing for Robstown residents. It still operates in this capacity today. Moreover, in 1978 Solomon P. Ortiz, the first Mexican American on the county commission, helped transform the main section of the camp into a public park. Robbins and Robbins argue that today the park represents an important space of community inclusion, which counters the camp's history as a place reflecting farmworkers' structural inequality.[85] The civic engagement and collective effort Mexican Americans exercised to transform the site, and the community formation it now supports, represents exactly what FSA officials envisioned the camps' democratic experiment might produce. Although it materialized generations later, it has historical roots in the New Deal era.

Alcario Samudio, who lived at the camp in Weslaco, Texas, as a young boy, described the camp's impact on his life and activist work in these communal and progressive ways. In 1952, after spending much of his childhood traveling to Wisconsin for migrant work, he settled there and worked as a recruiter and foreman at a seed potato company. Then, in 1971, he became the state supervisor of migrant programs for Wisconsin's Bureau of Migrant and Rural Services. According to Samudio, within the first couple of years in this position, his office "closed down over five hundred migrant camps due to substandard conditions."[86] In 1977, as vice chair of the governor's Commission on Migrant Labor, he played an instrumental role in passing Wisconsin's "Migrant Labor Law," which specified certain guidelines regulating migrant farmworkers' employment and housing, including mandatory inspections and certifications of all migrant labor camps.

One year later, Samudio returned to South Texas and began working as a paralegal for the Texas Rio Grande Legal Aid (TRGLA). In this capacity, he advocated against farm labor abuses concerning migrant workers across South Texas, Louisiana, Mississippi, Alabama, Tennessee, Kentucky, and Arkansas. It would be overstating the point to claim that Samudio's career was a direct result of his early experience in the FSA's camp program. Yet Samudio acknowledged that the program left a lasting imprint, which served as a powerful reminder of the government's willingness and ability to intervene to improve migrants' welfare. Not all of his camp memories were positive, but Samudio better understood throughout his career how exceptional it was that the federal camps' afforded farmworker families certain protections, resources, and advantages. "Today," he stated, "migrant workers are still unable to secure the most basic things," including fair treatment, livable housing, health care, and a living wage.[87]

The agrarian New Dealers who envisioned the camp program's reformist objectives were also inspired by the FSA's progressive accomplishments long after the program ended. Many of them went on to have significant careers advancing social reform programs domestically and abroad. The agency's top officials offer good evidence of this, but there are ample examples among the supporting staff as well.[88] Will Alexander, who followed Rexford Tugwell as administrator, left the FSA in June 1940 after accepting a position as vice president of the Rosenwald Fund, dedicated to advancing African Americans' educational opportunities in the rural South.[89] In January 1944, when Laurence I. Hewes left the FSA, Alexander recruited him. According to Hewes's memoir, Alexander sent him to Fisk University, a historically black university in Nashville, Tennessee, to "establish a better understanding of American race relations." After his month-long study, Hewes's principal job with the fund in D.C. involved working with urban public administrators and industrial leaders seeking technical aid in reducing racial tensions. Before too long, however, he was back in San Francisco as the West Coast director for the American Council on Race Relations, which formed out of the fund. He remained in this role until 1947, addressing the problems of labor discrimination, residential segregation, and police brutality affecting blacks and Mexicans.[90] After that, Hewes, like many of his FSA colleagues, went abroad as a rural development expert and an agricultural economic adviser for the USDA and the United Nations.

After C. B. Baldwin's departure in August 1943, he accepted a position as the director of Sidney Hillman's CIO political action committee where he worked to support Henry Wallace's vice presidential nomination for the following election. He went on to manage Wallace's presidential campaign in 1948 and became the national secretary for the Progressive Party during the early 1950s. Robert "Pete" Hudgens, who became acting administrator when Baldwin left, remained with the agency until 1946—one of the only original officials to do so. Soon after he resigned, he became director of the American International Association for Economic and Social Development, which was devoted to agricultural reform in Latin America. As Sidney Baldwin writes, "For several years, Hudgens, with a number of other veterans of the FSA, found great satisfaction in applying the methods of the FSA in Venezuela and other Latin American countries."[91] Indeed, several scholars have written important histories detailing how much of the ideological foundation of the agrarian New Deal, especially its community planning principles, lived abroad after the 1940s and returned home during the War on Poverty.[92]

The activities of the División de Educación de la Comunidad (DivEdCo), a government program that existed in Puerto Rico from 1949 to 1991, offer a useful example of how the FSA's community efforts and democratic intentions endured in other forms through the postwar period. DivEdCo was an agency under the Department of Education modeled directly after the FSA that sought to carry out a similar experiment in socioeconomic reform, mainly through cultural and artistic enterprises, among Puerto Rican rural families. In creating DivEdCo, Luis Muñoz Marín, Puerto Rico's first elected governor, drew heavily on his knowledge of the New Deal and his close relationship with Tugwell, who served as Puerto Rico's appointed governor from 1942 to 1946. Other central figures in the FSA, including photographers Edwin Rosskam and Jack Delano, also played a pivotal role in DivEdCo's administration.[93]

According to Muñoz, DivEdCo would teach the Puerto Rican community "the way of making use of their own aptitudes for the solution of many of their own problems of health, education, cooperation, [and] social life through the action of the community itself."[94] DivEdCo promoted the ideological basis of the Popular Democratic Party (PPD), the new commonwealth administration. Through a series of educational workshops, short films, booklets, posters, poems, and musical recordings, for instance, DivEdCo agents sought to instruct rural populations on how best to adapt to the changes brought on by industrialization and modernization and become a model democratic and participatory citizenry. The agency was a part of the broader efforts supporting Operation Bootstrap, a political program to modernize and industrialize the Puerto Rican economy.[95] The subject of DivEdCo's initiatives included "the self-management of health, nutrition, and family planning as well as self-reliance, and education."[96] In transforming people's customs, values, culture, and civic identity to better meet the ideals of the developing state, DivEdCo represented a key battleground between Puerto Ricans' desire to maintain a traditional sense of self and the intense process of Americanization imposed by U.S. imperialist forces.

The FSA's congressional fight weakened the agency and increasingly compromised its legitimacy in the shifting political climate that formed between 1935 and 1946. In response to the constant hostility they encountered, FSA officials deliberately molded their purpose and programs to more deliberately serve growers' interests and the nation's priorities in agricultural production. They did this mostly out of necessity, realizing that in order to save the FSA from further financial cuts and possible elimination, Congress needed to see the agency's contributions to efficient labor mobilization, not costly social experimentation. The FSA's willingness to refashion itself as a labor regulator and supplier not only saved the agency but also enabled it to expand its influence by building the camp program nationally. As the camp program developed in the early 1940s, it reached a greater number of farmworker families who had long labored as migrants and were routinely denied basic labor protections and civic entitlements based on their race and class status.

Consequently, the great irony in the FSA's political strength as the agency best suited to coordinate the nation's farm labor needs during wartime is that it allowed the FSA more resources from which to serve needy and forgotten farmworkers, even as it sowed the seeds to undermine their continued security. Beginning in 1942, FSA officials were forced to launch and manage the Emergency Farm Labor Supply Program, which involved the recruitment and importation of thousands of foreign guest workers. In the process, FSA officials did their best to protect domestic migrant families from the adverse effects that would likely arise. Yet by 1943 the agency lost considerable authority to manage farm labor conditions when it was transferred to the Office of Labor and the WFA. In camps across the country the FSA continued to aid domestic farmworkers providing important welfare services, such as medical care. Over time, however, the camps' bureaucratic shift to the WFA manifested itself in significant ideological and material ways. The camps increasingly became spaces from which to maximize farmworkers' productive power with minimal care for workers' social welfare.

Hewes captured the tragedy in the camp's progression when he published his memoir in 1957. As he observed:

In the thirties, when I was a young man, there was much sympathy for the migratory agricultural workers. But last winter in the cotton-field section of the San Joaquin, when I saw the wretched squalor and despair of one of our old migrant camps, I was sorry we had ever built them. And only a week or two ago an overloaded truck turned over. It was hauling Mexican beetfield workers and their families from Texas to Worland, Wyoming. The highway was a shambles of bloody broken bodies, according to the newspapers.

And who was to blame? . . . A Governor swore it was Federal responsibility and the Federal people said they were powerless. But the real
trouble was that no one really cared.[97]

Hewes's reflection expressed the loss many of the FSA's progressive New
Dealers felt in witnessing the agency's political transformation during the
1940s. In the face of constant conservative congressional pressure, budgetary reductions, organizational realignments, and wartime demands, the
agency was forced to concede its vision for democratizing rural America.
Although they had achieved remarkable improvements in migrants' daily
lives by providing farmworkers the economic resources and sociopolitical
opportunities they needed to contest their exploitation, there was no doubt
that they had left farmworkers in a precarious condition with few (if any)
federal allies to defend their interests. Although many FSA officials went on
to continue fighting to expand the nation's democratic ideals, in the immediate decade they largely abandoned the cause of American farmworkers.

Of course, migrant families had no choice but to keep fighting to
improve their labor and civil rights. While the FSA's retreat weakened their
power to collectively bargain against employers, farmworkers were more
accustomed to organizing without government support than with it. In the
1960s several events materialized to aid their struggle—namely, the end of
the bracero program, the rise of the civil rights movement, and the resur-
gence of the welfare state. Farmworker families residing in former FSA
camps called on their long history and demanded their rights.

Epilogue

On the surface Farm Security makes loans to small farmers—
owners, tenants, and workers—who cannot get fair credit
elsewhere. But it means much more than that. It signifies
democracy's faith in the ability of its humblest citizens to regain
their lost social status, to become part of the nation, to walk with
heads erect as free men.
  —"Pillar of Democracy," *Commonweal*, December 17, 1943

The FSA's farm labor camp program was more than just a short-term solution to the chronic problem of rural poverty and the farm displacement caused by the Great Depression. It was also more than just a rare example of the New Deal's approach to economic recovery and reform. For the FSA's progressive officials, the program was part of a social reform movement intent on pushing the limits of U.S. democracy in more expansive, inclusive, and participatory terms. Against seemingly insurmountable odds—especially the racist and classist structure of white supremacy delimiting New Deal policies, and the rise of corporate agriculture and its solidifying political influence—the FSA succeeded in advancing its experiment in democracy and improving migrant farmworkers' everyday lives. In the camps, tens of thousands of diverse migrant farmworker families across the country experienced a sense of security, stability, and promise they had rarely encountered because of the FSA's willingness to intervene on their behalf. As the epigraph above suggests, the FSA helped migrant farmworkers trapped in a condition of statelessness—what Carey McWilliams described in terms of their status as "alien Americans" and "federal homeless"—regain their social worth, self-determination, and full citizenship.[1] In the process, FSA officials forced U.S. society to see migrant farmworkers beyond their economic value.

The FSA's commitment to establish farmworkers' democratic rights was extraordinary, particularly in its disruption of the status quo. Against the forces deliberately excluding farmworkers from key labor and social welfare provisions under the New Deal, FSA officials defended migrant farmworkers' entitlement to full political and social participation in the United States. Their devotion to a more inclusive democratizing project is reflected in an article Rexford Tugwell wrote for the *New York Times* on January 10, 1937, on retiring from the Resettlement Administration. Although referring specifically to the New Deal's approach to farm tenancy, the claim he made captured the attitude many of his colleagues embraced in the FSA. As Tugwell contended, "If we have no intention of attacking poverty at its source . . . the administration ought not to have credit for helping really forgotten families: only for doing what democracies have usually done—help those who needed help less because those who needed it more did not count politically."[2] The FSA's camp program was built on the premise that migrant farmworkers, in their very dislocation physically and politically, exposed the contradiction of equality and opportunity rooted in the nation's democratic ideals. To participate as full citizens, FSA administrators argued, migrant farmworkers required a modicum of security against their exploitive bosses and the discriminatory local officials who set structural barriers preventing them from acting as contributing members of society.

To this end, the camp program provided farmworker families with more than just immediate economic relief. As dual-purpose domestic and labor spaces, the camps also granted migrants safe housing, a steady diet, modern medical care, educational opportunities, and social outlets in the form of dances and organized sports. Moreover, the program encouraged migrants' collectivization and broader political awareness in the form of camp councils and committees, and by supporting farmworkers' community and labor organization. The social activities and lessons in self-government were intended to model the FSA reformers' visions of a more expansive, participatory democracy. In these spaces the FSA taught migrants that civic membership and responsibility came in the form of everyday action, not simply through electoral power. The FSA insisted that through migrants' participation as invested members of their community, school, union, and church, for example, they were important political actors who determined how institutions operated. By seeking to enfranchise farmworkers in this way, the FSA pushed the possibilities of New Deal liberalism beyond what many wanted or considered possible.

Migrants embraced the FSA's program, not as destitute, dependent, or "abstract citizens" devoid of political identity but as mindful actors determining what would most benefit their family's welfare.[3] To be sure, many arrived at the federal camps in a desperate condition—some having lost their former way of life as farmers, others evicted from grower-owned housing, and most deeply malnourished, exhausted, and poor from constant movement. Yet they made a decision to enter the camps, which others avoided, understanding that it required them to relinquish some autonomy they maintained outside of the government's direct influence. For as much as the FSA sought to stabilize and empower migrants, it did require that they subject themselves to the program's conceptions regarding appropriate domestic, economic, cultural, and political behavior. Most camp managers tried to work with migrant families to determine their needs, but the camp staff occasionally behaved as experts who knew what was best for the purportedly ignorant people they served.

As migrants participated in the camp program and engaged the state's plan for their rehabilitation, they challenged how the FSA positioned their status as different racialized minorities, exploited workers, and disenfranchised citizens. Embracing the FSA's notion of participatory citizenship meant abiding by its moralist, nationalist, and assimilationist discourse. Many migrants were disposed to do this because they wanted to achieve the democratic inclusion FSA reformers envisioned, and because they saw themselves as members of the national polity who should have equal access to public services and civil rights as Americans. Yet at different times, migrants also articulated alternative versions of U.S. citizenship that reshaped the camp program's democratic intentions and outcomes. Most notably, migrant families, especially those that had long followed the crops, forced FSA officials to recognize that they were part of well-established social and political regional communities that existed locally, in movement, and transnationally. FSA officials began to understand how as migrants they navigated their status as noncitizens and claimed community belonging in their own terms.

While undoubtedly the FSA's camp program brought meaningful improvements to migrant farmworkers' daily lives, expanded their labor and civil rights, and made them visible beyond their role as temporary workers, as a social democratic movement the program was imperfect. The program's shortcomings are most evident when analyzing how FSA officials responded to farmworkers with varied experiences of racialization and legal status as citizens, and with distinct civil rights struggles rooted in specific histories of exclusion. Although farmworkers residing in the camps encompassed, among other groups, white "Dust Bowl refugees," Mexican and black "habitual laborers," Japanese American "evacuees" and "enemy aliens," and Filipino former "U.S. nationals," the FSA's liberal democratic script universalized their access to citizenship and equal representation. As Lisa Lowe explains, the narrative of "political emancipation through citizenship . . . requires the negation of a history of social relations that publicly racialized groups and successively constituted those groups as 'nonwhites ineligible for citizenship.'"[4] More specifically, it requires that noncitizen men and women ignore how civic membership and political democracy were constructed through a framework of white supremacy. The FSA's limitation was not that its officials disavowed the differences existing among the farmworkers they served; in fact, they often reinforced these differences through segregated practices and racist discourses concerning migrants' behavior. Rather, despite knowing how migrants experienced different forms of disenfranchisement, the FSA's democratic script promised all farmworkers equal opportunity.

A key factor underlying the FSA's political contradictions stems from the challenge its reformist officials faced in managing the camp program to promote migrants' economic democracy at the height of capitalist agriculture's expansion. From its inception, the program was forced to operate in the interest of agricultural production in order to legitimize its unprecedented social welfare intervention. Although many of the FSA's agrarian reformers recognized the exploitative structure sustaining industrial agriculture's growth, they knew their agency was not politically strong enough to reverse its course. And certainly, many did not see factory farming as the problem—as federal bureaucrats, they often spoke positively of its modern, efficient, and productive benefits. For these reasons, the FSA's New Dealers focused instead on reforming migrant farmworkers. They argued that the only way migrants would ever see an improvement in wages, living conditions, and access to public aid would be by strengthening their political voice. Accordingly, FSA officials insisted that farmworkers needed federal protection under the National Labor Relations Act (NLRA) and the Fair Labor Standards Act (FLSA), among other New Deal policies, if they were ever truly to stabilize their situation and achieve full citizenship.

After 1942, however, rather than seeing their labor rights improved, domestic migrant workers watched their condition worsen with the arrival of foreign farmworkers the FSA recruited. FSA officials lamented this fact and worked as best they could to contest the guest worker programs' adverse effects. Yet they became increasingly compelled to accommodate growers' labor supply (and control) demands, especially after the farm bloc succeeded in transferring the FSA to the more conservative WFA in 1943. At this point, the FSA lost much of its radical potential to advance farm-workers' democratic power. By 1946 the FSA's grower opponents and their allies in Congress succeeded in terminating what was left of the reformist agency. Without any meaningful federal regulation, the abusive and exploitative aspects of the industrial agricultural system hardened in the postwar period. It increasingly favored flexible, powerless, and disposable workers. The system centered ever more on extracting farm labor produc-tivity without any of the costs of farmworkers' social reproduction.

Although the FSA failed both in its fight to maintain the camp program as a site of farmworker empowerment and in its struggle for political sur-vival, its democratic experiment was not hollow. In addition to the essential amenities the agency afforded migrant families, the FSA challenged the dominant view in agriculture and U.S. society that farmworkers were not entitled to basic rights or equal protection under the law—including sani-tary and affordable housing, medical care, quality education, and fair labor standards. The FSA's efforts to grant farmworkers expanded rights is espe-cially important considering that the discriminatory intent codified in New Deal federal policies guaranteeing workers' rights continues to allow for well-known abuses in farm labor today. Farmworkers labor under some of the worst conditions imaginable—in jobs that are increasingly dangerous, poorly paid, and inhumane. Because farmworkers are still excluded from the NLRA, they cannot organize in most U.S. states without retaliation or discrimination. Yet even without federal backing, migrant farmworkers continue to exert collective action that defies their appellation as cheap, tractable labor. Recent actions by the United Farm Workers, Farm Labor Organizing Committee, Coalition of Immokalee Workers, Pineros y Camp-esinos Unidos del Noroeste, and Migrant Justice offer strong evidence of their continued activism. In their struggle, farmworker families force us as consumers and beneficiaries of their labor to see them beyond their eco-nomic value.

In upstate New York, where I live, the dairy industry has exploded in the last two decades following a national trend. Recently, a report by the Workers' Center of Central New York and the Worker Justice Center of

New York revealed that New York ranks third nationally in terms of the number of dairy farms. In the upstate region, milk sales represent 50 percent of total agricultural sales, generating about $14 billion a year, with milk production increasingly concentrated among fewer and larger farms.[5] About 70 percent of the dairy farms in New York operate with a majority Latino/a immigrant workforce (accounting for anywhere from 50 to 100 percent of the employees).[6] Dairy work is grueling—it is 24/7, year-round, dirty, and dangerous. Accordingly, most of the workers I have met as part of the Cornell Farmworker Program feel proud of the work they perform. They know they are integral to the economy, and they view their work as highly skilled. While workplace grievances account for much of their discontent, a matter of greater concern for many dairy workers involves their compromised quality of life.[7]

Under a boldly anti-immigrant federal administration that has only intensified the punitive forces of noncitizenship, many dairy workers describe feeling "locked up" and hidden away on farms. The day-in, day-out work often adds up to seventy-two-hour work weeks, which leaves most exhausted and with little time for a social life. Even if they did have time to head into town, the cost of a *raitero* willing to drive them averages about forty to fifty dollars per person.[8] One worker explained, "My daughter was born in the back of a car because we spent so much time debating going to a hospital."[9] The worker described how he and his wife did not know if they would receive help due to their unauthorized status. Other workers lament wanting to support their children in school by attending sporting events or parent-teacher conferences but feeling too afraid to expose themselves to possible deportation and long-term separation from their children. My intention in highlighting the suffering dairy workers in my community experience is not to suggest that they are helpless victims—they are most definitely not. Rather, I want to demonstrate how they struggle for basic human rights that should be available to any worker in a so-called democratic society.

In establishing the federal labor camps, FSA officials recognized that they would only ever reach a small fraction of the migrant population that needed aid. Because of the program's limited potential, they touted the camps as "models" of what could be done. As Carey McWilliams aptly noted in 1939, the camps were never meant to be solutions to the farm labor problem but were merely "demonstrations of what might be accomplished." In other words, they were valuable "prefigurations," as Michael

Denning has argued, of the future social democratic order McWilliams and most FSA leaders envisioned.[10] So what do they teach us? What can they help us imagine? In the contemporary context, it may appear we have no hope for a federally funded migrant camp program of this nature. In today's repressive state environment, it seems unlikely the federal government would intervene to advance marginalized workers' and noncitizens' labor and civil rights, especially against corporate interests. Still, can the FSA and migrant farmworker families' experiment in democracy help us envision an alternative way for current migrants to articulate political power, self-determination, and civic participation beyond their status as laborers?

The possibilities for migrant empowerment and inclusion have greater implications beyond the U.S. context. The numbers of refugees, asylum seekers, and internally displaced and stateless persons continues to rise globally as a result of persecution, war, imperialism, violence, economic despair, and environmental destruction. In 2018 the United Nations High Commissioner for Refugees estimated that by the end of the year, 70.8 million people worldwide had been forced to flee their homes.[11] First-asylum countries have responded to persons seeking refuge from the Middle East, South Asia, Africa, and Latin and Central America by, among other things, building "temporary" encampments that offer minimal services and developing resettlement strategies involving "guest worker" arrangements that are most often highly exploitive and sometimes coercive.[12] Both solutions exemplify a nonintegrative approach to "welcoming" refugees and other displaced people. These approaches most often ensure that migrants remain vulnerable and disenfranchised in a liminal condition of citizenship, despite their immediate economic and social contributions to the communities they inhabit in diaspora.

The United Kingdom and the United States claim to represent a liberal approach to the growing crisis of human displacement. Nevertheless, they have responded to the arrival of refugees at their borders with very aggressive nationalist claims concerning security, expressed in broad economic, social, and political terms. In 2015, for example, British prime minister David Cameron referred to Syrian refugees as "swarms" trying to "break into [the] country." Concurrently, his foreign secretary, Philip Hammond, warned of "marauding" African migrants. More recently, Theresa May has talked about asylum seekers as "foreign criminals" and sent vans painted with the words "go home" into communities with high levels of immigrants.[13] In the United States, President Donald Trump responded similarly in October 2018 to a mostly Central American caravan of roughly 3,500 migrants seeking asylum. Trump assigned approximately 5,200 military troops to help U.S. immigration officers patrol the U.S.-Mexico border and threatened to "close the whole thing!" if necessary, to keep the refugees out. The U.S. president also repeatedly posted inflammatory remarks concerning the asylum seekers on social media, including one claiming that they "can't be serious if they're waving flags from their home countries" and calling their plea for refuge a "BIG CON."[14] Far from offering the world's refugees a "safe haven," these influential global leaders have mounted public hostility and intolerance against them. This is not a situation we can ignore.

The FSA experiment in democracy that progressives and migrant farmworkers aimed to realize was a response to the intense dislocation rural Americans experienced as a result of economic depression, capitalist agriculture, and long-standing political disempowerment. Although it was limited in significant ways, the experiment is instructive and offers an important precedent for those seeking to advance migrants' basic rights and privileges today. Through the camp program, FSA officials sought to include migrant farmworkers who "did not count politically" in the national polity, even as some remained tied to their distant homelands. The leaders of the FSA believed migrants should have the right "to walk with heads erect as free men," and they argued that a nation with a large disenfranchised community did not represent a true democracy. Moreover, their efforts sought to restore the human dignity migrant families lost in their displacement by considering migrants as contributors beyond their economic potential. There is a real capacity to build on this experiment. As communities of workers, immigrants, refugees, and others committed to social justice unite to establish a stronger social democracy in today's world, they carry this history forward.

Location of Farm Security Administration Migratory Farm Labor Camps (July 1942)

Information concerning camp locations appears here as it was reported by the FSA for this month. As a result, some variations may occur concerning the position of mobile facilities at different times in the year depending on harvesting seasons.

Region I

Maryland

(Mobile Camps)

Hebron
Pocomoke City
Vienna
Westover

New Jersey

(Mobile Camps)

Big Oak
Burlington
Swedesboro

Region IV

North Carolina

(Mobile Camps)

Currituck
Hermitage

Virginia

(Mobile Camps)

Black Bay
Great Bridge
Lynnhaven
Timberville

Region V

Florida "(N) denotes Negro Camp"

Everglades (N)	S Canal Point, State Highway 143
Okeechobee (N)	(Belle Glade, Unit 2, Negro) 3.7 mi. S Belle Glade, State Highway 25
Osceola	(Belle Glade, Unit 1, White) ¼ mi. E Chosen on county road NE Belle Glade, and ¾ mi. from State Highway 143 N Belle Glade
Pahokee	SE Canal Point, State Highway 194
Pompano (N)	NW Pompano, U.S. Highway 1

Region VI

Arkansas

Springdale	off U.S. Highway 540

Region VIII

Texas

Crystal City	N Crystal City, U.S. Highway 83

Harlingen	S Harlingen, U.S. Highway 83
Lamesa	off U.S. Highway 87
McAllen	NE McAllen, U.S. Highway 83
Princeton	SE McKinney, State Highway 24
Raymondville	2 mi. W Raymondville, U.S. Highway 96
Robstown	2 mi. N Robstown, State Highway 44
Sinton	¼ mi. W Sinton, State Highway 44
Weslaco	at N end of town of Weslaco

Region IX

Arizona

Agua Fria	16 mi. W Phoenix, State Highway 77
Eleven Mile Corner	3½ mi. E Casa Grande and ½ mi. N of State Highway 84
Yuma	12 mi. SW Yuma

(Mobile Camps)

Friendly Corners
Gilbert

California

Arvin	17 mi. SE Bakersfield, U.S. Highway 99 // In Kern Co. about 10 mi. South and 7 mi. East of Bakersfield.
Brawley	at N end of town of Brawley // In Imperial Co.
Ceres	at NW end of town of Ceres, 3 mi. SE Modesto, U.S. Highway 99 in Stanislaus Co. North City Limits of Ceres
Firebaugh	at N end of town of Firebaugh
Gridley	3 mi. E Gridley in Butte Co. out of Gridley West Bank Feather River
Indio	1 mi. SE Indio, U.S. Highway 99 in Riverside Co. ½ mi. southeast of Indio
Mineral King	43 mi. S Fresno on U.S. Highway 99, left on State Highway 198, 3 mi. E Visalia
Shafter	1½ mi. NW Shafter and 19 mi. NW Bakersfield

Thornton	at S end of town of Thornton in San Joaquin Co. South City Limits of Thornton
Tulare	4 mi. SE Visalia, State Highway 198 in Tulare Co. 4 miles East and 1 mile South of Visalia
Westley	at W end of town of Westley in Stanislaus Co. ½ mi. Southwest of Westley
Windsor	1 mi. W Windsor in Sonoma Co. 1 mi. West of Town of Windsor
Winters	1 mi. NE Winters in Yolo Co. out of Winters on Davis Highway
Woodville	7 mi. NW Porterville, State Highway 190 in Tulare Co. near Poplar Southeast of Woodville
Yuba City	1 mi. SE Yuba City in Sutter Co. ½ mi. South and East of Yuba City

(Mobile Camps)

Brentwood
Cupertino
San Jacinto
Santa Maria
Sebastopol

Region X

Colorado

Fort Lupton

Region XI

Idaho

Caldwell	2 mi. W Caldwell, junction Highways 18 and 20
Twin Falls	2 mi. S Twin Falls, Highway 26

(Mobile Camps)

Blackfoot
Donnelly

Emmett
Jerome
Marsing
Nampa
Payette-Ontario
Pocatello
Rupert
Shelley
Sugar City
Wilder

Oregon

Yamhill   4 mi. S Dayton, Highway 223 (Dayton-Amity
                 cutoff)

(Mobile Camps)

Athena
Brewster
The Dalles
Coburg
Gresham
Nyssa
West Stayton

Washington

Granger   2 mi. NW Granger, U.S. Highway 410
Walla Walla   5 mi. SW Walla Walla, Oregon State Highway 11
                 (1 mi. N Oreg. Line)
Yakima   2 mi. W Union Gap on Ahtanum Road, U.S.
                 Highway 410

(Mobile Camps)

Auburn
Burlington
Dayton
Dixie
Kennewick
Wapato

Other States the Mobile Camps Would Have Served in 1942 (in other months)

Connecticut
Michigan
New Mexico

FSA Proposed Camp Construction for Fiscal Year 1940–41

Michigan	2 permanent camps, one for African American migrants (near Sodus), one for white migrants (in Riverside)
New Mexico	2 permanent camps
New Jersey	2 permanent camps
Arkansas	1 permanent camp (in Springdale)
Waco, Texas	1 permanent camp
Palisade, Colorado	1 permanent camp
Atlantic Seaboard	additional mobile camps to serve Florida, South Carolina, North Carolina, Virginia, and Maryland
Mississippi Valley	mobile camps to serve Louisiana, Arkansas, Tennessee, and Kentucky

Source: Farm Security Administration, "Camp Occupancy Report," box 19, folder AD-124 All Regs. 183 Migratory Labor Social Security Tables on Interstate Migrants 1937, FmHA, Record Group 96, National Archive at College Park, Md. (NACP). See also "Location of Migratory Farm Workers Camps," box 8, folder AD-124 Migratory Labor All Regs. Eastern Seaboard Report, FmHA, RG 96, NACP.

NOTES

Introduction

1. "A Petition and Explanation of Reason for a STAY of Execution on Certain Orders of this U.S.D.A. Camp of Recent Date," July 2, 1941, box 486, file TX-35-912-035, Records of the Farmers Home Administration (FmHA), Record Group (RG) 96, National Archives at College Park, Md. (NACP).

2. FSA Acting Director of Resettlement Division to C. M. Evans, Regional Director, August 7, 1941, Weslaco Files, FmHA, RG 96, National Archives at Fort Worth, Tex. (NAFW).

3. "A Program for the South," by Dr. W. W. Alexander, Farm Security Administrator, January 25, 1940, box C-R 1, ctn. 9, file Sharecroppers 1938–42, folder 8, 1940–42, Ralph W. Hollenberg Collection of Materials Relating to the Farm Security Administration (hereafter Hollenberg Collection), Region IX, San Francisco, Calif., Bancroft Library, University of California, Berkeley (BANC).

4. Carey McWilliams, "Americans Without a Country," *Nation* 153, no. 11 (1941): 420–22; Carey McWilliams, *Ill Fares the Land: Migrants and Migratory Labor in the United States* (Boston: Little, Brown, 1942), 343.

5. This is what historian David Gutiérrez refers to as "the politics of the interstices." Gutiérrez defines these politics as "the way in which individuals caught up in various diasporas have tried to negotiate the difficult transition between different formal systems of membership by devising conceptual frameworks that allow them both to describe their situation and to make rights claims despite their tenuous and ever-changing social circumstances." David G. Gutiérrez, "The Politics of the Interstices: Reflections on Citizenship and Non-Citizenship at the Turn of the Twentieth Century," *Race/Ethnicity: Multidisciplinary Global Contexts* 1, no. 1 (2007): 89–120. In this reasoning, I have also relied on Luisa Moreno, "Non-Citizen Americans of the Southwest," in David Gutiérrez, ed., *Between Two Worlds: Mexican Immigrants in the United States* (Wilmington, Del.: Scholarly Resources, 1996); Lisa Lowe, *Immigrant Acts: On Asian American Cultural Politics* (Durham, N.C.: Duke University Press, 1996); Mae M. Ngai, *Impossible Subjects: Illegal Aliens and the Making of Modern America* (Princeton, N.J.: Princeton University Press, 2004); Alicia R. Schmidt Camacho, *Migrant Imaginaries: Latino Cultural Politics in the U.S.-Mexico Borderlands* (New York: New York University Press, 2008); and the various essays in Rachel Buff, ed., *Immigrant Rights in the Shadows of Citizenship* (New York: New York University Press, 2008).

6. "The Fifth Migration," by Dr. George Gleason, *Report Submitted to Select Committee to Investigate the Interstate Migration of Destitute Citizens, Hearings Before the Select Committee*

to Investigate the Interstate Migration of Destitute Citizens, 76th Cong., 3d Sess., 1940–41, Part 7 (Washington, D.C.: Government Printing Office, 1941), 2998. These were known as the Tolan Hearings.

7. See, for example, Thomas G. Moore, FSA regional supervisor, as quoted in Michael R. Grey, *New Deal Medicine: The Rural Health Programs of the Farm Security Administration* (Baltimore: Johns Hopkins University Press, 1999), 174; John Steinbeck, *Their Blood Is Strong* (San Francisco: Simon J. Lubin Society of California, 1938), 16.

8. Jacquelyn Dowd Hall, "The Long Civil Rights Movement and the Political Uses of the Past," *Journal of American History* 91, no. 4 (2005): 1233–63. On the New Deal origins of the black civil rights movement, see Harvard Sitkoff, *A New Deal for Blacks: The Emergence of Civil Rights as a National Issue* (New York: Oxford University Press, 1981); Robert Korstad and Nelson Lichtenstein, "Opportunities Found and Lost: Labor, Radicals, and the Early Civil Rights Movement," *Journal of American History* 75, no. 3 (December 1988): 786–811.

9. On the RA's origins in the South, see Sitkoff, *New Deal for Blacks*; Patricia Sullivan, *Days of Hope: Race and Democracy in the New Deal Era* (Chapel Hill: University of North Carolina Press, 1996); Jarod Roll, *Spirit of Rebellion: Labor and Religion in the New Cotton South* (Urbana: University of Illinois Press, 2010); Ira Katznelson, *Fear Itself: The New Deal and the Origins of Our Time*, 1st ed. (New York: Liveright, 2013); Charles Kenneth Roberts, *The Farm Security Administration and Rural Rehabilitation in the South* (Knoxville: University of Tennessee Press, 2015).

10. John Steinbeck, *The Harvest Gypsies: On the Road to the Grapes of Wrath* (Berkeley: Heyday Books, 1988), x.

11. I use the ethnoracial terms "Mexican," "Filipino," and sometimes "Japanese" when referring to migrants with personal or family origins in Mexico, the Philippines, and Japan because it corresponds to prevalent use at the time. I am careful, however, to differentiate between U.S.-born citizens, longtime residents, and foreign-born persons when a distinction is possible and necessary. According to the FSA, noncitizens were eligible to receive the privileges of camp occupancy, but many likely avoided the camps out of fear of deportation.

12. Katznelson, *Fear Itself*; Juan Perea, "The Echoes of Slavery: Recognizing the Racist Origins of the Agricultural and Domestic Worker Exclusion from the National Labor Relations Act," *Ohio State Law Journal* 72, no. 1 (January 1, 2011): 95–138.

13. Steinbeck, *Harvest Gypsies*, 22, 56.

14. Sidney Baldwin, *Poverty and Politics: The Rise and Decline of the Farm Security Administration* (Chapel Hill: University of North Carolina Press, 1968), 158; Jess C. Gilbert, *Planning Democracy: Agrarian Intellectuals and the Intended New Deal* (New Haven, Conn.: Yale University Press, 2015), 88, 91–93.

15. Studies in agrarian New Deal history that consider the FSA's democratic intentions, particularly through rural community development, include Donald Holley, *Uncle Sam's Farmers: The New Deal Communities in the Lower Mississippi Valley* (Urbana: University of Illinois Press, 1975); Paul Keith Conkin, *Tomorrow a New World: The New Deal Community Program* (New York: Da Capo Press, 1976); Brian Q. Cannon, *Remaking the Agrarian Dream: New Deal Rural Resettlement in the Mountain West* (Albuquerque: University of New Mexico Press, 1996); Michael Johnston Grant, *Down and Out on the Family Farm: Rural Rehabilitation in the Great Plains, 1929–1945* (Lincoln: University of Nebraska Press, 2002); Sarah T. Phillips,

This Land, This Nation: Conservation, Rural America, and the New Deal (New York: Cambridge University Press, 2007); Roll, *Spirit of Rebellion*; Jason Manthorne, "As You Sow: Culture, Agriculture, and the New Deal" (PhD diss., University of Georgia, 2013); Gilbert, *Planning Democracy*; Roberts, *Farm Security Administration*.

16. Gilbert, *Planning Democracy*, xiv.

17. John W. Jeffries, "A 'Third New Deal'? Liberal Policy and the American State, 1937–1945," *Journal of Policy History* 8, no. 4 (January 1, 1996): 405.

18. Alan Brinkley, *The End of Reform: New Deal Liberalism in Recession and War* (New York: Alfred A. Knopf, 1996), 3–4, 8; Otis Graham, Jr., "Franklin D. Roosevelt and the Intended New Deal," in Thomas E. Cronin and Michael R. Beschloss, eds., *Essays in Honor of James MacGregor Burns* (Englewood Cliffs, N.J.: Prentice Hall, 1989).

19. Brinkley, *End of Reform*, 8–11, 164–66. See also James Patterson, "The Rise of Rights and Rights Consciousness in American Politics, 1930s–1970s," in Anthony J. Badger and Byron E. Shafer, eds., *Contesting Democracy: Substance and Structure in American Political History, 1775–2000* (Lawrence: University Press of Kansas, 2001); Roger Biles, *The South and the New Deal* (Lexington: University Press of Kentucky, 1994).

20. "FSA Migratory Camp Population Reports and Employment and Earnings of Families Living in FSA Camps," box 19, file AD 124 All Regs. 183 Migratory Labor Social Security Tables on Interstate Migrants 1937, FmHA, RG 96, NACP; U.S. House of Representatives, *Select Committee of the House Committee on Agriculture, to Investigate the Activities of the Farm Security Administration, Part 3, 78th Cong., 2nd sess., 1944* (Washington, D.C.: Government Printing Office, 1943–44), 1164–67.

21. Don Mitchell, *They Saved the Crops: Labor, Landscape, and the Struggle over Industrial Farming in Bracero-Era California* (Athens: University of Georgia Press, 2012), 59, 113; Cindy Hahamovitch, *The Fruits of Their Labor: Atlantic Coast Farmworkers and the Making of Migrant Poverty, 1870–1945* (Chapel Hill: University of North Carolina Press, 1997), 167. Additional studies that explore the FSA's camp program in some detail, yet through a mostly labor-control perspective, include Baldwin, *Poverty and Politics*; Linda C. Majka and Theo J. Majka, *Farm Workers, Agribusiness, and the State* (Philadelphia: Temple University Press, 1982); Don Mitchell, "La Casa de Esclavos Modernos: Exposing the Architecture of Exploitation," *Journal of the Society of Architectural Historians* 71, no. 4 (December 1, 2012): 451–61.

22. On the marginalization of women's interests during the New Deal, see Linda Gordon, *Pitied but not Entitled: Single Mothers and the History of Welfare, 1890–1935* (New York: Free Press, 1994); Suzanne Mettler, *Dividing Citizens: Gender and Federalism in New Deal Public Policy* (Ithaca, N.Y.: Cornell University Press, 1998); Alice Kessler-Harris, "In the Nation's Image: The Gendered Limits of Social Citizenship in the Depression Era," *Journal of American History* 86, no. 3 (December 1999): 1251–79. On the problem of a dual-systems approach to the study of class and gender, see Ava Baron, "Gender and Labor History: Learning from the Past, Looking to the Future," in *Work Engendered: Toward a New History of American Labor* (Ithaca, N.Y.: Cornell University Press, 1991), 1–46; Joan Wallach Scott, *Gender and the Politics of History* (New York: Colombia University Press, 1988); Gay L. Gullikson, "New Labor History from the Perspective of a Women's Historian," in Lenard R. Berlanstein, ed., *Rethinking Labor History: Essays on Discourse and Class Analysis* (Urbana: University of Illinois Press, 1993), 200–214; Alice Kessler-Harris, "A New Agenda for American Labor History: A Gendered Analysis and the Question of Class," in Carroll J. Moody and Alice Kessler-Harris, eds.,

Perspectives on American Labor History: The Problems of Synthesis (DeKalb: Northern Illinois University Press, 1990), 55–79; Alice Kessler-Harris, *Gendering Labor History* (Urbana: University of Illinois Press, 2007).

23. Based on a compilation of weekly population reports for the camp in Raymondville, Texas. The camp occupancy reports are scattered within FmHA, RG 96, NACP.

24. To be clear, my analysis does not focus on the study of popular or expressive culture but rather examines culture in terms of a field in which competing concepts and practices were struggled over and given meaning, ultimately shaping migrants' material reality and daily lives. My understanding of culture in these terms is informed by Paul Gilroy's *"There Ain't No Black in the Union Jack": The Cultural Politics of Race and Nation* (Chicago: University of Chicago Press, 1987), 17. Cultural studies analysis of the camp program include Walter J. Stein, *California and the Dust Bowl Migration* (Westport, Conn.: Greenwood, 1973); James N. Gregory, *American Exodus: The Dust Bowl Migration and Okie Culture in California* (New York: Oxford University Press, 1989); Anne Loftis, "Steinbeck and the Federal Migrant Camps," *San Jose Studies* 16, no. 1 (Winter 1990): 76–90; Brian Q. Cannon, " 'Keep on A-Goin': Life and Social Interaction in a New Deal Farm Labor Camp," *Agricultural History* 70, no. 1 (1996): 1–32; Charles J. Shindo, *Dust Bowl Migrants in the American Imagination* (Lawrence: University Press of Kansas, 1997).

25. Chicana/o studies scholars have long noted the intrinsic relationship between ethnic Mexican farm labor and civil rights organizing. Key scholarship includes Gilbert G. Gonzalez, *Labor and Community: Mexican Citrus Worker Villages in a Southern California County, 1900–1950* (Urbana: University of Illinois Press, 1994); Devra Weber, *Dark Sweat, White Gold: California Farm Workers, Cotton, and the New Deal* (Berkeley: University of California Press, 1994); Matt Garcia, *A World of Its Own: Race, Labor, and Citrus in the Making of Greater Los Angeles, 1900–1970* (Chapel Hill: University of North Carolina Press, 2001); Zaragosa Vargas, *Labor Rights Are Civil Rights: Mexican American Workers in Twentieth-Century America* (Princeton, N.J.: Princeton University Press, 2005); José M. Alamillo, *Making Lemonade Out of Lemons: Mexican American Labor and Leisure in a California Town, 1880–1960* (Urbana: University of Illinois Press, 2006); Marc S. Rodriguez, *The Tejano Diaspora: Mexican Americanism and Ethnic Politics in Texas and Wisconsin* (Chapel Hill: University of North Carolina Press, 2011); Mario Jimenez Sifuentez, *Of Forests and Fields: Mexican Labor in the Pacific Northwest* (New Brunswick, N.J.: Rutgers University Press, 2016). On farmworkers' use of the Mexican government to navigate rights in the United States, see Gilbert G. Gonzalez, *Mexican Consuls and Labor Organizing: Imperial Politics in the American Southwest* (Austin: University of Texas Press, 1999); Francisco E. Balderrama, *In Defense of La Raza: The Los Angeles Mexican Consulate and the Mexican Community, 1929 to 1936* (Tucson: University of Arizona Press, 1982); George J. Sanchez, "The 'New Nationalism,' Mexican Style," in *Becoming Mexican American: Ethnicity, Culture, and Identity in Chicano Los Angeles, 1900–1945* (New York: Oxford University Press, 1993).

26. McWilliams, *Ill Fares the Land*, 249, 257; John Weber, *From South Texas to the Nation: The Exploitation of Mexican Labor in the Twentieth Century* (Chapel Hill: University of North Carolina Press, 2015), 7; Rodriguez, *Tejano Diaspora*, 4. On the central importance of South Texas in determining the national migrant stream and system of farm labor enforcement, see also Selden C. Menefee, *Mexican Migratory Workers of South Texas* (Washington, D.C.: U.S. Government Printing Office, 1941); David Montejano, *Anglos and Mexicans in the Making of*

Texas, 1836–1986 (Austin: University of Texas Press, 1987); Emilio Zamora, *The World of the Mexican Worker in Texas* (College Station: Texas A&M University Press, 1995); and Cristina Salinas, *Managed Migrations: Growers, Farmworkers, and Border Enforcement in the Twentieth Century* (Austin: University of Texas Press, 2018).

27. Stein, *California and the Dust Bowl Migration*, 173–77; Don Mitchell, *The Lie of the Land: Migrant Workers and the California Landscape* (Minneapolis: University of Minnesota Press, 1996), 186; Shindo, *Dust Bowl Migrants*, 28; Devra Weber, *Dark Sweat, White Gold*, 134.

28. In using the term "democratic script" I am borrowing from Natalia Molina's "racial scripts" analysis to underline the process of politicization the FSA employed among different farmworkers concurrently to bring them into the fold of national belonging. Molina uses the term "racial scripts" to "highlight the ways in which the lives of racialized groups are linked across time and space and thereby affect one another, even when they do not directly cross paths." Natalia Molina, *How Race Is Made in America: Immigration, Citizenship, and the Historical Power of Racial Scripts* (Berkeley: University of California Press, 2013), 6. On this approach, also see Natalia Molina, "Examining Chicana/o History through a Relational Lens," *Pacific Historical Review* 82, no. 4 (2013): 520–41.

29. Baldwin, *Poverty and Politics*, 4; Richard A. Couto, *Ain't Gonna Let Nobody Turn Me Round: The Pursuit of Racial Justice in the Rural South* (Philadelphia: Temple University Press, 1991), 306.

30. Don Mitchell has usefully labeled such state systems a form of "benevolent repression" or "progressive repression." Mitchell, *Lie of the Land*, 42, 55–56.

31. Katznelson, *Fear Itself*, 18.

32. The term "alien citizen" comes from Mae Ngai's discussion on the important relationship between juridical and cultural citizenship. According to Ngai, it refers to a person who is an American citizen by virtue of his/her birth in the United States but whose citizenship is questioned or denied on account of racial identity, immigrant ancestry, culture, or politics. Mae Ngai, "Birthright Citizenship and the Alien Citizen," *Fordham Law Review* 75, no. 5 (April 2007): 2530.

Chapter 1

1. Carey McWilliams, *Factories in the Field: The Story of Migratory Farm Labor in California* (Berkeley: University of California Press, 1939), 306; John Steinbeck, *The Harvest Gypsies: On the Road to the Grapes of Wrath* (Berkeley: Heyday Books, 1988), xi, 57; Dorothea Lange and Paul S. Taylor, *American Exodus: A Record of Human Erosion* (New York: Arno Press, 1975), 148–49.

2. Benson Y. Landis, "Where the Grapes of Wrath Are Stored," February 17, 1940, box C-R 1, ctn. 1, file 1.38 FSA Background Material Miscellaneous Bibliographies—U.S. Department of Agriculture 1938–39, Ralph W. Hollenberg Collection of Materials Relating to the Farm Security Administration (hereafter cited as Hollenberg Collection), Region IX, San Francisco, Calif., Bancroft Library, University of California, Berkeley (BANC).

3. Dr. W. W. Alexander, "A Program for the South," Farm Security Administrator, January 25, 1940, box C-R 1, ctn. 9, file Sharecroppers 1938–42, folder 8, 1940–42, Hollenberg Collection, BANC. On the politics behind the report, see Patricia Sullivan, *Days of Hope: Race and Democracy in the New Deal Era* (Chapel Hill: University of North Carolina Press, 1996),

64–67. For more specific statistics, see Charles Kenneth Roberts, *The Farm Security Administration and Rural Rehabilitation in the South* (Knoxville: University of Tennessee Press, 2015), xxvi.

4. Lange and Taylor, *American Exodus*, 40–41.

5. Lange and Taylor, *American Exodus*, 144.

6. Laurence Hewes, "Notes for a Talk on the Migrant Problem," box C-R 1, ctn. 1, file 1.2 FSA Background Material, p. 4, Hollenberg Collection, BANC.

7. As Neil Foley explains, "the notion of a ladder was a fundamental tenet of American agriculture from the Civil War to the New Deal. It held that the young male farmhand could climb, rung by rung, through the stages of hired hand, sharecropper, and tenant farmer to farm owner. It guaranteed opportunities for all farmers, in theory at least, to move across social and economic boundaries toward farm ownership, which was both the symbol of and the passport to full citizenship in the democracy of rural America." Neil Foley, *The White Scourge: Mexicans, Blacks, and Poor Whites in Texas Cotton Culture* (Berkeley: University of California Press, 1997), 10.

8. I am defining noncitizen farmworkers as both those who were of foreign nationality and those U.S. born but nonetheless considered "alien citizens" on account of their racial and immigrant ancestry. Mae Ngai, "Birthright Citizenship and the Alien Citizen," *Fordham Law Review* 75, no. 5 (April 2007): 2521.

9. Steinbeck, *Harvest Gypsies*, 39, 25, 57.

10. Marc Treib and Dorothée Imbert, *Garett Eckbo: Modern Landscapes for Living* (Berkeley: University of California Press, 1997), 102.

11. The Popular Front was "a radical social-democratic movement forged around anti-fascism, anti-lynching, and the industrial unionism of the CIO." See Michael Denning, *The Cultural Front: The Laboring of American Culture in the Twentieth Century* (New York: Verso, 1997), xviii.

12. McWilliams, *Factories in the Field*, 303; Denning, *Cultural Front*, 266–67.

13. On this topic, see Anne Loftis, "Steinbeck and the Federal Migrant Camps," *San Jose Studies* 16, no. 1 (Winter 1990): 76–90; Denning, *Cultural Front*; Douglas C. Sackman, *Orange Empire: California and the Fruits of Eden* (Berkeley: University of California Press, 2005); Kathryn S. Olmsted, *Right Out of California: The 1930s and the Big Business Roots of Modern Conservatism* (New York: New Press, 2015).

14. Devra Weber, *Dark Sweat, White Gold: California Farm Workers, Cotton, and the New Deal* (Berkeley: University of California Press, 1994), 138; Don Mitchell, *The Lie of the Land: Migrant Workers and the California Landscape* (Minneapolis: University of Minnesota Press, 1996), 179.

15. Steinbeck, *Harvest Gypsies*, 22.

16. Denning, *Cultural Front*, 266–68; Sackman, *Orange Empire*, 243; Olmsted, *Right Out of California*, 105, 222–23.

17. Carey McWilliams, *Ill Fares the Land: Migrants and Migratory Labor in the United States* (Boston: Little, Brown, 1942), 10–11.

18. Lange and Taylor, *American Exodus*, 133.

19. Sackman, *Orange Empire*, 233, 236; Denning, *Cultural Front*, 228.

20. Hewes, "Notes for a Talk," 2–3.

21. Walter J. Stein, *California and the Dust Bowl Migration* (Westport, Conn.: Greenwood, 1973), x; James N. Gregory, "Dust Bowl Legacies: The Okie Impact on California, 1939–1989," *California History* 68, no. 3 (Fall 1989): 76. Despite the inaccuracy of the term "Dust Bowl refugee," I use it to emphasize the intended depiction consistent with historical usage.

22. Because of their economic position, not everyone viewed California's new migrants as white Americans deserving of the highest benefits and best treatment employers and state officials could offer. In fact, their impact on Depression-era California created much anxiety in their host communities, resulting in what was commonly referred to as "the Okie problem." For more, see James N. Gregory, *American Exodus: The Dust Bowl Migration and Okie Culture in California* (New York: Oxford University Press, 1989), 78–113. Other scholars have similarly argued that Dust Bowl migrants' descension from farm owners, tenants, and sharecroppers to migratory farmworkers resulted in a racialization that transformed white farming families to "off-white" farmworkers. On the loss of agrarian whiteness, see Foley, *White Scourge*, 183–201.

23. Linda Gordon, *Dorothea Lange: A Life Beyond Limits* (London: W. W. Norton, 2009), 226; Sackman, *Orange Empire*, 244; Olmsted, *Right Out of California*, 105.

24. McWilliams, *Factories in the Field*, 211.

25. Sidney Sufrin, "A List of the Agricultural Unions and Strikes in the United States," Labor Relations Division, September 5, 1935, box C-R 1, ctn. 4, folder 39, file Unions and Strikes 1935, Hollenberg Collection, BANC; Weber, *Dark Sweat, White Gold*, 79–80; Devra Weber, "Raiz Fuerte: Oral History and Mexicana Farmworkers," in Ellen Carol DuBois and Vicki Ruiz, eds., *Unequal Sisters: A Multi-Cultural Reader in U.S. Women's History*, 2nd ed. (New York: Routledge, 1994); Olmsted, *Right Out of California*, 6, 42, 52.

26. Cindy Hahamovitch, *No Man's Land: Jamaican Guestworkers in America and the Global History of Deportable Labor* (Princeton, N.J.: Princeton University Press, 2011), 25; Weber, *Dark Sweat, White Gold*, 103, 109, 118; Jarod Roll, *Spirit of Rebellion: Labor and Religion in the New Cotton South* (Urbana: University of Illinois Press, 2010); Olmsted, *Right Out of California*, 71, 73, 127–28, 138.

27. "Statement of Regional Office of Resettlement Administration on Possible Establishment of Migrant Camps," November 18, 1935, box 11, file AD-124 Reg. 9 Migratory Labor General 1936 thru 1939, Records of the Farmers Home Administration (FmHA), Record Group 96 (RG 96), National Archives at College Park, Md. (NACP).

28. Paul S. Taylor, *Adrift on the Land* (New York: Public Affairs Committee, 1940), 22; McWilliams, *Factories in the Field*, 225, 316.

29. Gordon, *Dorothea Lange*, 158, xx.

30. Paul S. Taylor and Dorothea Lange, Establishment of Rural Rehabilitation Camps for Migrants in California, March 1935, Library of Congress, https://www.loc.gov/item/2004 678009/; Gordon, *Dorothea Lange*, 164.

31. Steinbeck, *Harvest Gypsies*, 52–57; McWilliams, *Factories in the Field*, 129.

32. Although the deportations were mostly urban based, many farmworkers spent the off-season working in cities rather than going back to Mexico as most growers assumed. Francisco E. Balderrama and Raymond Rodriguez, *Decade of Betrayal: Mexican Repatriation in the 1930s* (Albuquerque: University of New Mexico Press, 1995), 149–51; Abraham Hoffman,

Unwanted Mexican Americans in the Great Depression: Repatriation Pressures, 1929–1939 (Tucson: University of Arizona Press, 1974), 174–75; George Kiser and David Silverman, "Mexican Repatriation During the Great Depression," *Journal of Mexican American History* 3 (1973): 139–64; McWilliams, *Factories in the Field*, 129. The Filipino Repatriation Act (1935) resulted in a much smaller effort to deport workers: only about 2,190 returned to the Philippines. However, the effects of displacement from California's agricultural fields, and society more broadly, were likewise significant. Howard A. DeWitt, *Violence in the Fields: California Filipino Farm Labor Unionization During the Great Depression* (Saratoga, Calif.: Century Twenty One Publishing, 1980), 12.

33. Carey McWilliams, *North from Mexico: The Spanish-Speaking People of the United States* (Philadelphia: J. B. Lippincott, 1949), 176. McWilliams cites Clements from a letter provided to the La Follette committee dated December 18, 1936. However, tracing it back to the La Follette hearings, I found that the letter is actually from A. G. Arnoll, secretary and general manager of the Los Angeles Chamber of Commerce. That letter can be found at United States Congress, *Violations of Free Speech and Rights of Labor: Hearings Before the United States Senate Committee on Education and Labor, Subcommittee on S. Res. 266, 76th Cong., 3d Sess., on Jan. 13, 1940, Part 53* (Washington, D.C.: Government Printing Office, 1940), 19714.

34. Gordon, *Dorothea Lange*, 171; Stein, *California and the Dust Bowl Migration*, 150–52; Charles J. Shindo, *Dust Bowl Migrants in the American Imagination* (Lawrence: University Press of Kansas, 1997), 26; Sidney Baldwin, *Poverty and Politics: The Rise and Decline of the Farm Security Administration* (Chapel Hill: University of North Carolina Press, 1968), 62.

35. Weber, *Dark Sweat, White Gold*, 133.

36. Olmsted explains that although Tugwell was sympathetic to farmworkers' struggles, he confessed in his private diary in late December 1934 that "the problem of agricultural labor is one which is avoided by everyone." Olmsted, *Right Out of California*, 211.

37. Stein, *California and the Dust Bowl Migration*, 152.

38. "Statement of Regional Office of Resettlement Administration on Possible Establishment of Migrant Camps," November 18, 1935.

39. Baldwin, *Poverty and Politics*, 117, 125; Stein, *California and the Dust Bowl Migration*, 153–54; Wayne D. Rasmussen, *A History of the Emergency Farm Labor Supply Program, 1943–47*, Agricultural Monograph No. 13 (Washington, D.C.: Department of Agriculture, 1951), 10–11.

40. Baldwin, *Poverty and Politics*, 222.

41. Baldwin, *Poverty and Politics*, 39; Sullivan, *Days of Hope*, 57; Roberts, *Farm Security Administration*, xxiv.

42. Sullivan, *Days of Hope*, 59; Baldwin, *Poverty and Politics*, 45, 122. On Raper's relationship to Alexander, see Jason Manthorne, "As You Sow: Culture, Agriculture, and the New Deal" (PhD diss., University of Georgia, 2013).

43. Laurie B. Green, *Battling the Plantation Mentality: Memphis and the Black Freedom Struggle* (Chapel Hill: University of North Carolina Press, 2007), 2.

44. Jonathan Garst, Regional Director, to C. B. Baldwin, August 19, 1938, box 11, file AD-124 Reg. 9 Migratory Labor General 1936 thru 1939, FmHA, RG 96, NACP.

45. Ira Katznelson, *Fear Itself: The New Deal and the Origins of Our Time*, 1st ed. (New York: Liveright, 2013), 170.

46. Sullivan, *Days of Hope*, 22. According to Foley, "The rural South lost 2,275,000 people through migration between 1930–1940. Oklahoma suffered the worst out-migration, followed by Texas, Georgia, and South Carolina." Foley, *White Scourge*, 177.

47. Southern historians have produced a vast historiography documenting the socio-economic and political changes the South underwent during the 1930s. Key works include Pete Daniel, *Breaking the Land: The Transformation of Cotton, Tobacco, and Rice Cultures Since 1880* (Urbana: University of Illinois Press, 1985); Jack Temple Kirby, *Rural Worlds Lost: The American South, 1920–1960* (Baton Rouge: Louisiana State University Press, 1987); Donald H. Grubbs, *Cry from the Cotton: The Southern Tenant Farmers' Union and the New Deal* (Chapel Hill: University of North Carolina Press, 1971); Harvard Sitkoff, *A New Deal for Blacks: The Emergence of Civil Rights as a National Issue* (New York: Oxford University Press, 1981); Roger Biles, *The South and the New Deal* (Lexington: University Press of Kentucky, 1994). In my analysis, I also relied on the more recent works by Foley, *White Scourge*; Sullivan, *Days of Hope*; Greta de Jong, *A Different Day: African American Struggles for Justice in Rural Louisiana, 1900–1970* (Chapel Hill: University of North Carolina Press, 2002); Nan Elizabeth Woodruff, *American Congo: The African American Freedom Struggle in the Delta* (Cambridge, Mass.: Harvard University Press, 2003); Roll, *Spirit of Rebellion*; Roberts, *Farm Security Administration*.

48. Sullivan, *Days of Hope*, 42; Baldwin, *Poverty and Politics*, 47.

49. Sitkoff, *New Deal for Blacks*, 45.

50. Sullivan, *Days of Hope*, 43.

51. Baldwin, *Poverty and Politics*, 50–53. Since the AFBF took on much of the responsibility of administering the early New Deal agricultural programs, it gained considerable power. Consequently, its membership more than doubled between 1933 and 1938. Roberts, *Farm Security Administration*, 10.

52. As Manthorne explains, the AAA was aimed at helping the nation's struggling farmers by raising prices for the basic commodities they produced. Nevertheless, by restricting cotton and tobacco acreage, the AAA assured the widespread displacement of southern sharecroppers and farm tenants. And in leaving control over local AAA committees in the hands of powerful landowners, it also made sure that they would have little opportunity to file their grievances and ensure their rightful share of AAA payments. Jason Manthorne, "The View from the Cotton: Reconsidering the Southern Tenant Farmers' Union," *Agricultural History* 84, no. 1 (2010): 21; Baldwin, *Poverty and Politics*, 76–80; Juan Perea, "The Echoes of Slavery: Recognizing the Racist Origins of the Agricultural and Domestic Worker Exclusion from the National Labor Relations Act," *Ohio State Law Journal* 72, no. 1 (January 1, 2011): 108.

53. Hahamovitch, *No Man's Land*, 25.

54. Perea, "Echoes of Slavery," 104–5.

55. Katznelson, *Fear Itself*, 25.

56. Testimony of H. L. Mitchell, Secretary, Southern Tenant Farmers' Union, Memphis, Tenn., in U.S. House of Representatives, *Select Committee to Investigate the Interstate Migration of Destitute Citizens, Hearings Before the Select Committee to Investigate the Interstate Migration of Destitute Citizens, 76th Cong., 3d Sess., 1940–41, Part 2* (Washington, D.C.: Government Printing Office, 1941), 623 (hereafter cited as Tolan Hearings); Manthorne, "View from the Cotton," 21, 36–37.

57. Mitchell described the displacement as follows: "In 1934, 99 percent of the members of this organization [STFU] were either tenant farmers or sharecroppers, but by 1937, 60

percent of the members had become day laborers, and today [1940] over 75 percent are working for wages." Tolan Hearings, 626. See also Robin D. G. Kelley, *Race Rebels: Culture, Politics, and the Black Working Class* (New York: Free Press, 1994); Greta de Jong, "'With the Aid of God and the F.S.A.': The Louisiana Farmers' Union and the African American Freedom Struggle in the New Deal Era," *Journal of Social History* 34, no. 1 (2000): 105–39.

58. Baldwin, *Poverty and Politics*, 80.

59. Gordon, *Dorothea Lange*, 275.

60. The "liberal faction," according to Baldwin, included Jerome N. Frank and his legal staff in the Office of the General Counsel; Frederic Howe and Gardner "Pat" Jackson in the Office of Consumers' Counsel; and Tugwell, at the time the undersecretary of agriculture. Baldwin, *Poverty and Politics*, 54–55, 76, 83.

61. Baldwin, *Poverty and Politics*, 85, 122, 237.

62. Gilbert has written most extensively on the ideological influences shaping some of the FSA's top administrators. For more on this topic, see Jess C. Gilbert, *Planning Democracy: Agrarian Intellectuals and the Intended New Deal* (New Haven, Conn.: Yale University Press, 2015), 74–78, 90–91.

63. Baldwin, *Poverty and Politics*, 244–46.

64. Baldwin, *Poverty and Politics*, 95–96.

65. Gilbert, *Planning Democracy*, 91; Baldwin, *Poverty and Politics*, 131.

66. Baldwin, *Poverty and Politics*, 96, 333; Sullivan, *Days of Hope*, 124.

67. Sidney Baldwin aptly writes that the FSA's ideology was a double-edged sword: "It sustained and unified the agency in a time of crisis, and, as the tide shifted, it helped to cleave the rock on which the agency was built." Baldwin, *Poverty and Politics*, 267, 270.

68. It is possible that Baldwin was a communist, or developed a communist philosophy after leaving the FSA, at which time he went to work for the CIO-Political Action Committee. Indeed, several FSA officials may have sympathized with the U.S. communist movement as growers claimed. Don Mitchell, for example, explains how N. Gregory Silvermaster, who worked for the California State Emergency Relief Administration to establish the first camps and later became chief of the FSA's Labor Division, was eventually outed as a Soviet spy. Still, according to Sidney Baldwin, it is unlikely that the FSA ever served the cause of communism wittingly or otherwise because American communists opposed the New Deal fairly consistently, including some of the FSA's programs. This would not, of course, protect the agency from zealous anticommunists trying to undermine its leaders and activities. Baldwin, *Poverty and Politics*, 356–59; Thomas W. Devine, *Henry Wallace's 1948 Presidential Campaign and the Future of Postwar Liberalism*, 1st ed. (Chapel Hill: University of North Carolina Press, 2013), 40, 302n11; Don Mitchell, *They Saved the Crops: Labor, Landscape, and the Struggle over Industrial Farming in Bracero-Era California* (Athens: University of Georgia Press, 2012), 32.

69. Baldwin, *Poverty and Politics*, 199–211; Lee J. Alston and Joseph P. Ferrie, "Resisting the Welfare State: Southern Opposition to the Farm Security Administration," *Research in Economic History*, Supplement 4, no. 0 (1985): 98.

70. Alston and Ferrie, "Resisting the Welfare State," 99.

71. Baldwin, *Poverty and Politics*, 208, 266; Sullivan, *Days of Hope*, 105.

72. John A. Fitch, "Now I've Got Rights," *Survey Midmonthly* 78, no. 8 (August 1942): 210, 212.

73. de Jong, "'With the Aid of God and the F.S.A.,'" 105. In some cases, the FSA reinforced racial segregation and contributed to black tenants' displacement by evicting them to

make room for white rehabilitation clients. On this topic, see Jane Adams and D. Gorton, "This Land Ain't My Land: The Eviction of Sharecroppers by the Farm Security Administration," *Agricultural History* 83, no. 3 (2009): 323–51.

74. Gordon, *Dorothea Lange*, 266–67; McWilliams, *Ill Fares the Land*, 14.

75. Richard L. Neuberger, "Who Are the Associated Farmers?" *Survey Graphic* 28 (September 1939), http://newdeal.feri.org/survey/39b12.htm; "The Associated Farmers," Institute for Propaganda Analysis, Inc., vol. 2, no. 12, August 1, 1939, box C-R 1, ctn. 6, file Farmer Organizations, 1936–1945, folder 1, Associated Farmers 1939, Hollenberg Collection, BANC; Olmsted, *Right Out of California*, 126. According to Weber, an earlier organization of small farmers existed in 1933 under the name AF, but they were gone (or pressured out) by the time the new organization emerged. Weber, *Dark Sweat, White Gold*, 118–19.

76. Olmsted, *Right Out of California*, 65–82.

77. According to one study, "The cry of Communism is their chief propaganda stock-in-trade. Of 375 items published in their monthly bulletin, the *Associated Farmer*, 190 were devoted to Communism." In their estimation, anyone who wanted to organize farm labor was a communist. "Associated Farmers," Hollenberg Collection, BANC.

78. Stein, *California and the Dust Bowl Migration*, 247.

79. Beginning in 1938, the House Committee on Un-American Activities led by Texas congressman Martin Dies, Jr., subjected UCAPAWA to intense scrutiny for its alleged communist politics. For more, see Vicki Ruiz, *Cannery Women, Cannery Lives: Mexican Women, Unionization, and the California Food Processing Industry, 1930–1950* (Albuquerque: University of New Mexico Press, 1987), 46–47.

80. Camp reports show that many local farmers and ginners, typically producing on a smaller scale, did appreciate the FSA's efforts. Some claimed that if it had not been for the domestic amenities provided by the camps, workers would not have stayed in the area for as long as they needed." Statement of Regional Office of Resettlement Administration on Possible Establishment of Migrant Camps," FmHA, RG 96, NACP.

81. McWilliams, *Factories in the Field*, 298.

82. "Coastal Bend Group Advices on Labor Camp," *Robstown Record*, March 27, 1941, http://newpaperarchive.com.

83. C. B. Baldwin, FSA Administrator, to Payson Irwin, Acting Regional Director [Pennsylvania], March 21, 1941, box 8, file AD-124 All Regional Migratory Labor General 1941, FmHA, RG 96, NACP. The same letter was sent to all regional directors, regional labor relations advisers, and regional information advisers across the country.

84. Paul H. Freier, Crystal City Acting Camp Manager, to W. A. Canon, FSA Assistant Regional Director, May 3, 1941, Crystal City Files, FmHA, RG 96, National Archives at Fort Worth, Tex. (NAFW).

85. Nan Elizabeth Woodruff, "Mississippi Delta Planters and Debates over Mechanization, Labor, and Civil Rights in the 1940s," *Journal of Southern History* 60, no. 2 (May 1994): 263. The FSA's Farm Transportation Program particularly troubled southern planters. They claimed that the FSA was working closely with unions to move workers around to earn the best wages. The FSA's correspondence with the STFU suggests that some coordination may have occurred. The FSA was aware, for example, that the STFU was recruiting southern farmworkers to work in Florida and requiring them to join the union and wear the union button if they wanted the job. In response, the FSA stated that it would neither "discourage

[nor] encourage such activity." Albert Maverick, Jr., Acting Director, to Jesse B. Gilmer, Regional Director, January 22, 1943, box 7, file Migratory-120-Southern Tenant Farmers Union, FmHA, RG 96, NACP.

86. Quoted in Jeffery B. McDonald, "Following the Harvest: Migrant Workers in Texas and the New Deal" (master's thesis, Stephen F. Austin State University, 1993), 42.

87. U.S. House of Representatives, *Select Committee of the House Committee on Agriculture, to Investigate the Activities of the Farm Security Administration, 78th Cong., 1st Sess., 1943, Part 4* (Washington, D.C.: Government Printing Office, 1943), 1547–48, 1552.

88. Woodruff, "Mississippi Delta Planters and Debates," 277.

89. Monthly Narrative Report (MNR), Harlingen, Texas, FSA Camp, April 9, 1942, box 486, file RP-TX-36-183-01 Monthly Narrative Report of Home Management—September 1941, FmHA, RG 96, NACP.

90. Major Walker, Director of Resettlement Division, and Mercer Evans, Director of Labor Relations Division, to C. B. Baldwin, November 2, 1937, box 2578, file Labor, Records of the Office of the Secretary of Agriculture (OSA), RG 16, NACP; Administrative Letter 161, "Policy regarding administration of FSA labor camps in California," to all administrators from Will W. Alexander, Administrator, April 18, 1938, box 14, FmHA, RG 96, NACP.

91. Stein, *California and the Dust Bowl Migration*, 252.

92. Stein, *California and the Dust Bowl Migration*, 250–52; Linda C. Majka and Theo J. Majka, *Farm Workers, Agribusiness, and the State* (Philadelphia: Temple University Press, 1982), 127.

93. Phil Ohanneson to Charles Barry, March 23, 1939, box 28, file RF-CF-27-160, FmHA, RG 96, National Archives at San Francisco, San Bruno, CA (NASF).

94. Interestingly, Fisher wrote to Dorothea Lange on January 4, 1939, requesting help getting the paper out to sympathetic audiences to raise funds for the migrants. Charles E. Barry to R. W. Hollenberg, March 24, 1939, and related correspondence, box 28, file RF-CF-27-160, FmHA, RG 96, NASF.

95. Weber, *Dark Sweat, White Gold*, 292n24, 184.

96. Gregory, *American Exodus*, 159; Stein, *California and the Dust Bowl Migration*, 264–72.

97. Sometimes UCAPAWA divided members into Spanish and English locals. This does not appear to have occurred at Shafter. Many of its members were veterans of the 1933 strikes and members of the Mexican American civil rights group El Congreso de Pueblos de Habla Español. Weber, *Dark Sweat, White Gold*, 183–84.

98. Ruiz, *Cannery Women*, 51.

99. Stein, *California and the Dust Bowl Migration*, 273.

100. James H. Ward, Chairman of Camp Council, to Earl R. Beckner, Acting Chief Labor Relations Division, n.d., box 206, file AD-CF-25 Arvin Migratory Labor Camp General (000–900), FmHA, RG 96, NACP.

101. "Migrant Workers Thinkers," *San Francisco Chronicle*, March 10, 1937, box C-R, ctn. 3, file Clippings 1937–1938, folder 40–41, Hollenberg Collection, BANC.

102. Stein, *California and the Dust Bowl Migration*, 270–71; Gregory, *American Exodus*, 164–71; Weber, *Dark Sweat, White Gold*, 148–49.

103. Donald Henderson, General President, UCAPAWA, to Henry A. Wallace, Secretary of Agriculture, November 29, 1938, box 8, file AD-124 All Regs. Migratory Labor General 1937 & 1938, FmHA, RG 96, NACP.

104. R. Friedan, UCAPAWA Press Bureau Chairman, to Henry A. Wallace, August 31, 1938, box 13, file AD-124 Washington Migratory Labor Commendations and Complaints, FmHA, RG 96, NACP.

105. Ruiz, *Cannery Women*, 48.

106. B. J. Walker, Labor Relations Specialist, to Dr. N. Gregory Silvermaster, FSA Director of Labor Division, February 24, 1942, box 10, file AD-124 Reg. VIII Migratory Camps 1941, FmHA, RG 96, NACP.

107. Donald G. Kobler, UCAPAWA Texas Regional Director, to Claude A. Wickard, Secretary of Agriculture, October 14, 1942, box 16, file Migratory-160–02 General, FmHA, RG 96, NACP.

108. On farmworkers' formal organizing efforts in South Texas between 1930 and 1940, see Victor B. Nelson-Cisneros, "La Clase Trabajadora en Tejas, 1920–1940," *Aztlán: A Journal of Chicano Studies* 6 (1975): 239–65; Victor B. Nelson-Cisneros, "UCAPAWA Organizing Activities in Texas, 1935–50," *Aztlán: A Journal of Chicano Studies* 9 (1978): 71–84; Foley, *White Scourge*, 183–201; John Weber, *From South Texas to the Nation: The Exploitation of Mexican Labor in the Twentieth Century* (Chapel Hill: University of North Carolina Press, 2015); Zaragosa Vargas, *Labor Rights Are Civil Rights: Mexican American Workers in Twentieth-Century America* (Princeton, N.J.: Princeton University Press, 2005).

109. In his memoir, Laurence I. Hewes admits that when he arrived in California in late 1939 to work as FSA regional supervisor, one of the first things he did was try to rid the camps of the more communist-leaning migrants in addition to the rabble-rousing managers. This would have included Arvin's manager, Fred Ross, who would famously go on to organize the Community Service Organization that trained Cesar Chavez and Dolores Huerta. Laurence I. Hewes, *Boxcar in the Sand* (New York: Knopf, 1957), 114–15.

110. "Tulare FSA Camp, 'No Union-Smashing!' Farm Workers Warn," *People's World*, n.d., box 37, file CF-31-01, FmHA, RG 96, NASF.

111. Box 8, file RP-M-121-02 Reg. 9 1941 Lemon Pickers Strike—Ventura C., FmHA, RG 96, NASF. According to Jose Flores, a Mexican American migrant worker involved in the strike, "Okie" migrants served as strikebreakers. "Interview about FSA camp governance, camp work, non-FSA migrant camps, labor issues, attitude toward 'Okies'," in Charles L. Todd and Robert Sonkin Migrant Workers Collection, "The Migrant Experience: Voices from the Dust Bowl, 1940–1941," Library of Congress, American Folklife Center, AFC 1985/001. For more on the lemon strike, see Frank P. Barajas, *Curious Unions: Mexican American Workers and Resistance in Oxnard, California, 1898–1961* (Lincoln: University of Nebraska Press, 2012), 167–84.

112. "Ventura County on Sucker List," *Port Hueneme Herald*, February 14, 1941, in correspondence regarding "Huelga piscadores de limón en el condado de Ventura," box 1457, file 1457-7 Huelga de Rigeadores de Limón, Archives of the Mexican Consul (AEMEAU), Secretaria de Relaciónes Exteriores (SRE), Mexico City, Mexico.

113. Rodolfo Salazar, March 1, 1941, in "Huelga piscadores de limón en el condado de Ventura."

114. The Delmo project was critical to the FSA's planned intervention in the rural South. P. G. Beck, FSA regional director, claimed that if the group labor homes proved successful, the agency planned to extend the program throughout the region. Roll, *Spirit of Rebellion*, 133–59; McWilliams, *Ill Fares the Land*, 282–98.

115. McWilliams, *Ill Fares the Land*, 295.

116. Several scholars have documented the wide variety of informal actions Mexican farmworkers employed to protest their working conditions. On this topic, see David Montejano, *Anglos and Mexicans in the Making of Texas, 1836–1986* (Austin: University of Texas Press, 1987); Weber, *Dark Sweat, White Gold*, 48–78; Gilbert G. Gonzalez, *Labor and Community: Mexican Citrus Worker Villages in a Southern California County, 1900–1950* (Urbana: University of Illinois Press, 1994); Emilio Zamora, *The World of the Mexican Worker in Texas* (College Station: Texas A&M University Press, 1995), 55–85; Vicki Ruiz, *From Out of the Shadows: Mexican Women in Twentieth-Century America* (New York: Oxford University Press, 1998); Matt Garcia, *A World of Its Own: Race, Labor, and Citrus in the Making of Greater Los Angeles, 1900–1970* (Chapel Hill: University of North Carolina Press, 2001); Stephen J. Pitti, *The Devil in Silicon Valley: Northern California, Race, and Mexican Americans* (Princeton, N.J.: Princeton University Press, 2003); Vargas, *Labor Rights Are Civil Rights*.

117. MNR, Crystal City, Texas, FSA Camp, May 9, 1941; Paul H. Freier, Acting Camp Manager, to W. A. Canon, FSA Assistant Regional Director, May 21, 1941, box 487, file RP-TX-38-183 Reports, FmHA, RG 96, NACP.

118. Freier to Canon, May 21, 1941, box 487, file RP-TX-38-183 Reports, FmHA, RG 96, NACP.

119. Arthur Eggleston, "The Labor Scene: La Follette Committee's Strike Quiz a Scratch on Surface of Deepening Problem of Farming," *San Francisco Chronicle*, December 27, 1939, box C-R 1, ctn. 1, file 1.18 FSA Background Material La Follette Committee 1939, Hollenberg Collection, BANC.

120. As Sullivan shows, "In 1939 the House also increased appropriations fourfold for the Special Committee on UnAmerican Activities, headed by Texas Democrat Martin Dies, thus sanctioning Dies's widely publicized search for Communists in the government and in the CIO." Sullivan, *Days of Hope*, 104–5.

121. "FSA Migratory Camp Population Reports and Employment and Earnings of Families Living in FSA Camps," box 19, file AD 124 All Regs. 183 Migratory Labor Social Security Tables on Interstate Migrants 1937, FmHA, RG 96, NACP; U.S. House of Representatives, *Select Committee of the House Committee on Agriculture, to Investigate the Activities of the Farm Security Administration, 78th Cong., 2nd sess., 1944, Part 3* (Washington, D.C.: Government Printing Office, 1944), 1164–67. In 1942 the FSA was operating labor camps in Washington, Oregon, Idaho, California, Arizona, Texas, Florida, Virginia, Maryland, New Jersey, and New York. The agency also planned to expand the camp program to the Pacific Northwest, the Mississippi delta, the Panhandle and High Plains areas of Texas, and New Mexico, Georgia, South Carolina, upstate New York, Ohio, Colorado, and Montana. Mason Barr, Director, Resettlement Division, to Emery Jacobs, Assistant to the Secretary, February 12, 1942, box 8, file Housing (Not Construction) AD-124, FmHA, RG 96, NACP; Hahamovitch, *No Man's Land*, 38.

122. "Origins and Problems of Texas Migratory Farm Labor," 26.

123. Memorandum to C. B. Baldwin, "Migratory Labor Camp Construction, Fiscal Year 1940–41," p. 3, box 8, file RP-M-124 Housing, FmHA, RG 96, NACP; Cindy Hahamovitch, *The Fruits of Their Labor: Atlantic Coast Farmworkers and the Making of Migrant Poverty, 1870–1945* (Chapel Hill: University of North Carolina Press, 1997), 166.

124. U.S. House of Representatives, *Select Committee to Investigate the Interstate Migration of Destitute Citizens, Hearings Before the Select Committee to Investigate the Interstate*

Migration of Destitute Citizens, 76th Cong., 3d Sess., 1940–41, Part 5 (Washington, D.C.: Government Printing Office, 1941), 2199.

125. "Recommendations Concerning Labor Camps," June 1936, box 19, file G Labor Non-Administrative & Non-Appointive AD-120, FmHA, RG 96, NACP.

126. The FSA and USES signed a "joint statement of policy formalizing a coordination of activities" on January 23, 1942. The purpose was to serve as "a framework through which each agency may complement the services of the other insuring labor for the production of defense food and fibre [*sic*] products." Rasmussen, *History of the Emergency Farm Labor Supply Program*, 25.

127. MNR, Harlingen, Texas, FSA Camp, April 9, 1942.

128. Zamora, *World of the Mexican Worker*, 30; Gunther Peck, *Reinventing Free Labor: Padrones and Immigrant Workers in the North American West, 1880–1930* (Cambridge: Cambridge University Press, 2000), 193–97; Hahamovitch, *No Man's Land*, 38. On the politics of farmworkers' mobility, see also Cristina Salinas, *Managed Migrations: Growers, Farmworkers, and Border Enforcement in the Twentieth Century* (Austin: University of Texas Press, 2018).

129. Mason Bar, Director of the Resettlement Division, to C. M. Evans, FSA Regional Director, October 23, 1941, General Camp Files, FmHA, RG 96, NAFW.

130. Henry C. Daniels, Robstown Camp Manager, to W. A. Canon, FSA Assistant Regional Director, November 7, 1941, Robstown Files, FmHA, RG 96, NAFW.

131. W. A. Canon to Henry C. Daniels, November 28, 1941, Robstown Camp Files, FmHA, RG 96, NAFW.

132. W. A. Canon to C. B. Baldwin, FSA Administrator, March 10, 1942, Robstown Camp Files, FmHA, RG 96, NAFW.

133. Alice Kessler-Harris, "In the Nation's Image: The Gendered Limits of Social Citizenship in the Depression Era," *Journal of American History* 86, no. 3 (December 1999): 1253, 1256, 1259. On the Depression's "feminization" of dependency, also see Robert S. McElvaine, *The Great Depression: America, 1929–1941* (New York: Times Books, 1984), 339.

134. Ruth Alice Allen, *The Labor of Women in the Production of Cotton*, Bulletin no. 3134 (Austin: University of Texas, 1931), 71.

135. Nancy Grey Osterud, "Gender and the Transition to Capitalism in Rural America," *Agricultural History* 67, no. 2 (Spring 1993): 14–29; Foley, *White Scourge*; Elizabeth H. Pleck, "Two Worlds in One: Work and Family," in Nancy F. Cott, ed., *The Intersection of Work and Family Life* (Berlin: De Gruyter, 2013).

136. Jack H. Bryan, Acting Chief Information Division, to Mason Barr, Director Resettlement Division, October 27, 1941, on the topic of "Rural Women and National Defense," box 13, file 165 Publicity, FmHA, RG 96, NACP; "War Weapons for War Workers," assembled and organized by Iva M. Caldwell, Associate Home Management Specialist, A. E. Scott, Jr., Chief Community and Family Services, Dallas, Texas, July 1942, box 17, file RP-M-88-163 Newspapers and Magazines, FmHA, RG 96, NACP.

137. "Corpus Christi, Texas. Mexican girl helping to save the crop which was threatened with ruin because of wartime manpower shortage," photograph by Howard R. Hollem, November 1942, Prints & Photographs Division, FSA/OWI Collection, Library of Congress, LC-USE6-D-007285. Also see the following sample images by Rothstein (by negative number): 024833-D; 024835-D; 024836-D; 024837-D; 024848-D; 024849-D; 024856-D; 024858-D; 024860-D; 024867-D; 024868-D; 024871-D; 03622-M1; 03622-M4; 03622-M5; 03623-M3;

03623-M5; 03624-M5; 03639-M1; 03627-M5. On the role of the FSA's Photographic Division, see James Curtis, *Mind's Eye, Mind's Truth: FSA Photography Reconsidered* (Philadelphia: Temple University Press, 1989); Pete Daniel, *Official Images: New Deal Photography* (Washington, D.C.: Smithsonian Institution Press, 1987); Nicholas Natanson, *The Black Image in the New Deal: The Politics of FSA Photography* (Knoxville: University of Tennessee Press, 1992); Wendy Kozol, "Madonnas of the Fields: Photography, Gender, and 1930s Farm Relief," *Genders* 2 (Summer 1988): 1–23; Gordon, *Dorothea Lange*, 423–30.

138. Emphasis in original. They also failed to acknowledge the conscious decisions migrant women made as laborers. For example, in one monthly narrative report, camp officials noted that while "there have been some calls for maids, none of the women will go as they can make more in the fields." MNR, Harlingen, Texas, FSA Camp, January 8, 1942, box 486, file RP-TX-36-183-01 Monthly Narrative Report of Home Management—September 1941, FmHA, RG 96, NACP. For a sample of the employment records, see folders titled "Weekly Employment Reports," boxes 484–89, Texas Project Records 1935–1940, FmHA, RG 96, NACP.

139. On the significance of this point, also see Foley, *White Scourge*, 146.

Chapter 2

1. Talbot Hamlin, "Farm Security Administration: An Appraisal," *Pencil Points* 22, no. 11 (November 1941): 709–20.

2. Nelson H. Cruikshank, "Suggested Changes in Annual Report for Uniform Projects," May 31, 1940, box 8, file RP-M-124 Housing, Records of the Farmers Home Administration (FmHA), Record Group 96 (RG 96), National Archives at College Park, Md. (NACP).

3. "Migratory Labor Camp Program as of September 1, 1939" and "Memorandum for Mr. Leonard Othwaite," April 17, 1941, box 8, file RP-M-124 Housing, FmHA, RG 96, NACP.

4. Hamlin, "Farm Security Administration," 709.

5. See, for example, Howard Gillette, "The Evolution of Neighborhood Planning: From the Progressive Era to the 1949 Housing Act," *Journal of Urban History* 9, no. 4 (August 1, 1983): 421–44.

6. USDA-FSA Division of Information, "Rural Housing in the West," box C-R 1, ctn. 1, file 1.11 FSA Background Material Press Releases 1939–43, Ralph W. Hollenberg Collection of Materials Relating to the Farm Security Administration (hereafter cited as Hollenberg Collection), Region IX, San Francisco, Calif., Bancroft Library, University of California, Berkeley (BANC).

7. Sara M. Gregg, *Managing the Mountains: Land Use Planning, the New Deal, and the Creation of a Federal Landscape in Appalachia* (New Haven, Conn.: Yale University Press, 2010), 176–77.

8. Gregg, *Managing the Mountains*, esp. chap. 6 on reforming submarginal lands.

9. Jason Manthorne, "As You Sow: Culture, Agriculture, and the New Deal" (PhD diss., University of Georgia, 2013), 45, 104, 142–49.

10. As Laurence Hewes would later recall, "I liked to think of our problems as exercises in social engineering which could be solved by precise objective techniques of administration. Too much respect for orderly procedures prevented any lush flowering in me of sentiments and emotions as guides to action." Laurence I. Hewes, *Boxcar in the Sand* (New York: Knopf, 1957), 136.

11. Eckbo designed approximately fifty migrant camps during his time with the FSA. Marc Treib and Dorothée Imbert, *Garrett Eckbo: Modern Landscapes for Living* (Berkeley: University of California Press, 1997), 44, 102.

12. Treib and Imbert, *Garrett Eckbo*, 122.

13. Vernon Armand DeMars, "A Life in Architecture: Indian Dancing, Migrant Housing, Telesis, Design for Urban Living, Theater, Teaching," an oral history conducted in 1988–1989 by Suzanne B. Riess, Regional Oral History Office, 1992, BANC, 99–102.

14. During his interview, when asked about how he would define himself politically on graduating from Berkeley, DeMars responded: "I got my religion as I went along in Farm Security, thinking there was something awfully wrong, if one part of the population (was homeless). I mean, this was not like the homeless and so forth now; here were people who were part of the working force, and living like animals. And the notion of doing anything to correct that just didn't occur, that at least minimum decent housing was a necessary thing. But I didn't come out of school with that, because I just wasn't exposed to it, quite." Similarly, Jack Kent recalled of his work at Telesis, "To my amazement—it's funny, I hadn't thought about this earlier—but as a student, I knew nothing about the Farm Security Administration. We were not in touch, aware, with all of our emergent social concern, we didn't know that there was such an office across the bay dealing with the needs of migrant farmers." DeMars, "Life in Architecture," 164, 175.

15. Noted Telesis members included William Wurster, Catherine Bauer Wurster, Vernon DeMars, Thomas Church, Garrett Eckbo, Grace McCann Morley, Geraldine Knight Scott, Joseph Allen Stein, Jack Hillmer, Francis Violich, and T. J. Kent. Philosophically, the group evolved from several larger international architectural movements, which included the International Congress of Modern Architecture (CIAM) and the Modern Architectural Research Group (MARS).

16. DeMars, "Life in Architecture," 145. Mumford was a leading authority on cities and their design history and communal purpose. He was a committed modernist who believed that society could be improved through rational and ecologically sound planning. Although he himself was a sociologist and journalist, he became the spokesman for the Regional Planning Association of America, an informal group of architects, planners, economists, and writers who came to prominence during the 1920s and 1930s. For more, see Robert Wojtowicz, *Lewis Mumford and American Modernism: Eutopian Theories for Architecture and Urban Planning* (Cambridge: Cambridge University Press, 1996).

17. Elizabeth Mock, *Built in USA since 1932* (New York: Museum of Modern Art, 1945), 61, cited in Treib and Imbert, *Garrett Eckbo*, 121, 129.

18. Hamlin, "Farm Security Administration," 718.

19. The Bauhaus school developed one of the most influential currents of modern art and architecture. It emerged during the post–World War I era when Germany was searching for a new social order by which to rebuild. Treib and Imbert, *Garrett Eckbo*, 13–20.

20. Garret Eckbo, "Farm Security Administration Projects," *Arts and Architecture* 1, no. 4 (1982): 42.

21. Treib and Imbert, *Garrett Eckbo*, 176.

22. DeMars, "Life in Architecture," 135, 102. The Chandler Project was not technically a migratory labor camp, though the distinction is minimal. It was set up as a cooperative subsistence farm for displaced farmers who were laboring as migratory workers. The Chandler Project was built before migrant camps were developed in Arizona.

23. Paul Keith Conkin, *Tomorrow a New World: The New Deal Community Program* (New York: Da Capo Press, 1976), 186.

24. Conkin, *Tomorrow a New World*, 148–49.

25. Conkin, *Tomorrow a New World*, 307.

26. Conkin, *Tomorrow a New World*, 102.

27. "Collapse of New Deal's 'Crackpot Utopias' Revealed," *San Francisco Examiner*, June 10, 1946, box C-R 1, ctn. 2, file 10 1937–38, Hollenberg Collection, BANC.

28. Conkin, *Tomorrow a New World*, 85.

29. Jess C. Gilbert, *Planning Democracy: Agrarian Intellectuals and the Intended New Deal* (New Haven, Conn.: Yale University Press, 2015), 76–77; Daniel Immerwahr, *Thinking Small: The United States and the Lure of Community Development* (Cambridge, Mass.: Harvard University Press, 2015), 47.

30. Baird Snyder to Nathan Straus, November 11, 1939, box 4, file AD-124, FmHA, RG 96, NACP.

31. C. B. Baldwin, FSA Administrator, to Senator Sam Rayburn, February 16, 1942, box 488, file TX-39-124 (Not Construction), FmHA, RG 96, NACP. To limit local resistance, the FSA collaborated with local officials from the regional chamber of commerce and with the city planning committees they formed to survey potential sites and give their recommendations. "Progress of Labor Camp Program in Region VIII" submitted by C. M. Evans, Regional Director, to W. W. Alexander, February 14, 1939, box 487, file RP-TX-37 000–900 McAllen Migratory Labor Camp, FmHA, RG 96, NACP.

32. Arthur J. Edwards to FSA Administrator, April 30, 1941, box 9, file AD-124 Reg. I Migratory Labor General 1941, FmHA, RG 96, NACP.

33. See, for example David Montejano, *Anglos and Mexicans in the Making of Texas, 1836–1986* (Austin: University of Texas Press, 1987), 197–219.

34. USDA, FSA, Division of Information Report, "Rural Housing in the West," box C-R 1, ctn. 2, Hollenberg Collection, BANC.

35. Mrs. Effie Ball Magurn to President Franklin D. Roosevelt, April 17, 1940, box 11, file AD-124 Reg 9 Migratory Labor Commendations & Complaints, 1940, FmHA, RG 96, NACP.

36. V. O. Key to USDA, FSA, Attention J. V. Warring, Assistant Administrator, Washington, D.C., May 3, 1941, box 489, file AD-TX-41 160–02 Lamesa Labor Camp and AD-TX-41 160-02 V. O. Key, FmHA, RG 96, NACP. It is very likely that this is V. O. Key, Sr., father to the well-known political scientist V. O. Key, Jr., who taught at Harvard and came of age in Lamesa, Texas.

37. Nate Brant to Board of Supervisors, January 17, 1941, and Committee on Resolution, J. E. McGrath, The Farmers Protective League to Senator Prentiss M. Brown, January 23, 1941, box 9, file AD-124 Reg II Migratory Labor General 1941, FmHA, RG 96, NACP.

38. "Petition Protesting Establishment of McAllen Farm Family Labor Camp," originally mailed to Secretary of Labor Henry Wallace, box 487, file RP-TX-37 McAllen Migratory Labor Camp, FmHA, RG 96, NACP. See also "Resettlement—Petition Protesting Establishment of McAllen Migratory Labor Camp," submitted to Dr. W. W. Alexander on February 15, 1940, McAllen Camp Files, file TX-37-160-02, FmHA, RG 96, National Archives at Fort Worth, Tex. (NAFW).

39. Memorandum for Major J. O. Walker, Director, Resettlement Division, from Nelson H. Cruikshank, Administrative Officer in charge of Migratory Labor Program, June 13, 1940, box 487, file RP-TX-37 000-900 McAllen Migratory Labor Camp, FmHA, RG 96, NACP.

40. C. McNallie to Migratory Labor Division, FSA, Dallas, Texas, May 16, 1941; C. McNallie to Hon. Milton West, House of Representatives, Washington, D.C., May 20, 1941; Tulane S. Smith, Acting Regional Director, to Mr. C. B. Baldwin, Administrator, FSA, June 18, 1941, in McAllen Camp Files, file TX-37-160-02, FmHA, RG 96, NAFW.

41. W. A. Canon, Acting Regional Director, to Dr. W. W. Alexander, Administrator, FSA, May 7, 1940, box 487, file RP-TX-37 000-900 McAllen Migratory Labor Camp, FmHA, RG 96, NACP.

42. Paul T. Vickers to W. A. Canon, February 2, 1940, box 487, file RP-TX-37 000-900 McAllen Migratory Labor Camp, FmHA, RG 96, NACP.

43. *Evening Valley Monitor*, n.d., news clipping found in box 487, file RP-TX-37 000-900 McAllen Migratory Labor Camp, FmHA, RG 96, NACP.

44. H. P. Hallsteen, District Engineer, to John F. Donovan, Acting Chief Engineer, January 12, 1940, box 8, file AD-124 All Regs Migratory Labor General 1940, FmHA, RG 96, NACP. Responding to the question of whether it would have been possible to put the camps right along the edge of town so as to serve as an extension of the town, FSA architect Vernon DeMars explained: "Probably the town wouldn't have allowed it in the first place." When further questioned: "Were these pariahs, all these people who were coming in [the migrants]?" DeMars replied: "Yes, that's partly it." DeMars, "Life in Architecture," 87–88.

45. John Beecher to J. H. Wood, "Memorandum Re: April Report, Florida, Migratory Labor Camps," May 2, 1940, p. 3, box 9, file AD-124 Reg. V Migratory Labor 1940, FmHA, RG 96, NACP.

46. Christine Reiser Robbins and Mark W. Robbins, "Spatial Relations in Oral History: The Robstown Migrant Labor Camp beyond the Federal Period," *Oral History Review* 42, no. 2 (September 4, 2015): 10, 13.

47. DeMars, "Life in Architecture," 106; Lois A. Craig, *The Federal Presence: Architecture, Politics, and Symbols in United States Government Building* (Cambridge, Mass.: MIT Press, 1978), 386.

48. U.S. House of Representatives, *Select Committee of the House Committee on Agriculture, to Investigate the Activities of the Farm Security Administration, 78th Cong., 1st Sess., 1943, Part 2* (Washington, D.C.: Government Printing Office, 1943), 624.

49. Treib and Imbert, *Garrett Eckbo*, 126.

50. Le Corbusier was a Swiss-French architect and one of the pioneers of modern architecture. He was a founding member of CIAM and a leading scholar on urban planning. DeMars, "Life in Architecture," 105; Greg Hise, "From Roadside Camps to Garden Homes: Housing and Community Planning for California's Migrant Work Force, 1935–1941," *Perspectives in Vernacular Architecture* 5 (1995): 257, doi:10.2307/3514258.

51. Greg Hise, *Magnetic Los Angeles: Planning the Twentieth-Century Metropolis* (Baltimore: Johns Hopkins University Press, 1997), 106.

52. Treib and Imbert, *Garrett Eckbo*, 123; Hamlin, "Farm Security Administration," 710.

53. Short to Mr. L. B. Arnold, Sinton, Texas, Camp Manager, May 23, 1940, in Sinton Camp Files, file TX-34-183-01, FmHA, RG 96, NAFW.

54. Box 1, file Arvin Administration (7-1-40) [Camp committees and meeting minutes, investigation 1936 w. 10 photos of camp buildings, 1 arch. drawing] [1936–1939], p. 3, FmHA, RG 96, National Archives at San Francisco, San Bruno, Calif. (NASF).

55. Letter to Jonathan Gast, FSA Regional Director, June 6, 1936, box 19, file G Labor Non-Administrative & Non-Appointive AD-120, FmHA, RG 96, NACP.

56. Diane Ghirardo, *Building New Communities: New Deal America and Fascist Italy* (Princeton, N.J.: Princeton University Press, 1989), 151–52.

57. Don Mitchell, *They Saved the Crops: Labor, Landscape, and the Struggle over Industrial Farming in Bracero-Era California* (Athens: University of Georgia Press, 2012); Cindy Hahamovitch, *The Fruits of Their Labor: Atlantic Coast Farmworkers and the Making of Migrant Poverty, 1870–1945* (Chapel Hill: University of North Carolina Press, 1997).

58. Don Mitchell, "La Casa de Esclavos Modernos: Exposing the Architecture of Exploitation," *Journal of the Society of Architectural Historians* 71, no. 4 (December 1, 2012): 451–61.

59. Treib and Imbert, *Garrett Eckbo*, 106, 135.

60. As Imbert suggests, "Everyone everywhere needed a tree, especially when 'everywhere' was not home." Treib and Imbert, *Garrett Eckbo*, 121.

61. Hamlin, "Farm Security Administration," 711.

62. Hise, *Magnetic Los Angeles*, 107.

63. Hamlin, "Farm Security Administration," 711.

64. W. A. Canon to Mr. Si Casady, Publisher, *Valley Evening Monitor*, McAllen, Texas, October 30, 1941, in McAllen Camp Files, file TX-37-160-02, FmHA, RG 96, NAFW.

65. Agnes E. Meyer, "Camps Aid to Valley Workers: Projects at Robstown Are Transformation for Migrants," *Texas Spectator*, May 5, 1946, 3.

66. On the origins of the "minimal house" idea in the camps, see DeMars, "Life in Architecture," 133.

67. Hise, *Magnetic Los Angeles*, 107. By 1942 there were approximately 1,960 homes constructed across the United States, 80 percent of which were occupied. "FSA Migratory Camp Population Reports and Employment and Earnings of Families Living in FSA Camps, Weeks Ending July 18 and July 25, 1942," box 19, file AD 124 All Regs. 183 Migratory Labor Social Security Tables on Interstate Migrants 1937, FmHA, RG 96, NACP.

68. "Labor Camp Open to Agricultural Workers," *Valley Evening Monitor* (McAllen, Tex.), n.d., p. 12, as found in box 487, file RP-TX-37 000-900 McAllen Migratory Labor Camp, FmHA, RG 96, NACP. Some of the labor homes at the McAllen camp were actually "duplex homes" that were composed of all of the same amenities as the single units, with the exception of an individual porch. These rented for seven dollars a month. The McAllen project, unlike any of the other Texas camps, was predominantly a labor home layout having 85 labor homes and only 48 temporary shelter units. This was atypical for the program, which usually had between 25 and 50 labor homes and an average of 200 to 400 shelter units.

69. DeMars, "Life in Architecture," 143; Hamlin, "Farm Security Administration," 716.

70. James T. Collins to R. T. Magleby, FSA Assistant Regional Director, n.d., box 13, file AD-124 Reg. XI Migratory Labor General 1940, FmHA, RG 96, NACP.

71. U.S. House of Representatives, House Report No. 1430, *Report of Select Committee of the House Committee on Agriculture to Investigate the Activities of the Farm Security Administration, 78th Cong., 2d Sess.* (Washington, D.C.: Government Printing Office, 1944), 16.

72. Texas Historical Commission (THC), "Report on Lamesa Farm Workers Community Historic District," Texas Recorded Historical Landmark Files, Texas Historical Commission Library, (Austin, 1991), 13; "Lamesa Farm Workers Community, Los Ybanez, Dawson County, Texas, U.S. Department of the Interior, National Register of Historic Places Continuation Sheet, Figure 54, Quadruplex Shelter—Floor Plan, Source FSA Plans, 1941," both in Lamesa File, THC.

73. "U.S. Sets Rent at a Dime a Day," *Philadelphia Inquirer*, February 1939, box 12, file AD-124 California Migratory Labor General 1939, FmHA, RG 96, NACP.

74. Monthly Narrative Report (NMR), submitted June 3, 1941, Sinton Migratory Labor Camp, Sinton Files, FmHA, RG 96, NAFW.

75. Ghirardo, *Building New Communities*, 151.

76. Paul Freier, Acting Camp Manager, to W. A. Canon, Assistant Regional Director, February 25, 1942, box 488, file TX-39-126-01 Project Inspection Report, FmHA, RG 96, NACP. Camp rules and regulations were outlined in an "occupancy agreement" that migrant residents were asked to sign on entrance to the FSA camp. Such occupational agreements outlined the responsibility of residents in the "normal labor of policing and maintaining [camp] premises . . . as a condition of occupation." The guard or "watchman" on site supervised this work. See "Farm Family Labor Camps," box 16, file RP-M-150-01 1941 Procedure, FmHA, RG 96, NACP.

77. Francis T. McSherry, Camp Manager, to Harvey M. Coverley, Assistant Regional Director, January 15, 1941, box 16, file RR-CF-37-789-18, FmHA, RG 96, NASF.

78. MNR, Weslaco, Texas, submitted on November 9, 1940, Weslaco Files, FmHA, RG 96, NAFW.

79. Paul Taylor to Garst, May 22, 1937, box 5, file RF-CF-16(25) 913, FmHA, RG 96, NASF.

80. "Humanity, U.S.A.: Farm Security Administration Tackles Biggest Job on Home Front," n.d., box C-R 1, ctn. 3, file 35, Newsletters 1941, Hollenberg Collection, BANC.

81. *Athena Breeze*, Migrant Camp Newspaper for Athena, Oregon, June 27, 1942, p. 2, box 17, file RP-85-163 1941 REG. 11 Newspapers & Magazines, FmHA, RG 96, NACP.

82. Gladys Murphy Graham, "The Migrants Are Americans," *Journal of the American Association of Women*, December 1940, p. 2, box 1, Archives Identifier: 4499583, Correspondence Relating to Migratory Labor Camps, FmHA, RG 96, National Archives at Boston, Waltham, Mass. (NAB).

83. "Social & Economic Survey of RA Migrant Camp Site at Brawley Imperial County, California," submitted to R. G. Tugwell, October 9, 1936, box 9, file RF-CF-16-201-2, FmHA, RG 96, NASF.

84. Labeling ethnic Mexican farmworkers as "Mexican Indians" reinforced the fact that they were racially not white despite any legal claims they may have had to citizenship if they were in fact American-born Mexicans. In other words, in an important example of the intersectionality of race, citizenship, and coloniality, in this context the depiction of Mexicans as Indians did not help them claim any "native" relation to the land; rather, it actually worked to affirm their "foreignness."

85. "Social & Economic Survey of RA Migrant Camp Site at Brawley."

86. Thomas Collins to Eric Thomsen, October 12, 1936, box 3, file RF-CF-16(25) 550 [+597], FmHA, RG 96, NASF.

87. In Florida, these were located in and around Belle Glade and Pompano. At Belle Glade, Camp Osceola consisted of 150 metal and concrete shelters and 20 labor homes for white families. Camp Okeechobee contained 304 metal and concrete shelters and additional duplex labor homes for 42 African American families. Camp Pahokee consisted of 30 labor homes and additional wooden duplex houses for 150 white families. Camp Everglades contained 13 labor homes and additional duplex wooden shelters for 300 African American

families. Finally, at Pompano, Camp Pompano contained duplex shelters for 300 African American families (no labor homes). "United States Department of Agriculture, Farm Security Administration Region V, Florida Migratory Labor Camp Program, 3-7-41," box 9, file AD 124 Reg. V Migratory Labor General, 1941, FmHA, RG 96, NACP. Missouri's "Delmo Labor Homes" Project—which some documents classified as migrant camps—also segregated facilities by race. The projects at Grayridge, North Lilbourne, Wardell, and Wyatt were also considered "colored units." See Memorandum to Mr. C. B. Baldwin, FSA Administrator, from Constance E. H. Daniel, Senior Administrative Assistant, March 26, 1942, box 16, file RP-M-132 Appts. & Actions, FmHA, RG 96, NACP. It should be noted, however, that other FSA camps were also distinctly racialized. For example, the federal labor camps in Rupert, Idaho, and Nyssa, Oregon, contained solely Japanese American farmworkers and their families. Similarly, the FSA camp at Del Rio in Oxnard, California, was designated for "Mexican fruit pickers."

88. Edward J. Rowell, Social Science Analyst, to Dr. Earl R. Beckner, Acting Chief Labor Relation Section FSA, November 16, 1939, box 10, file AD-124 Reg. 8 Migrant Camps, 1939, FmHA, RG 96, NACP.

89. FSA, "Migratory Farm Workers Camps," box 8, file AD-124 Migratory Labor All Regions Eastern Seaboard Report, FmHA, RG 96, NACP. See also "Proposal for Construction of Migratory Farm Workers Camp at Lamesa, Texas," February 25, 1941, box 489, file AD-TX-41-432 Budgets, FmHA, RG 96, NACP; "Report of a Committee Study Made Recently of Migratory Labor Camp Conditions around Phoenix, Arizona," box 484, file RP-TX-32 (000-900) Raymondville Migratory Labor Camp, FmHA, RG 96, NACP.

90. MNR, Princeton Camp, June 6, 1942, box 488, file RP-TX-38-183-01, FmHA, RG 96, NACP.

91. Baldwin to Evans, April 19, 1940, box 488, file AD-TD 39 432 Princeton Migratory Camp, FmHA, RG 96, NACP.

92. Robbins and Robbins, "Spatial Relations in Oral History," 5.

93. F. V. Meriwether, Senior Medical Officer, FSA, to Dr. R. C. Williams, Chief Medical Officer, FSA, November 4, 1940, box 10, file AD 124 R-8 Migratory Camps Medical Care, FmHA, RG 96, NACP.

94. Claude R. Wickard to Donald M. Nelson, May 8, 1942, box 6, file Foreign Labor Migratory, FmHA, RG 96, NACP; Hahamovitch, *Fruits of Their Labor*, 167.

95. Lynne Horiuchi, "Dislocations: The Built Environments of Japanese American Internment," in Mike Mackey, ed., *Guilt by Association: Essays on Japanese Settlement, Internment, and Relocation in the Rocky Mountain West* (Powell, Wyo.: Western History Publications, 2001), 255.

96. U.S. House of Representatives, *Select Committee Investigating National Defense Migration: Problems of Evacuation of Enemy Aliens and Others from Prohibited Military Zones, Hearings, 77th Cong., 2d Sess., Part 33* (Washington, D.C.: Government Printing Office, 1943), 11654 (hereafter cited as NDMH). Asian American studies scholars have long debated the correct terms to discuss Japanese internment, which are especially important in the context of spatial analysis. Mostly, I use the terms in use at the time to situate the process in historical context. I do, however, challenge the various euphemisms used to soften the experience of internment by emphasizing how the camps operated to regulate, contain, and police people of Japanese ancestry despite the state's democratic rhetoric. See Roger Daniels, *Prisoners Without Trial: Japanese Americans in World War II*, rev. ed. (New York: Hill & Wang, 2004).

97. By this time, the FSA had also gained wide experience in building defense housing and had become an industry leader in prefabricated housing and other construction technologies. For more, see Hise, *Magnetic Los Angeles.*

98. NDMH, 11659.

99. In this consideration, I was influenced by Robert Wilson's study on the history of the Klamath Basin Project along the Oregon-California border, in which he demonstrates how state agents have both constructed and blurred spatial binaries in environmental terms. Robert Wilson, "Landscapes of Promise and Betrayal: Reclamation, Homesteading, and Japanese American Incarceration," *Annals of the Association of American Geographers* 101, no. 2 (March 16, 2011): 424–44.

100. DeMars, "Life in Architecture," 224.

101. Hewes, *Boxcar in the Sand*, 159.

102. DeMars, "Life in Architecture," 225.

103. Horiuchi, "Dislocations," 172.

104. John Provinse and Solon Kimball, "Building New Communities During War Time," *American Sociological Review* 11, no. 4 (August 1946): 397.

105. Horiuchi, "Dislocations," 137.

106. DeMars would later reflect on how the army engineers came in to the San Francisco office and "were looking at rolls of blueprints and things [concerning the migrant camps], for the relocation camps." DeMars, "Life in Architecture," 226.

107. Mae Ngai, "'An Ironic Testimony to the Value of American Democracy': Assimilationism and the World War II Internment of Japanese Americans," in Marisha Sinha and Penny Von Eschen, eds., *Contested Democracy: Freedom, Race, and Power in American History* (New York: Columbia University Press, 2007), 239.

108. Ngai, "Ironic Testimony," 240. Horiuchi also suggests that Eckbo's landscape design for Manzanar might have been a protest of sorts. She writes that "place names appear in the plant list, particularly among tree species, that seem to leave no doubt that the landscape plan had a place name and international theme: Cottonwood Carolina, California Black Walnut, Chinese Elm, Arizona Ash, Norway Maple, London Plane, Russian Olive, English Private, Japanese Barberry. They seem to function as a cosmopolitan plant family alluding to a kind of postwar dream of international peace." Horiuchi, "Dislocations," 174–75.

109. Horiuchi, "Dislocations," 173.

110. Provinse and Kimball, "Building New Communities," 143.

111. Carey McWilliams, "What About Our Japanese-Americans?" (Public Affairs Committee, 1944), 16, California State University Japanese American Digitization Project; California State University, Dominguez Hills, Archives and Special Collections, Calisphere, accessed July 16, 2019, https://calisphere.org/item/ba286d625f170da307465ab7a6f9f5c8/.

112. Statistical information comes from Jeffery F. Burton, Eleanor Roosevelt, and Irene J. Cohen, *Confinement and Ethnicity: An Overview of World War II Japanese American Relocation Sites* (Seattle: University of Washington Press, 2002); see also Emily Brosveen, "World War II Internment Camps," Handbook of Texas Online, last modified May 23, 2016, https://tshaonline.org/handbook/online/articles/quwby; for information specifically on the transfer of the Crystal City camp to the INS, see box 488, file 88-TX-38-240, FmHA, RG 96, NACP.

113. Horiuchi, "Dislocations," 217.

114. Hise, "From Roadside Camps to Garden Homes," 210.

115. Arnold R. Hirsch, *Making the Second Ghetto: Race and Housing in Chicago, 1940–1960* (Chicago: University of Chicago Press, 1998); Kenneth T. Jackson, *Crabgrass Frontier: The Suburbanization of the United States* (New York: Oxford University Press, 1987).

Chapter 3

1. Evaristo Gonzalez, Jr., interview by author, Edinburg, Texas, July 19, 2008. After introducing the individuals I interviewed by their complete names, I subsequently refer to them by their first names. While this informal practice is unusual because they are now elders in the community, I use their first names to emphasize the fact that most were children at the time they lived in the labor camps.

2. Geographers created the term "mental map" in the early 1970s as a means of introducing differential perception into their spatial analysis. They were influenced by theories on cognitive mapping originated by psychologists. On this subject, see Elspeth Graham, "What Is a Mental Map?" *Area* 8, no. 4 (1976): 259–62. Social and cultural studies scholars have since built on such theories in an attempt to interrogate the varied meaning people assign to the spaces they inhabit and share. In this consideration, I was influenced by Elsa Barkley Brown and Gregg D. Kimball, "Mapping the Terrain of Black Richmond," *Journal of Urban History* 21, no. 3 (March 1995): 296–346. In a similar way, oral historians have captured the intersections of the biographical and geographical by mapping memories through the way individuals experience place, scale, and movement filtered through the lens of time. For more, see Paula Hamilton and Linda Shopes, eds., *Oral History and Public Memories* (Philadelphia: Temple University Press, 2008).

3. Israel Longoria Gonzalez, phone interview by author, March 27, 2015. Israel's "mental map" also included a video he made with his daughter, Debbie Gonzalez Santana. The video was taken at the private property of an individual who owns two of the original migrant shelters from the Harlingen camp. This person purchased the shelters from the county in the early 1970s for fifty dollars each. The shelters are in excellent condition. In the video, Israel describes where his family kept their beds and stove, and where they stored their belongings. He also told stories about events that happened in the shelter, including a time when he played a prank on his father by pulling a chair out from under him. Debbie posted the video on Facebook, which then invited extended family members to comment on their memories of the camp space.

4. USDA-FSA Division of Information, "Rural Housing in the West," box C-R 1, ctn. 1, file 1.11 FSA Background Material Press Releases 1939–43, Ralph W. Hollenberg Collection of Materials Relating to the Farm Security Administration (hereafter cited as Hollenberg Collection), Region IX, San Francisco, Calif., Bancroft Library, University of California, Berkeley (BANC).

5. Deutsch argues that, beginning in the late nineteenth century, continued migration and the development of a regional community was a necessary strategy New Mexican Hispanos used to deal with Anglo incursion and settlement. She concludes, contrary to my study, that New Deal–era programs severely limited the power Hispanos' regional communities maintained by destroying their cultural independence and making them increasingly reliant on government subsidies. Sarah Deutsch, *No Separate Refuge: Culture, Class, and Gender on an Anglo-Hispanic Frontier in the American Southwest, 1880–1940* (New York: Oxford University Press, 1987).

6. Israel Longoria Gonzalez, phone interview by author, April 3, 2018. See also family tree of Maria Balli Gonzalez available on Ancestry.com.

7. Andrew Herod, "From a Geography of Labor to a Labor Geography: Labor's Spatial Fix and the Geography of Capitalism," *Antipode* 29, no. 1 (1997): 24–25; Andrew Herod, "Workers as Geographical Actors," *Labor History* 53, no. 3 (August 2012): 335–53. In my analysis of farmworkers' "labor geography," more specifically, I have benefited from Don Mitchell, *The Lie of the Land: Migrant Workers and the California Landscape* (Minneapolis: University of Minnesota Press, 1996); Wendy Jepson, "Spaces of Labor Activism, Mexican-American Women and the Farm Worker Movement in South Texas Since 1966," *Antipode* 37, no. 4 (September 1, 2005): 679–702.

8. Charles J. Shindo, *Dust Bowl Migrants in the American Imagination* (Lawrence: University Press of Kansas, 1997), 30.

9. Brian Q. Cannon, " 'Keep on A-Goin': Life and Social Interaction in a New Deal Farm Labor Camp," *Agricultural History* 70, no. 1 (1996): 21.

10. Stein writes, "When the needs of the group conflicted with the desires of the individual migrant, however, the group invariably took second place. In this, the Okies were basically no different from other Americans." Walter J. Stein, *California and the Dust Bowl Migration* (Westport, Conn.: Greenwood, 1973), 172.

11. James C. Scott, *Seeing Like a State: How Certain Schemes to Improve the Human Condition Have Failed* (New Haven, Conn.: Yale University Press, 1998), 191.

12. Jess Gilbert similarly questions the applicability of Scott's analysis when considering the agrarian New Dealers involved in planning new community programs during the late 1930s and early 1940s. See Jess C. Gilbert, *Planning Democracy: Agrarian Intellectuals and the Intended New Deal* (New Haven, Conn.: Yale University Press, 2015), 62–63, 78–79.

13. Carey McWilliams, *Ill Fares the Land: Migrants and Migratory Labor in the United States* (Boston: Little, Brown, 1942), 230, 250.

14. Stein, *California and the Dust Bowl Migration*, 171, 175, 172–73. For a similar claim, see Shindo, *Dust Bowl Migrants*, 32; James N. Gregory, *American Exodus: The Dust Bowl Migration and Okie Culture in California* (New York: Oxford University Press, 1989), 139.

15. Stein, *California and the Dust Bowl Migration*, 243–74; Gregory, *American Exodus*, 154–64.

16. Gregory, *American Exodus*, 162–63.

17. Stein, *California and the Dust Bowl Migration*, 176.

18. Cannon, " 'Keep on A-Goin,' " 19, 21; Shindo, *Dust Bowl Migrants*, 33.

19. The Todd and Sonkin collection offers a rich perspective on the FSA camp experience in spatial and audio terms. The ethnographers recorded everyday sounds (including passing trains, kids playing, fans blowing, and people conversing) that help the listener situate themselves in the camp's particular landscape. On the origins of the project, see "The Charles L. Todd and Robert Sonkin Collecting Expedition," Library of Congress (LOC), accessed June 12, 2019, https://www.loc.gov/collections/todd-and-sonkin-migrant-workers-from-1940-to -1941/articles-and-essays/the-charles-l-todd-and-robert-sonkin-collecting-expedition/.

20. Charles L. Todd, Robert Sonkin, and J. W. Becker, "Interview About Life in the Government Camp, Shafter FSA Camp, August, 16, 1940," LOC, accessed June 12, 2019, https://www.loc.gov/item/toddbib000181/.

21. Todd et al., "Interview About Life in the Government Camp."

22. Charles L. Todd, Robert Sonkin, and Wayne "Gene" Dinwiddie, "Interview with Wayne 'Gene' Dinwiddie, Visalia FSA Camp, August 30, 1941," LOC, accessed June 12, 2019, https://www.loc.gov/item/toddbib000335/.

23. Charles L. Todd, Robert Sonkin, and Rosetta Spainhard, "The Government Camp, Arvin FSA Camp, August 1, 1940," LOC, accessed June 12, 2019, https://www.loc.gov/item/toddbib000039/.

24. Charles L. Todd, "Trampling Out the Vintage: Farm Security Camps Provide the Imperial Valley Migrants with a Home and Hope," *Common Sense*, July 1939, 30.

25. Monthly Narrative Report (MNR), Sinton, Texas, January 1941, Sinton Camp Files, file TX-34-183-01, Records of the Farmers Home Administration (FmHA), Record Group 96 (RG 96), National Archives at Fort Worth, Tex. (NAFW).

26. Russell Lee, "Migrant Camp, Weslaco, Texas," Prints & Photographs Division, FSA/OWI Collection, LOC (hereafter cited as FSA/OWI), LC-USF34-032108-D, February 1939.

27. James A. Moore to W. A. Canon, May 21, 1940, Robstown Camp Files, file TX-33-060, FmHA, RG 96, NAFW.

28. John Fisher, Director of Information, FSA, to Victor Weybright, Managing Editor, Survey Graphic, December 12, 1939, box 10, file AD-124 Reg. 8 Migratory Camps 1939, FmHA, RG 96, National Archives at College Park, Md. (NACP).

29. Albert K. Short, Camp Manager, Raymondville, Texas, to W. A. Canon, Director, Resettlement Division, March 1, 1941, Raymondville Camp Files, file TX-32-060, FmHA, RG 96, NAFW.

30. MNR, Mobile Unit #5, Oxnard, California, for June 1941, appendix A, box 224, file AD-CF-41 (000-900) California Mobile #4 General, FmHA, RG 96, NACP.

31. "Why Not Live Better," *Belle Glade Herald*, December 12, 1941, p. 6, box 17, file RP-85-163 Newspapers & Magazines, FmHA, RG 96, NACP. It is unclear if Williams or other *Herald* staff members had any direct relationship with the FSA, perhaps as local labor and community advisers, but it is evident that they were strong advocates of the camp program.

32. A *comadre* is a close female relative or friend, typically serving as a godmother to one or more children in the family. Alcario Samudio, phone interview by author, May 13, 2008.

33. The Suárezes moved from the Harlingen camp to the Weslaco camp in what their children described to be the late 1930s but was more likely the early 1940s, given that the camps were not built until 1941 and 1940, respectively. Mr. Suárez eventually became a foreman at the Weslaco camp, which partially explains Alcario's comment that he and his wife were "the ones really in charge." Also, by the late 1940s, when federal management of the camps waned, Mr. Suárez remained a central figure at the Weslaco camp. An individual by the name of Otto Belcher, who had previously worked for the Weslaco camp under the FSA, continued to manage the camp through the mid-1950s, but it was Mr. Suárez on whom most campers relied on a daily basis. Bertha Suárez, interview by author, Weslaco, Texas, February 29, 2008.

34. For a closer discussion of the familial and fictive kinship bonds Mexican farmworkers created across the South Texas borderlands, see Cristina Salinas, *Managed Migrations: Growers, Farmworkers, and Border Enforcement in the Twentieth Century* (Austin: University of Texas Press, 2018), 50, 57.

35. Israel Longoria Gonzalez, phone interview by author, March 27, 2015.

36. Evaristo Gonzalez, Jr., interview by author, Edinburg, Texas, July 19, 2008; Maria Guadalupe G. Barrera, interview by author, Harlingen, Texas, July 19, 2008.

37. Mrs. Ofilia Cantu Ramírez was married to Noel Ramírez, Fortunato's son. Herón Ramírez, interview by author, Pharr, Texas, July 18, 2008; Ofilia Cantu Ramírez, interviewed by Victor Ramírez (her son) on the author's behalf, Roma, Texas, July 27, 2008.

38. Maria Guadalupe G. Barrera, interview by author, Harlingen, Texas, July 19, 2008.

39. Monica Perales discusses the importance of analyzing childhood memories as both nostalgia and historical truth in *Smeltertown: Making and Remembering a Southwest Border Community* (Chapel Hill: University of North Carolina Press, 2010), 265–68, 271.

40. Israel Longoria Gonzalez, phone interview by author, Harlingen, Texas, March 27, 2015.

41. The James L. Landrum House in Cameron County, Texas, is now a historical landmark because of Landrum's significance as a business and civic leader and the originality of the home's architecture. Historic American Buildings Survey, James L. Landrum House (Rancho Ciprés), National Park Service, accessed June 12, 2019, http://lcweb2.loc.gov/master/pnp/habshaer/tx/tx1100/tx1125/data/tx1125data.pdf.

42. Aubrey Clyde Robinson and Glenore Fisk Horne, "Florida Migratory Workers," Confidential Report to the Administrator, June 1937, pp. 24, 26–27, box 9, file Copy #1 R-5 AD-124 Resettlement Administration Confidential Report to the Administrator FLORIDA MIGRATORY WORKERS Robinson and Horne, FmHA, RG 96, NACP. Linda Gordon suggests that similar "car groups" existed among the Dust Bowl refugees traveling to California, further contesting the notion that they were fiercely independent. As she writes, "Families and groups often drove in tandem, because their cars broke down so often. At other times, groups formed in roadside encampments, where they could share resources and exchange information." Linda Gordon, *Dorothea Lange: A Life Beyond Limits* (London: W. W. Norton, 2009), 249, 255.

43. FSA/OWI, LC-USF34-083067. Similar images can be found as part of Lot 44 in the same collection.

44. "Council Meeting," *Migrant Worker*, published at Migratory Labor Camp Unit #17, Bridgeton, New Jersey, October 19, 1942, box 17, file RP-M-163 1941 Reg. 1 Newspapers & Magazines, FmHA, RG 96, NACP.

45. "Migratory Farm Labor in Texas Agriculture," report conducted by Members of the Staff of the Agricultural and Mechanical College of Texas, College Station, Texas, prepared at the request of Hon. W. Lee O'Daniel, Governor of Texas, in U.S. House of Representatives, *Select Committee to Investigate the Interstate Migration of Destitute Citizens, Hearings on H. Res. 63 and H. Res. 491, 76th Cong., 3d Sess., 1940, Part 5* (Washington, D.C.: Government Printing Office, 1941), 1925.

46. Memorandum to Major J. O. Walker, Director Resettlement Division, from Nelson H. Cruiksank, Administrative Officer in charge of Migratory Labor Program, June 13, 1940, box 487, file RP-TX-37 000-900 McAllen Migratory Labor Camp, FmHA, RG 96, NACP.

47. United States Department of Agriculture, FSA, Migratory Farm Labor Docket, Region 8, Part I: Outline of the Social-Economic Part of Justification, N. Gregory Silvermaster to Dr. Mercer G. Evans, Director Labor Relations Division, September 7, 1938, p. 4, box 10, file AD-124-Reg. VIII Migratory Camps 1941, FmHA, RG 96, NACP.

48. Silvermaster to Evans, September 7, 1938.

49. Silvermaster to Evans, September 7, 1938. On the significance of South Texas as a home base for large numbers of Mexican migrant farmworkers, Marc Simon Rodriguez

importantly argues that we must "challenge the geographically settled understanding of US History and consider the vast diaspora that made Mexican American life a rich tapestry of interrelated and overlapping communities." Marc S. Rodriguez, *The Tejano Diaspora: Mexican Americanism and Ethnic Politics in Texas and Wisconsin* (Chapel Hill: University of North Carolina Press, 2011), 2.

50. Herón Ramírez, interview by author, Pharr, Texas, July 18, 2008.

51. Dell M. Caver, Home Management Supervisor (HMS), MNR, Harlingen, Texas, July 8, 1942, box 486, file RP-TX-36-183-01, FmHA, RG 96, NACP.

52. Genevieve A. Rhodes, HMS, and Robert L. Elliot, Camp Manager, MNR, Crystal City, Texas, May 4, 1942, box 488, file RP-TX-38-183-01 Monthly Narrative Report, FmHA, RG 96, NACP.

53. Genevieve A. Rhodes, HMS, MNR, Crystal City, Texas, January 3, 1942, box 488, file RP-TX-38-183 1941 Crystal City Migratory Labor Camp Population Report, FmHA, RG 96, NACP.

54. Robert L. Elliot, Camp Manager, MNR, Crystal City, Texas, March 9, 1942, box 487, File RP-TX-38-183 Reports, FmHA, RG 96, NACP.

55. Dell M. Caver, HMS, MNR, Harlingen, Texas, July 8, 1942, box 486, folder RP-TX-36-183-01, FmHA, RG 96, NACP.

56. It is also possible that Israel's paternal grandmother, Inocencia or "Chenchita," was present at Estefana's passing because she was a midwife, and although the camp had a medical clinic, Israel stated that many people depended on his grandmother's pre- and postnatal care. Israel Longoria Gonzalez, phone interview by author, Harlingen, Texas, March 27, 2015. Information about Estefana's case also came from her death certificate, available through Ancestry.com.

57. James H. Martin, Camp Manager, MNR, Princeton, Texas, December 8, 1941, box 486, file RP-TX-36-183-01 Monthly Narrative Report of Home Management—September 1941, FmHA, RG 96, NACP.

58. Henry C. Daniels, Robstown Camp Manager, to W. A. Canon, FSA Assistant Regional Director, October 24, 1941, Robstown Camp Files, file TX-33-060, FmHA, RG 96, NAFW.

59. Lillian P. Erwin, Grant Supervisor for the Sinton, Robstown, and Crystal City, Texas, Camps, MNR, December 5, 1941, box 486, folder RP-TX-36-183-01 Monthly Narrative Report of Home Management—September 1941, FmHA, RG 96, NARA.

60. Dell M. Caver, HMS, MNR, Harlingen, Texas, January 8, 1942, box 486, file RP-TX-36-183-01 Monthly Narrative Report of Home Management—September 1941, FmHA, RG 96, NACP. Israel considers Meliton his cousin. One of Israel's sisters later married one of Meliton's uncles. Israel remembers some of the Ontiveros children, including Meliton's sisters Martina and Eudelia and a brother whom they nicknamed "la caserolita." Israel Longoria Gonzalez, phone interview by author, September 5, 2017.

61. Longoria Gonzalez, phone interview by author, September 5, 2017; "Weekly Activities Reports," box 484, file RP-183 TX-32 Camp Population "Weekly Activities Report," FmHA, RG 96, NACP. Incidentally, Narciso Martínez was himself the son of migrant farmworkers. For many years prior to the 1940s, he played in farm labor camps throughout Texas and much of the Southwest. Teresa Palomo Acosta, "Narciso Martínez," Texas State Historical Association, Handbook of Texas Online, last modified August 3, 2016, https://tshaonline.org/handbook/online/articles/fmadk.

62. Glen Housley, for example, remembers having his high school senior year dance at the community center in the Raymondville, Texas, camp. He graduated in 1941, and at that time he recalls that this was the only big auditorium available in the area. Glen Housley, interview by author, Weslaco, Texas, February 27, 2008.

63. John Collier, Jr., "Bridgeton, New Jersey. FSA (Farm Security Administration) agricultural workers' camp (June 1942). Dancing in the recreation tent." FSA/OWI, LC-USF34-083393-C.

64. In using this term, I seek to draw on an argument made by Robbins and Robbins, who found a "simultaneously celebratory and tense nature of nostalgia" among the people they interviewed from the Robstown camp. I agree with their observation that although many who lived in the camps as children remembered the experience as "the good old days," these same individuals acknowledged that for their parents it was likely "the hard days." Christine Reiser Robbins and Mark W. Robbins, "Spatial Relations in Oral History: The Robstown Migrant Labor Camp Beyond the Federal Period," *Oral History Review* 42, no. 2 (September 4, 2015): 8, 21. Monica Perales in *Smeltertown* also discusses the importance of Tejano/a workers' decision to recall their experiences as "the good old days."

65. Guadalupe Mena, interview by author, Weslaco, Texas, February 29, 2008. Ms. Mena's family was from Mathis, Texas. For a short time, they lived at the FSA camps in Sinton and Robstown, Texas, as well as the one in Weslaco, where they spent the most time.

66. Alcario Samudio, phone interview by author, Austin, Texas, May 13, 2008.

67. William A. Anglim, Acting Regional Director, to Mr. Ted Parker, Firebaugh Service Club, October 17, 1941, box 17 [new], file RR-CF-37-933 Firebaugh Migratory Camp, FmHA, RG 96, National Archives at San Francisco, San Bruno, Calif. (NASF).

68. Mrs. Bennett also drew a "mental map" of the Harlingen camp. Contrary to the maps drawn by Evaristo and Israel, Mrs. Bennett's map only features the administrative buildings and not the residential section of the camp. Her map is a telling indicator of how she experienced the camp space as an employee relative to the migrant families who lived there. Zora Mildred Bennett, interviews by author, Harlingen, Texas, February 25, 2008, May 3, 2008.

69. Maria Guadalupe G. Barrera, interview by author, Harlingen, Texas, July 19, 2008.

70. Dell M. Caver, HMS, MNR, Harlingen, Texas, June 6, 1942, box 486, file RP-TX-36-183-01 Monthly Narrative Report of Home Management—September 1941; *Camp Flashes*, Harlingen, Texas, FSA Camp Newspaper, January 23, 1942, box 486, file TX-36 000-900, FmHA, RG 96, NACP.

71. Minerva Suárez Capello, interview by author, Weslaco, Texas, May 2, 2008.

72. Aida Hinojosa, interview by author, Weslaco, Texas, May 2, 2008; Arthur Rothstein, "Younger Members of Drake Family Weslaco, Texas, FSA Camp (Feb. 1942)," FSA/OWI, LC-USF34-024994-D.

73. Guadalupe Mena, interview by author, Weslaco, Texas, February 29, 2008.

74. DDT stands for dichlorodiphenyltrichloroethane. During the 1940s it was commonly used as an agricultural and household pesticide. It was not until the mid-1960s that concerns over its harmful environmental and bodily effects became more popularized. In 1972 it was banned for agricultural use in the United States. For more, see Chapter 4. Aida Hinojosa, interview by author, Weslaco, Texas, May 2, 2008.

75. Charles L. Thomas, interview by author, Weslaco, Texas, May 2, 2008.

76. Evaristo Gonzalez, Jr., interview by author, Edinburg, Texas, July 19, 2008.

77. Israel Longoria Gonzalez, phone interview by author, March 27, 2015.

78. Segregation in Texas was an institutionalized practice that affected both African and Mexican Americans, particularly in the realm of education, housing, and access to public facilities. Even so, it is important to clarify that Anglo discrimination and segregation against ethnic Mexicans was based mainly on social custom and not legally sanctioned as would have been the case for African Americans. On this topic, especially as it concerns the Rio Grande Valley, see Jennifer R. Nájera, *The Borderlands of Race: Mexican Segregation in a South Texas Town* (Austin: University of Texas Press, 2015).

79. Herón Ramírez, interview by author, Pharr, Texas, July 18, 2008. While Herón provided specific names in this story, I chose to conceal them because of its sensitive nature. The name "Robert" is a pseudonym.

80. Anne Loftis, "Steinbeck and the Federal Migrant Camps," *San Jose Studies* 16, no. 1 (Winter 1990): 83; Cannon, "'Keep on A-Goin'," 23–25.

81. Dell M. Caver, HMS, MNR, Harlingen, Texas, May 8, 1942, box 486, file RP-TX-36-183-01 Monthly Narrative Report of Home Management—September 1941, FmHA, RG 96, NACP.

82. Israel Longoria Gonzalez, phone interview by author, September 5, 2017. Among former Robstown migrants, some recalled more meaningful interactions between the Mexican and African American families at the camp. One interviewee remembered, for example, sharing butter, cornbread, and molasses. Robbins and Robbins, "Spatial Relations in Oral History," 7.

83. Herón Ramírez, interview by author, Pharr, Texas, July 18, 2008. While Herón provided the family names in this story, I chose to conceal them because of its sensitive nature.

84. "You know, they would see us as, 'oh they get together with the Ang [stops herself from saying Anglo], the gringos. She thinks she's a gringa [i.e., white].'" Minerva Suárez Capello, interview by author, Weslaco, Texas, May 2, 2008.

85. Aida Hinojosa, interview by author, Weslaco, Texas, May 2, 2008.

86. Alcario Samudio, phone interview by author, May 13, 2008.

87. Migrant camp newspapers are disbursed throughout the FSA's archival holdings. For the largest concentration of papers, see boxes 16–17, FmHA, RG 96, NACP. The FSA was careful to stress that migrants produced the papers with little interference from camp management. The camp paper for Yuma, Arizona, *Migrant Mike*, for example, included a clause that stated: "The FSA does not accept responsibility for the opinions or remarks which appear in this paper. This is solely the camper's paper and it is their news which appears in the migrant mike." *Migrant Mike*, Yuma Farmworkers Community, box 97, file RP-AZ-11 (000-900) Yuma Migratory Labor Camp (hereafter cited as RP-AZ-11), FmHA, RG 96, NACP.

88. Harvey M. Coverley, Assistant Regional Director, to Mr. Evald L. Swanson, District Supervisor, April 15, 1941; Guy W. Griset, Community Manager, to Mr. Harvey M. Coverley, Assistant Regional Director, April 11, 1941, both in box 23 [new], file RR-CF-26-163-01, FmHA, RG 96, NASF.

89. Coverley to Swanson, April 15, 1941.

90. John Fischer, Chief Information Division, to Mr. Shelby Thompson, Regional Information Adviser, December 28, 1940, box 9, file Region II AD-124, FmHA, RG 96, NACP; Harvey M. Coverley, Assistant Regional Director, to Mr. Thomas Collins, Camp Manager, December 26, 1940, box 53 [old], file RR-CF-31-918-01, FmHA, RG 96, NASF; James S.

Moore, Camp Manager, to Mr. W. A. Canon, Chief Resettlement Division, April 15, 1940, Raymondville Project Records, file TX-32-163-03, FmHA, RG 96, NAFW.

91. MNR, Crystal City Camp, submitted by Robert L. Elliott, Camp Manager, September 3, 1941, box 487, file RP-TX-38-183 Reports, FmHA, RG 96, NACP.

92. Camp officials reported one festivity as follows: "The sixteenth of September is a national holiday in Mexico celebrating the day Mexico won its independence from Spain. The day is always celebrated by the Mexican population of Crystal City. This year the only celebration in town was the one held at the Community Center Hall [in the FSA camp]. The hall was decorated with crepe paper of Mexico's colors and those of the United States. The stage was decorated with flags of Mexico and the United States. The celebration was held at night. There were speeches and a program followed by a dance (with an orchestra). The attendance was large with many guests from town present." MNR, Genevieve A. Rhodes, HMS, Crystal City, Texas, September 2, 1941, box 487, file RP-TX-38-183 Reports, FmHA, RG 96, NACP.

93. Correspondence concerning "Resettlement—Proposal from Camp Council—Crystal City Migratory Labor Camp," May 3, 5, 8, and 9, 1941, box 487, file RP-M-88-49-38-060 1941 Crystal City Mig. Labor Camp Projects, FmHA, RG 96, NACP.

94. The *ejido* system was a process by which the Mexican government allotted the use of land (often in the hands of wealthy private owners) to landless people for the cultivation of community/collective farming. The system was enacted in 1934 by President Lázaro Cárdenas, but many rural Mexicans had long been engaged in the practice of communal farming.

95. Correspondence concerning "Resettlement—Proposal from Camp Council—Crystal City Migratory Labor Camp."

96. Tore C. Olsson, *Agrarian Crossings: Reformers and the Remaking of the US and Mexican Countryside* (Princeton, N.J.: Princeton University Press, 2017), 57.

97. "Gran Baile el 11 de Junio en el Labor Camp," May 27, 1943, and "Johnny Barry Con Sus Diez Musicos en el Baile LULAC," June 3, 1943, appearing in the "Sección en Español" of the *Willacy County News*, Raymondville, Texas, 1941–1944, Center for American History, Newspaper Collection, University of Texas at Austin.

98. *Migrant Mike*, January 7, 1942, vol. 3, no. 2, RP-AZ-11, NACP.

99. *Migrant Mike*, February 6, 1942, vol. 3, no. 6, RP-AZ-11, NACP.

100. Frederick R. Soule, Regional Information Adviser, to Mr. Thomas S. Montgomery, November 27, 1941, box C-R 1, ctn. 3, file Labor Camp Program, 1937–1948, folder 7, Hollenberg Collection, BANC; *Migrant Mike,* February 6, 1942, vol. 3, no. 6, and January 23, 1942, vol. 3, no. 4, RP-AZ-11, NACP.

101. "Consumer, Recreation, and Community Sanitation Group Case Histories," n.d., box C-R 1, ctn. 2, folder 6 (1938–1942), Hollenberg Collection, BANC. Information on migrant boxers found in various editions of *Migrant Mike*, RP-AZ-11, NACP.

102. Helene Louise Ritchie, Sec. Holtville Mobile Unit #4, to Mr. Thomas S. Montgomery, Community Manager, March 12, 1942, RP-AZ-11, NACP.

103. Laurence I. Hewes, Jr., Regional Director, to Mr. Mason Bar, Director Resettlement Division, March 27, 1942, RP-AZ-11, NACP.

104. "Case History," Region IX, n.d., box C-R 1, ctn. 2, folder 6 (1938–1942), Hollenberg Collection, BANC.

105. "I Am an American," *Migrant Mike*, January 7, 1942, vol. 3, no. 2, RP-AZ-11, NACP.

106. *Migrant Mike*, January 2, 1942, vol. 3, no. 1, RP-AZ-11, NACP.

107. *Migrant Mike*, January 2, 1942.

108. Mae M. Ngai, *Impossible Subjects: Illegal Aliens and the Making of Modern America* (Princeton, N.J.: Princeton University Press, 2004), 119–20.

Chapter 4

1. Bertha Suárez, interview by author, Weslaco, Texas, February 29, 2008.

2. Sidney Baldwin, *Poverty and Politics: The Rise and Decline of the Farm Security Administration* (Chapel Hill: University of North Carolina Press, 1968), 208.

3. Michel Foucault's theories on biopower and governmentality are useful for considering the state's role in managing the life of individual bodies for the sake of protecting the interests, welfare, and longevity of the composite body (i.e., the nation). Yet I am cautious in applying such theory because the FSA's health measures, and migrants' responses to them, operated in more complicated terms, as I hope to clarify. Michel Foucault, "Governmentality," in Graham Burchell, Colin Gordon, and Peter Miller, eds., *The Foucault Effect: Studies in Governmentality* (Chicago: University of Chicago Press, 1991), 100–103; Giorgio Agamben, *Homo Sacer: Sovereign Power and Bare Life* (Stanford, Calif.: Stanford University Press, 1998).

4. Susan M. Reverby, "Suffering and Resistance, Voice and Agency: Thoughts on History and the Tuskegee Syphilis Study," in Laurie B. Green, John Mckiernan-González, and Martin Summers, eds., *Precarious Prescriptions: Contested Histories of Race and Health in North America* (Minneapolis: University of Minnesota Press, 2014), xxiv, 262; Jeffrey Ferguson, "Race and the Rhetoric of Resistance," *Raritan* 28, no. 1 (Summer 2008): 4–32, 174.

5. For more, see Natalia Molina, *Fit to Be Citizens? Public Health and Race in Los Angeles, 1879–1939* (Berkeley: University of California Press, 2006).

6. Nancy Tomes, *The Gospel of Germs: Men, Women, and the Microbe in American Life* (Cambridge, Mass.: Harvard University Press, 1998), 205; Cyrus Edson, "The Microbe as a Social Leveller," *North American Review* 161, no. 467 (1895): 421–26.

7. FSA, "Migrant Farm Labor: The Problem and Ways of Meeting It," December 1939, p. 3, box 8, file AD-124 Migratory Labor All Regs. General 1939, Farmers Home Administration (FmHA), Record Group (RG) 96, National Archives at College Park, Md. (NACP).

8. Few changes in these statistics had occurred by the mid-1940s. According to the state health department, the tuberculosis rate in Texas during 1944 was as follows: "31 per 100,000 for Anglo Americans, 95 per 100,000 for Negroes, and 209 per 100,000 for Latin Americans." Quoted in Pauline R. Kibbe, "Coordinator of Inter-American Affairs Spanish Speaking People in the United States. Report of the Executive Secretary to Members of the Good Neighbor Commission, Austin, Texas, December 29, 1944," Manuscript No. 224/58/7, Ernesto Galarza Collection, Special Collections, Stanford University.

9. Nathan W. Robertson, Assistant Director Division of Information, to Joseph Singerman, Vice President of the General Science Association of New York, March 19, 1940, box 8, file AD 124 Migratory Labor All Regs. Eastern Seaboard Report, FmHA, RG 96, NACP.

10. Baird Snyder, FSA Chief Engineer, to Karl Buster, FSA District 5 Engineer, November 6, 1939, box 10, file AD 124 R-8 Migratory Camps Medical Care, FmHA, RG 96, NACP.

11. Karl Buster to Baird Snyder, November 22, 1939, box 10, file AD 124 R-8 Migratory Camps Medical Care, FmHA, RG 96, NACP.

12. "Migratory Labor Camp Near Completion," *Weslaco News*, December 7, 1939.

13. U.S. House of Representatives, *Select Committee to Investigate the Interstate Migration of Destitute Citizens, Hearings Before the Select Committee to Investigate the Interstate Migration*

of Destitute Citizens, 76th Cong., 3d Sess., 1940–41, Part 6 (Washington, D.C.: Government Printing Office, 1941), 2460 (hereafter cited as Tolan Hearings, Part 6).

14. Molina, *Fit to Be Citizens?*, 2; Howard Markel and Alexandra Minna Stern, "The Foreignness of Germs: The Persistent Association of Immigrants and Disease in American Society," *Milbank Quarterly* 80, no. 4 (December 1, 2002): 757–88; Alexandra Minna Stern, "Buildings, Boundaries, and Blood: Medicalization and Nation-Building on the U.S.-Mexico Border, 1910–1930," *Hispanic American Historical Review* 79, no. 1 (1999): 41–81; Nayan Shah, *Contagious Divides: Epidemics and Race in San Francisco's Chinatown* (Berkeley: University of California Press, 2001), 12.

15. James N. Gregory, *American Exodus: The Dust Bowl Migration and Okie Culture in California* (New York: Oxford University Press, 1989), 115, 102; Walter J. Stein, *California and the Dust Bowl Migration* (Westport, Conn.: Greenwood, 1973), 60.

16. Christy Galvin and Garth Milam, "A 'Flat Tired People': The Health of California's Okies During the 1930s," California Odyssey Project: Dust Bowl Migration Archives, Special Topic Series, California State University Bakersfield (January 12, 2017), accessed July 16, 2019, http://hdl.handle.net/10211.3/183557; Gregory, *American Exodus*, 100, 111.

17. Walter M. Dickie, M.D., Director California State Department of Public Health, and Ellen S. Stadtmuller, M.D., Chief Bureau of Child Hygiene, "Report of the Second Year of the Migratory Demonstration, July 1937–June 1938," p. 1, box C-R 1, ctn. 2, file 10 1937–38, Ralph W. Hollenberg Collection of Materials Relating to the Farm Security Administration (hereafter cited as Hollenberg Collection), Region IX, San Francisco, Calif., Bancroft Library, University of California, Berkeley (BANC).

18. Esther A. Canter, "California Renovates the Dust-Bowler," *Hygeia: The Health Magazine of the American Medical Association* 18, no. 5 (1940): 420–23, 454–55.

19. FSA Medical Report, box 17, file AD-169 All Regs. Migratory Labor General Information Requests 1939, FmHA, RG 96, NACP.

20. Memorandum to Mr. Estel H. Yetter, Regional Personnel Adviser, November 6, 1941, box 16, file RP-M-88-132-01 Standard Personnel Classifications, FmHA, RG 96, NACP, 5.

21. On Dust Bowl migrant imagery, see Wendy Kozol, "Madonnas of the Fields: Photography, Gender, and 1930s Farm Relief," *Genders* 2 (1988): 1–23. Linda Gordon convincingly argues that Dorothea Lange's photography represented an intent to depict all farmworkers with dignity as part of the FSA's greater democratizing project. Nevertheless, she acknowledges that as a whole the FSA's photographic unit produced varied and sometimes problematic narratives. Linda Gordon, *Dorothea Lange: A Life Beyond Limits* (London: W. W. Norton, 2009), 198, 219–20.

22. Russell Lee, Prints & Photographs Division, FSA/OWI Collection, Library of Congress (hereafter cited as FSA/OWI), LC-USF34-032352-D.

23. FSA/OWI, LC-USF34-032393-D; LC-USF34-032401-D; LC-USF34-032388-D.

24. For examples, see FSA/OWI, Lot 601.

25. FSA/OWI, LC-USF34-032755-D; LC-USF34-032703-D.

26. For more on the role of FSA photography in African American history, see Nicholas Natanson, *The Black Image in the New Deal: The Politics of FSA Photography* (Knoxville: University of Tennessee Press, 1992).

27. The best example of this concerns the epidemiology of venereal disease. Brandt writes that although evidence existed since the late nineteenth century that venereal diseases are

caused by microorganisms, society continued to associate the disease with dirt and uncleanliness, especially as it related to immigrants and African Americans. Allan M. Brandt, *No Magic Bullet: A Social History of Venereal Disease in the United States Since 1880* (New York: Oxford University Press, 1987), 5. On the biological and cultural origins of disease, also see Tomes, *Gospel of Germs*, and Samuel Roberts, *Infectious Fear: Politics, Disease, and the Health Effects of Segregation* (Chapel Hill: University of North Carolina Press, 2009).

28. U.S. House of Representatives, *Select Committee to Investigate the Interstate Migration of Destitute Citizens, Hearings Before the Select Committee to Investigate the Interstate Migration of Destitute Citizens, 76th Cong., 3d Sess., 1940–41, Part 2* (Washington, D.C.: Government Printing Office, 1940), 541–42 (hereafter cited as Tolan Hearings, Part 2). Florida consistently displayed one of the highest rates of syphilis among all U.S. states with 53 cases per 100,000 in whites compared with 406 cases per 100,000 in nonwhites. Michael R. Grey, "Syphilis and AIDS in Belle-Glade, Florida, 1942 and 1992," *Annals of Internal Medicine* 116, no. 4 (1992): 331.

29. Tolan Hearings, Part 2, 542.

30. Dr. Sy Axelrod, a venereal disease consultant sent by the USPHS to Florida in 1943, blamed the widespread availability of alcohol in these "juke joints" for fostering the VD epidemic by promoting both sexual and social intercourse. Grey, "Syphilis and AIDS," 332. For a typical local perspective, see Testimony of Luther Jones, realtor, farmer, and owner of the *Belle Glade Herald*, in U.S. House of Representatives, *Select Committee Investigating National Defense Migration: Problems of Evacuation of Enemy Aliens and Others from Prohibited Military Zones, Hearings, 77th Cong., 2d Sess., Part 33* (Washington, D.C.: Government Printing Office, 1943), 12666 (hereafter cited as NDMH).

31. Aubrey Clyde Robinson and Glenore Fisk Horne, "Resettlement Administration Confidential Report to the Administrator, Florida Migratory Workers," box 9, file R-5 AD-124, FmHA, RG 96, NACP; U.S. House of Representatives, *Select Committee of the House Committee on Agriculture, to Investigate the Activities of the Farm Security Administration, 78th Cong., 1st Sess., 1943, Part 1* (Washington, D.C.: Government Printing Office, 1943), 235 (hereafter cited as FSA Hearings, Part 1).

32. Tomes, *Gospel of Germs*, 131.

33. "Statement by Wm. H. Weems, M.D., County Physician for Palm Beach County, Fla.," Tolan Hearings, Part 2, 591, 600–601.

34. Brandt, *No Magic Bullet*, 160. In 1937 Surgeon General Thomas Parran published his best-selling book, *Shadow on the Land*, which identified syphilis as the nation's preeminent public health threat. Grey, "Syphilis and AIDS," 331.

35. Tolan Hearings, Part 2, 541; Grey, "Syphilis and AIDS," 331.

36. H. L. Haney to Colonel Phillip G. Bruton, Deputy Administrator, War Food Administration, September 26, 1943, box 5, file 44-M 18 1943, Records of the Office of Labor (War Food Administration) (WFA), RG 224, NACP.

37. FSA, "Migrant Farm Labor: The Problems and the Ways of Meeting It," p. 7, December 1939, box 8, file AD-124 Migratory Labor All Regs. General 1939, FmHA, RG 96, NACP.

38. On the link between race, health, and citizenship in these terms, I have also benefited from Jim Downs, *Sick from Freedom: African-American Illness and Suffering During the Civil War and Reconstruction* (New York: Oxford University Press, 2012); Gretchen Long, *Doctoring Freedom: The Politics of African American Medical Care in Slavery and Emancipation* (Chapel Hill: University of North Carolina Press, 2012).

39. Ralph Chester Williams, "Development of Medical Care Plans for Low Income Farm Families," *American Journal of Public Health* 30, no. 7 (1940): 725–35.

40. Although they complemented each other, the FSA's cooperative health plans for rural farmers (specifically the agency's rehabilitation clients and borrowers) and the FSA's migrant medical plans (for agricultural workers) were coordinated as separate entities within the FSA's Health Services Branch. Michael R. Grey, *New Deal Medicine: The Rural Health Programs of the Farm Security Administration* (Baltimore: Johns Hopkins University Press, 1999), 17.

41. Grey, *New Deal Medicine*, 7–9, 13.

42. Richard Hellman, "The Farmers Try Group Medicine," box C-R 1, ctn. 2, file 20 Publications 1942, Hollenberg Collection, BANC.

43. Tolan Hearings, Part 6, 2515, 2523.

44. R. C. Williams, Chief Medical Officer, to Dr. W. W. Alexander, Administrator, April 3, 1940, box 10, file AD 124 R-8 Migratory Camps Medical Care, FmHA, RG 96, NACP.

45. The FSA established the first AWHA in 1938 serving California and Arizona. In 1940 the FSA established the Texas Farm Laborers Health Association (TFLHA), though it did not begin operating until 1941. By that time an AWHA existed to cover Washington, Idaho, and Oregon. In 1943 the FSA formed the Atlantic Seaboard Agricultural Workers Health Association to cover Florida, North Carolina, Virginia, Maryland, Delaware, Pennsylvania, New Jersey, New York, and Connecticut (although Florida eventually had its own plan, the Migrant Labor Health Association). Finally, in 1944 the FSA helped organize the Midwest Agricultural Workers Health Association to serve migrants in Ohio, Indiana, and Illinois. Grey suggests that the Texas plan was formed in 1943, but I found earlier evidence of its existence. For more on the various plans, see Grey, *New Deal Medicine*, 83. On the establishment of the TFLHA, see "Articles of Incorporation of the Texas Farm Laborers Health Association," August 9, 1940, box 3, file Agricultural Workers Health and Medical Association [Location] Minute Book, WFA, RG 224, NACP.

46. FSA, "A Medical Clinic on Wheels—the FSA Mobile Camps and Clinics for Migratory Workers," box 78, file Farm Security 3-2 Migratory Labor Camps, Records of the Office of the Secretary of Agriculture (OSA), RG 16, NACP; Rosamond C. Timmons and C. J. Glacken, "Medicine Follows the Crops," *Survey Midmonthly* 75, no. 3 (1939): 71–72.

47. R. G. Leland, "Medical Care for Migratory Workers," *Journal of the American Medical Association* 114, no. 1 (1940): 49.

48. Agency officials reported that many migrants sent in a few dollars at a time as they found temporary jobs and saved up a little cash. FSA, "Migrant Farm Labor: The Problem and Ways of Meeting It," December 1939, box 8, file AD-124 Migratory Labor All Regs. General 1939, FmHA, RG 96, NACP, 7.

49. Grey, *New Deal Medicine*, 84. At its peak in 1942, the FSA's medical care plans covered an estimated 117,000 farm families, or more than 600,000 persons, and extended into more than one-third of the counties in the nation. Frederick Dodge Mott and Milton Irwin Roemer, *Rural Health and Medical Care* (New York: McGraw-Hill, 1948), 393, 396–97.

50. Mott and Roemer, *Rural Health and Medical Care*, 247.

51. Mott and Roemer, *Rural Health and Medical Care*, 237.

52. "List of Migratory Labor Camp Personnel," box 484, file RP-183 TX 32 Health Reports and file RP-TX-32 (000-900) Raymondville Mig. Labor Camps, FmHA, RG 96, NACP.

53. Frederick Dodge Mott, "Health Services for Migrant Farm Families," *American Journal of Public Health* 35, no. 4 (1945): 308–14; Mott and Roemer, *Rural Health and Medical Care*, 293; Grey, *New Deal Medicine*, 91.

54. Mott and Roemer, *Rural Health and Medical Care*, 293.

55. Grey, *New Deal Medicine*, 92.

56. Mott and Roemer, *Rural Health and Medical Care*, 239.

57. Grey, *New Deal Medicine*, 92.

58. Mott and Roemer, *Rural Health and Medical Care*, 239; F. D. Mott, Chief Medical Officer, to Colonel Philip C. Bruton, Deputy Administrator, September 27, 1943, box 5, file Office of Labor 36 Medical, WFA, RG 224, NACP, 4.

59. Mott and Roemer, *Rural Health and Medical Care*, 238.

60. R. C. Williams, "Nursing Care for Migrant Families," *American Journal of Nursing* 41, no. 9 (1941): 1028–32, quotation on 1032.

61. Wanda D. Mann, R.N., "Migrant Nursing," *Pacific Coast Journal of Nursing* 37, no. 11 (November 1941), found in box C-R 1, ctn. 1, file 23, Hollenberg Collection, BANC; Canter, "California Renovates the Dust-Bowler."

62. Adela J. Ballard, "Working for the Migrant Workers," *Missionary Review of the World*, 1935; Adela J. Ballard, *Roving with the Migrants* (New York: Council of Women for Home Missions and Missionary Education Movement, 1931).

63. The CWHM, representing a number of denominations, initiated a program of social service in migrant camps across the United States beginning in 1920. Testimony of Edith Lowry, Executive Secretary Council of Women for Home Missions, U.S. House of Representatives, *Select Committee to Investigate the Interstate Migration of Destitute Citizens, Hearings Before the Select Committee to Investigate the Interstate Migration of Destitute Citizens, 76th Cong., 3d Sess., 1940, Part 1* (Washington, D.C.: Government Printing Office, 1940), 299.

64. Mary Lee Brown, "Nursing in a Migratory Labor Camp," *American Journal of Nursing* 42, no. 8 (1942): 862–64.

65. Several scholars have written about the significance of black public health nurses. See Susan Lynn Smith, *Sick and Tired of Being Sick and Tired: Black Women's Health Activism in America, 1890–1950* (Philadelphia: University of Pennsylvania Press, 1995), 101; Susan Gelfand Malka, *Daring to Care: American Nursing and Second-Wave Feminism* (Urbana: University of Illinois Press, 2007). Some reports suggested that African Americans avoided the camps for reasons related to the medical program, but FSA officials found that grower pressure was a more influential factor. Testimony of Paul Vander Shouw, Supervisor for the FSA camps in Florida, NDMH, Part 33, 371.

66. NDMH, Part 33, 357.

67. Mott, "Health Services for Migrant Farm Families," 312; Grey, *New Deal Medicine*, 93.

68. Atlantic Seaboard Agricultural Workers Health Association, Inc., "Health Services Handbook," p. 2605, Box 4, WFA, RG 224, NACP.

69. Monthly Narrative Report for September 1941, Princeton Labor Camp, box 488, file 88-TX-39 000-900, FmHA, RG 96, NACP.

70. Like most of the FSA's medical staff, the HMSs were predominantly white and middle-class, except for the "negro camps" along the Atlantic coast. In those cases, the African American HMSs were typically recruited from the Southern Colored Home Economics Workers organization. These women were typically college-educated in the field of domestic science

and earned an annual salary of $1,800 for their work in the FSA camps. Like the nurses, the HMSs lived in the camp year-round. "Personnel Information, Migratory Labor Camp, Crystal City, Texas," box 487, file RP-Crystal City Farm Workers Camp TX-38 000-900, FmHA, RG 96, NACP. On the link between domestic science and citizenship, see Tomes, *Gospel of Germs*, chap. 6.

71. MNR, Harlingen, Texas FSA Camp, April 1942, box 486, file RP-TX-36-183-01 Monthly Narrative Report of Home Management—Sept. 1941, FmHA, RG 96, NACP.

72. "War Weapons for War Workers: Based on an Educational Program for Farm Laborer Families," July 1942, assembled and organized by Iva M. Caldwell, Associate Home Management Specialist, and A. E. Scott, Jr., Chief County and Family Services, with contributions by HMSs employed in the South Texas FSA camps, box 17, file RP-M-88-163 Newspapers and Magazines, FmHA, RG 96, NACP.

73. Charlotte Myrtle Tompkins, "Social Problems of Girls in Migratory Labor Camps in South and Central Texas" (master's report, Colorado Agricultural and Mechanical College, 1948).

74. Genevieve Rhodes, HMS, MNR, Crystal City, Texas FSA Camp, November 1941, box 488, file RP-TX-38-183 1941 Crystal City Mig. Camp, Camp Population Report, FmHA, RG 96, NACP.

75. *Spotlight*, Crystal City, Texas, camp newspaper, September 12, 1941, 6, box 17, file RP-M-163-1941 Newspapers and Magazines, FmHA, RG 96, NACP.

76. *Migrant Mike*, Yuma, Arizona, camp newspaper, November 28, 1941, box 97, file RP-AZ-11 (000-900) Yuma Migratory Labor Camp, FmHA, RG 96, NACP.

77. Box 6, file RF-CF-16 918-01, FmHA, RG 96, National Archives at San Francisco, San Bruno, Calif. (NASF).

78. In 1942 the Birth Control Federation of America became Planned Parenthood. Grace Naismith, "Birth Control Nurse," *Survey Graphic* 32, no. 6 (1943): 260.

79. James Reed, *The Birth Control Movement and American Society: From Private Vice to Public Virtue* (Princeton, N.J.: Princeton University Press, 1984), 266; "Florence Richardson Wyckoff (1905–1997), Fifty Years of Grassroots Social Activism," Vol. II, UC Santa Cruz Digital Collections, https://library.ucsc.edu/reg-hist/wyckoff, 49 (hereafter cited as Wyckoff, Vol. II).

80. Mildred Delp, R.N., "Baby-Spacing: Report on California and Arizona," March–August 1940, box C-R 1, ctn. 2, file Reports 8 1938–40, Hollenberg Collection, BANC.

81. Naismith, "Birth Control Nurse."

82. Monthly Narrative Report for Brawley, California, March 20, 1942, box 10, file RF-CF-16-789-02, FmHA, RG 96, NASF; also see Grey, *New Deal Medicine*, 98.

83. Delp, "Baby-Spacing Report."

84. Katherine F. Lenroot, chief officer for the Children's Bureau under the U.S. Department of Labor, testified that in the five counties where the migrant agricultural population was concentrated in California, IMRs averaged 113 per 1,000 live births in 1937, whereas the national average that year was 57 per 1,000 live births. U.S. House of Representatives, *Select Committee to Investigate the Interstate Migration of Destitute Citizens, Hearings Before the Select Committee to Investigate the Interstate Migration of Destitute Citizens, 76th Cong., 3d Sess., 1940–41, Part 10* (Washington, D.C.: Government Printing Office, 1941), 4013 (hereafter cited as Tolan Hearings, Part 10).

85. Carey McWilliams, *Ill Fares the Land: Migrants and Migratory Labor in the United States* (Boston: Little, Brown, 1942), 118, 160, 245, 286; Carey McWilliams, *Factories in the Field: The Story of Migratory Farm Labor in California* (Berkeley: University of California Press, 1939), 317–18.

86. Agnes E. Meyer, "Good Housing Attracts the Best Workers in the Valley," *Texas Spectator*, June 14, 1946.

87. Grey, *New Deal Medicine*, 33; McWilliams, *Ill Fares the Land*, 365.

88. Dr. R. C. Williams, Medical Director, Farm Security Administration, "Keeping the Baby Well," June 17, 1938, box 12, file 85-936 Health & Hygiene, FmHA, RG 96, National Archives at Atlanta, Morrow, Ga. (NAA).

89. Grey, *New Deal Medicine*, 86.

90. George St. J. Perrott, Principal Statistician, USPHS, "Medical Needs Revealed by the National Health Survey," an address before the National Conference of Social Work, Seattle, Washington, June 28, 1938, p. 10, box C-R 1, ctn. 2, file 19 Statements and Testimonies 1938–42, Hollenberg Collection, BANC.

91. Charlotte G. Borst, *Catching Babies: The Professionalization of Childbirth, 1870–1920* (Cambridge, Mass.: Harvard University Press, 1995), 157.

92. Agnes E. Meyer, "Camps Aid to Valley Workers: Projects at Robstown Are Transformation for Migrants," as reprinted in *Texas Spectator*, May 5, 1946.

93. While Meyer referred to the local healer as both a midwife and *curandera*, in Mexican communities distinct persons typically performed these roles. A midwife or *partera* was usually a woman who specialized in the practice of childbirth, whereas a *curandera/o* or local healer could be either male or female and performed health treatments for a variety of ailments. It is possible that the woman who attended to the Robstown family was, in fact, both a *partera* and *curandera*, as Meyer suggested; however, acknowledging the distinction between these practices is central to recognizing the medical knowledge such individuals maintained.

94. R. C. Williams, FSA Chief Medical Officer, to C. M. Evans, FSA Regional Director, "Suggestions with Reference to the Medical Care Program for the Migratory Labor Camps," March 26, 1940, box 10, file AD 124 R-8 Migratory Camps Medical Care, FmHA, RG 96, NACP.

95. Dr. W. W. Alexander, FSA Administrator, to R. C. Williams, FSA Chief Medical Officer, May 7, 1940, box 10, file AD 124 R-8 Migratory Camps Medical Care, FmHA, RG 96, NACP.

96. For more on this topic, see Loralee Lewis Philpott, "A Descriptive Study of Birth Practices and Midwifery in the Lower Rio Grande Valley of Texas" (PhD diss., University of Texas Health Center Science Center at Houston School of Public Health, 1979); Aída Hurtado, "A View from Within: Midwife Practices in South Texas," *International Quarterly of Community Health Education* 8, no. 4 (1988): 317–39.

97. In a similar way, Smith discusses how public health programs in the South sought to eliminate the use of herbal remedies and blamed black midwives for high IMRs when in actuality their birth rates were no worse than those of physician-attended births. It was easier to attack them than to challenge the medical establishment or the state for the poor medical conditions available to rural black women—if any were available at all. Smith, *Sick and Tired*, 124–25, 127.

98. For a short overview, see Edward J. Rowell, "The Child in the Migratory Camp—Health," box C-R 1, ctn. 2, file 19 Speeches 1938, Hollenberg Collection, BANC.

99. Tolan Hearings, Part 10, 4013.

100. John Beecher, Farm Security Supervisor, Florida Migratory Labor Camps, "Living and Working Conditions of Migratory Farm Workers in the Florida Vegetable Area," Testimony before the Tolan Committee, May 15 and 16, 1940, box C-R 1, ctn. 9, file 13 Southern Farm Labor 1938–40, Hollenberg Collection, BANC.

101. Beecher, "Living and Working Conditions."

102. Katharine F. Deitz, Regional Educational and Community Activities Advisor, to Mrs. Marion C. Dodge, State Technician of Nursery Schools, Works Projects Administration, July 31, 1941, box 23, file 85-934 Education July 1940 thru December 1940, FmHA, RG 96, NAA. The Works Progress Administration became the Work Projects Administration in 1939.

103. News clipping, "Nursery Offers Special Program of Planned Play," September 3, year unknown, box 13, file RR-CF-44 918-02, FmHA, RG 96, NASF; Mary C. Burt, Head Teacher, Woodville Nursery School, "A Comprehensive Survey of the Woodville Nursery School Project," box 38, file RR-CF-31-912-034, FmHA, RG 96, NASF; Deitz to Dodge, FmHA, RG 96, NAA; testimony of Paul Vander Schouw, NDMH, Part 33, 369.

104. At Woodville the girls' participation in the nursery school was organized under a "pre-parent program." Evidence also suggests that adolescent boys showed great interest in working at the nursery school. Some "boys' clubs" were recruited to help with maintenance and the cleaning and repair of cots, for example. "Woodville Nursery School Statistical Report, March 1943," box 39, file RR-CF-31-918-01, FmHA, RG 96, NASF. See various photographs under the general search topic "FSA Camp Nursery School," FSA/OWI.

105. Testimony of Paul Vander Schouw, NDMH, Part 33, 356, 369; Dietz to Dodge, FmHA, RG 96, NAA.

106. Katharine F. Deitz to Edith E. Lowry, July 13, 1940, box 23, file 85–934 Education July 1940 thru December 1940, FmHA, RG 96, NAA.

107. Tolan Hearings, Part 2, 551.

108. Agnes E. Meyer, "Life on the Rio Grande," *Washington Post*, April 22, 1946.

109. Ofilia Cantu Ramírez, audio interview by Victor Ramírez (her son) on behalf of the author, Roma, Texas, July 27, 2008.

110. Herón Ramírez, interview by author, Pharr, Texas, July 18, 2008.

111. Alcario Samudio, phone interview by author, May 13, 2008.

112. Zora Mildred Bennett, interview by author, Harlingen, Texas, May 3 and July 31, 2008; Aida Hinojosa, Minerva Suárez Capello, and Charles Thomas, interview by author, Weslaco, Texas, May 2, 2008.

113. Dell Caver, HMS, MNR, Harlingen, Texas FSA Camp, December 1941, box 486, file RP-TX-36-183-01 Monthly Narrative Report of Home Management—September 1941, FmHA, RG 96, NACP.

114. Owen H. Eichblatt, Camp Manager, MNR, Princeton, Texas, FSA Camp, May 1942, box 488, file RP-TX-38-183-01 Monthly Narrative Report, FmHA, RG 96, NACP.

115. As cited in Grey, *New Deal Medicine*, 94.

116. The FSA typically assigned each migrant patient a "medical record card" identifying what inoculations or conditions they received at the camp clinic, even if they did not reside there. G. B. Herington, FSA Labor Relations Representative, to Walter Duffy, FSA Regional Medical Director, January 7, 1941, box 13, file AD-124 Region XI Migratory Labor General 1941, FmHA, RG 96, NACP.

117. Unlike the Freedmen's Bureau (FB), and its Medical Division in particular, the FSA did not create the migrant medical program simply to ensure migrants' sustained labor power. For more, see Downs, *Sick from Freedom*. On the state's role in migrants' transformation "from diseased bodies to desired laborers," see Stern, "Buildings, Boundaries, and Blood."

118. "War Weapons for War Workers," assembled and organized by Iva M. Caldwell, Associate Home Management Specialist, A. E. Scott, Jr., Chief Community and Family Services, Dallas, Texas, July 1942, box 17, file RP-M-88-163 Newspapers and Magazines, FmHA, RG 96, NACP.

119. U.S. House of Representatives, *Select Committee of the House Committee on Agriculture, to Investigate the Activities of the Farm Security Administration, 78th Cong., 1st Sess., 1943, Part 3* (Washington, D.C.: Government Printing Office, 1944), 1006.

120. R. C. Williams, "Better Health for National Defense," speech before the National Conference of Catholic Charities, November 18, 1940, Chicago, box C-R 1, ctn. 2, file 26, Hollenberg Collection, BANC.

121. "Farm Flashes," KXO–El Centro, California, December 18, 1941, box 11, file RR-CF-28-918-02, FmHA, RG 96, NASF.

122. On this point, Davidson was quoting "Miss Elliot," the Consumer Commissioner of the National Defense Advisory Committee. *Farm Flashes*, FmHA, RG 96, NASF.

123. *Farm Flashes*, FmHA, RG 96, NASF.

124. Grey, *New Deal Medicine*, 135–36.

125. "Farm Labor Importation Program (September 4, 1942–December 15, 1942)," file Migratory 120-General- ; telegram, "Public Health—for Duty in Connection with Mexican Workers," November 9, 1942, file Migratory-92-120; "Agreement between U.S. and Mexican Governments on Use of Mexican Labor in the U.S.," file Foreign Labor Migratory; "Problems to Be Learned from the Transportation Program," especially the section titled "Are Not Physically Suited to Do the Work," file Labor General M-120 Migratory Vol. 1 1942, all in box 6, FmHA, RG 96, NACP.

126. Mason Bar, FSA Director, Management Division (of Transportation Program), to Walter L. Cline, November 10, 1942, box 6, file Labor General M-120 Migratory Vol. 1, 1942, FmHA, RG 96, NACP.

127. Wayne D. Rasmussen, *A History of the Emergency Farm Labor Supply Program, 1943–47*, Agricultural Monograph No. 13 (Department of Agriculture, Washington, D.C., 1951), 190–94.

128. "Report of the Activities of the Agricultural Workers Health and Medical Association," March 1938 through March 31, 1948, box C-R 1, ctn. 3, file 13 1942, Hollenberg Collection, BANC.

129. Grey notes that the FSA was never free of scrutiny, despite overwhelming support by the rural doctors and medical societies in which the migrant health plans operated. For example, in 1940 and again in 1941 Congress subjected the Agricultural Workers Health and Medical Association (covering California and Arizona) to a detailed audit. The investigations shed light on the plan's costs and services, procedures provided, and operational programming. The findings were mostly positive, but the close inquiry exemplified the growing political debate over the New Deal's social reforms and the FSA's health activities in particular. Grey, *New Deal Medicine*, 103.

130. U.S. House of Representatives, *Select Committee of the House Committee on Agriculture, to Investigate the Activities of the Farm Security Administration, 78th Cong., 1st Sess.,*

1943–44, Part 4 (Washington, D.C.: Government Printing Office, 1944),1589–90 (hereafter cited as FSA Hearings, Part 4).

131. Grey, *New Deal Medicine*, 148, 151; Thomas R. Clark, "The Limits of State Autonomy: The Medical Cooperatives of the Farm Security Administration, 1935–1946," *Journal of Policy History* 11, no. 3 (1999): 271–72.

132. FSA Hearings, Part 4, 1626–27.

133. Grey, *New Deal Medicine*, 143.

134. The 1943 Wagner-Murray-Dingell bill proposed adding universal health insurance to the existing old-age, unemployment, and disability insurance programs created by Social Security. Grey, *New Deal Medicine*, 153, 158. See also Clark, "Limits of State Autonomy."

135. In 1938, for example, Samuel Lubell and Walter Everett published a piece in the *Saturday Evening Post* titled "Rehearsal for State Medicine," in which they warned the American public that the FSA had "staged a gigantic rehearsal for health insurance" that would surprise "friends and foes of socialized medicine alike." Samuel Lubell and W. B. Everett, "Rehearsal for State Medicine," *Saturday Evening Post*, December 17, 1938.

136. Grey, *New Deal Medicine*, 154–58; Clark, "Limits of State Autonomy," 270.

137. Grey, *New Deal Medicine*, 154.

138. Clark, "Limits of State Autonomy," 272.

139. Clark, "Limits of State Autonomy," 272.

140. Grey, *New Deal Medicine*, 150.

141. "Report of the Activities of the Agricultural Workers Health and Medical Association," March 1938–March 31, 1948, p. 13, box C-R 1, ctn. 3, file 13 1942, Hollenberg Collection, BANC.

142. According to Florence Wyckoff, when the FSA camps in California were taken over by growers' associations, "they sent their workers to the county hospital or to the local health department for treatment. So health care went into a period of the dark ages. . . . It just wiped out the migrant health clinics right there." Wyckoff, Vol. II., 53.

143. FSA Hearings, Part 1, 345.

Chapter 5

1. Charles L. Todd and Robert Sonkin Migrant Workers Collection, "The Migrant Experience: Voices from the Dust Bowl, 1940–1941," Library of Congress, American Folklife Center, AFC 1985/001.

2. Arthur E. Scott, Jr., Acting Assistant Regional Director, to Mr. Estel H. Yetter, Regional Personnel Adviser, November 6, 1941, box 16, file RP-M-88-132-01 Standard Personnel Classifications, Records of the Farmers Home Administration (FmHA), Record Group 96 (RG 96), National Archives at College Park, Md. (NACP).

3. John Steinbeck, *The Harvest Gypsies: On the Road to the Grapes of Wrath* (Berkeley: Heyday Books, 1988), 39.

4. Carey McWilliams, *Ill Fares the Land: Migrants and Migratory Labor in the United States* (Boston: Little, Brown, 1942), 29, 31; Paul Schuster Taylor, "Again the Covered Wagon," *Survey Graphic* 24, no. 7 (1935): 348.

5. Taylor, "Again the Covered Wagon," 25; McWilliams, *Ill Fares the Land*, 29.

6. Ruth Annabel Lerrigo, "On Every Town's Doorstep," *Survey Graphic* 25 (June 1936): 365.

7. Carey McWilliams, *Factories in the Field: The Story of Migratory Farm Labor in California* (Berkeley: University of California Press, 1939), 311; McWilliams, *Ill Fares the Land*, 343.

8. Carey McWilliams, "Americans Without a Country," *Nation* 153, no. 11 (1941): 422.

9. Adela J. Ballard was the western supervisor of migrant work for the Council of Women for Home Missions, which provided the first nurses for the California FSA camps. Adela J. Ballard, "Working for the Migrant Workers," *Missionary Review of the World*, 1935, 283–84.

10. McWilliams, *Factories in the Field*, 286–99. On relief as a form of labor control, see Zaragosa Vargas, *Labor Rights Are Civil Rights: Mexican American Workers in Twentieth-Century America* (Princeton, N.J.: Princeton University Press, 2005); Cybelle Fox, *Three Worlds of Relief: Race, Immigration, and the American Welfare State from the Progressive Era to the New Deal* (Princeton, N.J.: Princeton University Press, 2012).

11. C. B. Baldwin, "Doors to Rural Democracy," October 22, 1941, box C-R 1, ctn. 1, file 1.7 FSA Background Material Speeches 1938–1941, Ralph W. Hollenberg Collection of Materials Relating to the Farm Security Administration (hereafter cited as Hollenberg Collection), Region IX, San Francisco, Calif., Bancroft Library, University of California, Berkeley (BANC).

12. "Our Migrant Workers Part I," University of California Radio Service, broadcast no. 3021, December 15, 1939, box C-R 1, ctn. 2, file 1.9 FSA Background Material Radio Talks, 1939, Hollenberg Collection, BANC.

13. U.S. House of Representatives, *Select Committee to Investigate the Interstate Migration of Destitute Citizens, Hearings Before the Select Committee to Investigate the Interstate Migration of Destitute Citizens, 76th Cong., 3d Sess., 1940, Part 7* (Washington, D.C.: Government Printing Office, 1941), 2926.

14. *Joint Committee on Reduction of Nonessential Federal Expenditures, Part 3, 77th Cong., 2nd Sess., February 1942* (Washington, D.C.: Government Printing Office, 1942), 700, 702. On this topic, see also Patricia Sullivan, *Days of Hope: Race and Democracy in the New Deal Era* (Chapel Hill: University of North Carolina Press, 1996), 105–8.

15. Memo from C. M. Evans, Regional Director, to B. J. Walker, Acting Chief Migratory Labor Camps, November 2, 1940; C. B. Baldwin, FSA Administrator, to C. M. Evans, November 28, 1940; Clay Cochran, Project Manager, "Some Positive Educational Needs of Migrants in the Weslaco Migratory Labor Camp," box 10, file AD-124 R-8 Migratory Camps Administrative Personnel, FmHA, RG 96, NACP.

16. Among the "real causes" Cochran listed were "the large corporation, absentee landlord, insurance company and other devices . . . [and] how the Supreme Court defined a soul into the corporation, which since that time has gained control over most of the resources of the country." "Some Positive Educational Needs," box 10, file AD-124 R-8 Migratory Camps Administrative Personnel, FmHA, RG 96, NACP.

17. Subsidiary camp committees included the "women's committee," "sanitation committee," "welfare/mutual aid committee," and "social committee." Such groups provided the labor that facilitated and executed many of the mandates proposed by the council for the betterment of the community. In some cases, elections were also held for leadership roles in these committees.

18. *Cornucopia*, Ceres, California, FSA camp newspaper, November 25, 1941, box 255, file RP-Ceres Migratory Labor Camp-CF-44, FmHA, RG 96, NACP.

19. Monthly Narrative Report (MNR), Crystal City, Texas, May 9, 1941, box 487, file RP-TX-38-183 Reports, FmHA, RG 96, NACP.

20. For example, see Walter J. Stein, *California and the Dust Bowl Migration* (Westport, Conn.: Greenwood, 1973), 173–77; Don Mitchell, *The Lie of the Land: Migrant Workers and the California Landscape* (Minneapolis: University of Minnesota Press, 1996), 186; Charles J. Shindo, *Dust Bowl Migrants in the American Imagination* (Lawrence: University Press of Kansas, 1997), 28; Devra Weber, *Dark Sweat, White Gold: California Farm Workers, Cotton, and the New Deal* (Berkeley: University of California Press, 1994), 134.

21. "Camp Committee Minutes," n.d., box 19, FmHA, RG 96, National Archives at San Francisco, San Bruno, Calif. (NASF).

22. "Camp Committee Minutes."

23. C. B. Baldwin, "Our Ultimate Defense," November 17, 1941, box C-R 1, ctn. 1, folder 1.7 FSA Background Material Speeches 1938–41, Hollenberg Collection, BANC.

24. Sidney Baldwin, *Poverty and Politics: The Rise and Decline of the Farm Security Administration* (Chapel Hill: University of North Carolina Press, 1968), 327, 352, 354, 357. It is important to note, since it was a matter that greatly affected the FSA's political legitimacy, that there is still some contention over whether C. B. Baldwin was a "concealed communist." There is evidence that he became a member of the U.S. Communist Party shortly after he left the FSA in 1943, but Sidney Baldwin claims that it is unlikely he ever was a communist. For more, see Thomas W. Devine, *Henry Wallace's 1948 Presidential Campaign and the Future of Postwar Liberalism*, 1st ed. (Chapel Hill: University of North Carolina Press, 2013), 40, 302n11; Baldwin, *Poverty and Politics*, 359n42, 390.

25. Mexican American scholars have previously distinguished between those who were forcibly removed under these campaigns and those who voluntarily repatriated to Mexico. I chose to describe the process as a "mass deportation" effort to highlight how even the "voluntary repatriations" were coerced through state tactics of intimidation and harassment. Abraham Hoffman, *Unwanted Mexican Americans in the Great Depression: Repatriation Pressures, 1929–1939* (Tucson: University of Arizona Press, 1974), 174–75; Francisco E. Balderrama and Raymond Rodriguez, *Decade of Betrayal: Mexican Repatriation in the 1930s* (Albuquerque: University of New Mexico Press, 1995).

26. On African Americans and their experience gaining relief under the New Deal, see Fox, *Three Worlds of Relief*, chap. 8.

27. Moreno significantly points to the role organized labor played in founding El Congreso, which demonstrates the important intersections between Mexican's labor and civil rights actions at this time (discussed in Chapter 1). She writes, "The United Cannery, Agricultural, Packing, and Allied Workers of America, with thousands of Spanish-speaking workers in its membership, and Liga Obrera of New Mexico, were the initiators of the Congress." Luisa Moreno, "Caravans of Sorrow: Noncitizen Americans of the Southwest," March 3, 1940, as cited in David Gutiérrez, *Between Two Worlds: Mexican Immigrants in the United States* (Wilmington, Del.: Scholarly Resources, 1996), 123. For more, see Vicki Ruiz, *Cannery Women, Cannery Lives: Mexican Women, Unionization, and the California Food Processing Industry, 1930–1950* (Albuquerque: University of New Mexico Press, 1987).

28. In her speech, Moreno also acknowledged that it was necessary "to inform the Spanish-speaking workers that FSA camps were to be established," as a way to improve their condition. Moreno, "Caravans of Sorrow," 119–23.

29. In fact, during this period, the state's reliance on Mexican farm labor actually increased as the development of large-scale industrial cotton production expanded from the

U.S. South to the West after 1920. Neil Foley, *The White Scourge: Mexicans, Blacks, and Poor Whites in Texas Cotton Culture* (Berkeley: University of California Press, 1997), 3–4.

30. "Monthly Narrative Report," December 12, 1941, box 486, folder RP-TX-36-183-01 Monthly Narrative Report of Home Management—September 1941, FmHA, RG 96, NACP.

31. H. H. Bashford to J. W. O'Banion, January 19, 1942, box 8, folder TX-33-934 Migratory Labor Camp Robstown, Texas, FmHA, RG 96, NACP.

32. Mae Ngai, "Birthright Citizenship and the Alien Citizen," *Fordham Law Review* 75 (April 2007): 2521–30.

33. Arthur E. Scott, Jr., to Mr. Estel H. Yetter, November 6, 1941, box 16, folder RP-M-88-132-01 Standard Personnel Classifications, FmHA, RG 96, NACP.

34. Stein, *Dust Bowl Migration*, 184.

35. Guadalupe San Miguel, Jr., *Let All of Them Take Heed: Mexican Americans and the Campaign for Educational Equality in Texas, 1910–1981* (College Station: Texas A&M University Press, 2000), 73–74.

36. Texas was not the only state in which the FSA carried out such work. The agency also conducted an extensive study in California titled "Racial Trends of the Population of the Bakersfield City Schools," which tracked, among other things, the nature of segregated schooling in the area and included data from 1930 to 1936. Box 7, file RF-CF-16(25) 934-06 "School directory and racial statistics," FmHA, RG 96, NASF.

37. Gilbert G. Gonzalez, "Segregation of Mexican Children in a Southern California City: The Legacy of Expansionism and the American Southwest," *Western Historical Quarterly* 16, no. 1 (January 1985): 75. For more on the OIAA, see Pauline R. Kibbe, *Latin Americans in Texas* (Albuquerque: University of New Mexico Press, 1946); Neil Foley, *Mexicans in the Making of America* (Cambridge, Mass.: Belknap Press of Harvard University Press, 2014); Emilio Zamora, *Claiming Rights and Righting Wrongs in Texas: Mexican Workers and Job Politics During World War II* (College Station: Texas A&M University Press, 2009).

38. Foley, *Mexicans in the Making of America*, 82–83.

39. Lee J. Alston and Joseph P. Ferrie, "Resisting the Welfare State: Southern Opposition to the Farm Security Administration," *Research in Economic History, Supplement* 4, no. 0 (1985): 83; Baldwin, *Poverty and Politics*, 279–86.

40. Baldwin, *Poverty and Politics*, 282.

41. U.S. House of Representatives, *Select Committee Investigating National Defense Migration: Problems of Evacuation of Enemy Aliens and Others from Prohibited Military Zones, Hearings, 77th Cong., 2d Sess., Part 33* (Washington, D.C.: Government Printing Office, 1943), 355.

42. "Florida Migratory Workers," Confidential Report to the Administrator, Aubrey Clyde Robinson and Glenore Fisk Horne, June 1937, p. 50, box 9, file AD-124 Reg. V Migratory Labor 1940, FmHA, RG 96, NACP.

43. Hahamovitch concludes that "by 1940, 40,000 to 60,000 farm labor migrants came to Florida annually. . . . As summer approached, most returned to their home states for the cotton planting and chopping seasons. A minority joined the East Coast's mobile army of harvest workers or went 'up the state,' as the pickers called migrating up the coast for other harvest work." Cindy Hahamovitch, *The Fruits of Their Labor: Atlantic Coast Farmworkers and the Making of Migrant Poverty, 1870–1945* (Chapel Hill: University of North Carolina Press, 1997), 114–15, 125, 129.

44. "U.S. Lends a Hand to Help Florida Migratory Workers," Associated Press, May 23, 1940, box 17, file RP-85-163 Newspapers & Magazines, FmHA, RG 96, NACP.

45. John Beecher, FSA Supervisor, Florida Migratory Labor Camps, "Testimony Before the Civil Liberties Committee," May 15 and 16, 1940, p. 9, box 9, file Medical Care General, FmHA, RG 96, NACP.

46. Beecher, "Testimony Before the Civil Liberties Committee," 9–10.

47. Telegram to Hon. Claude R. Wickard, January 29, 1943, box 2, file Office of Labor W.F.A. Organization—Administration; Records of the Office of the Office of Labor (War Food Administration) (WFA), RG 224, NACP.

48. Beecher, "Testimony Before the Civil Liberties Committee," 27.

49. Baldwin, *Poverty and Politics*, 283.

50. John A. Fitch, "Now I've Got Rights," *Survey Midmonthly* 78 (August 1942): 212.

51. Beecher, "Testimony Before the Civil Liberties Committee," 10.

52. Beecher, "Testimony Before the Civil Liberties Committee," 10–11.

53. Beecher, "Testimony Before the Civil Liberties Committee," 11–12.

54. Beecher, "Testimony Before the Civil Liberties Committee," 13–14.

55. MNR, Raymondville, Texas, May 10, 1941, Raymondville Files, FmHA, RG 96, National Archives at Fort Worth, Tex. (NAFW).

56. MNR, Harlingen, Texas, February 10, 1942, box 484, file RP-183-TX-32 Narrative Report, FmHA, RG 96, NACP.

57. MNR, Raymondville, Texas, March 10, 1942, box 484, file RP-183 TX-32 Narrative Report, FmHA, RG 96, NACP.

58. MNR, Robstown, Texas, December 19, 1940, Robstown Files, FmHA, RG 96, NAFW.

59. H. H. Bushford, Acting Assistant Regional Director, to J. W. O'Banion, Assistant State Superintendent, January 19, 1942, Robstown Files, FmHA, RG 96, NAFW.

60. C. B. Baldwin, Assistant Administrator, to Honorable John R. Murdock, December 18, 1939, box 95, file AD-AZ-9615 Arizona Migratory Labor Camps Payment in Lieu of Taxes, FmHA, RG 96, NACP.

61. C. M. Evans, Regional Director, to C. B. Baldwin, Administrator, June 13, 1941, box 486, file RP-88-49-35-935 1941 Weslaco Mig. Labor Camp School, FmHA, RG 96, NACP.

62. Former camp residents whom I interviewed did not recall anything extraordinary about the instruction they received in the camps. They did explain, however, that even after the government seized ownership of the labor camps during the 1950s, county officials continued to use the community center building to school migrant children during the first few grades. Alcario Samudio, phone interview by author, May 13, 2008; Minerva Suárez Capello, interview by author, Weslaco, Texas, May 2, 2008.

63. John P. Manning, Superintendent Robstown Public Schools, to W. A. Canon, Assistant Regional Director, May 30, 1941; W. S. Gandy, President Robstown Independent School District, to W. A. Canon and C. M. Evans, Regional Directors, May 19, 1941, Robstown Files, FmHA, RG 96, NAFW.

64. For more, see Vicki L. Ruiz, "Tapestries of Resistance: Episodes of School Segregation and Desegregation in the Western United States," in Peter Lau, ed., *From the Grassroots to the Supreme Court: Brown v. Board of Education and American Democracy* (Durham, N.C.: Duke University Press, 2004).

65. "Negro Section/Colored Edition," *Belle Glade Herald*, December 12, 1941, box 17, file RP-85-163 Newspapers & Magazines, FmHA, RG 96, NACP.

66. MNR, Crystal City, Texas, December 1, 1941, box 488, file RP-TX-38-183 1941 Crystal City Migratory Camp, Camp Population Report, FmHA, RG 96, NACP; W. A. Canon,

Assistant Regional Director, to Joseph N. Cowen, Sinton Camp Manager, March 9, 1942, Sinton Files, FmHA, RG 96, NAFW.

67. Canon to Cowen, March 9, 1942.

68. MNR, Crystal City, Texas, July 15, 1941, and August 6, 1941, box 487, file RP-TX-38-183 Reports, FmHA, RG 96, NACP. A long tradition existed among ethnic Mexicans in the United States in developing private community-based schools known as *escuelitas*. Teresa Palomo Acosta and Ruthe Winegarten, *Las Tejanas: 300 Years of History* (Austin: University of Texas Press, 2003), 152–55.

69. "Negro Section," *Belle Glade Herald*, December 12, 1941, box 17, file RP-85-163 Newspapers & Magazines, FmHA, RG 96, NACP.

70. C. B. Baldwin, FSA Administrator, to Hon. Claude Pepper, July 29, 1941, box 9, file AD-124 Reg. V Migratory Labor General 1941, FmHA, RG 96, NACP.

71. Interview with Augustus Martinez in Todd and Sonkin, *Voices from the Dust Bowl*.

72. Martinez interview.

73. Interview with Jose Flores in Todd and Sonkin, *Voices from the Dust Bowl*.

74. MNR, Crystal City, Texas, May 9, 1941, box 487, file RP-TX-38-183 Reports, FmHA, RG 96, NACP.

75. For more, see Emilio Zamora, *The World of the Mexican Worker in Texas* (College Station: Texas A&M University Press, 1995), 92; Zaragosa Vargas, *Labor Rights Are Civil Rights: Mexican American Workers in Twentieth-Century America* (Princeton, N.J.: Princeton University Press, 2005).

76. Albert K. Short, Camp Manager, to W. A. Canon, Chief Administrator, May 6, 1940, Raymondville Files, FmHA, RG 96, NAFW.

77. Dillon S. Myer, *Uprooted Americans: The Japanese Americans and the War Relocation Authority During World War II* (Tucson: University of Arizona Press, 1971), 128–29. Milton Eisenhower was one of several former USDA officials involved in the WRA. For more, see Daniel Immerwahr, *Thinking Small: The United States and the Lure of Community Development* (Cambridge, Mass.: Harvard University Press, 2015), 47–50.

78. Wayne D. Rasmussen, *A History of the Emergency Farm Labor Supply Program, 1943–47*, Agricultural Monograph No. 13 (Washington, D.C.: Department of Agriculture, 1951), 102. By July 20, 1942, the Seasonal Leave Program was limited to only American-born Japanese. Louis Fiset, "Thinning, Topping, and Loading: Japanese Americans and Beet Sugar in World War II," *Pacific Northwest Quarterly* 90 (Summer 1999): 131.

79. Rasmussen, *Emergency Farm Labor Supply Program*, 102.

80. "Oregon Plan," Densho Encyclopedia, accessed July 3, 2019, http://encyclopedia.densho.org/Oregon%20Plan/. For a chart of the seasonal leave contracts executed between 1942 and 1944, see Fiset, "Thinning, Topping, and Loading," 133. A recent oral history project by the Oregon Cultural Heritage Commission, titled "Uprooted: Japanese American Farm Labor Camps During World War II," captures several perspectives on the decision to participate in the SLP and individuals' experiences within the program. See "Uprooted," accessed July 3, 2019, http://www.uprootedexhibit.com/about/.

81. Albert H. Kruse to Claude R. Wickard, August 27, 1942, box 7, folder Migratory-120-H Thru M-, FmHA, RG 96, NACP.

82. E. B. Duncan to Claude R. Wickard, September 8, 1942, box 7, folder Migratory-120-A Thru G-, FmHA, RG 96, NACP.

83. R. T. Magleby to Walter A. Duffy, n.d., box 16, folder Migratory -91-160-, FmHA, RG 96, NACP.

84. "Evacuees to Farms," *Business Week*, September 19, 1942, 40.

85. Magleby to Duffy, n.d., box 16, folder "Migratory—91—160," FmHA, RG 96, NACP.

86. By 1942, the FSA's migrant labor camps in the region included one permanent migrant camp in Colorado; one permanent and seven mobile camps in Oregon; two permanent and nine mobile camps in Idaho; and two permanent and six mobile camps in Washington. Camp Shelter Occupancy Report, Weeks Ending July 18 and July 25, 1942, box 19, folder AD 124 All Regs. 183 Migratory Labor Social Security Tables on Interstate Migrants 1937, FmHA, RG 96, NACP.

87. Wilson Cowen to Joe Pickle, August 15, 1941, box 8, folder TX-41 Migratory Labor Camp Lamesa, Texas, FmHA, RG 96, NAFW.

88. Farm Security Information Division, "Calling Dachau—Little Nyssa Speaks!" August 27, 1942, box 454, folder Migratory-OR-26 000-900, FmHA, RG 96, NACP.

89. Farm Security Information Division, "Calling Dachau—Little Nyssa Speaks!"

90. George D. Renan, FSA Associate Labor Relation Specialist, to Dr. N. Gregory Silvermaster, Director of FSA Labor Division, January 25, 1943, box 2, file Office of Labor W.F.A. Organization—Administration; Office of Labor, WFA, RG 224, NACP.

91. Silvermaster to Renan, February 10, 1943, box 2, file Office of Labor W.F.A. Organization—Administration; Office of Labor, WFA, RG 224, NACP.

92. "Are Evacuees to Become Peons?" *Christian Century*, August 1942, 973. The author of this piece was likely Galen M. Fisher, who wrote on similar topics for *Christian Century*, but the original document includes no name.

93. Interview of Mathias Uchiyama by Morgen Young, November 21, 2014, Oregon Cultural Heritage Commission, "Uprooted."

94. Fiset, "Thinning, Topping, and Loading," 127.

95. W. T. Geurts, Sr., FSA Labor Relations Specialist, to Dr. N. Gregory Silvermaster, June 28, 1943, box 1, file 4-FLT-R36 Labor Estimates, Office of Labor, FmHA, RG 224, NACP.

96. *Rupert Laborer*, September 15, 1942, vol. 1, no. 2, box 13, folder MA-163-91-, FmHA, RG 96, NACP.

97. Fiset, "Thinning, Topping, and Loading," 127.

98. John V. Lannan to David S. Allshouse, October 19, 1942, box 454, file Migratory-OR-26 000-900, FmHA, RG 96, NACP.

99. Magleby to Duffy, n.d., box 16, folder "Migratory—91—160," FmHA, RG 96, NACP; Memorandum for C. B. Baldwin, July 30, 1941, box 382, folder AD-ID-9 934 Migratory Labor Camps Education, FmHA, RG 96, NACP.

100. "Letter from Laurence I. Hewes, Jr., Farm Security Administration, to Remsen Byrd [Bird]. Collection Number SCJAR," (May 23, 1942). Calisphere, accessed July 16, 2019, http://content.cdlib.org/ark:/13030/kt238nf09d/?&brand = calisphere.

101. Laurence I. Hewes, "Operation of Evacuated Japanese Farms by Farm Corporations," Online Archive of California, accessed July 3, 2019, www.oac.cdlib.org/ark:/28722/bk0014b1j30/FID1. For more information on Japanese farmers, see Valerie J. Matsumoto, *Farming the Home Place: A Japanese American Community in California, 1919–1982* (Ithaca, N.Y.: Cornell University Press, 1993).

Chapter 6

1. Irving Abkin, Center Manager, to Myer Cohen, Asst. Regional Director, "Narrative Report," May 11, 1943, box [old number] 53, file RR-CF-31-918-02, Records of the Farmers Home Administration (FmHA), Record Group 96 (RG 96), National Archives at San Francisco, San Bruno, Calif. (NASF).

2. In the years between 1942 and 1947, the United States contracted approximately 219,546 Mexican farmworkers and 69,834 additional guest workers from Jamaica, the Bahama Islands, and Barbados. Wayne D. Rasmussen, *A History of the Emergency Farm Labor Supply Program, 1943–47*, Agricultural Monograph No. 13 (Washington, D.C.: Department of Agriculture, 1951), 199–206.

3. Don Mitchell, *They Saved the Crops: Labor, Landscape, and the Struggle over Industrial Farming in Bracero-Era California* (Athens: University of Georgia Press, 2012), 77; Ernesto Galarza, *Merchants of Labor: The Mexican Bracero Story: An Account of the Managed Migration of Mexican Farm Workers in California, 1942–1960* (Charlotte and Santa Barbara: McNally & Loftin, 1964), 55.

4. Sidney Baldwin, *Poverty and Politics: The Rise and Decline of the Farm Security Administration* (Chapel Hill: University of North Carolina Press, 1968), 394, 391.

5. Rasmussen, *Emergency Farm Labor Supply Program*, 201.

6. Months later, Hewes would employ the same staff and equipment used during the Japanese evacuation out of San Francisco to set up the first World War II bracero processing center in Mexico City. Laurence I. Hewes, *Boxcar in the Sand* (New York: Knopf, 1957), 183.

7. Hewes, *Boxcar in the Sand*, 178.

8. Cindy Hahamovitch, "The Politics of Labor Scarcity," Center for Immigration Studies, December 1, 1999, https://cis.org/Report/Politics-Labor-Scarcity.

9. Galarza, *Merchants of Labor*, 43.

10. Hewes, *Boxcar in the Sand*, 178.

11. Galarza, *Merchants of Labor*, 51.

12. Rasmussen, *Emergency Farm Labor Supply Program*, 42.

13. "Move to Supply Cotton Pickers Called Failure," *New York Herald Tribune*, November 12, 1942, box 8, file Migratory-120-Tarver, Hon. M. (C), FmHA, RG 96, National Archives at College Park, Md. (NACP).

14. Baldwin, *Poverty and Politics*, 385; Mitchell, *They Saved the Crops*, 33.

15. Harvey L. Hansen, Asst. Secretary Farm Labor Subcommittee, to Laurence I. Hewes, Regional Director, November 7, 1942, box 16, file Migratory-160-02 General, FmHA, RG 96, NACP.

16. Letter to Secretary Calude [*sic*] Wickard, October 5, 1942, box 7, file Migratory-120-A Thru G-; James Horton to Wickard, August 24, 1942, box 7, file Migratory-120-H Thru M-, FmHA, RG 96, NACP.

17. Telephone conversation between Major J. O. Walker, assistant administrator, and Sen. Hayden, Ariz., September 26, 1942, box 6, file [120-Region 9-] Foreign Labor Migratory, FmHA, RG 96, NACP.

18. Galarza, *Merchants of Labor*, 44.

19. Cindy Hahamovitch, *No Man's Land: Jamaican Guestworkers in America and the Global History of Deportable Labor* (Princeton, N.J.: Princeton University Press, 2011), 45–46.

20. Knox Alexander, Employment Supervisor, to Myer Cohen, Assistant Regional Director, November 14, 1942, box 6, file [120-Region 9-] Foreign Labor Migratory, FmHA, RG 96, NACP.

21. Laurence I. Hewes, Jr., Regional Director, to C. B. Baldwin, Administrator, February 20, 1943, box 2, file 32-L1-Mexican, Records of the Office of Labor, War Food Administration (WFA), RG 224, NACP.

22. J. O. Walker, Assistant Administrator, to John A. Fitch, New York School of Social Work, Columbia University, November 13, 1942, box 7, file Migratory-120-A Thru G-, FmHA, RG 96, NACP.

23. Baldwin, *Poverty and Politics*, 378–79, 381; Hahamovitch, *No Man's Land*, 47; Charles Kenneth Roberts, *The Farm Security Administration and Rural Rehabilitation in the South* (Knoxville: University of Tennessee Press, 2015), 194–95.

24. Rasmussen, *Emergency Farm Labor Supply Program*, 235.

25. Carey McWilliams, *Factories in the Field: The Story of Migratory Farm Labor in California* (Berkeley: University of California Press, 1939), 299.

26. Telegraph from L. G. Ligutti to Secretary Claude R. Wickard, Des Moines, Iowa, November 4, 1942, box 7, file Migratory-120-N- Thru R-, FmHA, RG 96, NACP.

27. Baldwin, *Poverty and Politics*, 380–81. Record of these debates can be found in ctn. 40, file 30-Farm Labor Camp Program 1947, Paul S. Taylor Papers, Bancroft Library, University of California, Berkeley (BANC).

28. Rasmussen, *Emergency Farm Labor Supply Program*, 46.

29. Rasmussen, *Emergency Farm Labor Supply Program*, 44.

30. Hahamovitch, *No Man's Land*, 47.

31. Baldwin, *Poverty and Politics*, 382.

32. N. Gregory Silvermaster, Director, Labor Division, "The Farm Labor Situation in 1942 and Its Relation to FSA," November 26, 1942, pp. 20–22, Ralph W. Hollenberg Collection of Materials Relating to the Farm Security Administration, Region IX, San Francisco, Calif. (hereafter cited as Hollenberg Collection), box C-R 1, ctn. 3, file Folder 22 Labor Reports 1940–1942, Bancroft Library, University of California, Berkeley (BANC).

33. Warren M. Engstrand, Community Manager, to Myer Cohen, Assistant Regional Director, Monthly Progress Report, November 28, 1942, box 11, file RR-CF-28-918-02, FmHA, RG 96, NASF.

34. Glen Trimble, Community Manager, to Myer Cohen, Assistant Regional Director, Monthly Progress Report, January 2, 1943, box 11, file RR-CF-28-918-02, FmHA, RG 96, NASF.

35. Glen Trimble, Community Manager, to Myer Cohen, Assistant Regional Director, Monthly Progress Report, February 9, 1943, box 11, file RR-CF-28-918-02, FmHA, RG 96, NASF.

36. On the East Coast, as Cindy Hahamovitch describes, "an official of the Division of Farm Population and Rural Welfare reported [in 1943], after a visit to the Swedesboro, New Jersey, camp, that of the 300 or so people in the camp, all but 25 were Jamaicans. The African American migrants who had come to the camp in family groups early in the year 'were permitted to stay,' but no new native families were accepted. He noted, however, that 'the Jamaicans and the Negro migrants' were housed separately." Cindy Hahamovitch, *The Fruits*

of Their Labor: Atlantic Coast Farmworkers and the Making of Migrant Poverty, 1870–1945 (Chapel Hill: University of North Carolina Press, 1997), 175.

37. "Data on 21 Federally Owned Farm Labor Supply Centers in California," box C-R 1, ctn. 2, file 10 1937–38, Hollenberg Collection, BANC.

38. U.S. House of Representatives, *Select Committee of the House Committee on Agriculture, to Investigate the Activities of the Farm Security Administration, 78th Cong., 1st Sess., 1943, Part 2* (Washington, D.C.: Government Printing Office, 1943), 616.

39. "Farm Labor Camps Operation," December 1, 1950, ctn. 40, folder 32, Farm Labor Camps 1948–1950, Taylor Papers, BANC.

40. Rasmussen, *Emergency Farm Labor Supply Program*, 181–82.

41. Hahamovitch, *Fruits of Their Labor*, 175.

42. Jesse B. Gilmer, Regional Director, to C. B. Baldwin, Administrator, June 5, 1943, box 7, file Office of Labor W.F.A. Organization—Administration, WFA, RG 224, NACP.

43. Baldwin, *Poverty and Politics*, 394–98.

44. The only congressional committee that supported the FSA was the House Select Committee to Investigate National Defense Migration, which met in 1941. It was chaired by California Democratic representative John H. Tolan, who loyally defended the FSA. Baldwin, *Poverty and Politics*, 345.

45. Baldwin, *Poverty and Politics*, 347.

46. Baldwin, *Poverty and Politics*, 398.

47. Baldwin, *Poverty and Politics*, 391. In a typical statement, "Mr. Poage from Texas" testified in the House of Representatives on June 29, 1949: "The camps were established as part of the old Farm Security Administration under one Beanie Baldwin. . . . [He] established them in the promotion of a social philosophy and not for the promotion of hygiene, or the suppression of smallpox. . . . The people of the United States . . . made it rather plain that they did not support that type of philosophy." House Congressional Record, ctn. 40, folder 32, Farm Labor Camps 1948–50, Taylor Papers, BANC.

48. Samuel Bledsoe, "F.S.A. Head May Quit Post; New Deal Sacrifice Hinted," *Los Angeles Times*, August 31, 1943.

49. Memorandum for the President from Jonathan Daniels, June 14, 1943, box 134, file Farm Security Administration, Franklin D. Roosevelt, Papers as President: The President's Secretary's File (PSF), 1933–1945, Franklin D. Roosevelt Presidential Library and Museum, accessed July 3, 2019, http://www.fdrlibrary.marist.edu/_resources/images/psf/psf000584.pdf.

50. Hewes, *Boxcar in the Sand*, 203–4.

51. "Pillar of Democracy: The Meaning of the Fight Against the FSA," *Rural Observer*, December 1943.

52. Public Law 298—80th Congress, Chapter 413—1st sess., copy of law found in box 464, file Lamesa Camp A226.4A, George Mahon Papers, 1887–1986, Southwest Collection, Texas Tech University, Lubbock, Tex.

53. C. B. Baldwin, Administrator, to Honorable Mary T. Norton, June 11, 1941, box 9, file AD-124 Reg. I Migratory Labor General 1941, FmHA, RG 96, NACP; James G. Patton, Colorado State President, NFU, to John C. Henderson, Migratory Labor Camp Program, July 14, 1939, box 20, file RF-CF-32-900 [1], FmHA, RG 96, NASF.

54. "Migratory Labor Centers," *California Grange News*, n.d., ctn. 40, folder 30, Farm Labor Camp Program 1947, Taylor Papers, BANC.

55. Robert C. Wells, "The Valley's Dangerous Problem," *Texas Spectator*, July 28, 1947, ctn. 40, folder 33, Farm Labor Supply Centers, 1946–48, Taylor Papers, BANC.

56. Mitchell, *They Saved the Crops*, 108.

57. Carl C. Taylor, Head, Division of Farm Population and Rural Life, BAE, Washington, D.C., and William H. Metzler, "Present Operation of the Former USDA Farm Labor Camps in the San Joaquin Valley," November 18, 1948, ctn. 40, folder 32, Farm Labor Camps 1948–50, Taylor Papers, BANC.

58. Statement of Mr. Scudder, House of Representatives, June 29, 1949, House Congressional Record, ctn. 40, folder 32, Farm Labor Camps 1948–50, Taylor Papers, BANC.

59. Taylor and Metzler, "Present Operation of the Former USDA Labor Camps"; Robert R. Brunn, "Roving Farm Labor Poses New Problem for Western States," *Christian Science Monitor*, June 20, 1947, ctn. 40, folder 31, Clippings 1947, Taylor Papers, BANC.

60. Vernon O'Reilly, "Lonesome Road Again?" *San Francisco News*, June 26, 1947, ctn. 40, folder 31, Clippings 1947, Taylor Papers, BANC.

61. O'Reilly, "Lonesome Road Again?" The "Weekly Population Report for the Farm Labor Supply Centers" for June 6, 1947, showed 6,973 children under the age of sixteen in the California camps and another 737 in the Arizona camps. ctn. 40, folder 33, Farm Labor Supply Centers, 1946–48, Taylor Papers, BANC.

62. Mitchell, *They Saved the Crops*, 129.

63. Agnes E. Meyer, "A Look at the Camps," *Texas Spectator*, June 30, 1947, 6–7, 11. It is possible that O'Reilly and Meyer were recruited to write the stories. The stories appeared in a similar three-part format, and both were friends of Paul S. Taylor.

64. Otey M. Scruggs, "Texas and the Bracero Program, 1942–1947," *Pacific Historical Review* 32, no. 3 (1963): 251–64. To clarify, there was never one set moment when the Mexican ban was lifted. It was off and on for several years. In 1948, for example, El Paso, Texas, was banned once again. It was not until 1949 that braceros started entering Texas in larger numbers.

65. "Final Report, Southwest Area Program," Unitarian Service Committee, October 1948, ctn. 40, folder 33, Farm Labor Supply Centers, 1946–48, Taylor Papers, BANC.

66. Galarza, *Merchants of Labor*, 203–4.

67. Donald H. Grubbs, "Prelude to Chavez: The National Farm Labor Union in California," *Labor History* 16, no. 4 (September 1, 1975): 453–69.

68. H. L. Mitchell, "Agricultural Workers Strike," *Commonweal*, November 14, 1947, 117; Don Mitchell, *They Saved the Crops*, 123.

69. Andrew J. Hazelton, "Farmworker Advocacy Through Guestworker Policy: Secretary of Labor James P. Mitchell and the Bracero Program," *Journal of Policy History* 29, no. 3 (July 2017): 431–61.

70. Anonymous letter to Galarza, Arvin, California, March 1950, Ernesto Galarza Papers, 1936–1984, M0224, box 43, file Employment, Displacement of Workers by *Braceros*, Correspondence, 1951–54, Department of Special Collections, Stanford University Libraries, Stanford, Calif.

71. Hahamovitch, *No Man's Land*, 113.

72. Mitchell, *They Saved the Crops*, 190–97.

73. John H. Dunlap, Public Housing Administration, "Farm Labor Camps Liquidation," ctn. 40, folder 30, Farm Labor Program 1947, Taylor Papers, BANC; Mitchell, *They Saved the Crops*, 113.

74. "The Housing Authority of the County of Hidalgo," accessed July 3, 2019, http://www.hidalgocha.org/en/farm-labor-housing.html.

75. Texas Historical Commission, "Report on Lamesa Farm Workers Community Historic District," Texas Recorded Historical Landmark Files, Texas Historical Commission Library, Austin, 1991.

76. "Housing Authority of Tulare County," accessed July 3, 2019, http://www.hatc.net/farm-labor.php.

77. "The Caldwell Housing Authority," accessed July 3, 2019, http://chaidaho.org/aboutus.html.

78. In addition to the oral histories I collected, there are several oral histories of individuals who lived in the labor camps from the 1950s through the 1970s. See, for example, "Caldwell Labor Camp Oral Histories Part 1," n.d., accessed June 28, 2019, https://www.youtube.com/watch?v = rx_XaIr48fg; Mario Compean, "Mexican American and Dust Bowl Farmworkers in the Yakima Valley: A History of the Crewport Farm Labor Camp, 1940–1970," in Jerry Garcia and Gilberto Garcia, eds., *Memory, Community, and Activism: Mexican Migration and Labor in the Pacific Northwest* (East Lansing: Michigan State University Press and Julian Samora Research Institute, 2005); Anna Webb, "Hard Times at Chula Vista: Braceros Made Community in Wilder's Migrant Camps," accessed November 8, 2018, https://scholarworks.boisestate.edu/fac_books/482.

79. *El Malcriado: "The Voice of the Farm Worker,"* no. 17, n.d. (1965), p. 7, https://libraries.ucsd.edu/farmworkermovement/ufwarchives/elmalcriado/adair/No17.pdf. On the strike, see Mitchell, *They Saved the Crops,* 109; Matt Garcia, *From the Jaws of Victory: The Triumph and Tragedy of Cesar Chavez and the Farm Worker Movement* (Berkeley: University of California Press, 2012), 34.

80. Gabriel Thompson, *America's Social Arsonist: Fred Ross and Grassroots Organizing in the Twentieth Century* (Oakland: University of California Press, 2016), 33, 43–44, 51.

81. *El Malcriado,* no. 17, p. 2.

82. *El Malcriado,* no. 17, p. 15; Robert Korstad and Nelson Lichtenstein, "Opportunities Found and Lost: Labor, Radicals, and the Early Civil Rights Movement," *Journal of American History* 75, no. 3 (December 1988): 787.

83. Edward R. Murrow, *Harvest of Shame,* directed by Fred W. Friendly (1960; Los Angeles: CBS Home Entertainment, 2018), DVD. There has been some criticism of how this scene was possibly exaggerated. For instance, see Elizabeth Blair, "In Confronting Poverty, 'Harvest of Shame' Reaped Praise and Criticism," *Weekend Edition Saturday,* National Public Radio, May 31, 2014, https://www.npr.org/2014/05/31/317364146/in-confronting-poverty -harvest-of-shame-reaped-praise-and-criticism.

84. Christine Reiser Robbins and Mark W. Robbins, "Spatial Relations in Oral History: The Robstown Migrant Labor Camp Beyond the Federal Period," *Oral History Review* 42, no. 2 (September 4, 2015): 11, 14.

85. Robbins and Robbins, "Spatial Relations in Oral History," 18–19.

86. Alcario Samudio, phone interview by author, May 13, 2008.

87. Samudio interview.

88. For example, Nelson Cruikshank, who was a labor officer and then director of the Migratory Labor Camp Program from 1936 to 1942, went on to have an important career

with the AFL-CIO on leaving the FSA. After a brief position abroad as head of the Labor Division of the European Security System, which was part of the Marshall Plan, he became director of the AFL-CIO's Department of Social Insurance. In this capacity he was one of the most influential figures in the creation of Social Security Disability Insurance, commonly known as "workers' disability," in 1956, and of Medicare in 1966. Nelson H. Cruikshank, Howard S. Hoffman, and Alice M. Hoffman, *The Cruikshank Chronicles: Anecdotes, Stories, and Memoirs of a New Deal Liberal* (Hamden, Conn.: Archon Books, 1989), 104–5. Dr. Frederick Mott's experience also offers a notable example. In 1946 he was recruited to chair Canada's Health Services Planning Commission, which went on to establish the model for Canada's national health insurance system. Then, in 1951, Mott returned to the United States to work for the United Mine Workers of America (UMWA) as supervisor of the union's hospital program. He helped John L. Lewis, president of the UMWA, develop the union's Welfare and Retirement Fund, which included a comprehensive medical care delivery program for miners and their families. As many as twenty FSA Health Services staff members worked for the UMWA at some point in their career. In 1957 Walter Reuther of the United Auto Workers hired Mott to serve as executive director of the union's Community Health Association in Detroit. For more, see Michael R. Grey, *New Deal Medicine: The Rural Health Programs of the Farm Security Administration* (Baltimore: Johns Hopkins University Press, 1999), 175–79.

89. Baldwin, *Poverty and Politics*, 332.

90. Hewes, *Boxcar in the Sand*, 206, 214–15.

91. Baldwin, *Poverty and Politics*, 396–97.

92. Jess C. Gilbert, *Planning Democracy: Agrarian Intellectuals and the Intended New Deal* (New Haven, Conn.: Yale University Press, 2015); Daniel Immerwahr, *Thinking Small: The United States and the Lure of Community Development* (Cambridge, Mass.: Harvard University Press, 2015), 11.

93. Edwin Rosskam was DivEdCo's director, Jack Delano headed the film division, and Jack's wife, Irene Delano, was in charge of the graphic arts section. Donald Thompson, "Film Music and Community Development in Rural Puerto Rico: The DIVEDCO Program (1948–91)," *Latin American Music Review / Revista de Música Latinoamericana* 26, no. 1 (2005): 102–14; Cati Marsh Kennerley, "Cultural Negotiations: Puerto Rican Intellectuals in a State-Sponsored Community Education Project, 1948–1968," *Harvard Educational Review* 73, no. 3 (Fall 2003): 416–48.

94. Kennerley, "Cultural Negotiations," 420.

95. Alyosha Goldstein, "The Attributes of Sovereignty: The Cold War, Colonialism, and Community Education in Puerto Rico," in Sandhya Shukla and Heidi Tinsman, eds., *Imagining Our Americas: Toward a Transnational Frame* (Durham, N.C.: Duke University Press, 2007); Ismael García-Colón, "Playing and Eating Democracy: The Case of Puerto Rico's Land Distribution Program, 1940s–1960s," *CENTRO: Journal of the Center for Puerto Rican Studies* 18, no. 2 (2006): 167–89.

96. Arlene M. Dávila, *Sponsored Identities: Cultural Politics in Puerto Rico* (Philadelphia: Temple University Press, 1997), 34–36; Kennerley, "Cultural Negotiations," 431; Laura Briggs, *Reproducing Empire: Race, Sex, Science, and U.S. Imperialism in Puerto Rico* (Berkeley: University of California Press, 2002).

97. Hewes, *Boxcar in the Sand*, 258.

Epilogue

1. According to the United Nations High Commissioner for Refugees, "The *1954 Convention relating to the Status of Stateless Persons* establishes the legal definition for stateless persons as individuals who are not considered citizens or nationals under the operation of the laws of any country. A person's citizenship and nationality may be determined based on the laws of a country where an individual is born or where her/his parents were born. A person can also lose citizenship and nationality in a number of ways, including when a country ceases to exist or a country adopts nationality laws that discriminate against certain groups." For migrant farmworkers, a condition of statelessness arises when their labor, civil, and human rights are nullified by discriminatory policies and practices related to their race and class status as itinerant workers. United Nations High Commissioner for Refugees, "Statelessness," UNHCR, accessed July 3, 2019, https://www.unhcr.org/en-us/statelessness.html.

2. Rexford G. Tugwell, "Behind the Farm Problem: Rural Poverty," January 10, 1937, *New York Times Magazine*, 22, https://www.nytimes.com/1937/01/10/archives/behind-the -farm-problem-rural-poverty.html.

3. As Lisa Lowe explains, "According to liberal political theory and the Marxist critique, citizenship requires that the subject deny its particular private interests to become the 'abstract citizen' of the political state." Lisa Lowe, *Immigrant Acts: On Asian American Cultural Politics* (Durham, NC: Duke University Press, 1996), 26.

4. Lowe, *Immigrant Acts*, 27.

5. Carly Fox, Rebecca Fuentes, Fabiola Ortiz Valdez, Gretchen Purser, and Kathleen Sexsmith, "Milked: Immigrant Dairy Farmworkers in New York State," a report by the Workers' Center of Central New York and the Worker Justice Center of New York, 2017, 19, accessed July 16, 2019, www.iwj.org/resources/milked-immigrant-dairy-farmworkers-in-new-york-state. For more on immigrant dairy workers' experiences, see Teresa M. Mares, *Life on the Other Border: Farmworkers and Food Justice in Vermont* (Berkeley: University of California Press, 2019).

6. Thomas R. Maloney, Libby Eiholzer, and Brooke Ryan, "Survey of Hispanic Dairy Workers in New York State," Charles H. Dyson School of Economics and Management College of Agriculture and Life Sciences, Cornell University, 2016, http://publications.dyson .cornell.edu/outreach/extensionpdf/2016/Cornell-Dyson-eb1612.pdf.

7. For more, see Cornell College of Agriculture and Life Sciences, Community and Regional Development Institute, "Cornell Farmworker Program," accessed July 3, 2019, https://cardi.cals.cornell.edu/programs/farmworker/.

8. Fox et al., "Milked," 16, 34–36, 58.

9. Isabella Grullón Paz, "Invisible Hands," *Ithaca Times*, July 13, 2017, 10, https://www .ithaca.com/news/invisible-hands/article_c2c75d4e-672e-11e7-b0a2-6fbb26688d72.html.

10. Carey McWilliams, *Factories in the Field: The Story of Migratory Farm Labor in California* (Berkeley: University of California Press, 1939), 303–4; Michael Denning, *The Cultural Front: The Laboring of American Culture in the Twentieth Century* (New York: Verso, 1997), 266–67.

11. USA for UNCHR, UN Refugee Agency, "Refugee Statistics," accessed July 3, 2019, https://www.unrefugees.org/refugee-facts/statistics/.

12. For more, see the Critical Refugee Studies Collective, https://criticalrefugeestudies .com/.

13. "PM's Migrant 'Swarm' Remark Criticised," BBC News, July 30, 2015, https://www.bbc.com/news/uk-politics-33716501; Aditya Chakrabortty, "If Theresa May Really Wants to Protect Refugees Why Does She Fuel Such Hatred?" *Guardian*, April 11, 2017, https://www.theguardian.com/commentisfree/2017/apr/11/theresa-may-refugees-croydon-attack; Adam White, "Has the World Hit Compassion Fatigue for Syria's Refugees?" Huck, February 2, 2016, https://www.huckmag.com/perspectives/compassion-fatigue-forgotten-humanity-syrias-refugees/.

14. Elise Foley, "Trump Responds to Migrant Caravan by Deploying 5,200 More Troops to Mexican Border," *Huffington Post*, October 29, 2018, https://www.huffingtonpost.com/entry/trump-military-border-caravan_us_5bd78134e4b017e5bfd4df77; David Nakamura, Josh Dawsey, and Nick Miroff, "'Close the Whole Thing!': Border Tensions Boil Over as Trump's Frustrations Grow," *Washington Post*, October 19, 2018, https://www.washingtonpost.com/politics/close-the-whole-thing-border-tensions-boil-over-as-trumps-frustrations-grow/2018/10/19/afe45462-d3a6-11e8-8c22-fa2ef74bd6d6_story.html; Mary Papenfuss, "Trump Returns to Bashing the Migrant Caravan, Calling It a 'Big Con,'" *Huffington Post*, November 17, 2018, https://www.huffingtonpost.com/entry/trump-migrant-caravan-big-con_us_5bef79bfe4b0f32bd589b6da.

Figures are indicated by page numbers followed by *fig.*

ACKNOWLEDGMENTS

The journey to complete this book has been a long one. I am grateful to my family, friends, and colleagues who never stopped believing in this work despite the time it took see their encouragement materialize. I am especially indebted to the generous people who took the time to share their memories of life in and around the labor camps. In particular, I'd like to thank Maria Guadalupe Barrera, Zora Mildred Bennett, Guadalupe and Lupe Cantu, Minerva Suárez Capello, Carolina and Evaristo Gonzalez, Jr., Aida Hinojosa, Olga Lozano, Guadalupe Mena, Herón Ramírez, Ofilia Cantu Ramírez, Victor Ramírez, Alacario Samudio, Guadalupe Saucedo, and Charles Lee Thomas for their contributions. Bertha Suárez, Israel L. Gonzalez, and Mr. Gonzalez's daughter, Debbie Gonzalez-Santana, deserve additional recognition for the substantial help they provided in sharing their stories, verifying general information, and connecting me to others I could interview.

The encouragement and assistance of many scholars helped formulate this study from its inception. I owe a good part of the success I've had in academia to David G. Gutiérrez. David not only inspired me to become a historian; he backed me at every phase and remains instrumental to my development as a scholar. The direction of David Montejano and Gunther Peck at the University of Texas at Austin made a lasting impact on my work. Emilio Zamora first introduced me to this topic and guided me with profound care and intelligence. He remains an important model for rigorous scholarship grounded in its value beyond academia. At UT, I was also fortunate to work with Laurie B. Green, John McKiernan-González, and Toyin Falola. I thank Laurie for her continued support, thoughtful advice, and devoted friendship.

My *compañera/os* in the Advanced Seminar in Chicana/o Research at UT taught me what it means to be an activist scholar. Thank you to all of you who dedicated time to this space. Many thanks also to the participants in the UT Custodial Workers Struggle. The UT Center for Mexican American Studies provided the institutional backing and safe space I needed to succeed. Thank you to all of my dear friends whom I met through CMAS. "Las Girlfriends" Olga Herrera, Jennifer Nájera, Laura Padilla, Isabela Seong Leong Quintana, Virginia Raymond, Lilia Raquel Rosas, and Cristina Salinas, have been a core part of what keeps me steady in academia and in life. Special thanks go to Cristina for sticking by me since our first day at UT. She's advised nearly every idea in this book, read more drafts than anyone cares to, accompanied me on research trips, and visited regularly (despite the long distance) to write together.

At Cornell University's ILR School I was fortunate to join a department that has been welcoming and supportive. Thank you to all of my colleagues in the Department of Labor Relations, Law, and History, especially Maria Cook, Jeff Cowie, Ileen DeVault, Shannon Gleeson, Kate Griffith, Louis Hyman, and Risa Lieberwitz. I'm particularly appreciative of the help Rhonda Clouse provided to get this book done, including reminding me to go outside for a walk. Thanks also to my colleagues in the Department of History at Cornell, especially Derek Chang and Maria Cristina Garcia, who have set a good example as intelligent and kind historians. The Latina/o Studies Program has helped make Cornell feel like home. Thank you to the faculty and students in LSP. Thanks especially to my writing partners, Mary Pat Brady, Ananda Cohen-Aponte, and Sofia A. Villenas. My *compañeras* Mary Pat and Sofia have read over numerous drafts, advised me on important decisions, and encouraged me when I lacked confidence. Helena María Viramontes has been a guiding light on so many occasions. I'm also grateful to my colleagues in the Cornell Farmworker Program, especially Mary Jo Dudley. Various undergraduate and graduate students at ILR provided research assistance. I thank each of them for their help, especially Walter Omar Manky Bonilla. I've also leaned quite a bit on my good friends and faculty members in the Center for the Study of Culture, Race, and Ethnicity at Ithaca College. Thanks especially to Belisa Gonzalez, Paula Ioanide, Gustavo Licón, and Phuong Nguyen.

Additionally, I'd like to express my deep gratitude to the many scholars who read my work, commented on presentations, pointed me to new sources, and shared suggestions for improving this project. During my fellowship time at the Smithsonian, Pete Daniel taught me much I did not know about agricultural history. When I was a fellow at Rhodes College, the History Department chaired by Gail Murray created a supportive environment in which to work. My fellowship experience at Bryn Mawr College was equally rewarding. I am especially thankful to Ignacio Gallup-Díaz and Madhavi Kale, who went out of their way to assist me. Laura Briggs saved me from misreading some of my research when we met at a conference on race and medicine long ago. Natalia Molina and Matt Garcia have answered numerous questions concerning both this study and my career. Lorena Márquez kept me laughing through stressful times. And Luis Alvarez, Linda Gordon, Laurie Green, David Gutiérrez, Cindy Hahamovitch, Don Mitchell, and Zaragosa Vargas have written letters of recommendation that played a big part in securing the funding and time I needed to write this book.

Thanks also to the participants in various workshops where I presented early versions of chapters. For their helpful suggestions, I thank my colleagues from the Mexican American History Workshop at the University of Houston, Berkshire Conference of Women Historians, Brett de Bary Interdisciplinary Mellon Writing Group on Spaces of Permeability and Alternative Infrastructures, "Labor Camp" Workshop at Syracuse University, ILR/ICL Department Workshop, and the Comparative History Colloquium at Cornell. Fellow members in the Labor and Working-Class History Association, Southern Labor Studies Association, Organization of American Historians, American Historical Association, and American Studies Association also offered valuable feedback as commentators and conference participants. Thanks to all of the supportive friends and mentors I've met in these spaces.

I am especially grateful for the careful attention my manuscript reviewers afforded this book. Vicki L. Ruiz not only offered thoughtful recommendations for refining my manuscript but also somehow found the time to edit each page. While it seems out of reach, I hope to become the kind of brilliant scholar, committed mentor, and powerful academic rabble-rouser she has been. My second reader also provided critical insights and prompted me to push the manuscript's intervention further. This encouragement gave me the confidence I needed to complete the book. I must also thank the anonymous readers for my article "For Labor and Democracy" in the *Journal of American History*. Their pointed questions and suggestions redirected this book in important ways. My editor at the University of Pennsylvania Press, Robert Lockhart, has been remarkably supportive and attentive. I'm pretty sure I've used up much of my good karma in working with him, Erica Ginsburg, and others at Penn Press on this book. I'd also like to thank the editors of the Politics and Culture in Modern America Series—Margot Canaday, Glenda Gilmore, Matthew Lassiter, Thomas J. Sugrue, and especially Stephen Pitti, who offered continued encouragement and smart ideas to make this book better.

Funding from various institutions allowed me to research and write the book I envisioned. I gratefully acknowledge the early support I received from the Consortium for Faculty Diversity in Liberal Arts Colleges. Through the CFD, I was awarded a William Randolph Hearst Fellowship at Rhodes College and an Andrew W. Mellon Fellowship in the Humanities at Bryn Mawr College. The Smithsonian Institution's National Museum of American History granted me the luxury of extended research time at the National Archives. The President's Council of Cornell Women awarded me an Affinito-Stewart Grant to complete my book research. The Ford Foundation Fellowship Program provided support for my work at every stage. Thank you to the Ford staff and affiliated faculty for the work you do to sustain academics of color and to champion the scholarship we produce. The Woodrow Wilson National Fellowship Foundation awarded me a Career Enhancement Fellowship at a crucial juncture on my tenure clock. As a CEF fellow I made wonderful friendships that helped me through the final stages of writing this book. Thank you especially to my writing/accountability buddies Daniel A. Rodriguez and Claudia Rueda.

Many archivists, librarians, local community historians, and others shared their expertise and recourses to make this study possible. Thank you to the archivists and staff at the National Archives and Records Administration in College Park, Maryland, and at NARA's various regional archives—namely, Boston, Atlanta, Fort Worth, and San Francisco; Dolph Briscoe Center for American History and Nettie Lee Benson Latin American Collection at UT; Texas State Historical Commission; and Southwest Collection at Texas Tech University. Thanks also to Aliqae Geraci at ILR's Catherwood Library, and to George Gause at UT Rio Grande Valley. George put me in contact with a number of people who helped my research develop, including Frances Isbell and Glenn and Margaret Housley from the Weslaco Museum. I am also appreciative of the assistance extended by the *Valley Morning Star*, the *Monitor*, the *Valley Town Crier*, and KURV Radio. My research time in the Rio Grande Valley would not have been possible without the support I received from Delia and Armando Salinas, who graciously opened up their home on several occasions. I also thank Jacinto Barrera Bassols for inviting me to stay with his family during my research time in Mexico City.

On New Year's Day in 2014, the most magnificent thing happened in my life—I gave birth to triplets, one of whom was later diagnosed with cerebral palsy. Admittedly, I somewhat expected my career was over. What I have since discovered is that this experience has made me a much better historian. That's not to say it's been easy—I have yet to find so-called work-life balance. But it's been possible because many friends offered their help, good food, and humor. Thank you to the Brady-McCullough family, Bruno-Licón family, Eversley Bradwell family, Feldman-DeVault family, Gonzalez-Ashton family, Nguyen family, Pipa family, Villenas-Richardson family, and to Vladimir Micic and Angela Herrera. Emily Burrichter Vorstadt was brave enough to agree to care for triplets when we offered her one of the toughest jobs ever in 2014. I'm eternally grateful that she's stuck by us all of these years. Obviously, I could not have done this without her. Beyond my partner, the person I've depended on the most to complete this book is Shannon Gleeson. Shannon and Gabriel Carraher have created a second home for my children. In fact, it's entirely possible that Shannon has fed and bathed my children more times than I have in the past year. For this, I could never thank you enough, *querida hermana*.

For their ceaseless emotional support, their smart and practical advice, and their continued source of inspiration, my family deserves the greatest recognition. I'm thankful to all of the Matsuda family for cheering me on as they always have. In particular, I thank Mary and Ronald Matsuda for their regular visits, frequent care packages, and constant support. David, Cat, baby Deacon, Scott, and Mark Matsuda also deserve my utmost gratitude. I owe so much to Elisabeth Gaynor Ellis for helping me become a better New Yorker (kinda) and historian. Thank you, Gaynor, for reading drafts, talking over ideas, and showering us with your love. My parents, Esperanza and Liberato Martínez, and my sisters, Marcie, Teri, Olga, and Belinda, inspired and nurtured this work in more ways than I can express. They have always encouraged my explorations and remained enthusiastic even as I moved farther and farther away. Thanks also to my brothers-in-law, Manny, Victor, and Ben, and niece and nephews, Endria, Jasmin, Alejandro, Danielle, Olivia, David, Ariana, Andres, Adrian, and Eli. My *comadre* Araceli Loera Martínez has had my back since the first day we met in elementary school—thank you to all of the Loera Martínez family.

Not unlike many of today's migrants, my parents risked almost everything to journey to the United States from Durango, Mexico. My father, despite little formal schooling, taught me the most valuable lessons in life.

I'm saddened that he is no longer in this world to see what his efforts produced. To his sacrifice, and that of my mother, who has always championed my education, I dedicate this work. I'll never be able to repay them for all they did to afford me with more than they had available to them, but I promise to live my life in a way that honors their hard work.

I also dedicate this book to my partner, Michael Matsuda. Even before our children were born, he willingly moved to a handful of research, teaching, and fellowship destinations, which made the completion of this study possible. Since 2014, however, he's been our children's primary caregiver. It's hard enough managing three kids, but he also does all of the work to coordinate my daughter's extended health care and service needs, which regularly require long hours on the phone and on the road. Michael, this book would not exist without your labor. Thank you, my love, for all you do to bring me happiness. Finally, to my *cariñitos* Joaquín, Lucia, and Oscar, you are my everything. One day when you read this book, I hope you know that your sweet kisses and bear hugs helped me write it.

Parts of this book were previously published and are reprinted here, by permission, in revised or expanded form. Parts of Chapter 4 were published as "'A Transformation for Migrants': Mexican Farmworkers and Federal Health Reform During the New Deal Era," in Laurie B. Green, John McKiernan-González, and Martin Summers, eds., *Precarious Prescriptions: Contested Histories of Race and Health in North America* (University of Minnesota Press, 2014). Parts of Chapter 5 were published in "For Labor and Democracy: The Farm Security Administration's Competing Visions for Farmworkers' Socioeconomic Reform and Civil Rights in the 1940s" in the *Journal of American History* (September 2019).

Printed in the USA
CPSIA information can be obtained
at www.ICGtesting.com
JSHW081107310824
69089JS00002B/14